D1545382

SEX, GENDER, AND ILLEGITIMACY IN THE CASTILIAN NOBLE FAMILY, 1400–1600

*Women and Gender in
the Early Modern World*

SERIES EDITORS

Allyson Poska
Abby Zanger

Sex, Gender, and Illegitimacy in the Castilian Noble Family, 1400–1600

GRACE E. COOLIDGE

UNIVERSITY OF NEBRASKA PRESS   LINCOLN

© 2022 by the Board of Regents of the University of Nebraska

Material in chapter 1 was previously published as "Contested Masculinity: Noblemen and Their Mistresses in Early Modern Spain," in *Contested Spaces of Nobility in Early Modern Europe*, ed. Charles Lipp and Matthew P. Romaniello (Farnham, UK: Ashgate, 2011), 61–84, © Informa UK Limited, reproduced with permission of the licensor through PLSclear. Material in chapter 2 was previously published as "'A Vile and Abject Woman': Noble Mistresses, Legal Power, and the Family in Early Modern Spain," *Journal of Family History* 32, no. 3 (July 2007): 195–214, © 2007, SAGE Publications, DOI: 10.1177/0363199007300205. Poetry in chapter 5 is Diane Wright's translation of Cardinal Mendoza's poem quoted in Francisco Layna Serrano, *Historia de Guadalajara y sus Mendozas en los siglos XV y XVI*, 2nd ed. (Guadalajara: Aache Ediciones, 1993), 2:63–65.

All rights reserved

The University of Nebraska Press is part of a land-grant institution with campuses and programs on the past, present, and future homelands of the Pawnee, Ponca, Otoe-Missouria, Omaha, Dakota, Lakota, Kaw, Cheyenne, and Arapaho Peoples, as well as those of the relocated Ho-Chunk, Sac and Fox, and Iowa Peoples.

Publication of this volume was assisted by the Center for Scholarly and Creative Excellence at Grand Valley State University. Publication was also assisted by the History Department at Grand Valley State University.

Library of Congress Cataloging-in-Publication Data
Names: Coolidge, Grace E., author.
Title: Sex, gender, and illegitimacy in the Castilian noble family, 1400–1600 / Grace E. Coolidge, University of Nebraska Press.
Description: Lincoln : University of Nebraska Press, [2022]
Series: Women and gender in the early modern world
Includes bibliographical references and index.
Identifiers: LCCN 2022003528 | ISBN 9781496218803 (hardback)
ISBN 9781496233622 (epub) | ISBN 9781496233639 (pdf)
Subjects: LCSH: Illegitimacy—History—to 1500. | Illegitimacy—Spain—History—16th century. | Nobility—Family relationships—Spain—History—to 1500. | Nobility—Family relationships—Spain—History—16th century. | BISAC: HISTORY / Europe / Spain & Portugal | SOCIAL SCIENCE / Gender Studies
Classification: LCC HQ999.S7 C66 2022 | DDC 306.874094609/02—dc23/eng/20220131
LC record available at https://lccn.loc.gov/2022003528

Set in Arno by N. Putens.

To Jason and Max

CONTENTS

ILLUSTRATIONS

ACKNOWLEDGMENTS

This has been a very long-term project, and the book and I have been the recipients of an amazing amount of support, encouragement, and love while it was coming together. I am very grateful to a wonderful community of scholars, friends, and family who have generously given their time and expertise to make this project better. I am indebted to audiences at the Renaissance Society of America Annual Meeting, the Sixteenth Century Studies Conference, and the Association for Spanish and Portuguese Historical Studies for their insightful questions and comments that helped me think through some of the main issues. Thank you also to Jakob Ladegaard, Julie Hastrup-Markussen, and David Hasberg Zirak-Schmidt, the organizers of "Passing On: Property, Family and Death in Narratives of Inheritance," a conference held at Aarhus University, Denmark, and funded by the Independent Research Fund Denmark, as well as to all the participants. I owe a special debt to the participants in the Premodern Spanish History Association of the Midwest for workshopping several chunks of this book and for their unfailing encouragement throughout the project. Over the years Gretchen Starr-LeBeau, Scott Taylor, Valentina Tikoff, Kristy Wilson-Bowers, Miriam Shadis, Silvia Mitchell, Luis Corteguera, Irene Olivares,

Pam Beattie, and Jeffrey Bowman have all provided support and insight. Lyndan Warner was an amazing coauthor for an article that touched on this project and a supportive editor when I worked on illegitimacy in the context of stepfamilies. Thank you also to all my generous colleagues who have helped me with translations, including Anne J. Cruz, Gabriela Pozzi, David Stark, Keith Watts, and Diane Wright. Fletcher Coolidge gave me expert help with proofreading and copyediting, and Fletcher Coolidge and Max Coolidge Crouthamel drew the family trees.

Special thanks to Elizabeth Lehfeldt, who read and commented on an early draft of chapter 2 in addition to helping me think through the larger themes of change over time. I also greatly appreciate the help and support of Allyson Poska for her friendship, her expertise, and her careful reading of the entire manuscript more than once. Her insightful comments helped the book grow and expand in important ways. Thank you also to the anonymous peer reviewer for the University of Nebraska Press for very generous and helpful suggestions for revision. Emily Wendell, Bridget Barry, Haley Mendlik, Ann Baker, Erika Rippeteau, and Monica Achen at the University of Nebraska Press have been incredibly patient and helpful throughout the publishing process, and I am grateful for their expertise.

I am also indebted to several institutions that have supported my scholarship in different ways. First and foremost, I am extremely grateful to the archivists at the Archivo Histórico de la Nobleza, the Archivo Histórico Provincial de Toledo, the Archivo Histórico Nacional, and the librarians and other experts at the Biblioteca Nacional in Madrid who have generously helped me over a period of almost twenty years. Their expertise and skilled care for the documents they guard makes this project possible. I have received generous financial support over the years from Robert Smart and the Center for Scholarly and Creative Excellence at Grand Valley State University that made archival trips possible and helped pay for the cover image. Thank you also to the interlibrary loan staff at Grand Valley State University, especially Amy Duwe and Alex Smith, who can apparently find anything. Thank you to the *Journal of Family History* and Routledge for permission to use elements from previously published material.

Mary Jane Halloran keeps going out to breakfast with me and asking me about the book even though she knows I will answer at length. Jim Diehl asked all the right questions and helped me with my title, and Bobbi Diehl gave me moral support at a critical juncture. Thank you to Anne Carmichael for help working out my database. Alice Chapman clarified the church's rules on celibacy, and Michael Huner, my friend and colleague, has been immensely supportive. Muriel Nazzari and Helen Nader both supported the very beginnings of this project, and I wish I could have shared the end of it with them.

Finally, Fritz and Hermann von Wolfenstein were absolutely no help at all in getting the book done, but a huge help in keeping me sane. My parents, Fletcher and Eleanor Coolidge, and my brother, Austin Robinson-Coolidge, have been a font of encouragement, support, and expert technical help. And most importantly, my husband Jason Crouthamel and our son Max patiently accompanied me through several very hot summers in Toledo while I pursued elusive illegitimate children from five hundred years ago. Then they nursed me through hip-replacement surgery, we sat out the pandemic lockdown together, and all the plumbing in the whole house quit. Their impressive resilience made it possible for me to go on working in spite of all this. I thank Max for being genuinely interested in the scandalous stories behind the bishops' portraits in the Toledo cathedral, for sharing with me the ups and downs of doing creative work, and for his expert help with the family trees. Most especially I thank Jason for his expertise, the Post-it notes, the chocolate, the proofreading, the use of his tool kit metaphor, the Swedish treasures, and all the love and support. There are not enough words for how much he has contributed to this book and to my life.

A NOTE ON THE TEXT

I have transcribed archival sources as they appear in the documents without modernizing spelling or forms. Unless otherwise noted, all translations are my own. The most common units of money in these documents are maravedís, reales, and ducados. The maravedí was the smallest unit of account. A real was a silver coin worth 34 maravedís. A ducado was worth 11 reales or 375 maravedís.

SEX, GENDER, AND ILLEGITIMACY
IN THE CASTILIAN NOBLE
FAMILY, 1400–1600

Introduction

In 1469 Catalina de González was a maid in the household of the Count of Arcos. She had served the family for seventeen years, living within the household and caring for the count's children. The count was a widower, his second wife, Leonor Nuñez, having died before 1452. The count and Leonor had nine children. Their eldest son, Pedro, had died in 1457 fighting against the Muslims, so the count was also responsible for caring for his four orphaned grandchildren.[1] This large household, and the social status of the Count of Arcos, make it unsurprising that he would have a maid such as Catalina. However, the relationships within this household were much more complex than they appear on the surface. In addition to being the maid, Catalina de González was the mother of six of the count's children. The countess herself, Leonor Nuñez, had been the count's concubine for many years before he married her, and the count was also the father of about thirteen more children, none of whom had been born from a legal marriage.

Writing his will in 1469, the second Count of Arcos acknowledged the role that Catalina had played in his life and family. Referring to her as "Cathalina González in whom I have had these my sons and daughters," he wrote: "[She has] served me in my house, and been with me, and worked with my children." He left her a legacy of 142,000 maravedís from his unentailed goods.[2] It is impossible to know Catalina's thoughts, how she felt about the count, what it was like to be his concubine but never his wife, how she treated the two enslaved women in the household who also had children with the count, how involved she was in her children's lives, or what her daily life was like. What we can know, and what this study shows, is that the sheer complexity of the second Count of Arcos's family and household, which encompassed multiple sexual partners, full and half-siblings, children of multiple generations, death, remarriage, and slavery, was fairly typical of the early modern Spanish noble family.

The study of illegitimacy in the noble family is necessarily a study of rape, abuse, betrayal, and the abandonment of children by entitled, arrogant, wealthy, and powerful men. It is a story of shattered families, or families that never had a chance to develop, and it is overwhelmingly the story of women who paid a heavy social and emotional price for being raped or choosing to have sex with someone they were not married to. It is also, however unexpectedly, a study of family flexibility, of women's social and economic agency, of anxiously involved fathers, of maternity outside of marriage, of matriarchal grandmothers and powerful aunts, and of families who cherished and provided for many of their children. Illegitimacy's sheer complexity makes it a revealing window into the inner workings of the early modern noble family because it allows the historian a glimpse of families in the process of negotiating power and status.

Illegitimate children were a constant presence in the Spanish noble family from 1400 to 1600. This book explores a series of interrelated questions connected to the illegitimate members of the noble family. What kind of relationships did these children have with their parents and families? How much did gender affect their roles and futures? How was their social status and ability to function in the adult world affected by the illegitimacy of their birth? What happened to their mothers? How did issues of race and ethnicity affect the lives of children who might have nonnoble mothers even when born to noble fathers? How did illegitimacy as a category shape the noble family as an institution, and was it an asset or a liability to have extra children who did not fit neatly into the prescribed categories of the family?

This book argues that Castilian noble families systematically used illegitimate children as a tool to ensure dynastic power. The nobility was so focused on uninterrupted dynastic succession that, in pursuit of power, wealth, and the future of the lineage, they were willing to accommodate women's agency, accept violations of the honor code, and promote illegitimate children when these actions benefited the lineage as a whole. The nobility grouped themselves into families and perceived themselves as members of a larger lineage. They adopted the concept of dynastic succession (the right of the family to succeed to the property, wealth, and titles of their ancestors) as an effective method to guarantee the success of the entire kin group who commanded their loyalty. Their standard of behavior was not prescriptive literature about women's roles, masculine ideals of honor, or the doctrine of the Catholic Church, but rather what constituted the most advantageous actions for their family.

Relentlessly focused on the success of the lineage, the nobility had a toolbox of strategies to secure that success. Their assets included status, reputation, land ownership, seigneurial rights, people, and wealth, and they could choose from a wide range of tactics, such as arranging marriage alliances, creating entails, performing military service, maintaining connections with monarchs, empowering women to serve as guardians of minors, and recognizing and promoting illegitimate children.[3] The nobility sacrificed or advocated for individual family members according to what would be most beneficial to the lineage as a whole rather than according to gender or legitimacy. Their creative reworking of family structures, inheritance laws, and church doctrine was an effective strategy that made them both flexible and resilient and lessened their vulnerability to the chaos of the early modern world. Within this strategy, illegitimate children became additional resources to work with. If illegitimate children threatened dynastic continuity by making claims that disrupted an eldest legitimate son's right to inherit property and title, the nobility could be harsh in denying them property, title, or rights. On the other hand, if the nobility lacked a legitimate heir, their preoccupation with dynastic succession meant that they could be equally adamant about promoting their illegitimate children to that role to the detriment of collateral branches of the family (brothers or sisters or their descendants).

Illegitimate children of the nobility occupied an ambiguous space within the noble family, because they had the potential to either be assets or disruptive forces. On the one hand, illegitimate children of noble fathers (and sometimes of noble mothers) could expand a noble family's power and connections through illustrious careers and prestigious marriages, manage family property, serve as executors and guardians, and above all could be substitute heirs in a system of arranged marriages that depended heavily on the smooth transfer of property and titles between men in order to flourish. On the other hand, illegitimate children had immense potential for disruption. They could sue for recognition and support, they were public symbols of disrupted marriages and sexual immorality, and they could potentially interrupt the smooth transfer of titles, especially if they were male. Noble families had a range of relationships with their illegitimate offspring, but as a whole they systematically benefited from their presence. Noble families could control illegitimate children and use them for their own ends because these children had fewer legal rights than their legitimate half-siblings. The complexity of families and human relationships, however, meant that the nobility also formed relationships with these children from outside the bonds of marriage, and there is abundant evidence of affection and support for illegitimate children from their mothers, siblings, grandmothers, aunts and uncles, fathers, and even their fathers' wives.

The constant presence of illegitimate children in the noble family over two centuries reveals their importance as part of the noble family's resilience and flexibility, a key to noble success in perpetuating and repairing a patriarchal system that was damaged by war, disease, rebellion, political unrest, and turbulent political changes.[4] This was a social group whose attitudes toward gender and religion were fragmented, in part because of their implacable loyalty to their own social class. Although the nobility officially supported a traditional patriarchal system that gave the most power to older adult men, they did not hesitate to call on women to take on responsibility and thus authority when family circumstances demanded it. Likewise, they were sincerely devout Catholics who systematically disregarded or circumvented church law and doctrine if they felt it was in the best interest of their family to do so. This devotion to the lineage sacrificed individual choice and desire to an overriding concern for the advancement of the entire group, a fact that is exemplified by arranged marriages, in which young men and women were assigned partners based on criteria of wealth and family background and expected to marry and cohabit with them until one of the spouses died. The nearly constant presence of illegitimate children in the noble family is a predictable side effect of the arranged marriage, as men (and sometimes women) forced into lifelong partnerships with people they were indifferent to or incompatible with sought sexual satisfaction, affection, companionship, and children elsewhere.

This preoccupation with dynastic continuity had profound implications for gender roles and norms. Noble families were much more interested in a smooth inheritance process than in enforcing traditional gender roles on their wives, their daughters, or the mothers of their children. They valued and rewarded women for the part they played in dynastic succession and were perfectly prepared to support women in roles such as guardians of children, executors of wills, powerful matriarchs, and even mothers of illegitimate children if all those roles promoted dynastic succession. Most importantly, women produced the children that ensured the succession. Noblewomen, who were most likely to be the brides of noblemen, also brought with them prestige, wealth, property, and exalted family lineage, all things that could benefit their sons and daughters and enhance the family's reputation and power. Women of lower social status who did not command prestige, wealth, and property were less likely to be noble wives, but they could still produce children, even heirs, which might be the most important piece a family needed to achieve dynastic succession. Noble families were inconsistent in enforcing gender roles because they evaluated women's actions in relation to the dynasty. Chastity and fidelity were important, but they were not the nobility's overriding concerns. An unfaithful wife who left her son's paternity open to question was anathema because her actions could disrupt the succession, but other women might be treated surprisingly leniently, even rewarded, for sex outside of marriage. A concubine who produced a living son who could inherit or even a daughter whose extramarital liaison enriched the family or gained them valuable allies might be an asset to the nobility.

This study focuses on the Castilian nobility, a powerful group of families at the top of Castilian society who were seigneurial aristocrats (*señores* and *títulos*), warriors, and landowners.[5] By the fifteenth and sixteenth centuries, the main goal of the Castilian nobility (and indeed, of nobles and kings across Europe) was dynastic continuity. Sara McDougall dated the beginnings of this preoccupation to the twelfth century. By the twelfth century, dynastic rule had taken firm hold in the political culture of much of Western Europe. It had become increasingly common for powerful men and women to pass their lands and titles on to their children successfully and without being challenged. Secular and religious authorities alike developed various legal doctrines to support these practices.[6] Recent scholarship has demonstrated that, in the words of Matthew P. Romaniello and Charles Lipp, in the early modern period noble goals "were as much about dynastic prosperity as political authority or social privilege."[7]

The nobility in fifteenth-century Castile was born from chaos, bloodshed, violence, and the most brutal kind of fratricidal strife. Fourteenth- and fifteenth-century Castile was racked by civil war and conflict with the Muslims. The nobility who fought for the winning side gained land, political power, and vassals from these conflicts. For example, in the early fourteenth century the Mendoza family (as well as the Ayala, the Velasco, and the Orozco families) rose from being relatively minor noble families from the northern province of Alava, moved to Castile, and, in the words of Helen Nader, "incorporated themselves into the Castilian fighting force, and climbed the ladder of rewards available to those who gave military service to the king."[8] Following this logic of exchanging military service for rewards, the successful noble families abandoned their allegiance to King Pedro (1334–69) in 1366 and supported his rival, Enrique de Trastámara (1333–79). Enrique was Pedro's half-brother, an illegitimate son of Alfonso XI (1311–50), who claimed the Castilian throne. After the disastrous battle of Nájera in 1367, the heads of the Mendoza, Ayala, and Velasco families were taken prisoner, and Orozco was murdered by Pedro. Enrique, temporarily defeated, nevertheless regrouped and returned to defeat and murder Pedro, becoming King Enrique II of Castile. Pedro had murdered over sixty of the country's most powerful nobles during his nineteen-year reign (1350–69), but the nobles who had backed Enrique and survived (the men who had been imprisoned after Nájera) retained a common identity and a common path to success.[9]

The nobles who had suffered for Enrique at Nájera embarked on a contractual relationship with their new king. Enrique claimed that kings were obliged to reward loyal subjects and to increase their fortunes. Benefiting from this generosity, the Mendoza and their allies became some of the richest nobles in fifteenth-century Castile, a position they quickly consolidated with strategic marriage alliances. Their active support of the Trastámara dynasty earned them the highest political and military offices in the kingdom.[10] On the other hand, their memories of chaos and what Helen Nader described as their status as "newly arrived in a society of great social mobility" shaped their strategy. Nader characterized them as a social group who wanted to enhance their status through marriage, titles, and political positions. They were obsessed with acquiring and increasing wealth; they organized themselves around the extended family for social, political, and educational purposes; and they were proud of being as adept in letters as they were in arms.[11] Social mobility characterized the nobility throughout the sixteenth century, and as their numbers grew, they continued to feel the need to compete for wealth and power, demonstrating adaptability and innovation combined with self-interest.[12]

The Castilian nobility was driven by a ruthless pragmatism that served them well. In this, they were not that different from the nobility across Europe, whom Jonathan Dewald characterized as "a violent and exploitative ruling group, whose prosperity depended heavily on the coercion of others."[13] As the fifteenth century wore on, the nobility in Castile navigated weak kings and an eventual civil war by looking out for themselves. About half of the nobility supported the crown at all times, with loyalties constantly shifting as noble families, according to Nader, practiced "a politics of necessity and opportunism." For example, the Mendoza increasingly relied on family relationships as part of their strategy, given that they "bore many children, lived to ripe ages, and thus acquired personal influence to cover any political eventuality." Eventually this powerful family agreed to support Ferdinand (1452–1516) and Isabel (1451–1504) in exchange for a clear title to the Castilian lands they claimed and a cardinalate for their most distinguished member, Pedro González de Mendoza, the bishop of Calahorra. Together, Ferdinand, Isabel, and the Mendoza were able to win the ensuing civil war. The Mendoza emerged as the Dukes of Infantado, and Pedro González de Mendoza, now cardinal of Santa Croce, was eventually able to establish his illegitimate sons with estates and titles of their own.[14]

The conflicts on the frontiers and the civil wars of the fifteenth century created a high demand for warriors, which left Castile with a high proportion of nobility (about 10 percent of the population).[15] By the early part of the sixteenth century, Ferdinand and Isabel had established and held peace in the realm, and the Castilian nobility was thriving. The upper level of this social class consisted of thirteen dukes, thirteen marquises, thirty-four counts, and two viscounts, with a combined yearly income of 1,309,000 ducados. This meant that 2–3 percent of the Castilian population owned 97 percent of the land in Castile, and over half of that 97 percent belonged to just a few of the powerful noble families.[16] Below these most powerful families were cascading layers of more minor nobles, most of whom were connected to the top families through ties of family and patronage.

This powerful group of families presented a formidable political and economic obstacle to the plans of Ferdinand and Isabel when the monarchs finally brought the wars to an end and set about governing multiple Spanish kingdoms. The degree to which Ferdinand and Isabel managed to tame the Castilian nobility is debated. The Catholic Monarchs were able to limit the political power of the nobility by destroying feudal castles, declaring private wars illegal, reducing and carefully defining the roles of the officers of the crown, bringing the masterships of the military orders under the control of the crown, and exerting control over the justice system.[17] However, the nobility also benefited from the land distributed after the conquest of Granada in 1492 as well as from having the right to establish entails (*mayorazgos*) confirmed by the *Leyes de Toro* in 1505.[18] They fit neatly within the pattern that Dewald discerned for the European nobility as a whole, "a startlingly resilient group, which maintained wealth and power through apparently cataclysmic social changes."[19]

By 1600, when this study ends, the nobility were beginning to change, moving away from the medieval warrior ideal and their roles as estate owners, and embracing new avenues of success through diplomacy, court life, and administration.[20] The image of the noble (traditionally gendered male) changed from that of the armored knight who displayed his skill and strength through hand-to-hand combat to that of the courtier invoked by Baldessare Castiglione (1478–1529), who wore his undoubted military prowess lightly and displayed other virtues like education, charm, self-control, and discipline.[21] As this change slowly took place, the fifteenth- and sixteenth-century images of the nobility were unstable, spawning lively debates focusing on the role of arms, the importance of education, and the value of birth versus that of achievement. Writers such as the fifteenth-century Diego de Valera (a vassal of the Mendoza family), who wrote *Espejo de veradera nobleza* (Mirror of true nobility), examined ideals such as knighthood and chivalry as well as the more practical realities of status.[22] Castiglione also shifted cultural ideals by focusing on the perfect nature of a chaste love that was spiritual (not sensual) and focused on the mind (not the body), and in which women ruled and men were their devoted servants. This characterization bore little resemblance to the Castilian nobility's actual behavior or system of arranged marriages.[23]

In the midst of this changing, difficult world, the Castilian nobility continued to consistently focus on their own advancement. Convinced that they deserved to occupy the highest rung of the social, economic, and political hierarchy, the nobility (men and women) focused on dynastic succession and promoted ideas of lineage that were sustained by their inheritance practices. They acquired and passed on immense wealth in part through their military roles and in part through their relationship with the crown. They were devoutly Catholic unless this was inconvenient, they subscribed to idealized gender roles unless these got in the way of family goals, and their sexual lives were violent and irregular. Their pragmatism made them highly resilient, and in their inexorable focus on their own success they enlisted the entire family, men and women, legitimate or illegitimate, to participate in advancing the lineage through dynastic succession.

This book focuses on the entire range of the Castilian nobility from the highest seigneurial lords down to provincial lords of small territories who did not carry titles. Many of the fathers in this study come from the highest ranks of the nobility, the heads of powerful clans like the Zúñiga (Dukes of Béjar) and the Álvarez de Toledo (Dukes of Alba), who owned much of the land in Salamanca; the Mendoza (Dukes of Infantado), who dominated the Alcarria in Castile; the Enríquez (Admirals of Castile), who owned most of Valladolid and Valencia; the Pimentel (Counts of Benavente), who owned much of León; and the "great magnates of Andalucía," which included the Guzmán (Dukes of Medina Sidonia), the Cerda (Dukes of Medinaceli), the Ponce de León (Dukes of Arcos), the Fernández de Córdoba (Dukes of Sesa), and the Mendoza again (Counts of Tendilla and of Priego).[24] Many others came from a group that J. H. Elliott has defined as *segundones*, the younger sons of these great magnates who did not inherit titles and were more career oriented.[25] Their status, while less than that of their titled fathers and elder brothers, was still socially and financially significant, and this group absorbed many illegitimate sons as well. The nobility owned land across the Iberian Peninsula and they consistently married partners who could expand that geographical reach. Therefore this book, though it centers on Castile, sometimes ventures into other regions of Spain and occasionally into the Portuguese connections of the noble families. The Trastámara and the Habsburg monarchies practiced similar family strategies and used their illegitimate children in ways that parallel those of the nobility, and though this book focuses on the Castilian nobility, I occasionally draw parallels with the lives and actions of the royal families.[26]

The Castilian nobility looked at the world as a vast hierarchy. They staked their claim to the top of that hierarchy, to a position right below the monarch, based on the medieval idea stated by the thirteenth-century *Siete Partidas*: "Men who are noble are so called for two reasons, either on account of their descent, or because of their excellence." The nobility's traditional roles as warriors, strengthened in Castile because of the concept of Reconquista and the violence on the Castilian frontiers, led the *Partidas* to equate them with the virtues of "energy, honor, and power."[27]

Accepting this estimation of their quality, the nobility exercised power over vast households of servants and slaves, as well as over citizens of their seignorial towns (*vasallos*) and the farmers and workers on their estates.[28] They enjoyed many special privileges, such as the right to bear arms and wear a sword; the right to certain forms of dress; exemption from certain forms of taxation; the right to sit on royal councils or advise the monarch; judicial powers within their estates; the exclusive rights to certain political and military offices; and monopolies on some leadership positions in the church. These privileges were lucrative, rewarding the nobility with incomes, perquisites, and opportunities to turn a profit.[29] Their wealth was immense. The Duke of Medina Sidonia, for example, collected revenues from ninety thousand vassals, and the nobility as a whole received at least a third of the revenues collected in early modern Spain. Not content with the profits from traditional agriculture, the nobility demonstrated their resilience and willingness to move with the times by embarking on lucrative commercial ventures. These included wool, silk production, fishing, and mining both in Castile and in their lands in North Africa and the Americas.[30]

Not everyone accepted the nobility's self-conception as a privileged class descended from medieval heroes, however. Jonathan Dewald found that "from 1500 on, commentators proved ready to make fun of nobles' pretensions and proclaim the falsity of the myths with which nobles surrounded themselves," and writers such as Erasmus, Thomas More, Machiavelli, as well as the Spanish picaresque novels, all put forward substantial critiques of nobles.[31] Along with these literary critiques, in the late sixteenth century the royal prosecutor in Castile filed a formal complaint that attacked the noble status of several high-ranking citizens of Seville. Michael Crawford argued that "the royal prosecutor's willingness to deny privileges to titled lords demonstrates the scale and nature of resistance to privilege and the absence of a strict hierarchy."[32] These kinds of attitudes, along with a general decline in noble privilege over the early modern period and the changing cultural demands of the fifteenth and sixteenth centuries, challenged traditional noble ideals and images of superiority.

In the face of these changes, the Castilian nobility were simultaneously insecure and resilient. They coped by celebrating lineage, turning to the part of the definition in the *Partidas* quoted above that equated nobility with descent. Analyzing the nobility across Europe, Jonathan Dewald argued, "The noble derived much of his/her identity from his lineage, and had an obligation to preserve this legacy for his descendants." Francisco Precioso Izquierdo found that in their wills, Spanish noblemen claimed their status and identity through family, house, and lineage.[33] This adherence to the idea and obligations of lineage dated back to the Middle Ages. Sara McDougall argued that at that time, "lineage, both maternal and paternal lineage, played the primary role in determining inheritance rights and succession in Western Christian Europe between the ninth and the thirteenth centuries."[34] As they moved into the chaotic early modern period, the nobility found lineage to be a reliable way to consolidate power and status. Relying on a corporate identity of the family meant that even in the face of death and disaster someone would be there to transmit power, status, and property to a new generation. Individuals might die, but the family stood a better chance of being sustained.[35] The nobility built a culture of lineage that was displayed through a reverence for ancestors marked by repeating their names through the generations, passing on family heirlooms such as swords or libraries, displaying their portraits in family homes and castles, and building elaborate tombs.[36]

Two powerful tools that the nobility used to maintain and extend the power of their lineages were the entail and the arranged marriage. For the Castilian nobility, this meant an emphasis on the smooth transfer of property and title within the bloodline and a slow accumulation of land, wealth, and power over the generations. In order to facilitate this, they increasingly practiced primogeniture within a modified system of partible inheritance. The eldest son inherited the bulk of the entailed estate (mayorazgo), while his siblings were compensated from the remaining unentailed goods. According to David Warren Sabean and Simon Teuscher, this time period "witnessed a new stress on familial coherence, a growing inclination to formalize patron-client ties through marriage alliance or godparentage, and a tendency to develop and maintain structured hierarchies within lineages, descent groups, and clans and among allied families." Thus, during the fifteenth and sixteenth centuries, the Castilian nobility moved toward showing "indications of a greater stress on either patrilineality or other modes of passing goods from one generation to the other."[37] This stress on patrilineality through the expanding use of entail in a society that had traditionally practiced partible inheritance created pressure on families and individuals.

The death of one son or one male titleholder could disrupt the entire process of passing land and titles from one generation of men to the next. To cope with this problem, the ambitious Castilian nobility relied heavily on women because, as Erica Bastress-Dukehart argued, "the womb symbolized everything noble families stood for . . . it was the harbinger of family honor, the living room of lineal continuity."[38] Sabean and Teuscher agreed, pointing out, "A closer look reveals that even the perpetuation of radically patrilineal patterns of devolution seem[s], in reality, to have depended on complicated settlements among husbands and wives or sisters and brothers, and on sales or mortgages that allowed for paying dowries and compensations."[39] Those complicated settlements could be eased by the presence of illegitimate children who had limited inheritance rights and were not legally entitled to compensation but who could serve as back-up heirs, as well as useful members of the lower rungs of the family hierarchy whose careers (in church, military, or court) as well as their marriage alliances could shore up the power and wealth of the titleholder and lineage. Therefore, if the fifteenth and sixteenth centuries saw a shift toward a stricter patrilineal hierarchy, for the Castilian nobility they also saw an increased recognition of and reliance on illegitimate children (and thus on the women who bore them) as a practice that helped bring about the desired patrilineality. Although this system inevitably generated friction, large networks of family members worked together to support it across generations. Along with this careful control of inheritance, the Castilian nobility exercised strict control over marriages in the lineage, practicing an intense endogamy.[40]

Focusing on the noble family complicates and amplifies the mostly masculine image of the successful, powerful noble magnates of the fifteenth and sixteenth centuries by including the roles of women and children. Leonore Davidoff defined families and kin as "ongoing processes, flexible and variable, filled with contradictions and tensions."[41] In the early modern Spanish noble family these contradictions and tensions were complicated by gender and age. The Spanish nobility was organized on patrilineal lines. In general, men had more power than women or children, and it was adult men who benefited from the "legal, cultural, and institutional 'patriarchal dividend.'"[42] Using Mary Erler and Maryanne Kowaleski's definition of power as "the ability to act effectively, to influence people or decisions, and to achieve goals,"[43] it is clear that power could also be wielded by women, transferred at need, and even challenged, making it a slippery, shifting concept. Studying illegitimacy over several generations yields insight into how carefully cultivated family strategies about marriage and inheritance helped the Castilian nobility adapt to historical changes.

ILLEGITIMACY: IMPLICATIONS FOR GENDER AND FAMILY

Since both ecclesiastical and civil law accepted that the status of illegitimate children varied according to the severity of their parents' sin, parents and children worked hard to prove that illegitimate children were in the least sinful category of illegitimacy or, better yet, actually legitimate because of legal technicalities, misunderstandings, or timing. Canon law held that all illegitimate children bore a moral stain, and Spanish legal codes systematically discriminated against illegitimate children as lacking *fama*, or public reputation. This barred them from holding public office, joining the church, or taking government jobs, but illegitimate individuals could petition the Spanish crown to have the stigma associated with their birth removed, becoming (in the formulaic phrase of the petitions) "legitimated as if they were of legitimate marriage."[44] The fact that people could be legitimated created a space within canon and civil law where women and men could recreate their social and legal identities to accommodate their own needs and those of the dynasty, and to compensate for past mistakes or irregularities.

Looking at illegitimacy in a comparative context, historian Thomas Kuehn argued that in early modern Italy, legitimation was a "social and legal paradox" that "was carefully managed and maintained," a definition that highlights its two-fold importance in inheritance strategies.[45] This paradox also existed in Spain. Kuehn's definition demonstrates the active ways in which people in both Renaissance Italy and Spain were able to control the social and legal aspects of their environment: "Illegitimacy and legitimation . . . were a means for people to craft an ambiguity that could be used to advantage. Creative manufacture, maintenance, and management of such ambiguities was one of the hallmarks of life in a Renaissance city-state, if not of all societies."[46] Illegitimacy, which on the surface might seem a quite straightforward matter of whether an individual's parents were married at the time of his or her birth, could in fact be hidden, contested, removed, overlooked, changed, and manipulated by the social and legal conventions of the early modern world. The fact that under Spanish law there were various different categories of illegitimate children demonstrates what a carefully crafted ambiguity illegitimacy was. Categories of illegitimacy are also found in Italian, Portuguese, French, Swedish, and German law, but not in English law.[47]

In Spain, if there was no legal impediment to their parents' marriage, illegitimate children were known as *hijos naturales* and had some legal rights of inheritance if they were acknowledged by their father. This was the least burdensome category of illegitimacy, partly because if the parents of hijos naturales subsequently married, then these children were automatically legitimated.[48] The thirteenth-century *Siete Partidas*, which is not very clear on the various categories of illegitimacy, nevertheless notes that natural children "are those not born of a marriage according to law." The seventeenth-century bishop of Mallorca, Juan Antonio Bacó, wrote that they were called natural "because they [were] engendered solely in nature and not in the honesty of marriage."[49] The other, and much more problematic, category of illegitimate children was that of *hijos bastardos*, or "bastards," whose parents were legally unable to marry at the time of their birth. Both the *Leyes de Toro* and Bacó referred to these children as *espurios*. The various types of bastards were again classified by the nature of their parents' sins. *Incestuosos* were children of parents who were related within the prohibited degrees of consanguinity provided by the Catholic Church, *adulterinos* were children who had at least one parent who was married to someone else, and *sacrílegos* were children who had at least one parent bound by religious vows. Ann Twinam's study on illegitimacy in colonial Spanish America found that these divisions were ranked according to increasing stigma. Hijos naturales were the least problematic and most likely to be legitimated, while sacrílegos carried the heaviest stigma.[50]

The attempt to systematically study illegitimacy and the nobility runs the risk of imposing a false consciousness on the Spanish nobility. The Spanish nobility did not intend to practice polygamy nor did they intentionally set out to create heirs-in-waiting. They were not consistently careful to make sure their illegitimate children were hijos naturales rather than hijos bastardos, although they were fully aware of the implications that this difference in status had for potential inheritance issues. The same men who had mistresses also arranged their children's marriages in the firm belief that this was the best way to protect both the children and the family property. Spanish noblemen, while depending heavily on individual women to protect their property, their children, and their power, rarely acknowledged this fact and never intended to empower women as a group. It is only when their behavior is observed over a period of roughly two hundred years, from 1400 to 1600, that patterns emerge in their ways of thinking about gender, family, and inheritance that demonstrate how their flexible attitudes gave them options that made them more resilient.

The Spanish nobility constructed a patrilineal inheritance system that publicly affirmed the power of older men and at the same time depended heavily on the loyalty and abilities of women in order to survive. Spanish men were vulnerable. They died in battles and from accidents, political intrigues, and disease. In order to ensure that the premature death of one male would not dismantle the power and prestige of an entire family, Spanish noblemen expected their wives, mothers, and sisters to be able and willing to take on male roles as they became guardians of children, managed noble estates, represented their families politically, arranged marriages, and sometimes even led revolts. Spanish noblewomen were able and willing to support their families. They shared the same conservative goals as their husbands, brothers, and fathers: preserving power and property and protecting children.[51]

Extramarital affairs and illegitimate children complicated this cooperative effort that made the Spanish nobility function so effectively. Sometimes the presence of a mistress and her offspring kept a noble title within a family and supported the conservative goals of the nobility, but at other times the presence of a mistress who had social and economic power of her own or of illegitimate male children in a family with only legitimate daughters could disrupt the entire process. Spanish society had some crucial ambiguities about issues of morality, honor, status, and gender that allowed male and female Spaniards to manipulate social attitudes as skillfully as they manipulated the law. Studying the way that the nobility responded to the challenges of illegitimacy complicates our understanding of the patrilineal family, revealing the experiences of women and of men with less power and status within the hierarchy as well as the clash between individual desires and the rules imposed by the church, the state, and the culture of the noble dynasty. As Allyson Poska said about studying women, studying illegitimacy means that "marriage appears more fragile and gender ideologies in the family more conflicted."[52]

The historiography of illegitimacy in Spain and in Europe in general has tended to focus on the legal aspects of legitimacy or on illegitimate individuals in isolation. Illegitimacy has often been studied through the lens of lawsuits about status or inheritance, which necessarily highlights moments when illegitimacy created crises.[53] In contrast, this study uses family records such as wills and legitimations as well as genealogies to examine the social and legal implications of illegitimacy as they played out within the context of the noble family over the course of two centuries, not just in moments of crisis. The fifteenth and sixteenth centuries in Spain saw many events that affected family structure, including the end of the Reconquista with its increasing emphasis on a unified, Christianized, and homogenous Spain, and the beginning of the Catholic Reformation, which increased focus on regulating the behavior of women and confining sexuality to marriage. The expansion of Spain's territories into the Atlantic world exposed Spaniards to new peoples, introduced them to new ways of structuring marriage and sexual relationships, and created complex Iberian families whose existence challenged the hierarchy of the Spanish empire.[54]

Historians of Latin America have produced a rich historiography on illegitimacy and its impact on Spaniards, Native Americans, and colonial life and social structures,[55] but there has not been an equivalent study of illegitimacy in peninsular Spain.[56] Historians of Spain have noted illegitimate children, often in relation to biographies of famous fathers (such as the Duke of Alba, the Count-Duke of Olivares, or the poet Garcilaso de la Vega)[57] or as part of the strategies of royal fathers such as Charles V, whose illegitimate daughter, Margaret of Parma, served as regent of the Netherlands and whose illegitimate son, Juan of Austria, commanded the Christian fleet at the Battle of Lepanto in 1571.[58] Illegitimate children also appear as actors in histories of particular Spanish noble families, usually when they play a role in the inheritance strategies of their fathers, and a few historians have noted illegitimate children in relation to their aristocratic mothers.[59] More systematic approaches have included some work on the legal aspects of illegitimacy and the ways in which illegitimacy interacted with the need to prove *limpieza de sangre*, or purity of blood.[60] Discrimination against people who had Jewish or Muslim ancestors or a family history of heresy increased steadily during the fifteenth century in Spain and made it more and more difficult for anyone who could not prove the identity of both their parents to gain entrance to the church or hold government positions (such as the office of notary public), complicating life for illegitimate persons.[61] There has also been some groundbreaking work on illegitimacy and the clergy in Spain during the medieval period that studies the concept of illegitimacy instead of simply focusing on individual illegitimate people or their parents.[62]

Scholars have noted the presence of illegitimate children and unorthodox ideas about marriage in social classes further down the hierarchy in early modern Spain. Allyson Poska argued that in Galicia for many peasants, "the restrictive sexual norms of the Catholic Church had little in common with the world they knew. According to most Galegas, marriage was no more reliable than living together and a child born out of wedlock was every bit as good as a child conceived after a blessing by the parish priest."[63] Abigail Dyer found that 1,804 women who had had premarital sex and been abandoned by their partners litigated to recover their honor in seventeenth-century Navarre, where they "were not social outcasts, nor were they rejected by family and neighbors. In nearly all cases the plaintiffs had friends and family testify to their good names and reputations."[64] Studying Castile, Scott Taylor suggested that "perhaps chastity was the only requirement for the honor of noble and wealthy women, but for peasant and artisan women ... engagement in the larger world outside their families meant that a wide array of characteristics contributed to their reputations."[65] Moreover, Renato Barahona found that in early modern Vizcaya, women of modest rank who were victims of sexual assault could repair their honor, turning to the courts to obtain "tangible remedies to their damaged reputations" a solution that "redressed lost sexual honour and reputation to a considerable extent."[66]

It seems that women and communities from across Spain rejected, reshaped, or were not aware of official prescriptive doctrine about marriage and sexuality. It is difficult, however, to untangle the actual behavior of the aristocracy from the conduct set out in advice manuals, honor codes, and treatises about the education of women, which, as Poska noted, "spoke almost exclusively to and about aristocratic Spanish women."[67] Were aristocratic Spanish women and men more bound by the prescriptive literature that historians have increasingly found did not apply to peasants, artisans, and people of a middle social rank?

In reality, as this book demonstrates, the nobility were consistently sexually promiscuous. Using archival documents such as wills, legitimations, dowries, and guardianships in conjunction with the seventeenth-century genealogies of noble families written by Luis de Salazar y Castro and the eighteenth-century genealogy of the Mendoza family by Diego Gutiérrez Coronel, I was able to reconstruct the Castilian nobility's alternate families. I located 258 women from a wide range of social backgrounds (from the very highest nobility down to serving maids, vassals, and enslaved women) who had extramarital relations with 203 noblemen in Spain in the fifteenth and sixteenth centuries.[68] Like the peasants studied by Poska, some noblemen and women participated in *amancebamiento*, a consensual union or concubinage, even after it became a secular crime and was condemned by the Council of Trent, and like the Galician peasants, the nobility were often quite candid about these relationships.[69] The difference between the sexual behavior of the nobility and that of people of lower social status lies less in the quantity of extramarital sexual activity and more in the nobility's ability to use their status to initiate and facilitate extramarital liaisons. Another difference is the creative ways in which the nobility used the children born from their extramarital liaisons to enhance their power and advance their lineages. The 258 women mentioned above produced 464 illegitimate children in approximately two hundred years, creating a substantial group of people that noble families could draw on at need.[70]

ORGANIZATION OF THE BOOK

This study is organized around the structure of the noble family, and it starts with parenthood. Chapter 1 examines noble masculinity and paternity. Studying fatherhood outside the bonds of marriage reveals that Castilian noblemen often enacted multiple and even conflicting forms of masculinity, existing as they did in a world in which ideal masculinity was shifting from that of violent, sexually aggressive warriors to one that valued moderation, sexual restraint, and self-control. In this chaotic environment, noblemen could effectively demonstrate masculinity through the everyday behaviors of marriage, becoming heads of households, having sex and procreating, and raising and nurturing children. Illegitimate children fulfilled several roles that made them valuable to their fathers, such as demonstrating their fathers' virility, expanding family connections, managing family property, and serving as substitute heirs.

The second chapter examines mothers of illegitimate children, a much more diverse group than their noble fathers. This chapter challenges the traditional view that chastity was the defining feature of women's lives in late medieval and early modern Castile, arguing instead that women who had sex outside of marriage were not irretrievably excluded from reputable femininity or virtuous maternity. Unmarried mothers' capacity to make independent decisions about their sexuality or to survive sexual assault, their ability to produce children, their willingness to use the court systems, and their success in acquiring economic resources and status and passing them on to their children made it possible for them to achieve culturally recognized goals such as economic security, marriage and careers, increased status, and successful maternity. None of this was easy or uncontested. A woman's social class affected her chances of success, but the ambiguous space occupied by women who had sexual relationships and children outside the bonds of marriage gave women opportunities to exercise agency as well as presenting difficulties they had to overcome.

Chapter 3 shifts the focus to illegitimate children themselves, examining how noble families coped with illegitimate infants and dealt with the complexities that illegitimate children added to their households and family structure. Although illegitimacy had emotional, financial, and dynastic consequences and created potential problems and disputes that needed to be carefully managed, the nobility systematically turned the nearly constant presence of illegitimate children into an asset.

Chapter 4 follows these illegitimate children into adulthood, arguing that illegitimate adults' ability to navigate their identities in relation to the noble family was complicated in the fifteenth and sixteenth centuries by race, gender, and changing religious mores. Although they were children of noblemen, their mothers might be noble, elite, poor, servants, or even enslaved. Their class status could be questioned and their inclusion in the noble family was not guaranteed. Although they were generally recognized, loved, and cared for by their noble families, illegitimate adults often occupied lower rungs on the social hierarchy.

Finally, chapter 5 attempts to move beyond the economic and political implications of illegitimacy and analyze the emotional complications produced by a system in which many adults had children with multiple sexual partners over long periods of time. This chapter argues that illegitimacy gave the noble family the emotional flexibility needed to make a patrilineal system of arranged marriages function by creating alternate families that gave the nobility a space for emotional attachments and relationships. At the same time, illegitimacy created human complications, conflicting emotions, and disruptions such as failed marriages, jealous spouses, and even violence that led to lawsuits and feuds that threatened the smooth transfer of property within a patrilineal family system.

1

Complex Masculinity

Noblemen, Illegitimate Children, and Fatherhood

By the time Diego Hurtado de Mendoza, the third Duke of Infantado, had retired to his palace in Guadalajara to write his will in 1531, he was riddled by gout, racked by religious guilt, and consumed by his passion for his unsuitable second wife. His adult children were alienated by and angry about his obsession with a stepmother whose social status was so far below their own. He had quarreled publicly with his influential cousin, the Count of Tendilla, over the succession crisis that followed the death of Isabel of Castile (1451–1504) in 1504, and with his eldest son over the *comunero* revolt in 1520. The family who had commanded his loyalty was increasingly divided, angry, and slowly moving away from their traditional position of power within the monarchy.

In spite of his dismal prospects in 1531, however, the duke could look back on a long and illustrious career as one of the heads of the powerful Mendoza clan. He had enough foresight and arrogant assurance to carry out a "hardheaded and carefully calculated" policy of remaining neutral in the succession dispute over the crown of Castile after the death of Queen Isabel, sure that whoever emerged as the new ruler would not be able to afford to have him as an enemy. The duke was apparently unmoved by questions of what Helen Nader described as "legal rights, Castilian nationalism, loyalty to the monarchy, or even loyalty to [King] Fernando." His commitment lay only with his own lineage, the extensive Mendoza clan.[1] Allied with his distant cousin the constable of Castile, he managed to carry most of that lineage to a favorable position under the eventual heir to the Castilian throne, Charles V, who awarded the duke the Toisón de Oro (Order of the Golden Fleece) in 1518.[2] The duke was also erudite, a patron of the University of Alcalá and described by the royal chronicler Hernando del Pulgar as writing "passages of great doctrine, sprinkling them with some funny things which give wit to the truth."[3]

Beyond being a politician, warrior, and scholar, the duke was also a concerned and responsible father. Archival evidence documents the duke's careful attention to the careers of all his children, from arranging for their educations to providing their dowries. In spite of his deathbed quarrels with his offspring, by 1531 he had succeeded in arranging marriages for seven of his children and had placed three others in religious careers where they flourished. His eldest son had married a niece of King Ferdinand of Aragón (1452–1516), creating new alliances and consolidating the power of the Mendoza, while another son, Martín, was the archdeacon of Guadalajara and of Talavera, and his daughter Brianda would become an abbess.

The duke's paternal care for all his children poses a challenge for historians and sheds light on the worldview of this prickly nobleman, who seems to have quarreled incessantly with the very lineage he was so implacably loyal to. Montserrat Rodríguez Posilio listed the third duke as having ten legitimate children with only one hijo natural, born before his marriage took place.[4] The mid-twentieth century chronicler of the Mendoza family, F. Layna Serrano, states that the duke had six legitimate children and eight illegitimate children.[5] The eighteenth-century genealogist Diego Gutiérrez Coronel recorded the existence of seven of the eight illegitimate children, and I have found documents in the Archivo Histórico de Nobleza in Toledo that confirm the existence of four legitimate children, but only four illegitimate children.[6] It seems that the existence and paternity of the youngest illegitimate daughter could reasonably be doubted.[7]

In a society obsessed by lineage, why is it so hard to uncover how many children one of the most famous and powerful men in the late fifteenth century had fathered and whether or not those children were legitimate? One response to that question seems to be that the distinction did not matter to the third duke in the same the way it has mattered to later historians. The third duke cared for all of his children, not equally, but attentively. His legitimate children made more prestigious marriages. As previously mentioned, his eldest son married Ferdinand of Aragón's niece. In addition, his legitimate daughter and another son married the children of other grandees (the highest ranking nobility in Spain), while his youngest illegitimate daughters married more local, minor nobility. Their marriages suggest a family hierarchy based on gender, age, birth order, and legitimacy, but the duke's careful attention to the futures of all his children (Martín, the archdeacon, and Brianda, the abbess, appear to have been illegitimate) incorporated even those who were born from his numerous extramarital relationships so firmly into the Mendoza lineage that generations of historians have struggled to untangle who was legitimate and who was not.

Studying the presence of illegitimate children in the sources about the nobility illuminates not only how the noble family hierarchy was structured, but also the nature of masculinity, and thus the patriarchy, in early modern Castile. Noble masculinity was based on a series of things that noblemen could only achieve by becoming fathers: lineage, succession, transmission of property and titles between generations, and ultimately the production of more men to create the next generation of the patriarchy. Noblemen were authoritarian in pursuit of their goals. They enforced a clearly defined hierarchy, demonstrating aggression toward the less powerful, and showing a contempt for women whom they raped, assaulted, and coerced into having sex and children with them. Simultaneously, noblemen could also be affectionate fathers who provided support for children of both genders, cared for and demonstrated attachment to their sexual partners, and enjoyed relaxed and affectionate family relationships. Categories of noble masculinity were dynamic, contradictory, and could coexist in complicated ways.[8] Additionally, the nobility's work of reproducing the patriarchy and maintaining male power was often disrupted or contested by death, by women's actions and agency, by disobedient children, and by the monarchy's efforts to consolidate its own power at the expense of the nobility.

This chapter argues that illegitimate children served several functions within the world of the noble family that could strengthen their ties with their fathers and that illuminate and complicate the nature of noble masculinity. Illegitimate children could demonstrate their fathers' virility; expand the family's connections through advantageous marriages or successful careers; manage family property; and above all provide the noble family with substitute heirs. These functions made illegitimate children a crucial part of the noble project of transmitting property, titles, and power between generations, and gave them a chance to form personal and even affectionate relationships with their fathers.

Fatherhood played an important part in shaping the complex noble lineages that dominated Spain's economic and political structures. Many Spanish noblemen were simultaneously fathers of legitimate and illegitimate children. The presence of illegitimate children makes the practice of fatherhood visible, because the care, feeding, and futures of children who existed outside of a legal marriage were not guaranteed. Men had to make special arrangements for the upbringing of these children, thus leaving records such as wills and legitimation petitions that, along with genealogies, chronicles, and secondary sources on noble families or noblemen, help illuminate what John Tosh refers to as the "social practice" of fatherhood in the nobility.[9] These records allow us to look beyond secular and canon law, the prescriptions of elite moralists such as Juan Luis Vives,[10] and the moral concerns of the Catholic Reformation to the actual practice of fatherhood and family in the fifteenth- and sixteenth-century Spanish nobility.

MASCULINITY AND PATERNITY

In early modern Castile, male identity was closely connected to both social status and fatherhood. These factors shaped how men performed masculinity and how others perceived their masculine character.[11] Masculinity is a nuanced, mutable concept that is socially constructed. In sixteenth-century Castile the masculine ideal was in flux, shifting from a more medieval concept of masculinity tied to the violence associated with the concept of Reconquista to a seventeenth-century idea that reflected concerns over Spain's experience of decline at home and on the world stage.[12] This chapter specifically examines the masculinity of noblemen who had unique powers and privileges (and pressures) that came with their place on the top of the hierarchy and their roles as warriors and councillors of state.[13] Noblemen's roles as warriors who embraced violence clashed with their equally important roles as the caring fathers of families.[14]

Scholars in late medieval and early modern Spain and Europe in general drew on their classical heritage to define men as biologically superior to women. Treatise writers stated that men should be big, have beards, be agile and strong, and have warm temperaments that led to better development in the more rational parts of their bodies, such as the soul and the brain.[15] They should also be virile and able to perform sexually, because, according to Vern L. Bullough, "it was a man's sexual organs that made him different and superior to the woman."[16] Medieval medical theories stressed the importance of penile erection and the production of sperm as elements that defined the male body and shaped ideas about a man's role in society, while also insisting on the health benefits of regular sexual activity for men.[17] Even St. Joseph, the holy husband of the Virgin Mary, became gradually younger and stronger in sixteenth-century art and was depicted in a Golden Age play as holding a staff that flowered, thus enabling him to win the hand of the Virgin. In spite of the church's emphasis on his holy virginity, images of St. Joseph took care to endow him with the physical characteristics of early modern manhood.[18]

Men's sexuality was often portrayed as assertive, even violent, and was used as a way to dominate women and perpetuate hierarchies. According to Michelle Armstrong-Partida, "Sex was seen as a masculine activity in which men were the initiators and the aggressors."[19] In medieval Castilian literary texts, Louise Mirrer found that masculinity is portrayed through menacing speech, force, and intimidation, and in the context of the concept of Reconquista, male sexuality was used as a tool for domination of groups like Jews and Muslims who were considered as irredeemably outside the Christian community.[20] The sexually aggressive male made a better warrior, an occupation that enabled the sexual conquest of women. Medieval

Castilian ballads made the connection overt. Mirrer pointed out that "the Cid's beard flourishes with every successful campaign against the infidel," while Muslim cities are portrayed as female in a powerful gesture that asserts male, Christian, military dominance over them. Christianity itself came to be portrayed as the more "muscular," "manly," or "potent" faith.[21] The warrior male was highly valued in medieval literature because of his aggressive and even violent traits, and war was seen as an opportunity for men to prosper, dominate, get rich, and demonstrate their masculinity.[22] Dian Fox argued that in literary sources in post-Reconquest Spain, virility was associated with "manliness and reproductivity" and defended through "competition with socially equal males, establishing hierarchy."[23] Paradoxically, the nobility's role as warriors pledged them to obey both the king and the church. In his will of 1530, don Luis Pacheco de Silva stated, "Always, with my person, my vassals, my servants, and my friends I have served and do serve the royal crown of these realms." The third Duke of Arcos asserted his paternal authority by threatening to curse his heirs unless they remained "obedient to the Holy Apostolic Faith and serve[d] the kings with all loyalty and fidelity." He commanded, "[Put] your blood and lives at all possible risk for the defense of the said Holy Apostolic Faith and the Catholic Faith and service to the kings and to the crown of Castile as our ancestors have always done."[24]

By the seventeenth century, the ways in which elites idealized masculinity had changed, although the shift was incomplete and inconsistent; the sixteenth century was a time of transition. Jennifer E. Barlow argued that "two models of Spanish masculinity collide[d] during the sixteenth century," as the medieval epic of the warrior (seen as virile) began to give way to the Renaissance, Italianate style of poetry of the courtier (criticized as effeminate). As an example of this, Barlow analyzed Garcilaso de la Vega's poetry, which simultaneously celebrates military victory (in Italianate verse) and identifies with those who suffer from it.[25] As early as 1521, Antonio de Guevara's *Relox de príncipes* directed young noblemen to receive military training but also to live virtuously and avoid immoderation. Other sixteenth-century texts, such as Castiglione's *Book of the Courtier* (1528, translated into Spanish in 1534), Luis Milán's *El cortesano* (1561), and Giovanni della Casa's *Galateo* (translated into Spanish in 1586), made similar arguments, stating that noblemen should hunt and fight, but with virtue, moderation, and control.[26] Castilian noblemen, whom Helen Nader characterized as engaged in the new Renaissance ideas, consciously casting "themselves and their ancestors as the spiritual heirs of the ancient Romans in Spain—men of arms and letters," must have wrestled with these contradictions.[27]

By the seventeenth century, moralists and *arbitristas* (who wrote commentaries on current affairs) increasingly recommended moderation, sexual restraint, and marital chastity. Whereas medieval noblemen were celebrated for their multiple affairs, seventeenth-century noblemen were urged to use more restraint and discretion.[28] St. Ignatius Loyola's autobiography, composed in the mid-sixteenth century, emphasized clerical chastity as unnegotiable and introduced more feminine models of emotion and spirituality. As the Jesuits established schools across Catholic Europe, they taught young noblemen a secular variation on this clerical model, emphasizing literature, elegant manners, and fluent speech.[29] St. Joseph was increasingly portrayed as a tender, nurturing father who cuddled the Christ Child and seemed almost to be taking away Mary's maternal duties.[30] Even in this new model, however, the seventeenth century continued to look back to the medieval world and envisage noble masculinity as being intimately tied to the importance of warrior values and training. The new courtier should be educated, politically active, graceful, and a skilled soldier.[31]

In Spain the actions of the elite and the understanding of noble masculinity have also been complicated by the existence of the noble honor codes articulated in advice literature as well as fictional texts such as the so-called wife-murder plays. These codes made a man responsible for the sexuality of his female dependents to the point that, in order to defend his honor, he had to kill any female under his control who was even perceived to be sexually deviant.[32] Although this code of behavior was long seen to represent a brutal early modern reality, Melveena McKendrick argued that "the honour code as depicted in the theatre was probably little more than a dramatic convention." Historians such as Allyson Poska and Scott Taylor have examined how honor codes and masculinity were perceived by peasants and nonelite members of society, demonstrating that elite honor codes, contradictory in themselves, did not translate directly (if at all) into the lives and daily behavior of the nonelite.[33] Indeed, Taylor has called into question the entire interpretation of an inflexible Spanish code of honor and vengeance that was based on male control over female sexuality, emphasizing instead that in daily life and disputes nonelite Castilians "could choose to invoke the language and gestures of honor—or not."[34]

Thus scholars have examined the honor codes, plays, and moral treatises of the elite and the daily behaviors of the nonelite, but there has been very little work done on the daily behaviors of the nobility, in particular what Pierre Bourdieu called "the embodied habits and practices of everyday experiences."[35] In the fifteenth and sixteenth centuries, while the prescriptive definitions of masculinity were shifting around noblemen, they demonstrated their masculinity through a set of behaviors that included marriage, becoming the head of a household, having sex and procreating, and raising and nurturing children. Many of the everyday experiences through which noblemen demonstrated and ensured their masculinity centered on their roles as fathers.

Marriage was an important characteristic of late medieval and early modern masculinity. Marriage was normative in medieval society, with the majority of men and women marrying and thus achieving adult status.[36] When a man married, he became the head of a household, which ideally would include his children, thus achieving several markers of masculinity at once by acquiring a position that asserted authority as well as demonstrating his sexual virility. Men who married accomplished what Michelle Armstrong-Partida called "an important public display of male governance over wives, children, servants, and slaves."[37] Marriage and setting up a household also advertised a man's ability to financially support his family, something that was important to Castilian masculinity across the social spectrum. Scott Taylor, arguing that male honor depended on other things in addition to control of female sexuality, found that "matters involving credit, debt, money, and property factored into male reputation" at the lower levels of society.[38] For noblemen, managing family property, resources, and wealth and passing them on intact to their descendants was the fundamental principle of dynastic succession and an obligation that they depicted as a Christian duty. In 1559 the Marquis of Cenete stated in his will that noblemen held goods "received from God" which they must therefore "dispose of . . . to their own advantage and that of their family and discharge their own conscience and leave order and clarity in their property."[39]

The importance of marriage to a man's status and the concern with preserving and passing on family property to the next generations connects masculinity to the production of children and fatherhood. Although the ability to have sex was a crucial sign of masculinity, becoming what Armstrong-Partida termed a "*paterfamilias*" who "protected and raised his sons and daughters, and ensured their future by providing them with an inheritance," was the sign that a man could form a household, procreate, exercise his authority in his family and the community, protect his dependents, and take on his full role as a man in his community.[40] It was fatherhood that ultimately proved masculinity beyond a doubt. Medieval medical authorities argued that the conception of a son meant that a father had strong sperm and was physically virile.[41] The importance of sons took on a special meaning for the nobility because of their preoccupation with dynastic succession, a process that depended on the procreation and survival of sons. As part of a larger lineage, noblemen who inherited a title had the fundamental responsibility of passing that title and property on to the next generation. The formulaic phrase that featured in the mayorazgos (entails) customarily drawn up by noblemen expressed their wish that noble property should descend "by degree through the eldest son in the direct line."[42] Therefore, successful noblemen had to be capable of procreation, demonstrating an ability to father children, preferably sons.

The ability to recreate the patriarchal family through the production of a living male heir was the stated goal of noble marriage. For example, in 1492 the Duke of Medinaceli stipulated that he would finish paying his daughter's dowry only after she and her husband had produced their first boy and that boy had lived at least sixty days, and in 1507 the second Duke of Frías stated that if his daughter Mencía's marriage produced no surviving children her husband had to return her entire dowry to her father.[43] Two centuries later the royal genealogist Luis de Salazar y Castro described Iñigo de Molina's prestigious first marriage as a failure because "this grand union had the misfortune to produce no more than a daughter."[44] All of these examples suggest that the lack of a son was perceived as a personal failure on the part of the married couple, one that was perhaps most problematic for the husband. But in a world where infant mortality was rampant, women frequently died in childbirth, and noblemen's roles as warriors, courtiers, or officials often separated them from their families, creating the next generation of children and sustaining the family within a legal marriage could be a difficult task.[45]

The emphasis on virility and sexual performance as an aspect of masculinity gave noblemen the privilege of being able to indulge in sexual relations outside of marriage. In Castile men who violated a woman's virginity could usually remedy the social problems they had created by paying a fine, something that was not a problem for the nobility. Indeed, the ability to have sex with women of inferior social status without intending to marry them was a sign of masculine and noble privilege.[46] These sexual interactions reenacted hierarchies of power in Castilian society that went beyond gender to include the inequalities between the nobility and lower-status women and men as well as the power of Christians over Jews and Muslims, thus enhancing the masculinity of the Christian noble at the top of the hierarchy.[47] Long-term sexual relationships also had the added benefit of allowing an unmarried man (such as a cleric or a younger son) to display some of the markers of adult masculinity that were usually reserved for marriage.[48] If sexual relations that existed outside marriage produced children, they were even more likely to enhance a man's masculinity. The ability to impregnate a woman was one of the most basic components of early modern masculinity, an action that demonstrated maleness in the moment, propping up a masculinity that could be fragile if a man had a childless marriage or was unable to marry.[49] Achieving fatherhood (legitimately or illegitimately), demonstrating it socially, and doing the work involved in this role enhanced a nobleman's masculinity.

Early modern Europe associated fatherhood with authority, care, and nurturing. Across the early modern Spanish empire, sermons celebrated the authority and importance of fathers who were owed obedience by their children, just as kings were owed obedience by their subjects. Noble fathers stood at the top of a family hierarchy that consisted of wife, children, and servants, what Francisco Precioso Izquierdo and Judit Gutiérrez de Armas refer to as a "small republic" that imitated the state.[50] The thirteenth-century *Siete Partidas* law code stated that a man legally had paternal authority, or *patria potestas*, only over his legitimate children, but this authority was often assumed by noble fathers in relation to illegitimate children whom they recognized and accepted as their own.[51] The *Leyes de Toro* (1505) laid out a procedure for this, stating that a father could publicly recognize his child as his own by acknowledging the child in his will, leaving a written record with a notary, or putting his name on the child's baptismal certificate.[52]

The *Partidas* also emphasizes the importance of paternal nurturing, admonishing fathers that their affection for their children would increase when they nurtured and cared for those children. The *Partidas* stated that fathers were legally expected to support the mothers of their children while they were pregnant and nursing, and both the *Partidas* and the later *Leyes de Toro* declared that fathers had to provide for the children once they reached the age of three, giving them the necessities of life, such as food, drink, clothing, shoes, and housing.[53] Furnishing this kind of support to a pregnant or nursing woman and her child was a social admission of paternity that could hold up in court, and failure to provide this kind of support was likely to draw censure from the community.[54] Debra Blumenthal found that neighbors and kin criticized men in fifteenth-century Valencia for neglecting or mistreating the enslaved women who bore their children and those children.[55] A father's primary responsibility was to provide for his family, causing the sixteenth-century writer Pedro Luján to comment, "In truth it would be better for a man to miss Mass than not to earn enough for his children in order to hear it."[56]

Fathers were also responsible for educating their children in a way that was appropriate to their social status. Noble fathers often sent their sons to school to learn to read and write and later to university (a sign of privilege), and many noble fathers also educated their daughters.[57] Writers before and during the Renaissance emphasized that fathers had a duty to educate children, especially sons, so that they gained skills to protect their family and their city when they became adults.[58] Castilian fathers could draw on writers such as Rodrigo Sánchez Arévalo, who wrote the first pedagogical treatise in the Iberian Peninsula in 1453; the humanist Antonio Nebrija, who wrote *On the Education of Children*; Erasmus, whose works were widely available in Spain; Juan Luis Vives, who wrote *The Education of a Christian Woman* for Catherine of Aragón; Pedro Luján, whose dialogues were published in eleven editions from 1550 to 1589; and fray Marco Antonio de Camos, who wrote *Microcosmia, y gobierno universal del hombre cristiano*.[59] These works emphasized the role of fathers as teachers and models, and humanists such as Leon Battista Alberti (himself an illegitimate son) wrote detailed advice about a father's obligation to observe the disposition, talents, and weaknesses of his sons so that he could tailor their education to their needs.[60] Noble children's education was designed to provide them with the literary and social skills they needed to prosper as adult members of the family. Fathers (and some mothers) provided tutors and subsequently sent promising children on to study at specialized schools and universities. Pedro González de Mendoza acknowledged his father's influence on his education by dedicating to his father a translation of Sallust that he completed in 1442 while studying with his uncle, the archbishop of Toledo.[61]

The logical outcome of a good education and the paternal responsibility to provide for the family was that as children grew to adulthood, fathers were also responsible for arranging their careers and marriages. Noble fathers sent sons to schools that would get them posts in the church or the government or they started them out on military careers while designating their daughters for convents or marriage. Helping to choose a spouse for a child and facilitating the marriage through a dowry were patriarchal responsibilities that often demonstrated paternity for illegitimate children.[62] Children owed their fathers obedience and elite fathers fought hard to retain control over their children's marriages.[63] This responsibility was reflected in the literature of the time, and it was often shared by mothers. Vives instructed young women to be guided by their parents when choosing a spouse, and both Giovanni Boccaccio and Leonardo Bruni used the tale of Ghismonda and her father Tancred to emphasize a father's negligence in neglecting to marry his daughter in time to prevent tragedy.[64] Men who failed to provide could be censured for not acting like proper patriarchs.[65] In order to be assets, illegitimate children had to be raised in a way that reflected their noble status and groomed them for their future roles. They needed the education, polish, manners, experience, and resources that would allow them to make good marriages or launch successful careers, manage family property, or even become the next titleholder in the lineage. Noblemen in early modern Spain consistently invested in their illegitimate children because it benefited their lineage and kin group.[66] In raising and educating them to play a part in the family strategy, men sometimes came to rely on these children and even developed bonds of affection with them.

ILLEGITIMACY AND THE LAW

Castilian inheritance law started from the "basic, immutable premise," stated in the seventh-century *Fuero Juzgo* and reiterated in the *Leyes de Toro* (1505), that all legitimate children, male and female, were entitled to share in the inheritance from four-fifths of their parents' goods as necessary heirs (partible inheritance).[67] This was complicated by the thirteenth-century *Siete Partidas*, which was based on Roman and canon law. The *Siete Partidas* made it easier to establish primogeniture and set up a mayorazgo, or entail, in which the monarch gave a nobleman a license that allowed him to put some of his property into an inalienable trust that was usually restricted to inheritance by the eldest son.[68] Creating an entail potentially restricted noble power, because every entail required permission from the monarch in order to waive the laws of partible inheritance in favor of one heir. But the nobility successfully co-opted this prerogative into a powerful tool of their own. According to John Lynch, when Ferdinand and Isabel set out to wrest political power from the medieval Castilian aristocracy, they compromised by recognizing "the aristocracy's immunity from certain types of taxation and its possession of seigneurial jurisdiction, and sanctioned its dominance over land." This compromise included confirming the right of mayorazgo in legislation of 1480 and the *Leyes de Toro* in 1505. The persistent use of entail "enabled landed proprietors to render their estates immune from alienation and tie them in perpetuity to their family," thus fitting neatly with the nobility's goals of dynastic succession. The nobility remained resilient, their political losses compensated by huge economic gains.[69]

The systematic use of entail meant that younger legitimate sons (and any daughters) were excluded from inheriting the entail, and thus were necessary heirs only of four-fifths of the unentailed goods (thus modifying the traditional practice of partible inheritance). The remaining one-fifth (*quinto*) of the unentailed goods could be used for funeral expenses, charitable works, and free bequests, so any inheritance that a parent wished an illegitimate child to have had to come from that one-fifth.[70] Illegitimate children born from an unmarried man who died intestate and had an established, monogamous relationship with the children's mother could inherit one-sixth of their father's property, or could inherit all, but only in the absence of legitimate children.[71] To further complicate this, illegitimate children who were born in "fornication, incest, or adultery" technically did not have the right to inherit from their fathers.[72] In practice the nobility overlooked this restriction, although it led to many lawsuits. Legitimate and illegitimate children thus had very different inheritance rights, and in order for illegitimate children to inherit at all, they needed formal recognition from their fathers, and their bequests needed to be clearly itemized in their father's will or given to them before their father's death.

Castilian inheritance law struggled to balance male sexuality and the resulting illegitimate children with the rights of children born from a legitimate marriage. The use of mayorazgo put a high value on male virility because the production of male children within a legally recognized marriage maintained the patrilineal system of inheritance. Outside of marriage, however, sexually active men complicated the inheritance system. Both church and state wanted men's sexual activities restricted to their legal marriages, but for different reasons. The church wanted men's virility to be restricted by the sacrament of marriage because of the possibility of sin. Frederico Aznar Gil pointed out that one of the most common concerns of canon law from the thirteenth century onward was "condemning the maintenance of extramarital relationships by clergy and lay people."[73] Secular law preferred legal marriage as the context for male and female sexuality because of the need to prove paternity and legal heirs. The *Siete Partidas* neatly summed up both these concerns: "The Holy Church forbids Christians to keep concubines, because they live with them in mortal sin. The wise men of the ancients, however, who made the laws, permitted certain persons to keep them [the concubines] without being liable to temporal penalty, because they considered it less wicked to have one than to have many, and in order that the children born of them might be more certain."[74] While acknowledging the church's concern with mortal sin, the *Partidas* took a more practical approach. It differentiated between different kinds of extramarital sexual relationships (concubinage, which produced "more certain children" whose paternity was clear versus shorter-term relationships), and it devoted an entire section (title XV of the fourth partida) to categories of illegitimate children and their legal status. The *Siete Partidas* also had economic concerns, stating: "Great injury results to children through their not being legitimate" because "they cannot share the honors of their fathers and grandfathers" and "they cannot inherit the property of their fathers or grandfathers, or that of any other relatives from whom they are descended."[75]

Religious and secular authorities also failed to restrict the sexual activity of men who had taken religious vows of celibacy. In the medieval period the Spanish church developed rather independently from the papacy, and in Castile-León, clerical concubinage was banned by canon law in the twelfth century but remained legal under secular law until the thirteenth century. Even when Alfonso X had incorporated the Fourth Lateran Council's ban on priestly marriage into the secular *Siete Partidas*, he still allowed clerics' children the right of inheritance in the dioceses of Salamanca and Guadalajara.[76] The change in law did not noticeably curtail the practice, and Armstrong-Partida's work on medieval Catalunya concluded that "clerical concubinage was a lived reality throughout the dioceses of Catalunya" through the fourteenth century, a "social practice" that was "a custom entrenched in Iberian society."[77] Frederico Aznar Gil characterized clerical concubinage across the Iberian Peninsula as "a true problem for the church during the thirteenth to the sixteenth centuries," and his study of petitions for legitimation found that in the sixteenth century, almost 60 percent of the petitioners were children of fathers who could not marry their mothers because they had taken religious vows.[78]

As Jane Mangan pointed out in the context of the Spanish empire, many illegitimate children (and their mothers) were probably abandoned by their privileged noble fathers, because the social structure empowered noblemen at the cost of women and of Indigenous peoples. Abandoning a child does not leave much (if any) in the way of archival records.[79] As a result of these social disparities, the records informing this chapter necessarily privilege children who were recognized and/or cared for by their fathers and do not reveal how many noblemen simply walked away from their paternal responsibilities. What these records do show is that some noblemen, in Mangan's words a "subset,"[80] took their paternal responsibilities seriously, caring for and sometimes developing relationships with their illegitimate children.

Noble fathers who recognized, maintained, and provided for their illegitimate children might do so for a variety of reasons, and their actions could produce complex results. Illegitimate children could be both a blessing and a burden. In a social group that was already struggling to balance the maintenance of their wealth and prestige across generations with their own fertility, younger children (whether legitimate or not) presented a challenge, especially as "the frontier closed and the entail became more general."[81] If recognized by their fathers, illegitimate children needed to be fed, housed, educated, and launched into suitable professions or marriages, all of which required substantial resources from noble families. On the other hand, illegitimate children could be of use to a nobleman in his efforts to promote family prestige, maintain social and political connections, manage the family's assets, and even enhance his personal reputation. William Maltby recognized this role for illegitimate children of royalty, commenting that Charles V "added to his future diplomatic capital by conceiving an illegitimate daughter, Margaret, who would become Duchess of Parma and then Regent of the Netherlands under Philip II."[82] The commitment needed to raise an illegitimate child in such a way that he or she could play a part in the noble family strategy might also create contact between father and child and even allow for closer relationships to develop.

The most basic service that a noble father could provide for his illegitimate child was recognition. There were a variety of ways in which fathers could grant recognition to children born out of wedlock, including a written statement acknowledging paternity, recognition in a will, testifying before a magistrate, and the father's participation in the baptismal ceremony (in person or through a representative). Jesús M. Usunáriz found other actions through which fathers in Navarre publicly and socially acknowledged paternity, such as providing for the mother when she was pregnant, feeding the newborn, and assuming responsibility for children over the age of three.[83] Noble fathers often made their paternity public by actions such as verbally claiming their children, raising them in the noble household, giving them a noble education, and seating them at the family table. Recognition by other relatives also helped to establish a child's ties to the family.[84] This recognition was vital to a child's survival, because if a father was certain that an illegitimate child was his, he was legally obliged to provide basic necessities for that child. The *Siete Partidas* stated that parents should provide enough "to eat, drink, and be clothed, shoes to wear, and a place to dwell," and the *Leyes de Toro* affirmed this. In the mid-seventeenth century Juan Antonio Bacó's legal commentary echoed the *Siete Partidas*, stating that illegitimate children are entitled to "food, drink, clothes, shoes, bed, house, medicine," and the other basics needed to survive, even if they were espurio. Clerical fathers who had no other goods were to use their benefices to provide for their sons and dower their daughters, and Bacó went as far as stipulating that fathers were also responsible for their grandchildren. The expectation was that mothers would support the child up until age three, at which time fathers would assume responsibility.[85]

The simple acknowledgment of paternity in a will gave an illegitimate child an identity and a documented connection to his or her noble father and thus to the father's lineage. In 1429 Pedro de Portocarrero, Lord of Moguer, gave the most succinct possible acknowledgment of paternity, referring to his illegitimate sons as "my son" every time either boy was mentioned in the will, but clarifying that his each of his legitimate daughters was "my daughter and the daughter of lady Beatriz Enríquez, my wife."[86] Pedro's careful delineation between the illegitimate status of his sons and the legitimate status of his daughters gave his sons an identity while simultaneously protecting his daughters' rights of inheritance. Gonzalo Ruiz de la Vega, who had three daughters, employed similar language in his 1456 will. He referred to Mencía and Leonor de la Vega (who were illegitimate) simply as his daughters while also protecting his legitimate daughter's rights by stating, "I leave and institute and establish as my legitimate daughter, universal heir of all my goods, the said my daughter doña Leonor de Mendoza, who is also the daughter of my wife, doña Mencía de Toledo."[87] Neither of these men provided any information about the mothers of their illegitimate children. The Count of Villalba was more forthcoming, stating in his will in 1540, "I had a son in Juana Fernández, both being single, who is called Martín Sanches."[88] This short phrase is illuminating. It conveyed to the count's contemporaries that Martín Sanches was his son and clearly identified the boy's mother. In addition, because both the count and Juana Fernández were single at the time of his conception, Martín was an hijo natural, a category of illegitimacy that carried less stigma (and potentially more possibility of inheritance) because it did not imply adultery or the breaking of religious vows on the part of the illegitimate child's parents.

Fathers concerned about the futures of their illegitimate children could also provide them with guardians, either instituting a formal guardianship with a notarized document or making a request in their will about the child's future custody. Noble fathers were not always in a position to raise their illegitimate children in their own households.[89] For example, the second Duke of Arcos left his two illegitimate children (both minors) in the custody of the religious institutions where they had been living before his death. His daughter was in the convent of Santa Clara on his estate, in the care of the abbess, doña María de Figueroa, and his son was in the care of the Jesuits. As well as making arrangements for their physical custody, he also appointed a formal guardian, Pedro de Pineda, to manage their property while they were underage.[90] Another solution to this issue was to have an illegitimate child serve in the household of a noble relative, usually a grandparent, aunt, or uncle, who took responsibility for raising them. Gonzalo Ruiz de la Vega recorded in his will in 1456 that his illegitimate daughter, Leonor de la Vega, was a maid for his sister, the Countess of Castañeda.[91]

This option was also used to care for orphans or children whose widowed parents had remarried.[92] It is not entirely clear if illegitimate children were treated differently from their legitimate counterparts in this situation, but it provided a solution for some fathers.

Noble fathers often demanded that their legitimate children house and support their illegitimate half-siblings. In 1530, for example, the fifth Duke of Benavente was asked by his father in his will to support his younger, illegitimate half-brother Alonso (identified as an hijo bastardo) until the age of twelve. When Alonso reached this milestone, the duke was to take his brother to court and present him to the king, presumably as a way of launching him into a career.[93] In another case, the third Duke of Gandía gave his heir sole responsibility for his illegitimate half-brother in 1538, stating, "We beg and charge our successor, [the next] duke, our son and heir, [to consider his illegitimate half-brother Juan Cristóbal] as a brother, and to treat him as such, even though he is a bastard. . . . We have not in our life, nor in this our current will, bequeathed him anything, trusting in our successor and heir."[94] The lack of an additional bequest for Juan Cristóbal's support put his entire future in the hands of his older half-brother.

Most noblemen who acknowledged illegitimate children in their wills or left them to the care and guardianship of others did so because they recognized these children's claim on them and were also providing for them financially. Both law and social custom established the financial support of children as a paternal responsibility and being able to provide for all his children, even those born outside of his marriage, enhanced a nobleman's masculine reputation. Noble fathers could apply also both to the church and to the monarchy to legitimate their illegitimate children, giving them additional legal rights to inherit goods and properties from their relatives.[95] Very powerful nobleman (like Cardinal Pedro González de Mendoza) might make personal requests to the monarch, but most of the royal legitimation petitions were processed through the Council of Castile and later the Council of the Indies. These petitions, called *gracias al sacar*, required a detailed deposition about the circumstances of the applicant's illegitimacy and a fee.[96]

Noblemen often requested legitimations (both papal and royal) as part of the process of leaving legacies to or arranging marriages for illegitimate children. The third Duke of Frías requested royal legitimations for all his illegitimate sons. This enabled him to further request royal permission in 1539 to provide for them from the income of his entailed estate. The Frías entail did not allow inheritance by legitimated sons or daughters, so the Duke of Frías's title and his entailed estate went to his nephew rather than to his illegitimate sons. But the third duke attempted to compensate for this by using some of his unentailed assets to create a new mayorazgo for his son Juan that consisted of "all of the valley of Arreba" with its fortresses, estates, meadows, and other appurtenances. After Juan's early death, this entail passed to his younger illegitimate brothers.[97]

Noble fathers' provisions for their illegitimate children ranged from yearly allowances to substantial inheritances. Don Diego de Arellano, a minor nobleman from northern Spain, left his illegitimate son an annuity (*censo*) in his will dated 1557.[98] The first Marquis de Santa Cruz, dying just months before he was to take charge of the great Spanish Armada in 1588, recognized his illegitimate son Diego in his will, identified him as an hijo natural, and left him a yearly allowance of 200 ducados.[99] The first Duke of Frías, suffering from a lack of legitimate male heirs, was more generous. In 1510 he applied for and received legitimations from Queen Juana of Castile for his four illegitimate sons, and he used this to leave his eldest legitimated son, Pedro, an extensive inheritance that included "the quinto of my estate" in addition to the town and castle of Castillo de Zeriego, vassals, land, and income in the town of Vanes, the town and great house of Rebilla de Campos, a house and meadow in Saldañuela, and 30,000 maravedís in cash.[100]

Bequests to illegitimate children often affirmed, in practical terms, a hierarchy of birth order and legitimacy, but they also reflect noblemen's anxieties about a lack of heirs. For example, in the mid-fifteenth century Dr. Pedro Gonçalez named his illegitimate son as a candidate in the line of succession to inherit the mayorazgo he had created if all his legitimate children died without succession. The young man in question did not inherit the entail, but his inclusion (even as a last resort substitute for his legitimate half-siblings) connected him publicly with his father's family and probably contributed to his success. He became a lawyer, was a member of the king's council, and married into the family of the Lords of Bonache.[101]

In turn, his presence was an additional reassurance for his anxious father that the lineage and the entail would continue.

When an arranged marriage failed to produce legitimate sons, noble fathers could attempt to fulfill their masculine role of perpetuating dynastic succession by creating entails for illegitimate sons. Many of these new entails were carved out of the incomes or free property (*bienes libres*) of entailed estates that had to be handed down intact to the next titleholder, and they demonstrated a man's wealth, power, and command of substantial economic resources. As previously noted, both the first and third Dukes of Frías did this. In an example of the nobility's farsighted view of family and lineage, in 1429 Pedro de Portocarrero, Lord of Moguer, left the estate of Moguer to his legitimate daughters, with the stipulation that his two illegitimate sons were to receive 3 million maravedís per year from the rents of the estate. In addition to this yearly stipend, however, his son Alfonso was also to receive 100 florins when he reached the age of twenty to help him make a good marriage, while Alfonso's brother Martín was to inherit the estate called Aljara "with its houses, and meadows, and pastures, and mountains, and waters." If Martín died without legitimate heirs, the estate of Aljara was to return to Pedro de Portocarrero's main mayorazgo of Moguer, but if the illegitimate Martín had legitimate children, they could inherit Aljara.[102] These provisions, which would help Alfonso make a good marriage and create an estate for Martín's future children, had the potential to create a new lineage even though Pedro de Portocarrero was facing death with two legitimate daughters and no legitimate sons.

Creating a new mayorazgo for an illegitimate child was a powerful tool that could create new titles, securing that child's place in the social hierarchy and expanding the family's influence and power. Álvaro de Luna, the notorious favorite of King Juan II of Castile, was an illegitimate son who had started life with little inheritance of his own. As he rose to power and influence, he made a prestigious marriage to Juana Pimentel, daughter of the Count of Benavente, and, like so many men of his time and class, had both legitimate children and illegitimate children (two of each). Although he was executed by the king in 1453, Álvaro had taken pains to protect his lineage. He used his will to create an entail for his legitimate son, Juan, who made a prestigious marriage with the daughter of the Duke of Béjar and became the Count of San Esteban; Álvaro's powerful widow protected their daughter, who eventually married the Duke of Infantado.[103] Juan had thought beyond his legitimate offspring, however, and also created entails for both of his illegitimate children, substantial inheritances that allowed his illegitimate son, Pedro, to become the first Lord of Fuentidueña, and his illegitimate daughter, María, to marry don Juan Mendoza y de Luna.[104] In spite of his own inglorious execution (and with considerable help from the women in his family), Álvaro de Luna had thus managed to extend his family's influence and connections through the alliances of both his legitimate and illegitimate children. In his analysis of the Fernández de Córdoba family, Yuen-Gen Liang argued for the importance of noble marriage, which "allowed parents to legally pass the social status, economic and material resources, and political offices that they had earned in their lifetimes to their progeny."[105] Ironically, this role was sometimes played by children born outside of the bonds of marriage, suggesting that illegitimate children were regarded as intrinsically part of the noble family, connected enough to the lineage that their own marriage could be seen as extending it.

In order for illegitimate children to fulfill this role, however, they needed the recognition and financial support of their fathers. Fathers who provided this assistance were enacting the role of paterfamilias and enhancing the lineage. As previously noted, a father's financial support for illegitimate daughters most often came in the form of a dowry, which would enable them to make advantageous marriages, even if illegitimate daughters might not receive the same dowry as their legitimate sisters. For example, the third Duke of Medina Sidonia gave his eldest legitimate daughter an extravagant dowry of 26 million maravedís, and her younger legitimate sister was part of a double-marriage contract that carried a payment from her father of 30 million maravedís.[106] Writing his will in the heat of July 1507 in Seville, the duke left his two still-unmarried legitimate daughters dowries of 6 million maravedís each, and his two illegitimate daughters dowries of 2 million maravedís each.[107] As for the children of the third Duke of Infantado discussed at the beginning of the this chapter, there was a hierarchy based in part on age and legitimacy operating within the Duke of Medina Sidonia's family, but all the daughters were provided with a dowry.

The marriages of illegitimate daughters also reveal the active role that some fathers played in their daughters' lives. The second Count of Feria was personally engaged in the marriage negotiations of his illegitimate daughter María Manuel, arranging for her to marry his first wife's nephew and when that engagement fell through, marrying her to the second Count of Medellín. He gave María two quentos in dowry at the time of her marriage, with another quento being given later on (probably after the marriage had been successfully consummated), and he financed this dowry by transferring 250,000 maravedís of annual income from the royal tithes that he had the right to collect in the town of Écija.[108] The Count of Feria's careful (and expensive) arrangements for the marriage of his illegitimate daughter demonstrate that he saw her as playing a role in his lineage. His first attempt to arrange a marriage would have married María to a close kin of his deceased wife (who was not María's mother), and his second choice for her marriage partner was a man whose title (count) was equal to his own. He also went to some pains to finance the marriage appropriately and provide María with a substantial dowry. Other noblemen also recorded the trouble and expense they went to in arranging the marriages of their illegitimate daughters. The fifth Duke of Benavente recorded in his will in 1530 that his illegitimate daughter María was an hija bastarda, meaning she was born during his marriage and was thus the product of adultery. Nevertheless, the duke had betrothed (*esta concertado*) María to don Antonio, the son of don Gonçalo Franco, and he made arrangements in his will to finish providing María's dowry after his death, according to the agreement he had with don Gonçalo.[109] This kind of material support shaped the lives of illegitimate daughters, whose carefully arranged marriages demonstrated a father's power and social standing among his peers and incorporated them into the network of noble alliances.

Noblemen in need of an heir or a marriage alliance with a powerful family were also quite capable of using their illegitimate children as pawns in the family strategy. In doing this they had a royal precedent. Charles

V, the Holy Roman Emperor, in pursuit of his own strategies, forced his illegitimate daughter Margaret of Parma into two marriages with men who were regarded as vicious and depraved by their contemporaries. Charles Steen argued that Charles was guided by the advice of his aunt Margaret of Austria, who "believed that the child of an emperor, even an illegitimate one, had great political value, for minor houses were always eager to marry into great dynasties without reservations, and happy in-laws made enduring allies."[110] Charles's chancellor, Mercurino Gattinara, wanted Charles to expand his influence in Italy. Therefore, Charles first married his thirteen-year-old daughter to twenty-seven-year-old Alessandro de Medici, whose opponents accused him of attacking people, confiscating goods at will, and inflicting "humiliation and rape even on nuns."[111] Fortunately for Margaret, Alessandro was assassinated in 1537 before the marriage was consummated, but her father promptly (the contract was concluded in June of 1538) rushed her into a new marriage with twelve-year-old Ottavio Farnese, grandson of Pope Paul III, whose father was accused of raping a bishop so violently that the young man died from the attack. Margaret was several years older than Ottavio, whom she described in a letter as "brutish, improper, unrefined, and a swine," and who proved incapable of consummating the marriage.[112] Although she was showered with jewels and favors from the Italian nobility and the papacy, Margaret's prestigious marriages were made to benefit her father who, according to Charles Steen, saw his daughter as "merely a pawn in the complicated game of dynastic chess."[113]

The nobility likewise saw their illegitimate children as chess pieces in their family strategy. In an example that illustrates both the fluidity of legitimacy and the importance of marriage in constructing dynasties, the second Count of Arcos had as many as twenty-eight illegitimate children with at least three different women, but no legitimate children. After the death of his wife, he married one of his mistresses, doña Leonor Nuñez, in 1448, and obtained a royal decree to legitimate their children that same year.[114] In addition to legitimating his children, he provided for them in his will and personally arranged the marriages of six newly legitimated daughters and two legitimated sons. The count, intent on preserving the dynasty, was involved to the point of being dictatorial when arranging these marriages. In 1457, the year his eldest legitimated son, Pedro, died in battle, the count arranged for his younger legitimated son, Rodrigo (now his heir), to marry doña Beatriz Marmolejo. Rodrigo was not yet fourteen, the legal age to contract a marriage, and he gave a deposition in Seville that his father, whom he said he was afraid of, was forcing him into the marriage against his will. Two years later, when he had reached the age of fourteen, he left another notarized legal document, complete with witnesses, stating that he had been forced to become engaged (*palabras de desposadas*) and had not consummated the marriage.[115]

These documents eventually allowed the marriage to be annulled, and Rodrigo went on to face the same dilemma that had haunted his father. He married a second time, to doña Beatriz Pacheco, but they had no children, leaving Rodrigo with three illegitimate daughters who had been born (between his marriages) from a liaison with Inés de la Fuente, daughter of a local elite (*hidalgo*) in Marchena. Rodrigo, in spite of resenting his father's interference in his own first marriage, used a very similar tactic to solve his own dilemma through the marriage of his daughter. Even illegitimate girls, because of the potential of their marriages, could be useful in the effort to pass on the title to one's male descendants. Rodrigo legitimated his eldest daughter, Francisca, and stipulated in his will that his title should pass to Francisca's son after his death. He then arranged for Francisca to marry a distant cousin, Luis Ponce de León, Lord of Villagracia. Their (legitimate) son, Rodrigo, inherited the title and estate at a very young age and became the first Duke of Arcos, thus carrying the dynasty safely into the future.[116]

Careers in the church were also part of noble family strategy, and a place where illegitimate children had the potential to reflect glory on their noble families and be of use to their fathers. Alonso de Aragón, the illegitimate son of King Ferdinand of Aragón, became the archbishop of Zaragoza, a position that he used to the benefit of his royal father. "A great military strategist and political bastion of his father, Fernando II of Aragón," he helped maintain control of Aragón during the absences of the king.[117] In turn, the careers of Alonso's own illegitimate children reflect several generations of a careful family strategy, combining prestigious marriages with brilliant careers in the church. Alonso's daughter Ana married the sixth Duke of Medina Sidonia, and his daughter Juana married the third Duke of Gandía.[118] Both of his illegitimate sons entered the church, and after Alonso's death in 1520, his elder illegitimate son, Juan, became the next archbishop of Zaragoza. In 1539 Alonso's younger illegitimate son, Hernando, held the post in his turn. Thus Alonso's four illegitimate children made alliances with two important noble families in Castile and retained control of a key church post in Aragón for the bulk of the sixteenth century. Alonso de Aragón was not the only noble clergyman to pass on his post to his son. Alfonso de Fonseca, the archbishop of Santiago de Compostela, had an illegitimate son who held the same post after his father and had at least one illegitimate child of his own, and Luis de Acuña, the bishop of Burgos, had an illegitimate son who became the bishop of Zamora.[119]

Many illegitimate daughters became nuns, often entering the convent at an earlier age than their legitimate sisters, probably in part because of difficulties over custody arrangements for illegitimate girls.[120] Convents could be a place to put illegitimate daughters who might otherwise be hard to place, providing them with a safe refuge and relieving other family members of their care. But the examples above demonstrate that many illegitimate daughters made prestigious marriages, suggesting that the convent could also be a deliberate choice of a career. An interesting example of an involved father who was thinking dynastically demonstrates the difficulty of untangling the life choices of illegitimate children from the plans their fathers had for them. Don Juan Pacheco de Silva, Lord of Villarejo de Fuentes, who had no legitimate children, wished his illegitimate daughter Gerónima to marry her first cousin don Luis Pacheco (the son of Juan's elder brother), who would eventually inherit a substantial part of Juan's estate because Juan had no surviving legitimate children. As in the Arcos family cited above, this marriage would have meant that Juan's legitimate grandchildren would inherit his estate even though he had no legitimate children. The young man, however, declined and married someone else instead, and Gerónima took the veil in the Dominican convent of Madre de Dios in Toledo, where her aunt was the prioress. Gerónima's father supported her choice financially, identifying her as Sister Gerónima de los Ángeles in his will in 1584 and leaving her 6,000 maravedís.[121]

Don Juan Pacheco de Silva took an active part in the future of his illegitimate daughter, an involvement that was undoubtedly increased by his lack of legitimate heirs. When the dynastic marriage he had planned for his daughter did not work out, Juan may have compelled his daughter to enter the convent, or he may have supported her wish to do so. He was a generous patron of religious institutions, founding a college for Jesuit novitiates, but his generosity (like his marriage plans for his daughter) tended to support his lineage and dynasty. He built a chapel in the church in Villarejo de Fuentes where he reinterred the bodies of his parents, moving them from Cuenca; he specified that the successors of his house should be buried there also.[122] The combination of dynastic concerns and religious sentiments that guided Juan Pacheco de Silva's building projects may also have guided his plans for the future of his daughter. If she could not extend his lineage, she could at least play her part in his religious projects. The mixture of social, financial, and religious motivations that ended in Gerónima becoming a nun was not unusual as families decided whether to devote their daughters to religious careers.[123]

Having sisters, daughters, aunts, and cousins in convents conferred both spiritual and financial benefits on families, who paid lower dowries for convent entry than for marriage, enjoyed the benefits of having female relatives who could act as spiritual intercessors, and had access to the convent's role in extending credit to lay people.[124] Family members who were prominent religious figures could be advantageous to the entire lineage. Ana Dorotea, the illegitimate daughter of Emperor Rudolph II, was a nun at the Descalzas Reales convent in Madrid where, Vanessa Cruz Medina argued, she "behaved as a full-fledged Habsburg, maneuvering and influencing the political scene from within" the convent.[125] Thus the resources invested in the church careers of illegitimate children were often rewarded. The Marquis de Santillana left a dowry of 2,000 maravedís to his illegitimate daughter Leonor, a nun in the convent of Santa Clara in Guadalajara. After Leonor's death the dowry would be donated to the convent. This investment paid off, as by 1480 Leonor had become the abbess of Santa Clara.[126]

Such investments might simply provide a living for an illegitimate child, but they also had the potential to launch careers that might benefit the entire family. The first Duke of Nájera stipulated that his illegitimate son Francisco should study for a church career and provided him with an entailed estate that was taken from the resources the duke had given in dowry to Francisco's elder, legitimate sister Guiomar, who had died childless. Francisco rewarded his father's investment, becoming the bishop of Orense, Salamanca, and Sigüenza and Charles V's chaplain and ambassador to France.[127] This is an interesting case of an illegitimate child making use of a previously failed investment. When Guiomar's prestigious marriage ended in her death without children, the substantial sum of her dowry came back to her birth family without benefiting the lineage by making the new and advantageous connection that had been hoped for from her marriage. When that dowry was reinvested in a younger, illegitimate brother's career, however, the dowry did bring a substantial benefit to the family lineage.

Like the church, the military could simultaneously provide for illegitimate sons and make the most of them as potential family assets. Service in the military could also bring these young men into proximity with their noble fathers. The third Duke of Alba's illegitimate son Hernando was a highly successful soldier who enjoyed the support and patronage of his father throughout his career. He served with the duke in Naples and by 1556 had received the title of grand prior of Castile of the Order of St. John of Jerusalem. In 1566 he was one of the military commanders who relieved the siege of Malta, and he served from 1567 to 1570 as his father's chief cavalry officer. Biographers of the famous duke maintain that the presence of his illegitimate son was "a profound solace to him" throughout his long military campaigns, and their shared military expertise meant that their lives ran along similar lines.[128]

PATERNAL REWARDS

Underlying all the possible roles that illegitimate children could perform within the family was the prospect that they could inherit the title. In Spain and across Europe, illegitimate children had the potential to provide their fathers and their lineage with an heir if the legitimate marriage failed to produce a son. As late as the eighteenth century, the French nobility and royalty occasionally, although not entirely successfully, "turned to extramarital offspring as reserve heirs."[129] Although in practice this rarely worked smoothly in the early modern period, it was a persistent idea and noble fathers sometimes tried hard to make it work.

For minor nobility, or noblemen who had not married, the legitimacy of their heirs might be less of an issue. In 1470 King Enrique IV of Castile gave the younger brother of the first Count of Aguilar permission to form a mayorazgo for his eldest son, Juan Ramírez. In 1534 Juan Ramírez wrote his will, testifying that as a result of this entail, he was the lord of a collection of small municipalities in La Rioja and Navarre, and that his heirs were his two illegitimate sons. Juan Ramírez's uncle Juan Enríquez (another younger brother of the first Count of Aguilar) was in a similar position. Both men were minor nobility, not the principal titleholders in this lineage, neither married, and both had illegitimate sons who inherited. Juan Enríquez's eldest son inherited "some places that his father had left him" and his second son entered the church. Juan Ramírez's sons did even better. Both of them were hijos naturales, their mother being single and a resident of one of the towns forming the entail. His will was not contested, and his sons, Juan and Carlos, flourished, dividing their father's municipalities between them. Carlos's descendants continued as local nobility, lords of the towns he had inherited, and Juan's descendants acquired titles, becoming the Counts of Murillo by the seventeenth century.[130] In this case the illegitimate grandsons of a younger son helped maintain the connection between an aristocratic family and a particular location in northern Spain that had endured since the mid-fourteenth century, and even managed to eventually elevate it to a title. This scenario helps explain why the nobility might invest in illegitimate sons; in the farsighted vision of a social class invested in hierarchy and lineage, any tool that contained the possibility of advancing the family was worth the effort.

Moving up the hierarchy, illegitimate sons could also be an asset to titled noblemen whose marriages had not produced the essential male heir who could carry on the title. As the stakes got higher, however, it became more complex and problematic to have an illegitimate child inherit. The first Duke of Medina Sidonia's marriage was childless, but he had eight illegitimate children. In 1457 the king gave him permission to form a mayorazgo for his eldest illegitimate son, Enrique. In order to ensure that Enrique would not suffer the disgrace of being labeled bastardo, the duke married Enrique's mother in 1468, after he was widowed and just before he died.[131] Legally, this marriage did not change Enrique's status, given that he had been born during the duke's first marriage and was in fact an hijo bastardo, but the duke seemed to feel that the marriage to Enrique's mother would strengthen Enrique's claim to the title. Perhaps it did have some social impact, since the sixteenth-century commentator Pedro Barrantes Maldonado scrupulously refers to Enrique's mother as "la duquesa Isabel" after the marriage.[132] The plan succeeded, and Enrique became the second Duke of Medina Sidonia, although his inheritance resulted in a lengthy lawsuit and eventual settlement between his father and his paternal aunt, who had claims on the inheritance due to the first duke's lack of legitimate children.

A few decades later, when the Medinaceli family was raised to the rank of duke, the first duke, finding himself without a legitimate male heir, tried to do the same thing. He recognized his illegitimate son Juan and then married Juan's mother, a nonnoble woman, just before he died in 1501. Technically this maneuver was illegal, as Juan (like Enrique before him) had been born while his father was married (making him an hijo bastardo), so marrying Juan's mother was not enough to legitimize him. In this case an intense legal battle ensued between Juan and his paternal uncle, creating a feud that spread beyond the immediate family and turned violent. The third Duke of Infantado enthusiastically joined in the fight, invading Medinaceli in support of Juan's uncle. Ferdinand and Isabel, the Catholic Monarchs, had to intervene to stop the growing violence, sending the case to court. Juan did eventually succeed in keeping the title.[133]

This case casts light on how the nobility viewed illegitimacy. For the nobility, illegitimacy and illegitimate children were not automatically either a problem or a sin. They were useful if an heir was needed and problematic only when they threatened to disrupt the inheritance process. An example of this is the second Count of Castañeda, who, having no legitimate children, legitimated his eldest son in 1453 and made him the heir to the title. The legitimation was promptly challenged by the second count's brother, the Count of Osorno (who had two illegitimate children of his own), who argued that he was the rightful heir because the Castañeda entail barred legitimated children from inheriting. The Count of Castañeda went so far as falsifying documents, adding the word "legitimated" to the original language of the entail in order to defend his son's inheritance.[134] In this case the presence of an illegitimate son was useful for his father, who wanted to hand his title down to his own offspring, but problematic to his uncle, who had a valid claim to that same title and estate.

The concern for lineage and dynasty and the need for male heirs also had personal implications. As previously mentioned, an important aspect of successful masculinity in early modern Castile was the ability to sire children. Illegitimate children could resolve the dilemma of young men unable to marry but needing to demonstrate their sexual potency in a society that valued virility as a sign of masculinity. In the winter of 1516–17, Juan de Velasco, a young nobleman from the ducal house of Frías, seduced Ana de Galves, who then gave birth to their son, Baltasar. Juan de Velasco formally acknowledged his paternity, giving Ana a dowry of 200 ducados, which enabled her to marry "a very honorable hidalgo."[135] Juan was a courtier, a role that combined with his unmarried status to challenge his masculinity even in the early sixteenth century. According to Elizabeth Lehfeldt, court life, which involved subjection to the king and an increasingly frivolous lifestyle based on conspicuous consumption, was "portrayed as decadent, and thus threatening to masculinity" by the seventeenth century.[136] In the winter of 1516–17, Luis de Herrera, the inquisitive servant of Cardinal Francisco Ximenez, wondered why Juan was spending so much time in the town of Bayona when the court was in Madrid. He asked various residents of Bayona, who obligingly informed him that "the cause was the daughter of the host where [don Juan] was staying who was very well dressed."[137] Luis de Herrera permitted himself to doubt this because, he claimed, "el señor don Juan had in court a reputation for being castrated [*en reputacion de Capon*]."[138] The hidalgo he mentioned this to "said to [him], 'look, the one you call castrated left the daughter of the host pregnant.'"[139]

The result of this pregnancy was Baltasar de Velasco, whom one witness "saw cared for in the said house where the said maiden was" and heard referred to as "Velasquito."[140] In the vicious world of court rumors, where courtiers like Luis de Herrera could openly speculate on another man's virility, the presence of Ana and her son served to restore Juan de Velasco's damaged prestige and affirm his masculinity.[141] By giving his son his name, Juan de Velasco did not need to marry his son's mother to reap the benefits of having a son, benefits that included repairing his masculine reputation. The archival documents refer to Juan as "castrated," probably indicating that he was considered impotent. Years later, after Juan was dead, Baltasar was able to collect the accounts of five witnesses who were prepared to swear under oath that Juan had been his father. The publicity surrounding this affair was part of Juan's performance of masculinity. The presence of his mistress helped him repair a damaged masculine reputation without the expense and difficulty of marriage, a burden that he perhaps could not afford at that time.

Another common fate for younger sons that precluded marriage and legitimate children was a career in the church. One man who brilliantly managed to balance the demands of a celibate career with the need to demonstrate virility was Cardinal Pedro González de Mendoza, son of the Marquis of Santillana and brother of the first Duke of Infantado. Pedro González de Mendoza rose rapidly from bishop of Sigüenza and abbot of Valladolid to the archbishop of Toledo and Seville and finally became a cardinal.[142] He was a key player in the success of Isabel of Castile's bid for power in the fifteenth century, fought for her in the civil war that ensued, and was a powerful member of her government.[143] His wealth, political power, military prowess, and service to the crown were well established. From 1469 to 1490 "the cardinal built a private fortune with an income one-quarter the size of that of the archbishopric of Toledo, the richest see in Spain."[144] In addition to these elements of masculinity, the cardinal was able to prove his sexual potency by fathering three sons by two different noblewomen.[145] He went on to further demonstrate his masculinity by successfully passing his wealth and status on to his sons. He obtained royal and papal legitimations for all three of his sons, finessing their legal status as children of an ordained Catholic clergyman by focusing on the unmarried status of their mothers.[146] In addition, he formed entails for them that they could inherit and pass down to their own children. One of his sons became the Marquis of Cenete, another the Count of Mélito, and both were patriarchs in their own right. This successful launch of two more noble dynasties gives an insight into the potential that illegitimate children held for their fathers' lineages. The fact that the cardinal had two extramarital families does not seem to have hampered his spectacular career in the Catholic Church, and his sons started important cadet branches of the powerful Mendoza family. For the nobility, verifiable masculinity was an important factor in retaining power in early modern Spain, and clerical celibacy, even at the very highest levels, was not a pressing concern.

These cases make abundantly clear the potential usefulness of illegitimate children, but it is more difficult to uncover any sense of the emotional dynamics of the noble family. Family strategies to use a son born out of wedlock as a substitute heir could create contact between father and illegitimate son, providing glimpses of possible personal relationships as well as insight into the complex families and households of the nobility. Left after two marriages with two legitimate daughters (who could not inherit his title because of the terms of the Frías mayorazgo) and four illegitimate sons, the first Duke of Frías (d. 1512) made a concentrated attempt to leave his title and the Frías entail to his youngest illegitimate son. In pursuit of this goal, the duke made his recognition of this youngest son very public, enabling various residents of the city of Burgos to affirm that Bernaldino de Velasco was indeed the youngest illegitimate son of the first Duke of Frías and leaving a record of actions that demonstrated his paternity. The duke provided Bernaldino with a wet nurse and then created a household for him under the supervision of a tutor, dressed him in silk and velvet "as befit the son of a duke," and arranged for him to go to court and serve as a page to Queen Germain de la Foix.[147] Subsequently, the duke petitioned for a legitimation for his son and tried to legally ensure that he would inherit through a deathbed marriage to the boy's mother. Although all these actions provided for the boy's daily needs, they also fulfilled the paternal responsibilities prescribed by Spanish law.[148]

In the end, the duke's brother inherited his estates and title, but in trying to pass his estates down to his illegitimate son, the duke became directly involved in his son's life and household, creating at least the possibility of a personal relationship between father and son. The duke also created a complex family situation in which he maintained at least three different households: one of which contained his second wife, their daughter, and his daughter from his first marriage, one containing his mistress, and one containing his youngest illegitimate son and that son's nurse and tutor. Although the Duke of Frías was clearly not changing diapers, he was directing his son's upbringing and, as Jane Mangan put it, "enacting the responsibilities of fatherhood," in part because he cared so much about who would inherit his title.[149]

The presence of a son and heir meant personal success for noblemen who defined themselves, at least in part, in relation to the dynasties they represented. Their strategies for successful inheritance and the promotion of their lineage could be undone in a moment with the death of a legitimate child but could also be repaired by the presence of illegitimate children. Personal affection for children (both legitimate and illegitimate) combined with an intense need for honor and a secure lineage gave some illegitimate children a role in the inheritance process. It is perhaps more surprising that illegitimate children who had no chance of inheriting the title so often carried out positions of trust and authority within families. We have already seen the long-standing relationship between the third Duke of Alba and his illegitimate son Hernando who fought and worked together for years on numerous royal campaigns. Other noble fathers also depended on their illegitimate children. The fifth Duke of Benavente named the elder of his two illegitimate sons as one of the executors of his will. The position of executor indicated that the duke trusted his illegitimate son Juan to carry out the provisions of his will and protect his younger legitimate half-siblings even though one of them would inherit the title that Juan was denied due to his illegitimacy.[150] Fernando de Andrade, Count of Villalba, had two illegitimate sons, one of whom was still a minor when he wrote his will in 1540. Fernando charged his elder illegitimate son (also named Fernando) with the guardianship of his younger brother: "To have and care for his person and goods until he comes of age, and to take charge of what he studies and learns and to arrange for him to become a clergyman." The younger, illegitimate

Fernando was to share this guardianship with his father's widow, who was not the mother of either of the boys, illustrating once again the complex intersection of formal and affective roles in the noble family.[151]

Another example of an involved father and a complex household is the case of Catalina de Mendoza, illegitimate daughter of the fourth Count of Tendilla. When she was two years old, her father removed her from her mother's care and took responsibility for her, sending her to live with his parents. Her grandmother, in turn, entrusted her to the care of her own youngest daughter, María (the Count of Tendilla's younger sister), who was only eighteen at the time. Again, the Count of Tendilla did not personally care for his daughter, or even provide her education, but he was directly involved in her life, and Catalina grew up in the context of his immediate family. When she rejected the prestigious marriage her family had planned for her and chose to become a *beata*, her father objected strenuously.[152] Catalina achieved her goal, however, and assumed the habit of a beata in 1571. The dispute must not have damaged their relationship substantially, because when her father was appointed viceroy of Naples later that same year, he asked Catalina to manage the vast Tendilla estates in his absence, even though he had several living legitimate male children.[153] In this particular case, father and daughter had developed a working relationship that depended on the count's trust in Catalina's skills and included the ability to disagree.

What is perhaps most striking about the careers and marriages of the illegitimate children of the nobility is not their individual brilliance, but rather the systematic attention paid to them by their families. The first Duke of Nájera, for example, had nine legitimate children and twenty illegitimate children, at least nine of whom are mentioned by name in his will. His paternal concerns, as articulated in his will, cover most of the categories discussed in this chapter. In spite of the death of his eldest legitimate son in early adulthood, he did not need to turn to his illegitimate sons as substitute heirs, because he had a second legitimate son who would eventually become the second Duke of Nájera, and with twenty-nine known children, his virility was not in doubt. But he recognized and supported his illegitimate children, naming their mothers in his will and leaving legacies to his sons. The duke left his eldest illegitimate son, Álvaro, a mayorazgo composed of the duke's houses in Burgos and Carrión, a substantial yearly income, and jurisdiction over one hundred vassals. He left similar legacies to his other illegitimate sons, as well as a dowry for one of his illegitimate daughters, Ana, provided that she marry someone approved of by his executors.

The duke also directed his son's careers, stating that Francisco should train to enter the church and leaving him a yearly income to support his studies, while his brother Jorge should serve the prince, later Charles V. Álvaro had already become a soldier, commanding the duke's troops in Navarre, and the duke recognized that by leaving him his gray horse and his arms in the will. Concerned about custody, the duke left several of his younger illegitimate sons to the care of their eldest legitimate half-brother, Antonio, and he stated that one of his mistresses, Espinosa, was housed in a convent with all of his illegitimate daughters. The duke gave his eldest illegitimate daughter, Ana, the option of going to Aragón with her legitimate half-sister Guiomar or staying in the convent with a group of about eight other sisters and half-sisters who apparently lived there. Although it is not clear what Ana chose to do, seven of the duke's illegitimate daughters became nuns, one becoming the abbess of Santa Clara in Burgos and another the prioress of the distinguished convent of Las Huelgas in Burgos. The remaining daughter married Diego Orense, Lord of las Villas de Amaya and mayor of Burgos. The duke's systematic attention to his illegitimate children provided for their support, custody, marriages, and careers, and was rewarded by the creation of a group of siblings based in and around Burgos who distinguished themselves militarily and religiously and apparently worked together with their legitimate half-siblings in pursuit of family interests. The duke provided all this care and support in addition to providing for his remaining legitimate son and heir, marrying off six legitimate daughters, and starting a seventh on a religious career that would culminate in her being the abbess of the convent of Las Huelgas in Burgos in company with her illegitimate half-sister, who was the convent's prioress.[154] The duke was known as a brilliant military strategist and a confirmed philanderer, but from this angle he also appears as a concerned, attentive, and responsible father.

The importance of this sense of obligation toward illegitimate children is captured in the will of the second Count of Tendilla, who wrote in 1575 that he was leaving an annual income to a boy who was being raised as his in another household, "although I do not think he is [my son]."[155] Even when their paternity was in doubt, it seems that some noblemen were concerned to appear to be providing for any child who might be their own offspring. Comments made by fathers throughout this chapter suggest a sense that their illegitimate children reflected their own status and reputation. The Count of Villalba asked that his illegitimate son be educated as was "required by his status and by whose son he" was and the third Duke of Gandía asked his heir to recognize his illegitimate brother "as a brother and to treat him as such."[156] Indeed, this issue of status was recognized by observers of the nobility as well, enabling a citizen of Burgos to relate (when asked years later by a lawyer) that the first Duke of Frías had dressed his illegitimate son "as befit the son of a duke."[157]

This sense of duty is easier to trace in the documents than paternal affection, but sometimes the two seem to have overlapped. Sixteenth-century historian and commentator Pedro Barrantes Maldonado, discussing the first Duke of Medina Sidonia's eight illegitimate children, stated, "And of these children there were three that he loved the most." Those three were his eldest son, Enrique, one of his much younger sons, Pedro, and his only daughter, Theresa, "because he did not have another daughter."[158] Having no legitimate children, the duke had the opportunity to decide which illegitimate child to leave the estate and title to. Whatever the duke may have thought, Barrantes Maldonado was at some pains to explain that Enrique got the title and estate mostly because he was the eldest, since the duke loved both Enrique and Pedro, finding them virtuous and mannerly. This was not true for all his sons, as Juan and Lorenço were described as "not having the manners to content the duke," in spite of their mother's elevated rank.[159] Barrantes Maldonado describes a clear sibling hierarchy, but the duke provided for all of his illegitimate children, with one of his less courteous sons marrying the daughter of the master of Santiago, while the other became a cleric.[160]

In spite of the widespread evidence of supportive and involved fathers, illegitimate children did not always smoothly integrate into noble families, and they were uniquely placed to disrupt that hallmark of noble masculinity, the smooth transfer of property between generations. Their presence could anger wives, they could sue their legitimate half-siblings over inheritance, and they did not always cooperate with their fathers' family strategies. Many of the tensions around the presence of illegitimate children occurred after a father's death, especially when the only legitimate heirs were female and the illegitimate children were male. Don Francisco de Ávila, lord of the estate of Ciudad-Rodrigo, had a legitimate daughter and an illegitimate son. After his death his adult son, now a councilman (*regidor*) in the city of Ciudad-Rodrigo, sued in 1558 to inherit his father's estate, and *his* son (Francisco's grandson) continued the lawsuit in his turn.[161] The lawsuit does not seem to have been successful, but it was lengthy and was doubtless also both disruptive and expensive. Other illegitimate children, however, did gain something from litigating against their father's families. In the late fifteenth century, don Juan Mateo, who had no surviving legitimate children, was the third Count of Lodosa and the younger brother of the second Count of Aguilar. His illegitimate son, Juan Hurtado de Mendoza, sued the Counts of Aguilar for part of the property (the estate of Soto) and won.[162] Although these lawsuits were disruptive to noblemen and noble families, they were also difficult and expensive for illegitimate children to pursue. Chapter 4 explores the lives and careers of illegitimate adults and analyzes these lawsuits from that perspective.

Noblemen could also face censure if their illegitimate children were an indication of unbridled or uncontrolled sexuality or a lack of self-control in general. Although early modern masculinity could accommodate and even be enhanced by the presence of illegitimate children, there were limits to how far noblemen could go in indulging their sexuality. The limits varied and were usually related to public perception and the ways in which a man's performance of masculinity was perceived. The Duke of Nájera could have twenty illegitimate children without incurring lasting censure in part because he was perceived as being in control of his family, his estates, his marriage, and his illegitimate children, whose futures he firmly dictated. But public scandals that disrupted families and created notoriety were not welcome.

The story of the third Duke of Infantado that began this chapter displays some of the complications that extramarital sexuality could precipitate. The third duke had a wife, multiple mistresses, and many children, both legitimate and illegitimate. Because he was virile, wealthy, and powerful, none of his illegitimate children damaged his reputation. He lost control of the situation only when, after his wife's death, he became infatuated with his daughter's maid, María Maldonado. When his adult children tried to intervene, the besotted duke married María, giving her both the title of duchess and a fair portion of his worldly goods. But the duke "did not consummate the marriage due to his many illnesses, weakness, and age."[163] In this case the lack of illegitimate children helped damage the duke's masculinity because it provided at least anecdotal proof of a lack of virility. An unconsummated marriage to a woman so far below him in social status made the duke the laughingstock of his contemporaries and complicated his ability to hand on his property to his heirs. After the duke's death his son and heir had to sue María to regain the property she had taken with her (the duke's movable goods that should have gone to his children) when she left the palace. The new duke won the lawsuit, but María made a successful second marriage, remained a wealthy woman, and continued to use the title of Duchess of Infantado throughout her long life.[164] In this case it was not the duke's illegitimate children that caused tension or legal disputes within the family, but his relationship with yet another woman. María's successful career is an interesting commentary on the opportunities that extramarital sexuality could sometimes provide women, a topic that the next chapter explores in depth.

Studying the relationships between noblemen and their illegitimate children presents a more nuanced view of the Spanish patriarchy and of the sometimes contradictory ways in which masculinity was practiced by noblemen. Although kings and noblemen were the primary beneficiaries of this patriarchy, having sexual access to a wide range of women both within and without the confines of marriage, they also seem to have had a sense that masculine obligations included being responsible fathers who provided financial support, education, dowries, and careers to their illegitimate offspring. For illegitimate children, the men at the top of the patriarchal family could (and sometimes undoubtedly did) skip this obligation, which was difficult to force them to perform. A surprising number of noblemen, however, did choose to support their illegitimate children. Their sense of obligation was not completely disinterested, given that illegitimate children could be substantial assets to the family strategy. Ultimately, illegitimate children had the potential to serve as heirs to property, money, power, and tradition, making them possible assets who could solve the most crippling dilemma that faced noblemen who were invested in the delicate task of building a lineage in an age of rampant child mortality. If that potential was to be realized, an investment in these children was necessary. They needed basic support (food, clothes, shelter, and education), careers and good marriages, and public recognition of their status as members of the nobility.

Sometimes this investment played out according to plan. A childless marriage could be redeemed and a nobleman's masculine reputation rescued by the presence of an illegitimate child, properly raised and recognized, who could inherit and keep the property within the family. More often, recognizing and supporting illegitimate children had unexpected consequences. Noblemen who took care to raise and educate their illegitimate children were sometimes pulled into more personal relationships with them, creating emotional and affective ties with those children and complex households that did not conform to the patrilineal model of a married couple and their legitimate offspring. Thus the men at the top of the social hierarchy who took advantage of the authoritarian model of patriarchy to have sex with multiple women and cheat on their wives could also be men embedded in a web of tolerant and even affectionate family relationships outside of marriage that had the potential to simultaneously sustain them emotionally and rescue their dynasties from extinction. Invested heavily in the success of the lineage, noblemen were active but often also controlling or even coercive fathers, and the illegitimate child who was publicly recognized was also ideally placed to disrupt the inheritance process by challenging the legal heir (especially if that heir was female) or making expensive claims on the next generation of a noble family. As sons and daughters of noblemen, but with mothers who embodied a wide range of social statuses, illegitimate children's flexible identities were both an asset and a threat to the noble lineage.

2

Beyond Chastity

Women, Illegitimate Children, and Reputation

Ana de Villagrán grew up in Guadalajara about the turn of the sixteenth century. As a young woman, she achieved a post as lady-in-waiting to the Duchess of Infantado, María de Luna, who presided over the luxurious Infantado Palace in the heart of the city of Guadalajara. Ana's family was not noble, but they must have had enough status to enable her to achieve that post. Young and beautiful, Ana attracted the attention of the duke's younger brother Juan, who at fifty years of age was disenchanted with his own wife, Beatriz de Zúñiga, with whom he already had three children. Ana's family had probably hoped that service with the duchess would yield a dowry and a marriage that would raise their social status. Instead, Ana became the concubine (*manceba*) of Juan de Mendoza, with whom she had five children. The affair was scandalous because Juan mistreated his wife, who was disgusted by his public infidelity. When Beatriz died, it was rumored that Juan and Ana had poisoned her. Juan made the scandal worse by marrying Ana in time for their sixth child to be born from a legitimate marriage.

Having finally achieved marriage into the ducal family, Ana neverthe-less faced a difficult situation when Juan died in 1517. Trying to adequately provide for two families from an entailed estate, Juan had attempted to break the entail and leave the town of Beleña to Ana and their illegitimate children. This attempt infringed on the property rights of his uncle, the Count of Coruña. After Juan's death the incensed count attacked his nephew's will in court and mounted a military assault on Beleña, threatening to kill Ana if she did not release her claim on the town. Ana was forced to relinquish Beleña and to retreat back to Guadalajara. In the end Ana and her five illegitimate children inherited the fifth (quinto) of Juan's belongings that were not entailed, while her sixth daughter (who was legitimate) inherited with her legitimate half-siblings from Juan's first marriage.[1] Ana lived on in Guadalajara as a widow until, in the bitter cold of early January, 1534, she signed her will with the formulaic phrase used by widows, "the sad doña Ana."[2]

Ana de Villagrán's life was difficult, but it was not unique. She was vilified in the legal documents from the dispute over Beleña as being "flighty" and having caused all Juan's troubles by enslaving him through her enchantments.[3] Her role as a concubine was public knowledge within her community of Guadalajara and damaged her reputation, and her economic situation remained troubled and uncertain. Guadalajara was, however, home to other women who had illegitimate children with the men of the Mendoza family. Doña Mayor Díaz de Mendoza had three illegitimate children with Ana's husband Juan before his first marriage.[4] Doña Ana de Barnuevo, daughter of an elite (hidalgo) family in the city had two children with don García Lasso de Mendoza, the abbot of Santillana y Santander, who could not marry her because of his clerical status.[5] Doña Leonor Beltrán had three children out of wedlock with the second Count of Tendilla, and doña Beatriz de Sacedón subsequently had another illegitimate son with the same Count of Tendilla.[6] As the ancestral home of the Mendoza clan, Guadalajara was the loose center of a wide network of families, both the official ones blessed by the church and the less formal ones that sprang up around them. However scandalous her initial sexual relationship was, Ana was not the only woman in Guadalajara with illegitimate children and an ambiguous connection to issues of honor and reputation. Her time as Juan de Mendoza's concubine was only a part of her longer life, which included marriage and seventeen years of widowhood. Ana was a mistress, but she was also a wife, a stepmother, and a widow, roles that many women played throughout their life cycle.

Studying the women who had illegitimate children with noblemen complicates our understanding of femininity and maternity. In a society that had a strong literary and legal tradition of strict chastity and enclosure as the prescribed behavior for women, a distrust of women's ability to be virtuous, and an understanding of upright motherhood that could only be enacted within Christian marriage, any woman with an illegitimate child should have been hopelessly compromised, or murdered, as often happened in the so-called Castilian "wife-murder plays."[7] But the evidence shows that, far from losing their lives because of a lack of chastity, most women with illegitimate children remained fully engaged in life, coping with unplanned parenthood, complex extended families, strained relationships with their partners, difficult economic situations, legal challenges, and often marriage, widowhood, careers, and relationships with grown children. The story of maternity outside the bonds of marriage challenges the notion of a good woman who was either chaste or dead, suggesting a more complex definition of femininity and a much wider array of female experiences. Analyzing the mothers of illegitimate children reveals a life cycle that could include sex and children both in and out of wedlock as well as multiple ways to enact motherhood. Success, and indeed survival, depended heavily on a woman's own agency, courage, determination, and resourcefulness. Like Ana, many women were concubines, wives, widows, stepmothers, and even nuns at different points in their lives.

This chapter argues that the mothers of illegitimate children and other women who had sex outside of marriage had a fluid and complex relationship with reputable femininity and virtuous maternity, but they were not incontrovertibly excluded from either concept. These women operated in a more nebulous social space that had potential for choice, agency, and social advancement as well as risks for themselves and for their children. The existence of illegitimate children proved a woman's fertility, which could make her a desirable marriage partner, but erased her chastity, which could compromise her ability to marry. Having illegitimate children and liaisons with men of high social status could provide women with economic resources that they could use to make honorable marriages and care for their families and children, or it could leave women legally unable to access their own resources or transmit them to family members. To complicate this, chastity was time sensitive. Although the birth of an illegitimate child could compromise a woman in the moment, twenty years later her reputation might depend not on the existence of that child but on her success or failure as a community member, a wife, a mother, a widow, or a nun.

Recent scholarship on early modern Spain has illuminated the ways in which specific groups of women (peasants in Galicia and Ybenes, women of middle status in Navarre, noblewomen in Castile, queens, and nuns) interacted with the prescribed ideals of chastity and enclosure.[8] Drawing on this body of work as well as the lives of the women in this study, it is possible to define femininity more broadly than the traditional, prescriptive idea that a good woman was chaste, enclosed, and silent. Allyson Poska argued for the existence of agentic gender expectations for women "that were familiar to early modern people and played an equally powerful role" as that of the patriarchy. She defined "agentic" as "expressing or having agency."[9] My analysis of the lives and actions of mothers of illegitimate children in Castile supports her argument by revealing a wide variety of women who, in Poska's words, lived up to "the early modern expectation that women had the opportunity to act independently, achieve success, and exert power and authority in many aspects of their lives."[10] The lives of women who had children out of wedlock reflect this definition of female agency in both the objectives these women achieved and the methods they used to gain those ends. The mothers of illegitimate children occupied a flexible moral, legal, and social space. Their capacity to make independent decisions about their sexuality or to survive sexual assault, their ability to produce children, their willingness to use the court systems, and their success in acquiring economic resources and status and passing them on to their children made it possible for them to achieve culturally recognized goals such as economic security, marriage, careers, status, and successful maternity.

A woman's social class made a difference in how she navigated the challenges posed by having illegitimate children. The women who had sexual relations with noblemen ranged from enslaved women to the wives, widows, and daughters of grandees, and the reasons they had sex outside of marriage were equally wide ranging. Women of higher social status had more access to economic resources and were more likely to pass both status and resources on to their children. Maternal lineage was a crucial factor in how illegitimate children fared in relation to succession and inheritance.[11] Noblewomen were also more able to use the legal system to their advantage and that of their children. Women of lower social status often gained economically but were less likely to pass on prestige to their children and had less access to the legal system. None of this was easy or uncontested, and not all women succeeded in achieving their goals, but the ambiguous space occupied by women who had sexual relationships and children outside the bonds of marriage gave women opportunities to exercise agency as well as presenting difficulties they had to overcome.

This chapter is based on the lives of 258 women who had extramarital relationships with noblemen. Of these women, 74 were noble,[12] 42 were not noble,[13] and the status of 142 of them is unclear.[14] Since the records used in this book track only illegitimate children whose fathers and families chose to acknowledge them and their mothers, they cannot give any concrete information on how many illegitimate children or mistresses existed for these families during this time. In addition, it is difficult to find records of women who had sexual relationships but not children with noblemen. Although some women had illicit sex with noblemen and did not get pregnant, their lack of offspring usually kept them out of inheritance strategies and disputes, making them hard for the historian to find beneath the language that shielded their honor and that of their families.[15]

FEMININITY, CHASTITY, AND MATERNITY

Unlike the definition of masculinity, which must be teased out of men's actions and extracted from the language in their wills, early modern Castile had a clear-cut definition of what constituted a good woman. In 1523 the Spanish humanist Juan Luis Vives, living not in Spain but in the Netherlands and then later in England, wrote a conduct manual for Katherine of Aragón titled *The Education of a Christian Woman*. On the one hand the book was remarkable for assuming that women needed an education, that they had the intellectual capacity to learn, and that they would be morally improved by learning.[16] On the other hand, Vives was unequivocal about the sole attribute that constituted a good woman. "A woman's only care is chastity," he proclaimed, "but in a woman, no one requires eloquence or talent or wisdom or professional skills or administration of the republic or justice or generosity; no one asks anything of her but chastity."[17] This point of view is supported by other moralists who did live in Spain, including fray Luis de León, author of *The Perfect Wife* (1583), who opined, "[Chastity is] the very being and substance of the wife, because, if she does not possess this, she is no longer a married woman but a perfidious harlot and the dirtiest mud, and the most foul-smelling and repulsive dirt."[18] Jesuit Gaspar Astete stated in 1597 that loss of virginity would result in "irreparable damage suffered by the virgin . . . whose [future] husband would be forever disgusted by her."[19] Other moralists of the time criticized any attempt to educate women, because it might endanger their chastity by allowing them to "wrongly learn other writings and secrets toward which the weak and curious feminine sex leans."[20] Secular law codes such as the *Fuero Juzgo* and the *Siete Partidas* defined the crime of "filial adultery" as "sexual relations willingly engaged in by a woman living under her father's roof" and classified this as a capital crime.[21]

By the sixteenth century, the fear of women's sexuality meant that the image of the Virgin Mary herself had become much more passive, with all symbols of sexuality or even motherhood removed and an increasing emphasis on her identity as pure and untouchable. According to Mary Elizabeth Perry, her presentation "denied the sexuality of woman and promoted the belief that it was dangerous and sinful," an idea that undermined her maternity. Charlene Villaseñor Black stated, "The cultural work performed by her [Mary] as mother was left undone."[22] This elevation of Mary separated her from ordinary women, who were identified with the female body and its tendency to sin and excess. Religious writers like fray Luis de León characterized women as lascivious, impetuous, and dangerous to men, associating them with uncontrolled sexuality. For male religious writers, the result of all this was that women should be inferior, below men in hierarchy just as the angels were below God.[23]

Early modern Castilian dramatists also emphasized the overwhelming importance of a woman's chastity. In the late sixteenth and early seventeenth centuries, Pedro Calderón de la Barca and Lope de Vega wrote plays in which a husband who believes that his wife has been unchaste feels compelled to kill her in order to defend his honor. The most famous and most gruesome of these is probably Calderón de la Barca's *The Surgeon of His Honor* (1629), in which don Gutierre has his wife, Mencía, bled to death because he thinks she has been unfaithful to him, a suspicion that is unfounded. The honor plays are still shocking and thus have received more than their fair share of attention when considering the roles of women. In point of fact, these "wife-murder" plays were only a small part of the output of either playwright, and they were only two among a multitude of successful dramatists. Their importance was exaggerated by nineteenth-century scholars, and their subject matter owed more to the thematic demands of contemporary drama than to the reality of women's lives. Melveena McKendrick argued that the impetus behind these plots was actually the increasing Castilian obsession with pure blood (limpieza de sangre), which was played out on the stage in the form of a sexual drama.[24] Murder of supposedly unfaithful wives at the hands of their husbands was rare in early modern Castile and was often severely punished with exile and disinheritance by the monarchy.[25]

These ideas and anxieties about the fundamental nature of women complicated the late medieval and early modern understanding of motherhood, as male writers were anxious about the importance of this role and the amount of agency it might give women. Before the Enlightenment religious writers in Spain (who were already wary of women) treated the mother as a secondary figure and approached motherhood with distrust, worrying endlessly about the effects a bad mother could have on her children.[26] Authors connected a mother's supposedly immoderate love for her children to a woman's tendency to excess and worried that too much maternal indulgence would endanger the children's moral education. In 1523 Juan Luis Vives fretted, "We imbibe with our mother's milk not only love but also a disposition toward certain behavior. . . . Mothers, I do not wish you to be unaware that it is your responsibility, for the most part, that evil men exist."[27] Vives's very anxiety about women's influence on their children highlights women's presumed agency in shaping the next generations. Fray Luis de León, writing toward the end of the sixteenth century, was concerned that women should give up any claims to agency by identifying first as wives and only second as mothers, submitting all familial decisions to the control of their husbands, who, as fathers of their children, exercised strict oversight in domestic affairs. In the eighteenth century the Jesuit writer Antonio Arbiol wrote about "barbarous women who, because they [did] not have even a little patience and [could not] restrain their animal love, wish[ed] their children to be raised as idiots, and hamper[ed] the father who would correct them or the teacher who would punish them as their transgressions deserved."[28] More private sources such as diaries and letters do not analyze motherhood, perhaps because, as Isabel Morant Deusa and Mónica Bolufer Peruga argued, in this time period "motherlove was considered a natural sentiment, about which there was little to say." On the other hand, letters can provide models of how mothers passed on values and knowledge to their children.[29]

These notions about motherhood raise problems for considering mothers of illegitimate children who were not married to the fathers of their children and were not necessarily even of the same social class of the men with whom they had children. Vives made one fleeting reference to illegitimate children, stating, "There are many bastard daughters who grew up with their paternal grandmothers, who were virtuous women, and deviating from their mother's character, took on the virtuous way of life of their grandmothers."[30] This characterization completely dismisses any possibility that an unmarried mother could be maternal in any positive way, and was endorsed in 1595 by Pedro López de Montoya, who felt that children could only be properly raised within a legitimate marriage.[31] And yet, with as many as one-fifth of households in various European locations headed by women (widows or never married),[32] motherhood often existed without the close supervision of a husband and father.

If we move away from the fears of religious writers like Vives and fray Luis de León, it is easier to see how a wide variety of women, both within and outside of marriage, could be maternal. The most basic component of maternity is childbirth itself, the act that makes a woman into a mother and an act that had immense importance in perpetuating noble families and lineages whether or not the child was legitimate.[33] There is evidence that the early modern world recognized childbirth as labor, a difficult but satisfying task that was deserving of support. Sixteenth-century Spanish and Mexican art includes numerous depictions of St. Anne, the mother of the Virgin Mary, resting in bed after giving birth to the Virgin while other women swaddle the Virgin, prepare her cradle, and offer St. Anne the *caldo*, or soup prescribed by Spanish doctors for women who had just given birth. Unlike the Virgin, who had a miraculous and pain-free birth, St. Anne had a normal human pregnancy with all the pain and labor that implies.[34] Pregnancy also had legal status and recognition as a condition that required support, even if the mother was unmarried. Jesús M. Usunáriz found numerous cases of fathers sentenced to provide support (food, grain, money) to their pregnant partners (who were not their wives) during their pregnancies and while they were nursing the illegitimate infants.[35]

Another appropriate area of maternal concern was the health and well-being of children, a sphere that could include managing wet nurses, the children's diet, the air and sanitation of their living areas, and any illnesses or accidents that might befall them.[36] Noblewomen were likely to carry out these responsibilities by supervising servants or retainers who did the hands-on care, sparking a debate about the appropriate role of mothers that can be most clearly seen in the practices of breastfeeding. Legal sources, including the *Siete Partidas*, recognized a mother's obligation to nurse her child herself to age three, even if that child was illegitimate, and starting in the fourteenth century, images of Mary breastfeeding the baby Jesus were popular in Spain.[37] Humanist writers across Europe (including Vives) encouraged mothers to breastfeed their children themselves, decrying the practice of relying on wet nurses, and early modern doctors increasingly emphasized the health benefits of breastfeeding.[38] In spite of this emphasis on the moral and health-related benefits of nursing, noble mothers often did not nurse their own children, turning them over to wet nurses soon after birth. Wealthier families brought the wet-nurse into the household, where the mother's role became supervisory as she oversaw a variety of caretakers who did the physical work of raising young children.[39]

After age three, the role of the mother and the nature of maternity is less clear. By the fourteenth century there were depictions of both St. Anne and the Virgin Mary with books and pens and ink, underscoring the potentially educational nature of the relationship between mother and child and providing possible models for ordinary women and their families.[40] But by the seventeenth century, in spite of Bartolomé Esteban Murillo's famous painting on the subject of St. Anne teaching the Virgin to read, humanist writers tried to present Mary as having learned to read from the Holy Spirit and advised fathers to take a more active role in teaching their children.[41] Nevertheless, there is abundant evidence that women of the period had a hand in their children's education, in the early years for their sons and throughout adolescence for their daughters.[42] Mothers across Spain provided their daughters with practical skills (such as housework, sewing, and cooking) and literacy.[43] Models of maternity such as Isabel of Castile (1451–1504) and St. Teresa enacted the maternal responsibility of teaching their daughters, their ladies in waiting, and their novices, and Juan Luis Vives invoked his own mother as a "model of maternal authority."[44] In addition to educating their children, noblewomen had maternal responsibilities that were specific to their social class. Noble mothers, especially if widowed, carried on the responsibility of ensuring the dynastic succession and increasing the family's wealth and influence.[45] Thus noble motherhood could include arranging children's marriages and careers, administering their estates and property until adulthood, prosecuting lawsuits on their behalf, and making decisions about family loyalties and alliances.[46]

The reality of women's lives does not support the drastic reduction of a woman's identity to her ability to remain chaste. In spite of the plots of early modern Spanish drama, conduct manuals such as those of fray Luis de León and Juan Luis Vives, and the expectations of church doctrine, a woman's chastity or honor was not an absolute quality, but was affected by her social status, her marital status, her perceived intentions, and a society that tended to view honor as "an elastic commodity."[47] Life required more of women than simply guarding their virginity. The act of bearing an illegitimate child or children shaped women's lives but did not necessarily define them, and most women who did bear illegitimate children were also called on to play other roles to secure their own futures and those of their children. Abigail Dyer found that although "premarital sexual acts, according to Catholic doctrine and contemporary notions of honor, should have caused a woman's descent into disgrace and, later, hell," women in eighteenth-century Navarre who sued for seduction by promise of marriage "were not social outcasts, nor were they rejected by family and neighbors."[48] A realistic definition of femininity in early modern Castile must take into consideration the rest of a woman's life cycle, her potential roles as wife, widow, mother, and even nun, her economic necessities, and her identity as part of a larger community.

This more complex definition of femininity applies across the social spectrum. Allyson Poska argued that historians would do well to consider the demographic, economic, class, and regional context when evaluating attitudes toward women's chastity or honor, because these attitudes varied so widely across Spain. Her work on peasant women in Galicia provides ample evidence of women who often chose concubinage over marriage and bore children out of wedlock. Far from being ostracized by their communities, these unwed mothers gained custody of their children, used the legal system to pursue their rights, and were free to marry after their initial relationships had dissolved.[49] Using criminal records and looking at the issue of reputation in relation to "lower-status women in a small town" in central Castile, Scott Taylor found that "the salient characteristics of female reputation" included "sexual purity, credit and property, a concern to protect the family, and a defense of legal rights."[50] Women and men in Taylor's study valued female chastity, and they used the Spanish terms for mistress or concubine (*amancebada*) as insults. Their use of sexual language was nuanced, however. Castilians extended the use of sexualized insults (including whore or *puta*) to attack women who appropriated not just another woman's husband but also her economic and social resources, and, more positively, they valued women's ability to participate in the economy and their role in the family as well as their sexual purity.[51] Both Poska and Taylor theorized that the nobility may have been more influenced by prescriptive gender roles than the average Spaniard,[52] but my research finds that in practice even the nobility did not always equate honor with female chastity.

Although Castilian noblewomen and their families were concerned with chastity, reputation, and honor, they could (like women and families of more modest status) accommodate women with less than perfect reputations. Ann Twinam affirmed that in colonial Latin America, even "elite women could live their lives 'in between' the dyad of the saint and the whore."[53] Looking at the brides of the noble Guzmán family (Dukes of Medina Sidonia), Miguel Ángel Ladero Quesada found that noblewomen's reputations extended beyond chastity and in fact included an ability to administer house and property; the provision of children who would give meaning and continuity to the patrimony and reputation achieved by the man; an augmentation of the lineage through pure blood and extensive property of their own; and their personal attributes of beauty, virtue, chastity, goodness, and kindness (*bondad*).[54] The dichotomy between honor and reputation was summed up by Abigail Dyer, who argued that honor was dependent on external factors while reputation was intrinsic, so that "Spanish justice systems separated the concepts of a woman's honor and her good reputation, tying only her honor, not her reputation, to her virginity."[55] A woman whose honor had been compromised through a lapse in chastity still had the potential to achieve a good reputation. Mothers of illegitimate children in this study occupy an ambiguous place in relation to idealized definitions of femininity and maternity both because of their behavior and because of their social class backgrounds. Although they had fallen short in the contemporary expectations of chastity, they were often successful in other ways.

MARRIAGE, SEX, AND THE LAW

Prior to the Council of Trent (1545–63), getting married in early modern Europe was a process rather than an act, and people's marital status was not always easy to define.[56] In 1179 the papacy accepted two ways to recognize a marriage. Betrothal (*palabras de futuro*) and consummation constituted a valid marriage, but so did a marriage ceremony (*palabras de presente*).[57] This two-stage model gave rise to an uncertain period between the betrothal and wedding in which popular custom deemed that sexual activity between betrothed partners was acceptable.[58] The thirteenth-century Castilian law code the *Siete Partidas* recognized both the distinction between future and present promises (palabras de futuro and palabras de presente) and the importance of consummation: "There is no difference or distinction, so far as the validity of a marriage is concerned, between one contracted by words relating to the present time, and the other which is consummated by the husband having carnal union with his wife."[59] By the fifteenth century the stages of the marriage ceremony in Castile also included the veiling (*velaciones*) that was celebrated in the presence of a priest, who said mass and granted his blessing to the pair. Contrary to popular custom, the church would have liked the couple to delay consummation until after this final ceremony.[60] But Heath Dillard argued that throughout the changes in the marriage law, in medieval Castile the popular opinion was that sex was "not condemned, unexpected or even unusual between betrothed couples," and this opinion persisted into the early modern period.[61] This attitude was not unique to Iberia, and indeed proved remarkably consistent across Western Europe, even surviving the changes made by the Reformation in Protestant countries.[62]

Thus, the exact moment when a marriage became legal and any offspring legitimate could be surprisingly ambiguous and might result in inheritance problems and uncertain status for women involved in sexual relationships with noblemen.[63] It remained common for noble couples (often eager for children to carry on the lineage) to consummate their marriages during the betrothal period. This practice was risky, especially for women. Lady Elvira de Guzmán, for example, died in childbirth in 1438 before the dispensation legalizing her marriage to the first Duke of Medina Sidonia was dispatched from Rome. Her daughter, Teresa, therefore, remained illegitimate.[64] The period of time after the betrothal (palabras de futuro) was solemnized in front of witnesses but before the public ceremony with palabras de presente took place and any needed papal dispensations arrived was an ambiguous space for women that was socially but not legally recognized as marriage, and in which sexual activity often took place.

To further complicate the fluid and contradictory marriage laws, the Iberian Peninsula had a long tradition of legal concubinage, which persisted into the early modern period. Although canon law moved slowly toward establishing concubinage among the laity as illegal,[65] all the major Spanish law codes since the Visigothic era had recognized a union of unmarried individuals who agreed to temporarily share bed and board and provide for any children born from the union.[66] Concubinage (called *barraganía* in Castile) existed in various forms across medieval Iberia and was practiced from royal courts down to the peasantry. The illegitimate children who resulted from concubinage enjoyed what Sara MacDougall termed "Mediterranean laxity," in which they were publicly recognized, provided for, and even became heirs to kingdoms.[67] In conjunction with barraganía, both Spain and Portugal had informal domestic partnerships (clandestine marriages) that, according to Jutta Sperling, were often created "in the absence of parental consent and formal legitimizing procedures." Sperling concluded that in both Catholic and Protestant Europe, "informal domestic partnerships were a widely practiced form of marriage," and domestic partnerships were quite common in Spain. In Sperling's study of papal dispensations for kinship prohibitions, 68 percent of Spanish petitioners in 1564 declared that they had married informally. This is in strong contrast to France (15 percent) and Italy (14 percent), and Sperling hypothesized that this was connected to inheritance laws and property regimes: "Wherever forms of joint ownership among spouses and equal inheritance among siblings prevailed, as in Portugal, Spain, and the Low Countries, informal domestic partnerships were common," thus giving women more control over their own sexuality in societies with high rates of concubinage.[68]

Concubinage could be risky, damaging a woman's reputation and leaving her at risk economically after the union ended. It also, however, provided advantages for women who could choose their sexual partners, engage in sexual activity, have children, form meaningful emotional bonds, and have access to economic support without being trapped in a permanent marriage.[69] Miriam Shadis found that, at the very top of the social scale, the position as the king's barragana provided noblewomen and their families with "special access to ruling power, unavailable to their male peers" in the medieval courts of Portugal, Castile, Aragón, and León, and the illegitimate descendants of these women formed some of the most important noble families in early modern Castile.[70] For example, after the death of the second Lord of Marchena in 1352, his widow, Beatriz de Jérica, became the concubine of Enrique II of Castile (1333–79). Their illegitimate daughter married the first Count of Niebla and Beatriz's grandson became the first Duke of Medina Sidonia.[71]

The degree of power that concubines could acquire had the potential to make them threatening. In an early example, doña Leonor de Guzmán was the beloved and favored concubine of King Alfonso XI of Castile (1312–50), who granted her and her family valuable concessions and promoted the welfare of their illegitimate children, who included the first Count of Albuquerque and Enrique II of Castile. The success of Leonor and her children was so threatening to Alfonso's wife and queen, María de Portugal, that after Alfonso's death in 1350, María had Leonor imprisoned and executed.[72] Both of these women exerted agency in support of what were acceptable maternal goals. Leonor used her power and authority to procure valuable royal concessions for her children and her family, while María acted to defended her young son, the legal heir, and ensure dynastic succession. In spite of being executed, Leonor succeeded in the long run. Her family became "the most powerful feudal line of Castile."[73]

Further down the social scale, concubines of noblemen could also be rewarded with grants of lands and titles that could be passed on to their offspring, in ways that resembled Leonor's success. In the late fifteenth century, doña María de Sandoval, the illegitimate daughter of the Lord of Villafrechos, married Ramiro de Guzmán, Lord of Villajimena, with whom she had two daughters. At some point during her marriage, María had a sexual relationship with her first cousin, the first Duke of Nájera and had two more children with him. The Duke of Nájera outranked both María's father and her husband, and was thus in a position to reward María and her apparently complicit husband. The duke granted María's husband the rights to the estate and houses of Villajimena and allowed María's legitimate daughters to inherit the estate after Ramiro's death.[74] Concubinage remained ingrained in Iberian culture into the early modern period as an acceptable alternative to marriage. Poska argued that even as late as the sixteenth century, Galician peasant women acted independently when it came to choosing concubinage: "[They] easily entered these relationships and bore illegitimate children because they knew that not only were they unlikely to be punished for their acts, but their choices would be supported by both the Castilian legal system and Galician culture."[75] The early modern nobility drew on this tradition, practicing a form of concubinage that was not legal (because one or both partners were often married), but was often quite stable and was part of a larger cultural tradition that would prove difficult for the Catholic Reformation to eradicate.

At the very end of the period covered in this study, the Council of Trent (1545–63) tried to change both traditional Spanish marriage customs and the status of concubinage. First, the council required the presence of a priest and two witnesses in order for a marriage to be legal.[76] Second, the council's catechism declared that fornication between unmarried people "was a grave sin, and [that] believing otherwise was a heresy subject to the Inquisition" and forbade all extraconjugal unions on pain of excommunication, thus putting any woman who was living in concubinage in theoretical danger of being prosecuted as a clandestine prostitute.[77] Susanna Burghartz argued that the Council of Trent and its subsequent changes created a "new concept of premarital sexuality" in a society that had previously accepted sexual relations between betrothed couples.[78] At almost exactly the same time, it becomes harder to find evidence of women having extramarital relationships with noblemen. I was able to locate 111 women for the fifteenth century and 145 women for the sixteenth century, but only 45 women for the seventeenth century, suggesting the possibility that the changing moral attitudes of the Council of Trent eventually helped to make extramarital relationships less publicly acceptable among the nobility. In Castile Philip II only reluctantly endorsed the decrees of the council, and the nobility continued to invoke earlier ideas about sexuality even as the decrees of the Council of Trent were being promulgated in Spain.[79]

SEXUALITY AND CHILDREN

The Castilian nobility's focus on dynastic succession put a high value on women's sexuality. In spite of all the prescriptive literature's insistence on chastity, it was sexual intercourse that produced children. Noblemen were often guilty of rape, but the records also reveal women exerting agency about both their own sexuality and what happened next. Most of the cases in this study occurred before the Council of Trent, but the women who had sex with the Castilian nobility also had to negotiate the changing legal times as they dealt with the complications resulting from their extramarital sexual relationships and any children that might result. An example that demonstrates both female agency and the limits of that agency in a sexual relationship, as well as the importance of children, is that of Luisa de Carvajal.

In 1564 Luisa de Carvajal, daughter of a local magistrate in Madrid, had a sexual relationship with Almirante Luis Colón, the first Duke of Veragua. The grandson of Christopher Columbus, Luis had been granted the title of duke in 1536 and had arrived in Castile from Santo Domingo in 1551. By 1563 he was under house arrest in Madrid because of a conviction for bigamy, and in April of that year he met the fourteen-year-old Luisa during an illicit nocturnal excursion.[80] Luis and Luisa's son Cristóbal was baptized on May 26, 1565. Both of Cristóbal's parents would have liked him to be legitimate. His father (whose two legitimate children were both girls) consulted legal experts to see if he could be regarded as legitimate and thus inherit the title, and Luisa and her family claimed in court that Luis had married her privately with palabras de presente in 1564.[81] Ann Twinam pointed out that before the Council of Trent, "the couple rather than the priest were the agents of matrimony," making it possible for an exchange of marriage vows without a priest to create a legal marriage if the couple were both single at the time. After the Council of Trent, however, "only marriages performed by clerics legitimized sexual liaisons."[82]

In a 1572 legal case about whether or not Cristóbal was legitimate, the judge referred directly to the decrees of the Council of Trent. He noted that Cristóbal was baptized on May 26, 1565, so he must have been conceived in September of 1564 and "the council [of Trent] was published in these regions in April or May of the same year [1564]."[83] The judge concluded, "In order to be legitimate the mother must have been in good faith not only at the time that she married, but also at the time of conception, because if she conceived in bad faith he is not legitimate; but I say that at the time of conception, it is impossible that doña Luisa had good faith [because she must have known about the decrees of the Council of Trent which invalidated her marriage]."[84] In reality Luis was married to someone else at the time of Cristóbal's conception, had been married at least three times, and was in extensive legal trouble for bigamy, so there was little possibility of Cristóbal being declared legitimate.[85] Indeed, don Cristóbal was described by his opponents in the case as "espurio and adulterino; and as such incapable of inheriting," and he ultimately lost his bid to be considered legitimate.[86] Considering the circumstances, Luis and Luisa made a bold bid for their son's legitimacy and the legality of their relationship. Before the Council of Trent's changes to the ways in which marriages were constructed, they might have had a better chance of succeeding. Although the judge in this case clearly understood the decrees of the Council of Trent and expected that Luis and Luisa should have abided by it as soon as it was promulgated in Castile, the idea that a private exchange of vows constituted a legal marriage persisted in popular practice and occasionally in civil and ecclesiastical courts into the seventeenth century.[87]

Luisa de Carvajal's relationship with Luis, the Duke of Veragua, illustrates both her agency and the limits of that agency. In the first place, the fourteen-year-old Luisa seems to have been out at night in a setting where she could meet Luis with relatively little supervision, demonstrating her ability to act independently. Then the judge in this case (who took quite a negative view of Luisa's agency) felt that she had chosen to ignore the decrees of Trent and to enter into a sexual relationship that she should have known was not marriage. The use of false names on Cristóbal's birth certificate suggests that Luisa participated in a deliberate concealment.[88] And when Luis and Luisa's father decided that the only solution was for Luisa to marry one of Luis's employees, Luis Buzón of Toledo, Luisa allegedly resisted to the point that her father had to use physical violence to force her to accept the marriage. Shortly after her marriage she attempted to get an annulment from the ecclesiastical judge of Madrid. In the end Luisa lost the lawsuit and the marriage endured for at least twenty more years, despite her active rejection of the union.[89] If we accept that agency does not necessarily guarantee happiness or success, however, we can see that Luisa demonstrated several ways in which women could influence their own futures. She made independent decisions about her sexuality, she had a son, she used the court system to try to change her situation, she gained economic resources in the form of a 3,000 ducado dowry awarded to her by Luis, and she married.[90]

Across the social spectrum, women's ability to produce children added to their value in society. In spite of the emphasis on virginity and chastity that prevailed in the prescriptive literature of the time, the nobility, obsessed with the need for male heirs, put a high value on women's fertility, and women who had illegitimate children were undeniably fertile.[91] Thus, motherhood was an important role for women that could provide them with advantages even when it occurred outside of marriage. Women who produced children for the nobility could gain social and financial status through marriage or public recognition. The goal of marriage in medieval and early modern Castile was offspring, and childless marriages were considered failures.[92] This position devalued lawfully wedded wives who were sterile and could invert social norms enough to give a fertile mistress a path to marriage.

Doña Catalina Enríquez de Ribera's life story includes the possibility of sexual assault, the insecurity that came with the role of noble concubine, and the advantages that producing children could gain for a woman in her situation. Catalina served as a lady-in-waiting to the childless doña Mencía Enríquez, Countess of Castañeda, who had married the count in 1430. When doña Mencía's husband, the count, evinced an interest in Catalina, Mencía arranged a marriage for Catalina with another, more minor, nobleman without her husband's knowledge. After the vows had been spoken in the present tense (palabras de presente) but before the marriage could be consummated, the count discovered the deception, kidnapped Catalina, and bore her off to his fortress of Villa-Lumbroso, where the couple subsequently had two sons and two daughters. This left Catalina in an awkward legal and social position as she was married but not to the man she was living with and it is not at all clear from the documents if she had been raped or which man (if either) she wanted to be with.

A similar case in which more information is available sheds some light on what might have happened to Catalina, given the power imbalance between herself and the count. After Rodrigo de Portocarrero's wife died, witnesses interviewed years later testified that he had tricked her friend and lady-in-waiting, doña Beatriz Vallejo, into being alone with him and had then raped her. Beatriz fled to her sister, but when she realized she was pregnant her sister insisted that she return to Rodrigo's house (he was the son of the second Count of Medellín), assuring her that Rodrigo would take responsibility for her and the child. Indeed, conforming to the standards of masculinity discussed in the previous chapter, Rodrigo cared for Beatriz during her pregnancy, gave her a dowry because she had been a virgin, arranged a marriage for her, and then raised their son in his own household.[93] His actions demonstrate both the vulnerability of young women in service in noble households and the ease with which noblemen could deal with their sexual transgressions without incurring loss of status or reputation. Rodrigo's actions also indicate the importance of children to the noble family, as he cared for his illegitimate son and even raised him with his legitimate ones.

The importance of children is also central to the story of Catalina and the Count of Castañeda. Whether or not the count had raped Catalina, he was delighted when she gave birth to sons (especially because he had no legitimate sons). The count obtained a royal legitimation for the eldest boy in 1453 so that he could inherit the title and estate. The ability to produce an heir earned Catalina long-term benefits also, giving her access to what historian Barbara Harris characterized as "female careers," in which marriage and motherhood "had as much political and economic as domestic importance."[94] When Mencía died in 1480 after fifty years of childless marriage, the count married Catalina as his second wife and left her the town of Santillana, "with its rents, and goods, and rights," for life. Their son became the fourth Count of Castañeda.[95] Catalina lived in the nebulous social and legal space that women who had extramarital relationships often occupied. She was noble herself, she held a position as a lady-in-waiting in a good household, she was part of an honorably arranged marriage from which she was either kidnapped or rescued by the Count of Castañeda, she was a concubine, she had four children outside of marriage, and she ended her life in a second marriage with the title of Countess of Castañeda and the promise of an inheritance. She had demonstrated her agency by either choosing a sexual relationship with the count or surviving his sexual assault on her. Ironically, her long-term and fruitful relationship with the count bears more resemblance to the ideal early modern marriage than the count's troubled and childless relationship with his first wife.

The marriages between women and the fathers of their children can also reveal the practical, transactional nature of noble marriage alliances. Isabel de Meneses, a young, beautiful, and poverty-stricken daughter of a Portuguese hidalgo, became the long-term concubine of the first Duke of Medina Sidonia, with whom she had two sons, Enrique and Alfonso. The duke was not a faithful partner. His marriage was childless, but he had at least eleven illegitimate children with nine different women. In 1444 the duke got permission from Juan II of Castile (1405–54) to annul the clause of the Medina Sidonia mayorazgo that required that the heir to the title be legitimate and chose Isabel's elder son, Enrique, as his heir. In 1466 the duke's wife died. On November 15, 1468, the duke married Isabel, and on November 29, 1468, the duke died. Isabel's marriage lasted only two weeks. On the duke's side the marriage was about their son, not about Isabel. It was designed to bolster the position of his illegitimate heir and hopefully avoid the lawsuits that inevitably followed when an illegitimate child inherited a title. And yet, Isabel gained too, achieving marriage and a slightly nebulous status by producing an heir for the house of Medina Sidonia. Hers was the most stable and long-term of the duke's nine extramarital relationships, lasting more than eleven years. The duke left her the town of Rociana, and she lived on its rents for the next twenty-six years until her own death in 1494. Her son became the second Duke of Medina Sidonia, and she styled herself as the "Duchess of Rociana," an imaginary title that nevertheless reveals her own sense of privilege.[96] From a young, impoverished concubine, Isabel became (briefly) a wife and then a widow with a secure source of income and some sense of status.

The importance of women's fertility to the patriarchal structure of the nobility put a high value on women's bodies and reproductive capabilities. The Count of Castañeda and the first Duke of Medina Sidonia rewarded their concubines for their ability to produce male children, an essential characteristic for successful noble masculinity that depended on women.

Even when mothers of illegitimate children were not able to achieve marriage or a title for themselves, they often accomplished some of the tasks that the early modern period identified with successful motherhood, thus benefiting their children. The labor of being a good mother was understood to begin with childbirth itself (as the images of St. Anne resting after the birth of the Virgin Mary imply) and proceeded to nursing and caring for an infant. Doña María de Guzmán cared for her son Juan until he was just over three years old, at which point his father, the archbishop of Santiago, rather reluctantly took charge of him as was stipulated by Spanish law. Juan survived and eventually applied to enter the Colegio de San Bartolomé when he was thirteen years old.[97] There is no record that he had any more contact with his mother, but she did provide maternal care for him during those essential first three years of his life.

Even the poorest and most socially disadvantaged women had the potential to contribute to the well-being of their children. Beatriz Núñez, an enslaved woman, had four children with the second Count of Arcos, and Marta Rodríguez (also enslaved) had one son with the count. Both women were owned by the count.[98] The count recorded in his will: "[Beatriz and Marta] have served me for a very long time, and been with my sons and daughters, and they know much about the style and customs of my house and understand and know much about governing the health of the children, my sons and daughters." The two women were so essential to the smooth running of what must have been a very complex household (the count had about twenty-eight illegitimate children with at least eight different women) that the count "prayed and commanded" them to remain with his children after his death, "helping to care for and cure the health of [the children]."[99] The practice of taking minority women (many of them slaves) as concubines was common throughout medieval Iberia and persisted into the early modern period. Canon lawyers denounced it, but the *Siete Partidas* did not forbid it and the laws of Sepúlveda, the *Costums* of Tortosa, and the *fuero* of Cuenca all refer to the practice as common.[100] Enslaved women were often valued for domestic skills, such as making the fruit preserves and jellies that were used to dilute the supposedly harmful effects of water on the human system. They were employed in the kitchen, in the laundry room, as seamstresses, as midwives, and (as in this case) as nursemaids for children, taking care of the routine drudgery of maternity for their own and other people's children.[101] Beatriz and Marta provided the daily labor and the skilled care that their children and their children's half-siblings needed, filling an important maternal role in the count's large household.

Noblewomen who were not in a position to fulfill these most fundamental maternal tasks were able to provide support for their children in other ways. Doña María de Ribera had an adulterous relationship and an illegitimate daughter, Magdalena, born in 1504 when her husband was absent from Toledo. Although it is unclear if her husband knew about her adultery, María felt unable to care for Magdalena in her own home. But she still undertook the work of motherhood and ensured that her daughter received a noble upbringing and a career. María confided the girl to the care of her sister (who had several children of her own) and then later arranged for her to enter the convent of Santo Domingo el Real, where Magdalena eventually professed as a nun. Although she never publicly acknowledged her daughter, when she wrote her will in 1525 María left 300,000 maravedís to the convent of Santo Domingo el Real.[102]

Evidence that women who had children outside of marriage could achieve successful maternity can also be found in their relationships with their adult children. On the most basic level, children were potentially an economic asset. In 1401 María Sánchez, a nun in the convent of Santa María de las Dueñas, received a legacy of 2,000 maravedís from her illegitimate son Fernando Ponce de León. Fernando stated that the legacy was in payment of a debt he owed her, suggesting that she had originally helped him. About a hundred years later doña Aldonza Iborra received an income of 50,000 maravedís from her illegitimate daughter, Juana de Aragón, who was the Duchess of Frías when she wrote her will in 1509.[103] These legacies signaled protection, respect, and recognition, implying that these mothers were included in the affective family even though they were not legally married to the fathers of their children.

In a more dramatic example, Inés de Sagredo had an ongoing sexual relationship and three illegitimate sons with the first Duke of Frías during both his marriages. Inés never married the duke, who supported her in a household of her own,[104] but she did maintain close ties to their sons. In 1512 when the duke lay dying in Burgos, he sent an urgent message to Inés asking her to rush to his bedside to marry him before he died, in an attempt to legitimize their youngest son, Bernaldino. The messenger found Inés in the household of her eldest illegitimate son, who was the dean of the cathedral in Burgos. Inés willingly rode out into the night escorted by her two eldest sons and in support of her youngest son's potential inheritance, although the duke died before she arrived at his residence in Burgos and the scheme failed. The duke valued Inés (whom he had been with for over fifteen years at this point), at least for the sons she had given him, and Inés had close relationships with her adult children. Although the notorious concubine (or as the witnesses for Bernaldino's legitimation put it, "well-known friend") of the duke, Inés was also a mother embedded in family life, welcomed and protected by her adult sons in spite of her dubious claims to traditional feminine honor or reputation.[105]

USE OF COURTS AND LEGAL STRATEGIES

Women from a range of social statuses in early modern Castile drew on their experiences as heiresses, as guardians of their children, and as executrixes of their husband's wills to protect their families.[106] Lapses in chastity could complicate their legal status but did not lessen their abilities. One of the most basic but also most useful tools that mothers of illegitimate children possessed was the ability to write a will.[107] We have already seen that doña María de Ribera was able to use her will to leave a legacy to her daughter's convent without ever needing to make their relationship public. Ana de Jaén, who had a sexual relationship with and then married the third Count of Paredes after the death of his first wife, used her will in 1558 to bolster her children's claim to legitimacy. There is some disagreement among historians about the legal status of Ana's children with the count. Rosa Montero Tejada wrote that all six of their children were illegitimate, but the seventeenth-century genealogist Luis de Salazar y Castro only stated that the eldest child was born before their marriage and was subsequently legitimated by that marriage.[108] Either way, Ana, who had started her career as a maid in the count's household and had no title, social standing, or fortune, attempted to quell the controversy over her children's status. Widowed by 1558, she wrote a will in which she asserted her own status, identifying herself both as a "comendadora de la Orden de Santiago" and also as the "wife of don Rodrigo Manrique, my lord and husband, who is in heaven, Count of Paredes de Nava." She went on to state unequivocally (adding an unusual extra clause to the formulaic language of her will to emphasize this point) that her children were legitimate, naming them as "my legitimate children whom I have at present and those of the said count don Rodrigo Manrique, my lord and husband, [children that] I had *during the marriage and the time that I was married* with the said count don Rodrigo Manrique, my lord" (emphasis added). Since it is not at all clear that Ana's children were legitimate (at least the eldest, Bernaldino, seems to have been born out of wedlock), Ana left a written record to try to bolster their status after her death.[109]

Women could also turn to the court system to assert their own status as legitimate wives, address broken promises of marriage, and (in an example of active maternity) protect their children.[110] An excellent example of this is doña Leonor de Guzmán, daughter of the Lord of Lepe and granddaughter of the first Duke of Medina Sidonia. In 1500 Leonor married the widowed Juan de Guzmán, her first cousin and the third Duke of Medina Sidonia, with whom she already had at least one son (it seems likely that Leonor was pregnant in 1500).[111] The couple had been living together for several years, having celebrated a private marriage and consummated it without waiting for the papal dispensation. This was a very public scandal with potentially damaging religious and secular consequences. When Pope Alexander VI finally issued the dispensation on April 13, 1500, he gave them permission to marry in spite of being related within the third and fourth degrees of consanguinity, absolved them of the sin of incest, which they had technically committed by having sex before the dispensation arrived, and legitimized their children. It took until 1504 for the Catholic Monarchs to agree that they would not confiscate half of the duke's property because of these offenses.[112] Once the issue was resolved, Leonor legally became a wife and the couple settled down together and had a daughter (who died young) and another son.

But when the duke died unexpectedly from the plague in Seville on July 10, 1507, at the age of forty, the troubled start to Leonor's marriage came back to haunt her. The duke left two families, and his eldest son and heir Enrique (the child of his first marriage) was a teenager who was engaged to be married to the daughter of the Count of Ureña.[113] The young count's brother-in-law, Pedro Girón, was one of his guardians and also a rapacious, power-hungry aristocrat with designs on the estate of Medina Sidonia. Leonor and her sons (the next potential heirs after Enrique) were a threat to his ambitions. The duke had left generous provisions to Leonor and their children, but Girón took Leonor to court, charging that her marriage was invalid and her children illegitimate.

Leonor promptly initiated a legal process to prove the legitimacy of her marriage in the archepiscopal court in Seville and to protect her children.[114] While this process dragged on, Girón's overwhelming ambitions earned him the anger of King Ferdinand to which Girón responded by kidnapping the young fourth duke and duchess (Enrique and his wife) and decamping to Portugal. By the time a royal pardon had been procured in 1512, the fourth duke was suffering from the upheavals of his travels, and he died shortly after returning to Spain in January 1513, without having had any children. His will left his entire estate not to Leonor's son (the duke's younger half-brother, who should have been next in line for the title) but to his sister Mencía, who was married to Pedro Girón. At the same time Girón sent three thousand armed men to occupy the town of Medina Sidonia. Again, Leonor took prompt action, appealing directly to King Ferdinand and securing an agreement from him that the rightful heir to the dukedom was her eldest son, Alonso, legitimate son of the third duke. The king forced Pedro Girón to surrender Medina Sidonia to the new duke, Alonso, and take his claims to the courts instead. Leonor and the king, working together, arranged a marriage between Alonso and the king's illegitimate granddaughter, both whom were under the age of fourteen, and Leonor took effective control of the estate and dukedom of Medina Sidonia in the name of her son. Leonor ran the estate until her death in 1515, keeping a captain and eight hundred cavalrymen in Medina Sidonia for fear of further attacks.[115]

Doña Leonor de Guzmán's story embodies the shifting and unstable nature of female chastity and reputation as well as the importance of a woman's own agency in negotiating these difficulties. She was a noblewoman of the highest rank, the Duchess of Medina Sidonia, a wife, and a widow. She had also technically been a mistress, having sexual relations with her fiancé before her marriage was legal, and producing two sons whose legitimacy was subsequently in doubt. This behavior had consequences for her and her future husband, causing a public scandal that had to be resolved by the pope himself, putting half of their estate at risk of royal confiscation, making Leonor and her children vulnerable to the ambitions of her greedy aristocratic peers, and threatening the inheritance of the estate and title of Medina Sidonia after the duke's death. Leonor's independent actions, skills, and social status helped save the situation and ensure both her children's legitimacy and their inheritance. She demonstrated an ability to fight for her family, using legal, diplomatic, and military skills to fend off enemies and restore order. In the process she also saved the dukedom of Medina Sidonia from being subsumed into the estates of the powerful Girón family, thus upholding the concept of dynastic succession that was so important to the high nobility.

Where Leonor succeeded, however, other noblewomen with equal status and willingness to use the courts, though still displaying considerable agency, did not fare as well. Doña Aldonza de Urrea, daughter of the Count of Aranda, had sex with her fiancé, don Manrique de Lara, the future third Duke of Nájera. The duke was only fifteen when he obeyed his parents' wish on June 12, 1520, and agreed in writing to marry doña Aldonza as soon as the papal dispensation authorizing their marriage (they were cousins) arrived from Rome.[116] Some time after that the young couple acted in accordance with the popular idea (discussed earlier in this chapter) that sexual activity after a betrothal but before a marriage was acceptable, and consummated their relationship. Doña Aldonza subsequently became pregnant with a son, also named Manrique. Rather than complete the marriage to Aldonza with a formal veiling ceremony and palabras de presente, at some point in this process the future duke jilted Aldonza. Now older, and perhaps inclined to make his own decisions, Manrique declared his intention to marry doña Luisa de Acuña, daughter and heiress of the Count of Valencia. Doña Luisa's status as her father's only legitimate daughter and heiress meant that several other noblemen also wanted to marry her. Charles V (1500–58) ordered that doña Luisa be sent to the monastery of Santo Domingo el Real in Toledo in order to have some space to make up her mind away from family coercion, a practice that was prescribed by canon law.[117] Doña Luisa declared that she wanted to marry don Manrique, who promptly asked the archbishop of Seville (who was his distant cousin) to perform the ceremony. On a warm August morning in Toledo in 1529, the men met doña Luisa in the parlor of the monastery and she slipped through a space in the grill and escaped into the visitor's parlor. Placing an altar in the parlor, the archbishop married (*velar*) the young couple in the presence of two witnesses (one of them the archbishop of Santiago, who had originally sent her to the monastery on the king's orders, and the other the chaplain of the Reyes Nuevos Chapel in Toledo Cathedral).[118]

Left with a broken promise and an infant, doña Aldonza took vigorous action to defend herself and her son. She sued her errant fiancé and claimed in court that she was his legal wife and that their son was legitimate and the heir to the dukedom of Nájera because the couple had exchanged vows in the future tense (of which she had written proof) and then consummated their relationship.[119] As this occurred long before the Council of Trent, doña Aldonza should have had a valid legal case, but she nevertheless lost. Three judgments went against her, and while her fiancé walked free, she was condemned to pay the court costs. The third Duke of Nájera remained officially married to doña Luisa de Acuña, and Aldonza's son remained illegitimate. By 1568 her son Manrique was forced to settle with his legitimate younger half-brother, the fourth duke, agreeing to drop the lawsuits and never marry in exchange for a yearly allowance from the Nájera estate.[120]

Aldonza's failure to restore her son to legitimacy or reclaim her marriage probably resulted at least in part from the difficulty of challenging a duke and his powerful family. Nevertheless, the affair and Aldonza's subsequent independent actions and lawsuit created long-term legal problems for the Dukes of Nájera. In the short term there was such a scandal that Charles V had to become personally involved in order to resolve it, and doña Luisa's father disinherited her in favor of her illegitimate half-brother. Subsequently, Aldonza's son pursued her original lawsuit, taking the issue all the way to the papal court (*la rota de su santidad*) and finally requiring Philip II to send the Duke of Pastrana to resolve what had by 1568 become a fight between two brothers.[121] The entire incident illustrates the ambiguity of marriage and the agency of noblewomen who made decisions about whom to marry, whom to have sex with, and when and how to go about challenging the decisions of their noble partners. Aldonza's initial action of making her fiancé give her a written promise of marriage before she had sex with him suggests a degree of legal savviness as well as an awareness of the vulnerability of her own position.

In these two cases the outcomes differed dramatically for the women involved, but the legal decisions both tended toward maintaining the dynastic continuity of the noble family. Because she did not subsequently marry her lover (as Leonor had done twenty years earlier), Aldonza's legal challenge disrupted the dynastic succession of the Dukes of Nájera by demanding the dissolution of the marriage the duke had established with Luisa de Acuña. It was also potentially very costly, because Luisa's disinheritance was eventually revoked and her extensive property became a permanent part of the Manrique family estate.[122] In contrast, Leonor's legal actions preserved the dynastic succession of the Dukes of Medina Sidonia, preventing them from being taken over by their noble rivals. Even if her initial marriage had been technically illegal, neither the monarchy nor the rest of the nobility wanted to see one noble family annex another, thus setting a precedent that disrupted traditional inheritance patterns. Regardless, both women showed agency and skill, using the courts to fight for themselves and their children. Their legal actions fit a model of noble maternity, since one of noblewomen's obligations as mothers (especially when widowed) was to prosecute lawsuits on their children's behalf.[123]

ECONOMIC RESOURCES AND STATUS

Women could also gain substantial economic benefits from their sexual relationships with noblemen. This might mean economic security for the women themselves as well as an ability to support their children and assist them with educations, marriages, and careers, all of which fell into the domain of early modern maternity. Helen S. Ettlinger argued that families of noblewomen who had sexual relationships with Italian princes "found these liaisons advantageous and actively cultivated such relationships," in spite of Italian ideas that honor was explicitly connected to virginity for women. This was also true in medieval Spain, where the nobility benefited when their wives and daughters became the concubines of the medieval kings of the Iberian kingdoms.[124] In addition, Ettlinger's study found that the women themselves benefited, "some even holding property in their own right and achieving a degree of independence not normally available to Renaissance women."[125] In France both Anne de Pisseleu, mistress to Francois I (1494–1547) and Diane de Poitiers, mistress to Henri II (1519–59), accrued power, land, and titles through their relationships with and proximity to the monarch. These assets enabled their independent decisions (Anne became publicly Protestant after the death of the king) and gave them the resources to fulfill maternal roles. Although neither woman had children, Anne used many of her assets to enrich and promote her nieces and nephews, while Diane voiced authority through her appropriately gendered concern for the welfare and health of the king's children.[126]

Like these noblewomen, Castilian women across the social-class spectrum could use their bodies and their potential to attract the attention of noblemen as economic assets to advance their own economic security. In his study of recognition of paternity in sixteenth- and seventeenth-century Navarre, Jesús M. Usunáriz found that there was a legal and social expectation that men provide for their partners and their children. According to Usunáriz, a sixteenth-century judge stated: "When the mother is poor the father is obliged to support the child and the mother."[127] We saw earlier in this chapter the social expectation that noblemen would care for their children and the mothers of those children when Beatriz Vallejo's sister, learning that Beatriz was pregnant after Rodrigo raped her, insisted that Beatriz return to Rodrigo because she was sure Rodrigo would take responsibility for Beatriz and the child, which he did.[128] Women who had children with the Castilian nobility, however, often benefited beyond receiving the basic necessities. For example, doña Inés Enríquez de la Carra had at least one daughter with the Lord of Valdenebro y Villafrechos, who left her 50,000 maravedís in his will in 1491, and Isabel de Leyma "had communication" and three children with the second Count of Oñate who, in turn, left her 300,000 maravedís in his will in 1541.[129] Further down the social scale, Isabel Ramírez had a son out of wedlock with Gonzalo Ruiz de la Vega, a member of the powerful Mendoza family. In his will in 1456, Gonzalo left Isabel (who did not carry the title doña) a lifetime income, "for her maintenance every year for her entire life thirty *fanegas* of wheat and 3,000 maravedís in money for wine and meat and fish and clothes," and a further 2,000 maravedís to provide for her mourning clothes after his death.[130] After Gonzalo died Isabel had economic security and the wherewithal to participate publicly in mourning his death, a legacy that might have been a mark of social status.

In a testamentary clause that gives insight into how these relationships might have been negotiated, the second Count of Arcos (d. 1471) claimed to have made a specific arrangement with Mencía de Fojeda and her parents (her father was a local official). The count could "have" Mencía, and in exchange the count left her an annual income made up of bread and 1,500 maravedís in addition to a one-time gift of an additional 40,000 maravedís from his unentailed possessions.[131] Mencía and her family made a business deal with the Count of Arcos that he later honored in his will, and she emerged from this encounter with an annual income and a considerable inheritance in cash. Whereas the Count of Arcos honored his promise to Mencía, other women had to use the courts, as discussed previously, to fight for their economic support. Doña Elvira González de Medina was the long-term concubine of the cathedral canon and archdeacon of Ávila, don Nuño González de Aguila. Don Nuño attempted to provide for her by selling her all or part of his property, but their son, who would otherwise have inherited the property, objected. Doña Elvira fought for nine long years in court before most of her wealth was restored to her, enabling her to found the Carmelite convent of la Encarnación. Her willingness to use the court systems and her success in that endeavor gave her economic security and gave the city of Ávila a crucially important convent that would later welcome the future St. Teresa.[132]

At the very bottom of the social hierarchy, enslaved women routinely suffered from sexual exploitation and rape. They had few choices about their own sexuality or indeed about their futures in a hostile society, but even here women exercised some agency in difficult circumstances. Brian Catlos argued that "consensual or semi-consensual [sexual] relations could be an important strategy for survival and advancement" for enslaved women. In Valencia, where bearing a master's child meant automatic manumission or freedom for an enslaved woman, Deborah Blumenthal found examples of women going to court to file what were essentially paternity suits to win their freedom.[133] Although manumission was not guaranteed under Castilian law, the lives of Beatriz and Marta, the enslaved women owned by the Count of Arcos and mentioned previously also exhibited some potential for agency. In his will the count acknowledged his children with both women, freed both of them, and left Beatriz a legacy of 30,000 maravedís and Marta 10,000 maravedís, with another 10,000 for her son Cristóbal. In contrast, though he also freed a third enslaved woman, Marina (who apparently did not have children with him), he left her only 1,500 maravedís. Thus the production of children for a noble family gained Beatriz and Marta increased economic resources. The count's will also hints at a possible future for Beatriz, Marta, and Marina, stating that after his death all three women might live together in "a life more honest" and not go astray or separate ("e non por otras partes descarriadas e apartadas").[134] At the time of the count's death in 1471, cities like Toledo and Castile included communities of freed slaves, and in many parts of southern Spain freed slaves "often came to form part of their former owners' network of patronage and dependence."[135] This was an uncertain and precarious position in society, but equipped with their freedom, economic support, and their intimate connections to the powerful Arcos family, Beatriz and Marta might have been able to end their days with a community that they identified with, some economic security, and more potential control over their own destinies.

Sexual exploitation and rape were a problem for women at every social level, but women further up the social hierarchy had better protection and a wider range of possible outcomes. The choices that Castilian women made about who to have sexual relations with and when to have them could damage their reputations for chastity, but also had the potential to put them in command of economic resources that could repair that reputation and give them the ability to achieve a reputable marriage. As discussed in the previous chapter, in the winter of 1516–17, Ana de Galves, daughter of a resident of Bayona, had sexual relations with a young nobleman (Juan de Velasco) from the house of Frías and gave birth to a son, Baltasar. This restored Juan's masculine reputation, but it also benefited Ana. Juan de Velasco did not marry Ana, but he did compensate her for the loss of her virginity with a dowry which one neighbor assessed at 200 ducados and another at 70,000 maravedís. Studying cases of *estupro* (sex with a virgin or a widow of good reputation against her will or through false promises) in Navarre, Jesús M. Usunáriz found that these cases were often compensated either with money (a dowry) or marriage to the offender. Before the Council of Trent, the compensations tended more toward the dowry, which allowed the woman to marry someone else, but the council's emphasis on completing promises of marriage meant estupro cases were more likely to end in marriage to the offender after the decrees of the Council of Trent took effect.[136]

In this case (which occurred well before the Council of Trent), the dowry Ana obtained from the incident gave her a chance at a secure situation in life. Ana and Juan's son was raised by Ana's parents, and Ana used the dowry she had gained to marry a "very honorable hidalgo."[137] The witness testimony implies that Ana made a better marriage than she might have without the dowry. Ana's sexual relationship with Juan was public enough that twenty-one years later, when their son wanted to prove his paternity, he could find several witnesses who remembered the details of these events and the identities of both his parents. Presumably, then, Ana should have been suffering from (at the very least) a damaged reputation, yet in reality the dowry she received from Juan enabled her to make an advantageous marriage and to go on with her life as a wife. It is less clear that she had contact with her son, who was raised by her father and stepmother. This arrangement was an attempt at secrecy, but Ana and her family had nosey neighbors. One witness testified that when he realized that Ana's father was much too old to have such a young son, he just kept asking questions until Ana's harassed father broke down and told him that the child was his illegitimate grandson.[138] Ana, then, was the mother of an illegitimate child and the wife of a respectable hidalgo. Her lapse in chastity was known in her community and was one part of her reputation, but it did not define her role, and the dowry she gained from that lapse in chastity had enabled her subsequent marriage and reputation as a wife.

There is abundant evidence that virginity, while important, was not the most crucial quality a woman could bring to her marriage in early modern Castile. Economic resources were seen as a solid start to a successful marriage, one that could outweigh the importance of a woman's virginity or her chastity. Isabel de las Casas had a long-term sexual relationship and four children with Pedro Girón, master of the Order of Calatrava. In his will written in 1466, Pedro ordered their eldest son Alfonso (who inherited his father's estate) to give his mother 500,000 maravedís, adding, "And if the said doña Isabel his mother will marry and wishes to live honestly, that the said don Alfonso will support her in living honestly." Pedro Girón's expectation was that a dowry of 500,000 maravedís would allow Isabel to marry and "live honestly" even though she was not a virgin and was not technically chaste, since she had been living in sin with him for some years.[139] The wording of his will frames feminine honor and chastity as things that could be repaired and reinstated, suggesting that the current concubine could become a chaste wife in the future, a direct contradiction of fray Luis de León's assertion that a loss of chastity was permanent, rendering a woman a "perfidious harlot and the dirtiest mud, and the most foul-smelling and repulsive dirt."[140]

As illegitimate children got older the records show their mothers planning for their futures. In 1513 doña Inés de Mendoza y Delgadillo left a careful and detailed bequest designed to augment the dowry of her illegitimate daughter Marina. In her will Inés stated that Marina should receive four new mattresses, a "Moorish" bedspread, new bedclothes made of linen and decorated with blackwork embroidery, a small cloth, two rugs, four cushions decorated with Holland-work embroidery, and eight new sheets. Inés's legacy provided her daughter with important household linens and presumed a future for her as a married woman.[141] Other mothers provided less detailed gifts but were even more generous. Doña María de Aguirre left her illegitimate son as her universal heir when she died in 1601, even though she did not know where he was. He could not be found when she died, so he did not inherit.[142] The failure of this bequest hints at tensions and divisions within the illegitimate family, but still highlights the agency of women who had economic assets at their disposal and wished to use them to provide for their children's futures. Mothers of illegitimate children could also take action to express their displeasure or disapproval of their children's course in life. In 1537 doña Guiomar Carillo made a donation of part of her property to her illegitimate son (Lorenzo) with the poet Garcilaso de la Vega. The seventeen-year-old Lorenzo had already inherited some support from his father, designed to provide him with a university education that would enable him to become a cleric or go into the law. When Lorenzo got in trouble, however, his mother indicated her displeasure by attempting to revoke the donation.[143]

If women who had illegitimate children did not subsequently marry, another career possibility for them was the convent. A successful convent career could put women in command of resources and people and demand of them some of the skills previously discussed, such as an ability to use the court system, manage land and incomes, and educate and care for younger women. In some ways early modern Spanish convents, "revered, sacred institutions that embodied their culture's piety and enshrinement of female chastity," were not obvious places for women who had illegitimate children to thrive. Yet Elizabeth Lehfeldt argued persuasively that the cloister walls were permeable and that "convent space was fraught with tension over female sexuality."[144] The same contradictions in ideas about women's reputation that could enable mothers of illegitimate children to thrive outside the convent also existed within convent culture. Convents had close connections to elite families and the titled nobility and often provided homes for female family members.[145]

Convents could therefore be a place to hide noblewomen who had violated the rules of chastity and brought shame on their families or a solution to the future of illegitimate daughters, but they could also be the focus for new lives and careers for talented women. Doña Elvira González de Medina was mentioned previously as "widowed" after a long concubinage with the cathedral canon and archdeacon of Ávila don Nuñez González del Aguila. She demonstrated her authority and ability to act independently by establishing a tiny *beaterio*[146] of fourteen women in her own house in 1479. By 1495 she had obtained a donation of land from Ferdinand and Isabel on which to build a new convent, and the beaterio transformed into the Carmelite convent of la Encarnación that opened in 1515. By 1535 la Encarnación had over a hundred nuns, including the young St. Teresa of Ávila.[147] Women who joined already existing convents also achieved success in this arena by rising to leadership positions. Doña Floriana de Portas Ossorio had an illegitimate daughter with the fourth Count of Benavente in the late fifteenth century. Her daughter married a minor nobleman, and doña Floriana ended her days as the abbess of the Cistercian monastery of Santa María de Carrizo, a distinguished role that indicated her success and commanded respect in her local community.[148]

In addition to being spiritually respected, abbesses of important convents participated in the Iberian economy in both the medieval and the early modern period. Doña María de Navarra and Aragón had an illegitimate daughter with the Lord of Lodosa and then went on to become the abbess of the convent of Santa Clara in Tudela. Her illegitimate daughter, Isabel, had an illegitimate son with the third Duke of Nájera and ended her days as the abbess of the prestigious convent of Las Huelgas in Burgos, an achievement that reflects her skills and ability as well as her noble status.[149] In the medieval period the office of abbess of Las Huelgas was, as Elizabeth Lehfeldt noted, the "pinnacle of the power conferred upon female monastics."[150] Isabel's role included both temporal and spiritual obligations and had a significant effect on the economy. In the villages under her jurisdiction she had the authority to appoint chaplains and priests, confer benefices, hear civil cases, decide matrimonial cases, and convene a synod. By the sixteenth century some of these powers had waned, but the position of abbess was still powerful enough to make it a substantial career.[151] Neither Isabel's own illegitimacy nor her liaison with the Duke of Nájera seems to have impeded her highly successful ecclesiastical career, demonstrating that having an illegitimate child could over time lessen in social importance as a woman accrued other skills and achievements on which to base her reputation.

Like Ana de Villagrán at the beginning of this chapter, many of the women who had illegitimate children with the Castilian nobility were concubines for only a part of their lives. Before she was a concubine, Ana was a lady-in-waiting to the Duchess of Infantado, and afterward she was a wife and then for seventeen years a widow. Likewise, Isabel de Meneses was the concubine of the Duke of Medina Sidonia for eleven years, his wife for two weeks, and his widow for twenty-six more years. Their lives were simultaneously complicated and enriched by their extramarital relationships and illegitimate children, and their paths were not always easy. Ana de Jaén, who had six children with the Count of Paredes, subsequently married him, and used her will to assert her children's legitimacy, had a bad widowhood. The count married her, elevated her to the status of countess, and left her a legacy of 1,000 ducados de oro, 500,000 maravedís, and a mill. But Ana's marriage was odious to her stepchildren who prevented her from receiving her inheritance and left her living neglected and struggling with debt in the town of Villapalacios for twenty-two years until her death in 1558.[152] Her story, and that of the other women in this chapter, is both more demanding and more ambiguous than the simple prescriptive dichotomy that erased all unchaste women with a shameful death. In reality Castilian society contained a wide variety of women with a wide variety of sexual histories, traumas, and choices, many of whom were fully integrated into the wider society in which they fulfilled multiple roles and exerted considerable agency.

A noble widow, with more freedom of movement and choice than her married or single sisters, might choose the longstanding Iberian tradition of a stable concubinage, as might a peasant woman with limited economic resources. But it was not that difficult for the most high-ranking noblewomen to find themselves on the wrong side of Castile's shifting marriage laws, while enslaved women living in a noble household had no choice about accepting their owner's sexual advances. Extramarital sex and the children that resulted from it had complex consequences for women's lives that varied according to a woman's family situation, social class, relationship with her noble lover, and relationship with her children. Women of higher social status often had more resources, were shielded by their family's reputation, and were more likely to be able to use the legal system to their advantage and that of their children. On the other hand, these women struggled with enforced secrecy (many of their names are still not known), damaged family reputations, shame, and limited contact with or ability to acknowledge their children. Women of lower social status could benefit economically from relationships with noblemen, but were less likely to pass on prestige to their children and often had less legal or familial support for themselves or their children. Running through the lives of all of these women was the fragile nature of the legal ties they had to their children who were born outside of marriage. Some women were able to bear and raise children in a relatively stable form of concubinage or as part of the same household, thus enacting a maternal role that their contemporaries could recognize and even applaud. Other mothers of illegitimate children had to leave them to the care of their fathers or other family members to preserve their own reputations.

A woman's claim to reputable femininity was not static but rather a long-term, continuous process of negotiation between behavior, perception, and status. Reputation varied over time, depending in part on chastity but also on a woman's marital status, her ability to participate in the economy, her ability to protect and provide for her family, and her ability to produce children. It is that last characteristic that I discuss in the next chapter, which focuses on illegitimate children and the complexities they introduced into the noble family.

3

"Send the Baby to Me"

The Care and Custody of Illegitimate Children

In January of 1542, Iñigo López de Mendoza, eldest son and heir of the Counts of Tendilla, married his cousin María, daughter of the Duke and Duchess of Infantado. Just three weeks later, on February 5, he became a father when his extramarital partner, doña Luisa de Mosquera, gave birth to their daughter Catalina in his parents' home in the Royal Palace of Granada. The baby was a complication in Iñigo's brand new marriage, so when she was old enough to leave her mother, she was sent to her paternal grandmother at the family palace in Mondéjar. Catalina grew up away from her mother but in the heart of the Mendoza family, where she was cared for by her grandmother and her father's sister María. The Mendoza women educated Catalina in the humanist tradition. She was sent to court as a lady-in-waiting to Princess Juana of Austria, and her father's brothers arranged a marriage for her with the heir to the Count of la Gomera.[1]

If the Mendoza family was generous to Catalina, their generosity was well repaid. Articulate, strong-willed, and religious, Catalina did not bow to her family's wishes or accept the future they had arranged for her, but she did prove an asset to their financial and emotional well-being. Catalina was raised by her aunt María, a strong-minded woman who refused an arranged marriage to live a religious life, taking a vow of chastity and becoming friends with Teresa of Ávila. Catalina's own mother lived and died in the habit of a beata despite having had an illegitimate child with the Count of Tendilla.[2] When Catalina and her aunt María discovered the dissolute life that Catalina's absent husband was living in Seville, Catalina appealed to the pope to have her marriage annulled. She succeeded, and subsequently devoted herself not to the customary Poor Clares but to the Jesuits, the new and exciting embodiment of religious reform at this time. The Jesuits do not admit women, but the Princess Juana, also a passionate admirer of theirs, had convinced the pope to allow her to take vows in secret in 1554. As one of the princess's former ladies-in-waiting and a well-accepted member of a prominent family, Catalina must have been aware of this, and she also eventually prevailed on the Jesuits to allow her to take their vows of poverty, chastity, and obedience in 1600, just two years before she died.[3]

While pursuing her religious goals, however, Catalina also worked on her family's behalf. In 1571 her father was called away to the royal post of viceroy and captain general of Naples, and he chose Catalina to administer the vast Tendilla estates for him until his return in 1580.[4] Her emotional connections to her father and her siblings were strong. When she fell ill in February of 1602 at age seventy-six, her younger brother Juan, the sixth Duke of Infantado, rushed to her bedside, using his power and wealth to bring her the best doctors available.[5] Catalina died as she had lived, religious, penitent, and surrounded by her family.

Catalina's experiences were typical of illegitimate children of noble families in several key ways. She was recognized by her father and was part of his large family (she would have eleven legitimate half-siblings). The complications her presence caused in Iñigo's family were managed by a team of family members that included her paternal grandmother and several of her father's siblings. When her intelligence and talent were recognized, the family invested in her future, arranging a marriage for her that would benefit the Mendoza lineage and create new familial alliances, and Catalina's own skills and actions made her an asset to her father's lineage.

Illegitimacy and the presence of illegitimate children in the noble family created incredibly complex households and family structures. Many noblemen had multiple wives, long-term, relatively stable relationships with concubines, and short-term affairs. Although all these relationships could produce children who were acknowledged and supported by their fathers, the resulting households were held together by the labor and economic resources of a wide variety of women, including mothers, wives, aunts, sisters, grandmothers, servants, and enslaved women. When illegitimate children were recognized by their fathers, they were often raised within the noble household along with legitimate siblings. One result of this physical proximity was strong sibling bonds. Children of different mothers within one generation developed long-term ties and often assisted and cared for each other. These bonds then stretched into the next generation as they helped raise, educate, and support the careers of each other's legitimate and illegitimate children. This entire intricate system persisted because it was advantageous to noble families, allowing them to develop a power base that consisted of a wide array of human resources and talent.

This chapter argues that although illegitimacy had emotional, financial, and dynastic consequences and created potential problems and disputes that needed to be carefully managed, the nobility systematically turned the nearly constant presence of illegitimate children into an internal asset. By investing in their care and education, the nobility used illegitimate children as strategic agents to advance the power, wealth, and connections of the entire lineage. Illegitimate children who were recognized by their fathers' families added an additional layer of complexity to already intricate noble family structures. In order to raise and educate these children, noblemen drew on the labor, financial resources, and goodwill of women, but they also relied heavily on sibling bonds. In return, the noble family expected to be able to count on illegitimate family members as cooperative, supportive, and useful members of the larger lineage. Noble strategies to gain political power and economic resources were enhanced by the talents, labor, military service, church careers, marriage alliances, and financial resources of illegitimate children. As the next chapter discusses, however, illegitimate children occupied an ambiguous space in relation to a family who could find them useful but was not obligated to support them.

Most noble families experienced illegitimacy as a matter of course. For example, in the Medina Sidonia family, the eight generations from the illegitimate founder of the dynasty, Guzmán "el Bueno" (d. 1309), to the third Duke of Medina Sidonia (d. 1507) produced twenty-one legitimate children and twenty-two illegitimate children. Five generations of the Dukes of Arcos produced twenty legitimate children and thirty-eight illegitimate children from roughly 1387 to 1573.[6] Although the numbers are not always that dramatic, they do speak to the persistent presence of illegitimate children. The Dukes of Frías had thirty-seven legitimate children and ten illegitimate children over seven generations (1418–1585) and the Dukes of Infantado had thirty-nine legitimate children and thirteen illegitimate children over five generations (1405–1531).[7] These numbers include only the children of the main titleholders, thus overlooking the illegitimate children of their younger brothers. Marie Claude Gerbet estimated that the nobility in Extremadura produced one illegitimate child for every seventeen legitimate children.[8] Any child growing up in those families would have had illegitimate half-siblings, illegitimate cousins, or illegitimate aunts and uncles.

Illegitimacy was an ambiguous, unstable, and complex legal and social condition in fifteenth- and sixteenth-century Castile. The futures of illegitimate children were affected by their own legal status, the social class of their parents, and the rising concern with purity of blood (limpieza de sangre) in Castilian society. As noted in the introduction, there were several different legal categories of illegitimacy in medieval and early modern Castile, ranging from hijos naturales (those whose parents were legally able to marry) to hijos bastardos (those whose parents were legally unable to marry).[9] Illegitimacy highlighted the failures of the noble system of arranged marriages, added to the sheer complexity of family relationships already complicated by endogamy, left illegitimate children vulnerable, and changed inheritance patterns. For example, in 1411 Alfonso de Guzmán, younger son of the first Count of Niebla, wed Leonor de Zúñiga in an arranged marriage that quickly broke down. Alfonso maintained Leonor honorably in the town of Gine outside of Seville, but he did not live with her or have children with her, and it is doubtful whether the marriage was consummated. Instead, he formed a long-term relationship with Mencía de Figueroa, an illegitimate daughter of nobleman Lorenzo Suárez de Figueroa. Mencía left her convent of Santa Clara in Seville to have five children with Alfonso. Some sources claim they were married, but Alfonso's first wife, Leonor, was still alive, doing business, and claiming her status as his wife in 1422, thus rendering his relationship with Mencía concubinage rather than marriage. To further complicate this family situation, Mencía's legitimate half-sister Teresa was married to Alfonso's brother Enrique, the second Count of Niebla (see figure 1).[10]

A generation later Castile was in chaos, caught up in the war between Juan II of Castile (1405–54), the Infantes of Aragón, and most of the high nobility. As the political situation deteriorated, Alfonso's illegitimate children were left without protection. In 1444 Alfonso's nephew Juan (the first Duke of Medina Sidonia—son of Teresa and Enrique) took him prisoner, forcing him to sign a will that disinherited his own children and left them at their cousin's mercy. Alfonso's illegitimate daughter Urraca, only eighteen when she was taken prisoner, had two illegitimate children with the first Duke of Medina Sidonia, who was her double first cousin.[11] Founding a legacy for Urraca's unborn child, the duke referred to Urraca's mother (his uncle's concubine) as "my aunt," suggesting that the family recognized that long-term relationship as a de facto marriage. In spite of that casual recognition, the questionable legitimacy of Alfonso's children was a problem for them. It is unlikely that the duke would have been able to disinherit them (even in the middle of a war) if they had been legitimate, and Urraca was more vulnerable in relation to her cousin and captor because of her illegitimacy. Illegitimacy also had implications for the family property. In 1454 the first Duke of Medina Sidonia (who had eight illegitimate children of his own) gave one of his illegitimate daughters, Teresa, a dowry as she prepared to marry the son of Álvaro de Zúñiga, Count of Plasencia. Teresa's dowry consisted of the rents from Lepe, Ayamonte, and La Redondela, the properties that had been settled on her great-uncle Alfonso in 1396 in preparation for his failed marriage with Leonor de Zúñiga, who was the great-aunt of Teresa's new husband. Historian Miguel Ángel Ladero Quesada suggested that the dowry could be considered a tardy compensation "to the honor and interests of the house of Zúñiga."[12]

Illegitimacy was a common characteristic of the Medina Sidonia family. In addition to his five illegitimate children, Alfonso had three illegitimate half-siblings, and his mother was the illegitimate daughter of King Enrique II of Castile (1333–79). His legitimate brother Enrique, the second Count of Niebla, had four illegitimate children, and, as previously mentioned his rapacious nephew Juan, the first duke of Medina Sidonia, had eight illegitimate children. By 1496 the scandal in the Guzmán family was the third duke's second marriage to his cousin Leonor de Guzmán, the daughter of the first duke's illegitimate daughter Teresa. The problem was not Teresa's illegitimacy, but the fact that the third duke and his second wife had lived together and had at least two children before the papal dispensation for consanguinity arrived from Rome to sanction their marriage.[13] The Medina Sidonia family had layers and generations of different kinds of illegitimacy to contend with.

Although illegitimacy could create problems for illegitimate individuals, for the smooth transfer of property, and for legitimate heirs, it was an ordinary complexity, one that noble families negotiated generation after generation and which created a web of relationships. Sometimes those relationships could be unexpectedly beneficial. Francisca Fernández Manrique, Lady of Frigiliana, benefited from the death of her father's mistress, María de Aguirre. María had left her son Carlos, Francisca's illegitimate half-brother, as her universal heir, but he could not be found when she died in 1601, and Francisca took possession of the estate because she was his closest relative.[14] At other times illegitimacy (even in the past) could complicate marriage and kinship. Juana de Valencia's marriage to García Manrique in 1525 required a dispensation because their grandmothers had been sisters—one the honorably married Margarita de Lemos and the other the acknowledged mistress of Cardinal Mendoza, Mencía de Lemos.[15] And sometimes (as in the case of the Dukes of Medina Sidonia) illegitimacy and remarriage could create family relationships that were so convoluted that early modern genealogists enjoyed writing riddles about them. In the mid-sixteenth century Juan de Benavides, illegitimate son

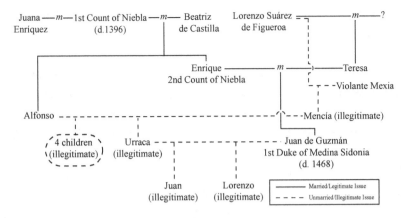

Juana —*m*— 1st Count of Niebla —*m*— Beatriz   Lorenzo Suárez ⚊ ⎤ ————— *m* ——— ?
Enríquez   (d.1396)   de Castilla   de Figueroa

Enrique ——————— *m* ————⎤————— Teresa
2nd Count of Niebla   ⎪
                                                  ⊢ – – Violante Mexia

Alfonso – – ⫟ – – – – – – – – ⫟ – – – – – – – – – – – – – ⌐⎤– – Mencía (illegitimate)

⌐ – – ⫟ – – ⌐   ⎪   ⎪
⎪ 4 children ⎟ Urraca – – ⫟ – – – – – – – ⫟ – – – – Juan de Guzmán
⎩(illegitimate)⎭ (illegitimate) ⎪   ⎪   1st Duke of Medina Sidonia
                                ⎪   ⎪   (d. 1468)
                                ⎪   ⎪
                               Juan   Lorenzo   ┌────── Married/Legitimate Issue
                           (illegitimate) (illegitimate) │ – – – Unmarried/Illegitimate Issue

1. Dukes of Medina Sidonia family tree. Composed by Grace E. Coolidge from Miguel Ángel Ladero Quesada, *Guzmán: La casa ducal de Medina Sidonia en Sevilla y su reino. 1282–1521* (Madrid: Dykinson, 2015), 95–96, 95n22, 160. Drawn by Fletcher Coolidge.

of the fourth Lord of Javalquinto, married his father's wife's sister.[16] The marriage was legal because the two were not related, but this technically made Juan his father's brother-in-law.

The family of Ana de Mendoza, the sixth Duchess of Infantado, displays several of the characteristics that made noble families so intricate, including remarriage, stepparenthood, uncle-niece marriage, and illegitimacy. Ana, heir to the title of Infantado, married her uncle Rodrigo in January of 1582. Rodrigo already had two illegitimate daughters, and the new couple quickly produced four more legitimate children, including a son who died young. Rodrigo died in 1587 and, lacking a son to inherit the Infantado title, Ana married her first cousin in 1594 and had two more daughters. After the birth of Ana's sixth child, this family included legitimate half-siblings, illegitimate half-siblings, and (if such a thing can exist) illegitimate stepsiblings, given that Ana's children from her second marriage were not actually siblings of her first husband's illegitimate children, although they were distantly related. In addition, because Ana's first marriage had been to her uncle, her illegitimate stepdaughters were also her first cousins.[17] It seems that all eight children were probably raised together in the family palace in Guadalajara, giving them an opportunity to form relationships and attachments throughout their childhoods.

The prevalence of illegitimacy and illegitimate children who were recognized by Castilian noble families raises the question of how these children were brought up and cared for. Although some illegitimate children were disowned, disinherited, abandoned, or even killed, a subset of illegitimate children were claimed as family members.[18] They often inherited unequally, but if claimed by a noble father or a noble family they were themselves noble, and they still needed physical care and the education that would allow them to live up to that status. The complex households of the nobility, containing, in the words of James Casey, "stepmothers, illegitimate children, maiden aunts, servants and slaves and so many other dependents," used female labor and financial resources to care for the illegitimate members of the group.[19]

Noble wives provided some of the labor when illegitimate children were raised in their married father's households. These wives were expected to support the family and to produce legitimate children. Barbara Harris found that for elite women in England, "wifehood constituted a career that incorporated reproductive, managerial, political, and social functions essential to the survival and prosperity of their husbands' patrilineages," and Castilian noble wives had a similar range of responsibilities.[20] Genealogist Luis de Salazar y Castro, writing in the late seventeenth-century, lauded "the happiness achieved by the House of Lara through the production of many excellent daughters who contributed highly to the ancient splendor of this heroic family by their [marital] alliances and their numerous progeny."[21] Pedro Barrantes Maldonado, writing the history of the Counts of Niebla in 1541, was even more explicit. He commended the marriage of twenty-seven-year-old Guzmán el Bueno to fifteen-year-old María Alfonso Coronel to prevent Guzmán's "falling into the sins of the flesh" and to produce legitimate children to "succeed to [Guzmán's] house and . . . memory."[22] The patriarchal expectations for wives demanded skill, self-sacrifice, and an acute awareness of the nobility and the status of one's family. Describing Leonor de Guzmán, wife of the fourth Prince of Mélito and Éboli, Salazar y Castro enthused, "[She] governed the estates of her husband and administered the guardianship of their children with notable skill during his journeys to France, Portugal, and Rome. She respected his traditions and finally [she] did everything in a manner that corresponded with the greatness of her birth."[23] A wife who attended to her obligations could hope for the kind of commendation and familial authority that don Luis de Requesens gave his wife when he wrote his will in 1573 in Milan, where he had been appointed as viceroy under Philip II: "I command my son don Juan and my daughter doña Mencía . . . to revere, serve, and comply with the said lady, my beloved wife, whom I have loved dearly as she has deserved from the quality of her person and the great love in which we have lived, and so I order and pray to my children to serve and obey her."[24]

The expectations for noble wives gradually incorporated the idea that the ideal wife would raise her husband's illegitimate children along with her own. In his chronicle of the Counts of Niebla mentioned above, Pedro Barrantes Maldonado included an admiring description of María Alfonso Coronel's behavior toward her husband's extramarital relationships and illegitimate children, which was by his account both practical and generous. Aware that her husband was both having an affair in Seville and living in an extravagant style that the estate could not afford, María, "like a sane and honorable woman," took action. She brought her husband's newborn illegitimate daughter Teresa into her own house "and cared for her as though she was her own daughter," and she suggested to her husband that they leave Seville and live somewhere else (presumably somewhere less expensive). Struck by María's goodness and virtue, Guzmán complied with both her actions.[25] This anecdote reflects the advice of moralist Juan Luis Vives, who told several stories about women who behaved with such exemplary patience toward their unfaithful husbands that the husbands were won over: "Modest and chaste, [a virtuous wife] bears hurts and injuries / From her spouse and hides his misdemeanors."[26]

Exemplary wives who bore in mind Vives's assurance that "human laws do not require the same chastity of the man as they do of the woman" received lavish praise in the early modern period and beyond.[27] In his late fifteenth-century will, Diego de Lemos asked his wife, doña Mayor de Ulloa, to take in and raise his two illegitimate sons.[28] The third Duke of Alba brought his illegitimate son Hernando (b. 1527) into his household during his lifetime, raising the boy to be a highly accomplished soldier who would eventually fight with his father on numerous campaigns. His wife, María Enríquez, became a legend for her gracious acceptance and support of Hernando, conforming to the narrative of the selfless wife who accepts her husband's bastards without comment or censure.[29] As late as 1947, Jacobo Fitz James Stewart y Falcó, the Duke of Berwick y Alba, published an article in the *Boletín de la Real Academia de la Historia* in which he recounted this story of María's acceptance of Hernando and lauded her as taking on the responsibilities of being the wife of a great man with "modesty, silence, resignation, and a Christian spirit," a list of virtues that comes straight from the sixteenth-century Vives.[30]

Noblemen found Vives's ideas convenient. When the first Duke of Infantado wrote his will in 1479, he asked that his second wife, Isabel Enríquez, would take in two of his illegitimate daughters after his death, "having them in her house and company . . . until they marry because I trust that out of her love and goodness she will guard, discipline, and honor them while they are with her."[31] The duke's language to Isabel is slightly ambiguous. Like Diego de Lemos (mentioned above) the duke stated authoritatively, "It is my will," but then adds, "I pray" or "I plea" (*ruego*), when asking for her help in this matter. These two illegitimate daughters, who were born before he married Isabel, were just one piece of his family's complicated structure, which included their illegitimate brother and another half-sister born out of wedlock to a different mother. Married to the duke in 1467, Isabel had two young legitimate daughters of her own by 1479 as well as an uneasy relationship with the duke's eight adult children from his first marriage.[32] Isabel had legal guardianship of her own two daughters along with custody of their slightly older illegitimate half-siblings, and might have raised all four girls to adulthood together.[33] The duke's will suggests that although he was fairly confident that Isabel would raise his illegitimate daughters as he had asked, he was less sure that his children from his first marriage would support Isabel. He spelled out Isabel's inheritance in precise detail in his will to prevent them from challenging her right to his property, but by 1480 Isabel and the new duke, her stepson, were already embroiled in a lawsuit over financial support for her legitimate daughters.[34]

In reality, the composite nature of the noble household demanded more from married women than silence, humility, and resignation. María Alfonso Coronel's saintly acceptance of her husband's illegitimate daughter Teresa, as told in the sixteenth century by a male commentator, is only part of her life story. After the death of her husband in 1309, María eventually grew into a powerful matriarch who controlled her dowry and half of the goods she and her husband had accumulated during their marriage. From this vantage point she directed her young son in the administration of his estates, gave generously to the poor, and bought and sold slaves. She also remained committed (and perhaps genuinely attached) to Teresa, arranging her marriage and paying for her dowry.[35] The reality of family relationships encompassed affectionate bonds between women and children who were not their own. The fifth Duchess of Nájera was so fond of her husband's illegitimate daughter Isabel that she referred to her as "my daughter" in her will in 1601.[36]

The relationships between women and their husband's illegitimate children also shed light on the complex identities that made up a noble household. When Juana de Aragón wrote her will in 1509, she was the Duchess of Frías with one legitimate daughter and the second wife of a husband who already had a legitimate daughter and at least four illegitimate sons by the time she married him. Juana left her husband as the universal heir of her estate, but with the caveat that if he died before she did, she left her goods to his illegitimate son, Pedro de Velasco. She said in her will: "His estate is small and the said don Pedro will be good."[37] This is an unusual legacy, made even more interesting by the fact that Juana herself was the illegitimate daughter of the king, Ferdinand of Aragón. Was Juana's legacy prompted by sympathy for another illegitimate child? Pedro was born during the duke's first marriage, not during his marriage to Juana, thus perhaps posing fewer emotional complications for Juana. Was Juana trying to pressure her husband into increasing Pedro's inheritance? Juana did not leave an explanation of her motives, but the incident sheds light on the complexity of a noble family in which two illegitimate individuals who were not related to each other were, for all intents and purposes, stepmother and stepson. In this odd situation Juana might very well have understood the uncertainties that Pedro was facing and sympathized with his difficulties.

Nevertheless, asking wives to care for illegitimate children created potentially volatile family situations. The small army of women who were part of any large noble household made it possible for noblemen to raise illegitimate children within their own households even while the presence of those children and their mothers could disrupt noble marriages. Don Juan de Guzmán, first Duke of Medina Sidonia, claimed that he had cared for all his illegitimate children (who had at least five different mothers) in his house "since they were born." The duke's marriage to María de la Cerda had been a failure and the couple did not live together, so care for his illegitimate children did not fall on María.[38]

An example of how noblemen without resident wives might construct a household that could care for their illegitimate children can be seen in the household of the second Count of Arcos. The Count of Arcos's wife, Leonor de Guzmán, left his household shortly after she had arrived there because of the count's obvious interest in her lady-in-waiting, Leonor Núñez. The count ignored his wife and lived openly with Leonor Núñez (whom he eventually married in 1448, after Leonor de Guzmán's death), and during this time the couple raised their nine children within the count's household. Unfortunately, Leonor Núñez died shortly after her wedding. The glue that held the count's household together from 1452 onward was Catalina González, his maidservant and the mother of six of his children, who was featured in the introduction to this book. She must have helped raise Leonor Núñez's youngest children as well as her own. In her turn, Catalina relied on the labor and skill of Beatriz Núñez and Marta Rodríguez, enslaved women owned by the count, both of whom were also the mothers of several of his children (see chapter 2).[39] When the count wrote his will in 1469, Catalina was still with him and his children. He left her a legacy that acknowledged her labor: "Because of the care I have for her, and for the sons and daughters I have had in her, and for the upbringing she has given them, and because of the seventeen years she has served here in my house and been with me and been working with my children. . . ."[40] The sheer number of illegitimate children fathered by the second Count of Arcos was unusual, but his reliance on the physical and sexual labor of female servants and slaves was not. In the absence of a compliant wife, women further down the social scale provided the daily work necessary to raise and feed the small children of the nobility.

In spite of Vives's moral doctrines and noblemen's hopes and expectations, noblewomen often did not appreciate their husbands' infidelity and sometimes refused to care for illegitimate children. By 1639 the moralist and writer Luisa de Padilla published a critique of noblemen's tendency to adultery, and even before this public criticism, some noblewomen resisted social pressure to patiently put up with their husband's extramarital liaisons.[41] One strategy available to a wife who was in charge of a large noble household was to use her influence to separate her husband from the other women he was involved with. The Countess of Castañeda, Mencía Enríquez, was a sister of the Count of Alva de Liste and the great-aunt of Ferdinand of Aragón, in addition to being closely related to the powerful Mendoza family. When Mencía realized that her husband was infatuated with her lady-in-waiting, Catalina de Ribera, she reasoned that the affair would end if Catalina was removed from the estate. Unbeknownst to her husband, Mencía arranged an honorable marriage for Catalina with Juan de San Pedro, alcaide de Ureña, a man "of known nobility."[42] Another strategy was to withdraw from the marriage and leave a husband's household (as Leonor de Guzmán, the second Countess of Arcos, did when her husband displayed his interest in her lady-in-waiting), but this option was only available if a noblewoman had somewhere else to go. The second Count of Oñate married Mencía de Velasco, daughter of the second Duke of Frías, in 1507, and the couple had eight children. In 1541 the count wrote a will in which he acknowledged a mistress and three illegitimate children, two of whom were still quite young. At about the same time, Mencía retired to her brother's estates, where she died in 1548. As her husband's affair became public, Mencía chose not to conform to the ideal of the wife who accepts and raises her husband's illegitimate children without complaint and instead withdrew from the situation entirely.[43]

These strategies reveal both the agency of noble wives and the limitations of that agency. None of these women was willing to accept the saintly behavior prescribed by moralists, but none of them could easily get a divorce. In the event (as detailed in chapter 2), the Count of Castañeda went after Catalina, kidnapped her, separated her from her husband, and had four children with her while the countess, Mencía, remained legally married but childless. The count's illegitimate children appear to have been raised by their mother, Catalina, whom he later married. Although the Countess of Oñate had support from her own powerful family and took refuge with her brother, the Duke of Frías, she could not stop her husband from acknowledging his illegitimate children and remembering them in his will. In this case, however, her husband had to make other arrangements for the custody of his illegitimate children, leaving custody of his youngest illegitimate daughter, Ana, to his aunt and entrusting his son Pedro to the Duke of Nájera, who was the senior nobleman of his house.[44] Ultimately, noblemen had the power to accept or reject their wives, but this behavior had consequences for them as well as for the women involved. Rejecting a woman who came from a powerful noble family and had some control over her own economic resources ultimately caused chaos, lawsuits, and damage to the family structure that did not benefit any children.

Usually the complexity of the family household, based on an arranged marriage, could stretch to take in and raise illegitimate children, but if this seemed ill-advised, noblemen had an extended family of households to turn to for help. Illegitimate children's gender, the social statuses of their mothers, and the circumstances and timing of their birth could shape where they were raised and educated. Returning to the Infantado household, the first duke did not ask his second wife to take in all his illegitimate children. In fact, the duke asked Isabel to raise only his two illegitimate daughters (Elvyra and Mariana) who had been born before he married her and whose mother, Juana de Lasarte, was noble enough to carry the honorific title "doña." His request to his wife was that she prepare these girls for marriage, something she was undoubtedly well qualified to do as a noblewoman with two daughters of her own. One of the daughters, Elvyra, did indeed eventually marry.[45]

After securing a place for his daughters within Isabel's household, the duke turned to his extended family for help with his other illegitimate children. Determining that his illegitimate son Alfonso was to be a priest, the duke asked his brother, Cardinal Pedro González de Mendoza, to raise and educate Alfonso for a post in the church. In his will the duke identified all three of these children as hijos naturales and asked that they be treated "as though they were legitimate children."[46] The duke had another illegitimate daughter, Leonor, who was born in different circumstances. For her care and upbringing he turned to his eldest son, Iñigo, and, specifically, to his daughter-in-law doña María de Luna. The duke requested that Iñigo and María raise and educate Leonor in their household, asking them to "dispose of her to marriage or religion, whichever seems best."[47] The duke made no mention of Leonor's mother, only of the town that Leonor lived in, and Leonor's inheritance was left to the discretion of her half-brother. The implication here is that the duke had sexual relations with someone on his estate, a nonnoble woman who could not give her children any help in the matter of status. Leonor's own status thus suffered from the status of her mother. Perhaps Leonor was not an hija natural, although the duke's will does not mention her legal status. Because she seems to have been the youngest of the four illegitimate children, it is also possible that she was born during his second marriage, and thus might have been an offense to his wife in a way that his two elder illegitimate daughters, born before his second marriage, were not. In any case, she was presumably raised within the household of the second Duke of Infantado after her father's death, with provisions made for her future. The first Duke of Infantado thus used a variety of strategies that were common among noble fathers. He turned to his wife, to his brother, and to his eldest son to ensure the future of his illegitimate children.

The larger noble lineage provided a wide variety of family members who could potentially raise and care for illegitimate children, many but not all of whom were women. For example, Mariana de Mendoza, the illegitimate daughter of the second Marquis de Montesclaros, was raised by her widowed, childless great-aunt Ana, who cared for Mariana and made the girl her heir. After Mariana's father died in 1570, his widow, Isabel Manrique, signed Mariana's marriage contract on behalf of the then seventy-year-old Ana. Working together, these two noblewomen ensured a secure future for the illegitimate Mariana by raising and educating her as a noblewoman and by marrying her to Juan de Baeza y Castilla.[48] Like the fates of the children of the first Duke of Infantado, Mariana's marriage demonstrates that her social status was judged in part on the identity of her mother, Luisa de Orozco, who came from a minor noble family in Guadalajara. Mariana's husband was also a minor nobleman with an entailed estate; he held public offices in Zamora, Valladolid, and Guadalajara.[49]

The actions of these women in raising and arranging a marriage for Mariana reveal some of the internal complexity of the Marquis of Montesclaros's family. The marquis's legitimate son, born posthumously, was raised by his widow Isabel, while his illegitimate daughter was raised by his wealthy aunt. As these two half-siblings grew up, Mariana (of lower status because of her mother's identity) married a local official in Guadalajara, while her half-brother inherited a title and married into the powerful Mendoza family, who had raised her. In this family illegitimacy created a liminal space where the social status of illegitimate children was in flux, changing over time from a more flexible childhood to what were deemed appropriate adult roles.

The care and custody of illegitimate children created multigenerational networks of women whose labor and resources helped sustain illegitimate children. Blanca de la Cerda, the widowed Countess of Cifuentes, was the guardian of her daughter and her son, who was vision-impaired and struggled with multiple health issues. Because of her son's poor health, Blanca administered her own dowry and joint share in the conjugal estate (returned to her after she was widowed) as well as the Cifuentes estate that her son had inherited.[50] The Counts of Cifuentes had jurisdiction over multiple towns throughout Guadalajara and Toledo, so from 1591–95 Blanca supervised the collection of *alcabalas* (sales taxes), *martiniegas* (a municipal annuity paid on St. Martin's Day), and *pechos* (head taxes), as well as legal fines, the fees paid by municipal councils, the rents and tributes from tenants on the estates, and the upkeep of several great houses and a fortress. In addition to managing these responsibilities and caring for her son's failing health (he died in 1602), Blanca granted an allowance to Isabel de Silva, the illegitimate daughter of her father-in-law, and contributed to the upkeep of her own husband's illegitimate daughter Ana de Silva, both of whom were nuns. Helping Blanca with these responsibilities, her mother-in-law, Ana de Ayala y Monroy, left a bequest to her illegitimate granddaughter, Ana.[51] In this case two generations of noblewomen committed to supporting two generations of illegitimate daughters, applying both their resources and their skilled labor to the task.

Noblewomen's skills and labor helped manage the problems that male promiscuity caused in marriages. In 1591 Diego de Mendoza got a little unsolicited advice from his mother, the Princess of Éboli, about how to conduct himself in relation to his new bride, the Countess of Salinas. After warning him to party less and stay away from his first wife (who had divorced him), his mother advised, "If you expect any living fruit from the wild oats you have sown, send the baby to me without your wife knowing about it; don't anger or displease her in any way, not even in thought by recalling such things."[52] The princess assumed that Diego's new wife would be angered and displeased if she encountered an unexpected illegitimate child of her husband, and she offered herself as the solution to a situation that she felt might endanger this promising new marriage.

As we saw in the case of the Count of Tendilla at the beginning of the chapter, noble grandmothers with large households and substantial financial resources could be immense assets to an illegitimate child and a way out of embarrassing difficulties for noblemen.[53] Antonio Enríquez de Navarra, Lord of Ablitas, had a relationship with doña Jerónima de Sarría. When Jerónima became pregnant, the couple traveled to Madrid where Antonio entrusted Jerónima to the care of his mother until their daughter was born.[54] In another example, the great Spanish poet Garcilaso de la Vega was an aristocratic younger son who had an extended sexual relationship and an illegitimate son, Lorenzo (born about 1520), with Guiomar Carrillo, the daughter of a distinguished noble family in Toledo. Garcilaso's mother, Sancha de Guzmán, stepped in to raise the young Lorenzo in her own household, claiming him as her nephew and thus helping to protect Guiomar's reputation.[55]

The role of noble grandmothers also emphasizes the complexity of the noble household over the generations. In 1499 the dowager Duchess of Medina Sidonia, Leonor de Guzmán, left each of her illegitimate granddaughters 1,000 maravedís in her will to augment their dowries. Leonor also remembered the girls' mother, Isabel de Melgarejo or de Zúñiga, who had been her lady-in-waiting and her son's lover before his marriage in 1488 and with whom the duchess was apparently still in contact eleven years later.[56] Another aspect of the complexity of the noble family is the way in which grandmothers often worked with other female family members to provide care, education, and material support to their illegitimate grandchildren. We have already seen how the dowager Countess of Cifuentes helped her daughter-in-law provide financial support to two generations of illegitimate daughters, and the third Countess of Tendilla and her unmarried daughter raised their young granddaughter and niece (respectively) Catalina de Mendoza, the illegitimate daughter of the fourth Count of Tendilla.[57] Grandmothers also supplied support, as in the case of doña Aldonça, the dowager Countess of Castañeda, who provided 10,000 maravedís to care for and educate her illegitimate grandson García Manrique. Doña Aldonça's bequest was a good investment, and the result helps demonstrate why nobles did invest in the illegitimate children of their lineages. By 1488 García was working for his legitimate elder brother, serving as the governor of Cartes, part of the estate inherited by the Counts of Castañeda.[58]

THE IMPORTANCE OF SIBLINGS

All of these strategies to provide for illegitimate children demonstrate that fathers worried about their children's futures. Mothers did, too. Illegitimate children often faced uncertain prospects, in part because their rights to inherit were not guaranteed. Under Castilian inheritance law, legitimate children were necessary heirs (*herederos forzosos*), meaning that four-fifths of a mother's or father's estate had to go to that person's legitimate children. Illegitimate children did not have such clear protection. The remaining one-fifth of the estate (the quinto) could be designated by the testator for funeral expenses and bequests to other people (including illegitimate children if the testator so chose).[59] The older Visigothic law code, the seventh-century *Fuero Juzgo*, discussed adultery but did not stipulate the inheritance rights of illegitimate children.[60] By the mid-thirteenth century, however, the *Fuero Real* and the *Siete Partidas* both addressed the issue. The *Fuero Real* stated that children born from concubinage to a man who also had children from a legitimate marriage could only inherit from the quinto.[61] The *Siete Partidas* endorsed this, stating that illegitimate children could not "inherit the property of their fathers or grandfathers, or that of any other relatives from whom they [were] descended."[62]

Nonetheless, illegitimate children's inheritance rights also depended on whether they had legitimate siblings and what category of illegitimacy they fell into. Despite the statement above, the *Siete Partidas* also stated that illegitimate children could inherit if the father had no legitimate children and the illegitimate child was classified as "natural," not born from "fornication, incest, or adultery." The *Siete Partidas* further stated that because maternity was always certain, illegitimate children could inherit from their mothers along with the mother's legitimate children unless they were born from incest or the mother had taken religious orders.[63] In 1505 the *Leyes de Toro* reiterated that illegitimate children could not inherit from their mothers if their mothers had legitimate children, but that their mothers and fathers could use the quinto to provide for their illegitimate children.[64] In practice the situation was much more confusing, not least because customary law also played a role in court. Castilian nobility often provided for illegitimate children (even those who were not hijos naturales) through the one-fifth of their property that they could designate at will, but they also manipulated both the law and their children's status to fulfill dynastic goals.[65]

If a parent used the quinto or other unentailed goods to provide for children born outside of marriage, those children often remained reliant on their legitimate siblings (the executors of their parents' wills) to actually receive their inheritance. In 1471 the second Count of Arcos anxiously begged his heir, Rodrigo (who had twenty-seven siblings, all illegitimate), "As a good eldest son, . . . treat lovingly and make the most of my sons and daughters, your siblings, and my grandsons and granddaughters, especially the little ones, who should be faithfully cared for."[66] He also asked Rodrigo to care for his servants, a request that was common in noble wills,[67] but which has a different implication in this household, where several of the servants and enslaved women were the mothers of Rodrigo's half-brothers and half-sisters. In his will in 1538, the third Duke of Gandía gave his heir sole responsibility for the duke's illegitimate son, stating, "We beg and charge our successor, [the next] Duke, our son and heir [to consider his illegitimate half-brother Juan Cristóbal] as a brother, and to treat him as such, even though he is a bastard," adding, "We have not in our life, nor in this our current will, bequeathed him anything, trusting in our successor and heir."[68] This trust that fathers put in their heirs suggests that illegitimate half-siblings were seen as part of the lineage and as having a legitimate claim on the noble estate. The first Marquis de Santa Cruz left his illegitimate son Diego an annual life income in 1588, stating: "The successor and [future] successors of this my mayorazgo will pay from the income of the estate."[69] The burden of supporting younger legitimate and illegitimate siblings, half-siblings, and stepsiblings, paying dowries for daughters, sisters, and aunts, finding careers for young relatives, and supporting the vast, sprawling network of noble patronage routinely fell on the eldest male titleholder as a charge on his inherited estate.

Noble culture, based as it was on an idea of patronage and a system of arranged marriages and routinely threatened by premature death, relied heavily on sibling bonds for political connections, financial arrangements, and child rearing.[70] From the late fourteenth century, the rise of a new inheritance strategy, that of the entail or mayorazgo, reinforced this tendency by creating a clear line of descent and by assigning the care of the younger siblings (who were disadvantaged by the consolidation of family property into an entail) to their eldest brother. In 1478 the Count of Tendilla stated in his entail, "The descendant who is to be lord of all should have more patrimony and power to gather to himself and shelter all our descendants." In 1612 the Duke of Frías stated, "Younger brothers depend on the elder and look to enhancing his authority and the grandeur of his house, so that the elder, in return for so much respect, should always look out for his brothers, always helping and favoring them."[71] Siblings were an especially valuable asset when coping with illegitimate children and their futures, and fathers impressed this obligation on their heirs in the strongest possible terms. In 1471 the second Count of Arcos threatened to withhold his paternal blessing if his son did not support his siblings, and the third Count of Parades stated in his will in 1558 that if he had not settled the futures of his illegitimate children before he died, his eldest legitimate son, Pedro, should "support them and feed them as befits my children" until they could be established in a career, and he added: "This I ask and pray that he do in service to God and to me."[72] Eldest sons took this responsibility (which was often a heavy one) seriously. The second Duke of Nájera, blessed with twenty illegitimate half-siblings, appealed to Charles V for help in 1516, stating, "In these vacancies that I have here put forward, you will agree that the duke, my father, left many children and relatives and spent much to serve your majesty and that I myself also have children." The duke specifically asked that the king provide captaincies for his illegitimate brothers.[73]

This expectation that eldest sons would look after their father's illegitimate children created family connections that stretched across the generations and embedded illegitimate children and their families within the hierarchy of the noble family. In 1487 the second Duke of Medina Sidonia arranged a marriage between his illegitimate half-brother, Juan de Guzmán, and Leonor de Cárdenas, an illegitimate daughter of Alonso de Cárdenas, the master of the Order of Santiago. The marriage had deep family roots, as another of Alonso's daughters, Juana, had been contracted to marry another one of the second duke's illegitimate half-brothers, but the young man died before the marriage could be completed. This second attempt at a marriage alliance between the two families was more successful. On this occasion, the second duke gave his brother 2 million maravedís in cash as well as the promise of an income of 100,000 maravedís per year for life. Twelve years later, in 1499, the second duke's widow left Juan an additional 200,000 maravedís in her will. As late as 1521 the second duke's great-grandson (the fifth Duke of Medina Sidonia) was still paying that 100,000 maravedís "in favor of don Juan, 'uncle of the duke.'"[74]

Thus the obligations of the eldest son or daughter could stretch over generations if illegitimate siblings lived long enough to need long-term support, something that heirs to the title understood. The fourth Duke of Nájera had two illegitimate children, Juan and Isabel, after the premature death of his wife in 1562. He didn't mention these children in his will, but hours before his death in 1600 he wrote a letter to his legitimate daughter, the future fifth duchess, confessing their existence. The duchess, who inherited after the deaths of her four legitimate brothers, formally recognized these two half-siblings in 1601, claiming them as members of the family who had the right to the name Manrique. Looking to the future, she requested her children to care for her half-brother and sister "with the greatness corresponding to their quality," and to "help, esteem and favor" Juan especially.[75] These two half-siblings were not the duchess's only responsibility. She also left a legacy to her eldest brother's illegitimate daughter Mariana and another to her husband's illegitimate daughter (also named Isabel).[76] The duchess's generosity and ideas about family duty created long-lasting relationships in the Manrique family. Twenty years later, as Juan wrote his will, he drew on family connections, naming as his executors his legitimate half-sister, the duchess, as well as his cousins the ninth Count of Paredes and don Manrique de Lara.[77]

Although the role of head of the family and supporter of illegitimate children usually fell to the eldest son, it could also to fall to women, as the story of the Duchess of Nájera demonstrates. In the 1570s Francisco Manrique de Lara, twin brother to the fifth Count of Paredes, came to an amicable resolution of a lawsuit with his niece Inés that gave Inés the title of Countess of Paredes as well as the obligation to provide for Francisco's illegitimate children and their mother. The dispute was over whether the Paredes entail privileged a woman who was the daughter of the last title-holder or a man who was a more distant relative. Because the fifth count had no surviving sons, Francisco (as his younger twin brother) had a claim on the estate. Francisco, however, was not married and was apparently not going to marry. So in 1579 he ceded his rights to the estate and title to Inés and her son Antonio in exchange for a promise that Inés would pay an income of 600 ducados a year to Francisco's illegitimate son, his two illegitimate daughters, and their unnamed mother. This was apparently a successful settlement. Francisco's eldest son, Rodrigo, got 450 of the 600 ducados every year (his sisters having both joined the convent of Nuestra Señora de Consolación in Calabazanos) and "kept a great friendship with the counts of Paredes, his nephews."[78]

These types of obligations extended over the generations. Rodrigo, the second Count of Arco's eldest son, fulfilled his father's request to look after his twenty-seven illegitimate siblings. By the time Rodrigo wrote his will in 1492, his legacies suggested a patriarch providing for the next generation, as he dowered his half-brother Diego's daughter as well as the daughter of his half-sister Florentina and two daughters of his deceased half-sister Constança.[79] As we saw in chapter 1, noble patriarchs were authoritative but were also commended for caring. The fourth Count of Paredes, Pedro, obeyed his father's instructions and continued to help his ten illegitimate half-siblings, arranging a marriage for his half-sister Catalina in 1535 and reminding his own son and heir in his will in 1539 to finish paying Catalina's dowry. As late as 1570, the fifth Count of Paredes, Pedro's eldest son Antonio, was doing business with Catalina's son, also named Pedro.[80] The actions of the fourth Count of Paredes met with the approval of the seventeenth-century genealogist Luis de Salazar y Castro, who commended Pedro for his "Christianity and prudence," because he "helped with much fondness the hijos naturales and bastardos that [his father] left, and either married them off or placed them in a convent or monastery [algunos puso en estado]."[81] This language of Christianity, prudence, fondness, and affection evokes the side of noble masculinity that expected men to be caring fathers who supported children and dependents in their households. Eldest sons extended this expectation to carrying on the fatherly role of the previous generation, finishing or passing on the responsibilities of parenting that their fathers had left incomplete.

An eldest son's failure to manage the responsibility of illegitimate brothers on top of other burdens could be a symptom of a true crisis of patriarchy. Juan de Guzmán, the third Duke of Medina Sidonia and progenitor of another complicated family, turned to his eldest son, as was customary, to care for and raise some of his five illegitimate children. Unfortunately, his own early death meant that his son inherited as a minor and was subject to the nobleman's worst nightmare, an unreliable and rapacious guardian. In his will, written a few days before his early death in 1507 aged only forty-one, the third duke asked his eldest legitimate son, Enrique, for help with the care and custody of his younger, illegitimate son. The language of the will suggests that Enrique (who was only twelve when his father died) might not have known about the half-brother he was now being asked to care for. The duke requested that Enrique raise his illegitimate half-brother Juan, identifying the boy as the one "who[m] Juan Manuel, my servant and mayordomo of my estates, knows about."[82] Enrique was to take Juan to court to secure an honorable post (and presumably career) for him. Enrique was orphaned just as Castile was suffering a crisis of succession after Queen Isabel's death, meaning that royal authority could only intervene belatedly to help a duke who was still a minor.[83] Already caught in a marriage he was too young to consummate, the motherless Enrique endured a short and turbulent minority under the disastrous guardianship of his brother-in-law and died in 1513 at the age of nineteen. He had little or no opportunity to look after his half-brother or launch him into the tumultuous world of the royal court. Although it is unclear what happened to Juan in the chaos of Enrique's short reign as the fourth duke, Enrique's wife, the young Duchess María Girón, apparently rescued Enrique's illegitimate half-sister Beatriz. María included 30,000 maravedís for Beatriz's clothes in her household accounts for 1509–13.[84] As discussed in chapter 2, after Enrique's death the succession of the house of Medina Sidonia was left in crisis. The next potential heir, Enrique's half-brother from his father's second marriage, had been born before his parents acquired the dispensation that legalized their marriage. In this case, the nobility relied on women to hold both the lineage and the immediate family together, as the succession crisis was resolved by the timely intervention of the dowager duchess.[85]

As the Medina Sidonia case demonstrates, the expectation that the heir to the title would support younger, dependent, illegitimate half-siblings was a difficult one. Early inheritance or the premature death of the titleholder (as in the case of the fourth Duke of Medina Sidonia above) meant that the most practical solution to raising and supporting illegitimate children was a team of family members, often siblings, aunts and uncles, or a combination thereof, who could help by providing custody, emotional support, education, careers, marriages, and financial support in general. As previously mentioned, don Rodrigo Manrique de Lara, the third Count of Paredes, charged his eldest son, Pedro, with taking care of his eight legitimate siblings, six legitimate half-siblings, and at least ten illegitimate half-siblings. Pedro fulfilled this charge with help from his sisters. Pedro supported his illegitimate half-brother don Geronimo by helping him make a good marriage, and Pedro's legitimate sister María Magdalena, the childless Countess of Deleytosa, also supported Geronimo by leaving his legitimate children legacies in her will dated 1587.[86] A seventeenth-century genealogist opined that don Geronimo "should praise the grace of his siblings" for these two substantial interventions that helped him and his children survive and thrive financially.[87] Juana, another legitimate sister of Pedro's, helped in 1588 by contributing three ducados per year to their illegitimate half-sister Aldonza, who became a nun in the convent of Santispiritas de Alcaráz.[88] This example highlights the importance of women's financial contributions to the well-being of the noble lineage. When they inherited titles and lands, women also inherited the family responsibilities that accompanied these possessions. Doña Isabel Manrique, the illegitimate daughter of don Juan Manrique de Lara, younger son of the second Duke of Nájera, professed as an Augustinian nun in Ávila with help from her eldest legitimate half-brother, don Antonio, who paid the 30 ducados of annual rent that her father had left her in his will in about 1570. Sixty years later, Isabel's legitimate half-sister, doña Juana Manrique, had inherited the family title and lands and the responsibility for Isabel's upkeep from their brother Antonio. Juana left Isabel 100 ducados of annual rent in her will.[89] Even fragmented, unhappy families often lived up to their obligations of supporting illegitimate siblings. As previously discussed, the fourth Duke of Medina Sidonia's marriage was, by all accounts, a colossal failure, but his wife still gave his illegitimate half-sister a home and financial support.[90]

Some of the ways in which siblings supported each other in the matter of raising illegitimate children centered on arranging appropriate marriages for the next generation. These children benefited from family connections that enabled them to make good marriages, and, in their turn, were often able to extend the power and influence of the lineage through their new alliances. In 1573 don Juan Manrique, the seriously ill archdeacon of Valpuesta in Burgos, noted, "the great love and brotherhood that I have with the reverend my lord brother the Bishop of Coria." This sentiment led him to make his brother the executor of his will, of which his illegitimate daughter Catalina was the beneficiary. In turn, his brother, don Iñigo Manrique, arranged a marriage for Catalina. Her husband, Juan Rodríguez de Rojas, was the brother of the archbishop of Granada, suggesting that Iñigo might have used his professional connections to help arrange a marriage that was advantageous to both families.[91]

Family members not only arranged marriages but often contributed to dowries for illegitimate children who could not legally inherit from their fathers' estates. María de Mendoza y de la Cerda stated in her will in 1565 that for reasons of propriety she had raised her brother's illegitimate daughter Isabel in her own household.[92] As an aunt, María integrated Isabel into a family network of legitimate female cousins and sisters, whom she supervised in her household and dowered to assist the nieces in marrying well. María bequeathed her illegitimate niece Isabel a dowry of 3,000 ducados, and she introduced Isabel to her older, legitimate half-sister Ana, the Princess of Éboli.[93] Both the marriage and the relationship between the two half-sisters must have endured into adulthood because Isabel and her husband stood as godparents to Ana's fifth child.[94]

The age gap between siblings of sprawling noble families meant that some older siblings were in a position to be as helpful as aunts and uncles when their illegitimate half-siblings needed assistance with marriages. Antonio de Mendoza, the first viceroy of New Spain and the fifth son of the second Count of Tendilla, arranged a marriage for his much younger, illegitimate half-sister María with Martín de Ircio, a wealthy *encomendero* (a colonist who held a royal grant of Native American labor) whom Antonio had encountered during his administration of Spain's overseas territories. María and Martín exchanged vows by proxy in Spain in 1537, and then María journeyed to Mexico to finalize the marriage in 1539. It was unusual for a Mendoza daughter to marry outside of Spain, and María was hesitant about this marriage, delaying it for two years because of a vow that she had taken. During those two years she lived within Antonio's household, perhaps getting to know her brother, who was twenty years older than she was, for the first time. Although María had a dowry befitting her social status and this unusual marriage benefited the Mendoza family's enterprises in the New World, it also suggests that illegitimate daughters might be sent to take risks that were not demanded of legitimate daughters.[95]

These legacies that created dowries for illegitimate daughters also suggest relationships and possible ties of affection and proximity that have been obscured over time. Doña Luisa Manrique, illegitimate daughter of don Francisco de Solis Manrique, Lord of Solis, received a dowry from her aunt, her father's sister-in-law, doña Luisa de Peralta, in 1598. Did the older Luisa have a special affection for her niece-by-marriage who bore the same name? In another example that suggests a personal relationship, doña María Manrique, Countess of Montijo and lady-in-waiting to Queen Isabel de Valois, had no children of her own and used her property to create an entail that she left to her illegitimate niece, also named María. The younger María contracted an advantageous marriage with the first Viscount of Castejón.[96] Was the younger María named after her generous aunt? Did the elder, childless countess have a hand in raising her while her unmarried military father pursued his duties? The legacy suggests that this might have been the case.

The connection between illegitimate children and their noble families can also be seen when (in keeping with the nobility's customary endogamy) illegitimate children married family members. Doña Antonia de Aguila, illegitimate daughter of Alonso de Aguila, a military man and member of the Order of Santiago, married her cousin Antonio de Silva. To put this in context, Antonia had two illegitimate brothers, both churchmen and both deans of Ciudad Rodrigo, careers that indicated a familial investment, so all three of these illegitimate siblings were recognized and provided for by their family.[97] Marriages like this created webs of relationships that included illegitimate members in the larger family identity. Doña Francisca de Mendoza was an illegitimate daughter of a prestigious military family, an identity that shaped her future. Her father was don Juan de Mendoza, commander of Mérida in the Order of Santiago and captain general of the galleys of Spain in the second half of the sixteenth century. Francisca married a knight from the Order of Santiago, and their eldest son married his first cousin, whose brother was also a member of the Order of Santiago. Doña Francisca's marriage was less prestigious than those of her legitimate sister Elvira, both of whose husbands carried minor titles, but even Elvira's second husband was a member of the Order of Santiago.[98] This web of marriages seamlessly incorporated an illegitimate daughter into the family network of military professionals and minor nobility, and then used that daughter's son to extend the connections.

ILLEGITIMATE CHILDREN AS GOOD INVESTMENTS

The cultural practice of recognizing and supporting illegitimate children across the generations gave the nobility a reserve of people and talents that they could draw on if needed.[99] Nobles used their illegitimate relatives as strategic agents, people who could represent the lineage, assist in times of transition between generations, and provide support for younger family members. Charged with creating a royal reception for King Enrique II of Castile's second wife, Juana of Portugal, as she crossed the Portuguese border into the Castilian city of Badajoz in 1455, the first Duke of Medina Sidonia rode out to meet the future queen accompanied by his illegitimate brother Alfonso and no fewer than six illegitimate sons.[100] This display of "prestige and luxury" was accompanied by the lavish distribution of pieces of silk, cloth of gold and silver, horses, and jewelry, as well as the adornment of his own house with "the most beautiful tapestries, the richest dinner sets and harnesses of the lineage."[101] The duke was obviously out to make an impression on the new queen and the bystanders, which suggests that he valued his illegitimate brother and sons and saw them as an integral part of the strength of his house. Writing his will some years later in 1463, the duke put this sentiment into words, telling his son and heir, Enrique, to raise his illegitimate half-brothers: "And treat them well and like brothers, because once they are of age they will serve him just as reason obliges them to do."[102]

The family connections created by recognizing, educating, and caring for illegitimate children within the family gave them allies in times of transition. Half-siblings were often entrusted with tasks pertaining to the execution of wills, the transfer of noble property, and guardianships. For example, don Juan Baptista Manrique, a canon of Toledo Cathedral and an illegitimate son of the third Duke of Nájera, attended the deathbed of his legitimate half-brother, the Count of Paredes, in 1574. Don Juan formally presented his brother's will to the judge in Madrid so that it could be opened, published, and executed.[103] Exhibiting a more spiritual form of support, Luis Fajardo, illegitimate son of the second Marquis de Vélez, left money in his will for masses for his father, his legitimate half-siblings, and his mother.[104] Illegitimate children could also stand as guardians to their half-siblings, an appointment that indicated a fair degree of trust on the part of fathers that illegitimate siblings would not compete with their legitimate half-siblings for the inheritance. In 1512, for example, the Lord of Orgaz y Santa Olalla appointed his illegitimate son Fernándo de Guzmán guardian of his nine legitimate children. Fernándo appears to have carried out this responsibility in cooperation with the children's mother, Isabel de Mendoza y Borbón.[105] In this case, rather than the widow caring for an illegitimate child or grandchild, the illegitimate child was positioned to help and support the widowed Isabel, who faced numerous legal challenges surrounding the estate of Orgaz. An even more unorthodox family arrangement was that of the second Count of Villalba who left his second wife, doña Juana de Leyva, and his elder illegitimate son, Fernando, coguardians of his younger illegitimate son, Martín. The count, who had no legitimate sons, charged the two of them solemnly to raise the young Martín, stating that they should proceed: "according to what is required by his person and because of whose son he is." Juana herself was childless and although Martín and Fernando were half-siblings, neither boy was related to her.[106]

The cross-generational networks of siblings also meant that illegitimate uncles could serve as useful assets to their half-siblings' children in issues of inheritance. Doña Ana Manrique de Luna, the Countess of Paredes, reached back two generations and appointed her grandfather's illegitimate brother (her great-uncle), fray don Bernardo Manrique, bishop of Malaga, as one of the executors of her will in 1541.[107] Years later, her husband, the fifth Count of Paredes, writing his will in May of 1570, appointed *his* illegitimate uncle don Luis Manrique as an executor.[108] Sometimes the benefits of having illegitimate relatives were financial, as don Alonso Fernández Manrique de Solis, the ninth Lord of Galisteo, inherited from his illegitimate half-brother, Gabriel Manrique, archdeacon and canon of Cuenca.[109]

In addition to executing wills, becoming guardians, or passing on legacies, illegitimate children could play the most crucial role in the central noble project of passing on title and property intact to the next generation by becoming legitimate(d) heirs. In the early fifteenth century, Álvaro de Bracamonte, the second Lord of Peñaranda y Fuente del Sol, married three times but ended up with twenty illegitimate children and no legitimate heirs. In a move that demonstrated the flexibility that illegitimate children granted the noble family, Álvaro applied to Ferdinand and Isabel for a legitimation for his son Juan so that the boy could inherit the title and estate, but the legitimation had not yet been granted when Álvaro lay dying. In this dire situation Álvaro turned to his own illegitimate half-brother, Alonso, the abbot of Medina del Campo, for help. In a complicated maneuver Álvaro designated his brother Alonso as his heir (making Alonso briefly the third Lord of Peñaranda y Fuente del Sol) but asked Alonso to hold the estate and title only until his young nephew could be legitimated. Alonso kept his word to his dying brother and turned the estate and title over to Álvaro's son, who became the fourth Lord of Peñaranda y Feunte del Sol as soon as he was legitimated.[110] Two generations of illegitimate sons enabled the title to stay within the immediate family, illustrating the bonds between illegitimate half-brothers and their children.

These kinds of transactions illustrate both the importance of illegitimate children to the succession of the noble family and the potential fragility that surrounded an illegitimate heir. The first Duke of Medina Sidonia, who commented above on the importance of brothers, left his title to his illegitimate son Enrique. Facing the chaos of civil war in Castile and worried about the transfer of power because of the boy's illegitimacy, the duke began the process of transferring the estate in January of 1463 as soon as Enrique was fourteen years old (the earliest age at which boys could be married under the *Siete Partidas*) and legally married. In his will in 1468 the duke clarified that his own illegitimate half-brother Alfonso (Enrique's uncle) should be Enrique's guardian and granted Alfonso the power to take possession of the estate in Enrique's name. The ceremonies that ensued after the duke's death in November of 1468 were elaborate, "charged with symbolism about the origin and hierarchy of the power and basis of the exercise, which made clear the preeminence of the office and justice of the lord over" the entire estate. Alfonso carefully took possession of each piece of the vast Medina Sidonia estate in his nephew's name, with the result that no force was needed to ensure the succession, although the new duke was later plagued by lawsuits put forth by other claimants because of his illegitimacy.[111] Thus, the illegitimacy of the heir was a problem that needed to be managed, but for many noblemen this was preferable to letting the title go to a brother, nephew, or cousin. The complex nature of illegitimacy is reflected in the presence of illegitimate uncles helping illegitimate nephews to inherit titles, a title that in this case might have been Alfonso's since before Enrique was born, Alfonso had been his brother's heir. Nevertheless, like the abbot of Medina del Campo above, Alfonso remained loyal to his half-brother, his nephew, and the lineage in general and protected his nephew's title. The first Duke of Medina Sidonia rightly felt that his half-brothers were his staunchest allies as Alfonso oversaw the transfer of power and his other illegitimate half-brother Fadrique was an executor of the duke's will.[112]

Noblemen preferred to pass titles from fathers to legitimate sons, but the existence of illegitimate sons and brothers gave them some flexibility in the face of early death or the lack of a legitimate male heir. Recovering from a long illness in November of 1540, the second Duke of Soma was moved to write his will. He left a legacy to his half-brother, an illegitimate son of his father, and, because in 1540 he had a young daughter but no sons, he also stated what should happen to his estate and title if he did not father a son. If he died without male children, the estate went to his widow during her lifetime, then to a close male relative, and then if that male relative failed to have children, to his illegitimate brother's legitimate children. In the event, none of this happened. The duke lived until 1571 and had two sons, both of whom inherited the title in their turn.[113] His illegitimate half-brother, however, formed part of a pool of male relatives who could keep the title and estate in the family in case of a dynastic disaster.

The family of the Marquises de Vélez also invested in an illegitimate child in an effort to keep a pool of male heirs available. Two noble sisters, Francisca and Mencía Fajardo, faced in 1579 with the death of their brother (the marquis) and the youth of their nephew (his heir), combined their resources to provide an entail for their illegitimate half-brother Luis, who had recently married. In the event, the young marquis survived and thrived, but (demonstrating the power of the entail) Luis's legacy enabled him to start a collateral line, the Marquises de Espinardo.[114] If dynastic disasters did happen, an illegitimate son could keep the connection between a family and their estate. An example of this is the estate of Sotomayor. Fernan Yañez, Lord of Sotomayor, married and had two legitimate children, who died young. The estate of Sotomayor then reverted to his sister, doña Mayor, who had no children. Doña Mayor dealt with this problem in 1476 by leaving the estate to Fernan's illegitimate son, don Pedro Alvarez de Sotomayor, who made a good marriage and became the Count of Camiña in Portugal.[115]

The Castilian nobility had the wealth, power, and social standing to turn their illegitimate children into assets who could advance the noble lineage. A skilled noble patriarch developed a power base of family members whose presence allowed him to be flexible and resilient in times of crisis. To do this, he depended on the labor and loyalty of a wide variety of women, who included his wife, mother, and sisters in addition to the mothers of his illegitimate children (discussed in chapter 2). Maids and enslaved women provided much of the physical caretaking of noble illegitimate children, whereas noblewomen might provide financial assets, education, training, and custody. One result of this approach was the creation of strong networks of siblings whose loyalties stretched across generations. Noblemen depended on their siblings to protect their illegitimate children; legitimate noble children often provided support and care for their illegitimate half-siblings; and illegitimate children returned the favor by participating actively in family affairs and helping to protect the family as a whole.

The nobility's conception of family stretched beyond the immediate family unit of parents and children to encompass an extended lineage that stretched back in time and included a hierarchy of people ranging from the male titleholder down to more humble but useful dependent cousins and younger sons and daughters. Illegitimate children often occupied the lower rungs of that hierarchy, but they could still be crucial assets to the noble patriarch, who might support them for reasons of both affection and practicality. This chapter documents family support and care (sometimes from unlikely sources) for illegitimate children as infants and children. The next chapter problematizes these relationships by looking at the noble family from the perspective of the adult illegitimate children, who might be closely connected to their noble father's family but who were also dependent on that family for their status, financial support, careers, marriages, and futures. Although many noble families acknowledged, supported, and even loved their illegitimate children, they were not legally obligated to do anything beyond provide basic maintenance. Illegitimate adults occupied an ambiguous space in relation to family, status, and wealth that could cause tensions and problems within the larger lineage.

4

A Person Not Born of Lawful Marriage

The Uncertainties Facing Illegitimate Adults

Born in 1501 and raised in luxury, don Bernardino de Velasco was the son and namesake of the first Duke of Frías. He was cared for by a wet nurse named Isabel, dressed "in crimson velvet and other times in silk," provided with a tutor, and eventually sent to court to be a page to the queen, Germaine de Foix.[1] In spite of all these highly visible connections to the house of Frías, however, by 1538 don Bernardino was worried enough about his economic future and that of his children to go to a notary in Burgos and make a formal statement that explained the circumstances of his birth and attempted to establish his identity beyond doubt or dispute:

> I, don Bernardino de Velasco, here present, do state that in as much as I am hijo natural of the Constable my lord don Bernardino de Velsaco [the first Duke of Frías] . . . and of my lady doña Inés de Sagredo my mother and at the time that my father and mother had me and I was born . . . [they] . . . were not married or engaged to anyone nor obligated by any religious vows, wherefore I am hijo natural of my mother and father. . . . Because I am afraid that the witnesses that I can avail myself of could die or go to other places where I could not reach them when I or

my heirs and successors might need the said proof, it suits me to make it in order [that we] might inherit all and whatever goods remain from the said lord D. Bernadino de Velasco my lord father after his death.[2]

Despite his luxurious upbringing, Bernardino was illegitimate, and his mother's status, although honorable, was far below that of his ducal father. As an adult, his illegitimate birth had the potential to cause him problems. He was the son of a duke, but his mother's family took in locksmiths as boarders. He was raised in luxury and trained for a court post, but he had no legal inheritance rights. His parents had not been married at the time of his birth, so he was an hijo natural and their subsequent marriage could have legitimated him—but they did not marry. He had reason to be anxious about his future, given that by 1538 his father was dead, his cousin had inherited the ducal title, and Bernardino was no longer the son of the current duke.

The nobility routinely exerted their influence on behalf of illegitimate children, making many of them an integral part of the family network.[3] As detailed in previous chapters, the nobility's sense of responsibility toward illegitimate children created complex, multigenerational households and mixed families. Even so, illegitimate individuals like Bernardino might experience difficulties demonstrating their status or getting the support they had been promised by their family. A mother of lower social status or who lacked purity of blood, the lack of an adult to advocate for them, or the perception that they could try to challenge the succession of their legitimate half-siblings might threaten their connection to their noble fathers. Moreover, these children might not be willing to accept the roles their family had designated for them. The way the nobility handled illegitimacy was contingent on dynastic strategies, and an illegitimate child's rank and status could fluctuate wildly depending on what part he or she was destined to play in the lineage as a whole. This complex system persisted because it was advantageous to noble families and it helped them develop a power base that consisted of a wide array of human resources and talent.

This chapter argues that for the noble family, illegitimate children functioned as one of the assets that the nobility routinely used to protect the lineage. Tools of the larger plan to ensure dynastic succession, many illegitimate children were provided with tools of their own, such as education, vocational opportunities, and arranged marriages. They were trained to be noble in traditionally gendered ways, with girls being bound for marriage or the convent and boys for the church or the military. They were given these advantages in part because their status reflected on the noble families of their fathers. For illegitimate children themselves, however, their role as tools of the lineage could be full of uncomfortable paradoxes. Illegitimate children who had the skills and education that marked them as noble were connected to the prestige and wealth of the larger lineage and could be called on for help, expertise, and support. On the other hand, if the dynasty did not need them they might spend their lives confined to lower levels of the family hierarchy with limited access to resources and status.

Illegitimate adults' ability to navigate their complex identities in relation to the noble family was further complicated in the fifteenth and sixteenth centuries by race, social status, gender, and changing religious mores. They were children of noblemen, but their mothers might be noble, hidalgo, poor, servants, or even enslaved women. Their class standing and their religious and ethnic identities could be questioned. Their acceptance as family members was not guaranteed. When they were recognized by their noble families, illegitimate adults often occupied lower rungs on the family hierarchy. Recognition that illegitimate children had a claim to being noble or at least part of the noble family had to be given, usually by their fathers. The power of illegitimate children to demand inclusion in the noble family was mainly negative, consisting largely of a threat to cause problems by taking their families to court over inheritance or maintenance issues. They could sue for support, for recognition, and even for a noble title, and in this litigious society they often went to court. But they were suing the most powerful people in Castile from a position of ambiguous identity.

In spite of their equivocal status and identity, there is abundant evidence of illegitimate children of both genders being accepted into family networks of affection and financial support, which launched them on careers, provided them with good marriages, and made use of them to advance the lineage as a whole. If the nobility needed their illegitimate children, they claimed them, overruling all considerations of identity except the nobility of their fathers, and evidence suggests that noble families often valued and even loved these children who could function as extensions of the noble lineage. But illegitimate children were not legally guaranteed an inheritance, and it could be difficult to hold powerful noblemen to their obligations if they chose to ignore them. This created a vulnerable situation for illegitimate children who were dependent on the goodwill of families who might need them to fulfill specific roles or might find them inconvenient, embarrassing, or threatening. Illegitimate children negotiated their social position and economic support, were recognized and accepted, and were the source of contention and strife. All this reveals the complex tensions over status, hierarchy, and gender at the heart of noble families as well as their intense focus on dynastic succession.

ILLEGITIMACY, THE LAW, AND SOCIAL STATUS

In addition to the varying legal categories of illegitimacy discussed in the last chapter, illegitimate adults occupied a changing social landscape in fifteenth- and sixteenth-century Castile, one that was slowly and unevenly becoming more concerned with limpieza de sangre, or supposed purity of blood.[4] This concern had immediate implications for the illegitimate children of the nobility, because Spanish noblemen often had children with women of lower status (maids, enslaved women, vassals), so that although their fathers were noble, their mothers sometimes were *conversas* or *moriscas* (the converted descendants of Jews or Muslims), were Jewish or Muslim, or their identity was unknown, leaving the illegitimate child unable to prove limpieza de sangre. Sara McDougall highlighted this important role for mothers, arguing that in medieval Europe before the twelfth century, the exclusion of some illegitimate children from royal inheritance was based on maternal lineage rather than "on whether their parents had married according to the strictures of the church." This changed over time, and by the thirteenth century, "ideas about legitimate birth increasingly contributed to the stigmatization of those born outside of marriage."[5] In the multicultural environment of Castile, however, the mother's ethnic and religious background and social class remained important.[6]

From the thirteenth century onward, the language of identity shifted in Castile, gradually connecting identity to legitimacy. The thirteenth-century *Siete Partidas* stated rather vaguely that a "person not born of lawful marriage [was] infamous from that very fact" and defined "infamous" as a condition in which "such persons [could not] again obtain any dignity or honor" and were unable to serve as "a judge or councilor of the king," although they could act as attorneys, guardians, and arbitration judges and hold all other offices.[7] During this same time the role of the nobility shifted slightly as growing government administrations needed university-trained administrators. These new jobs, which tripled over the course of the sixteenth century, offered rich rewards and status.[8] The nobility took advantage of these opportunities by educating their younger sons and their illegitimate sons to fill these posts, but illegitimate sons increasingly faced additional barriers. In 1414 Pope Benedict XIII approved the constitution of the new Spanish *colegio* of San Bartolomé, which demanded that entering members (young men studying law or theology in preparation for posts in the church or the royal government) had to prove that they were "of full fame and reputation" and also possessed "pure blood," but the constitution did not include any specific language about legitimacy.[9] By 1430, however, the college of Naples demanded that medical doctors had to prove that their ancestors were "good and serious men without spurious or otherwise illegitimate birth," and in 1449 a candidate for city council in Toledo ran into trouble under the new city statute that discriminated against conversos, because he was illegitimate and did not know who his parents were—he could not prove limpieza de sangre.[10] The Royal Pragmatic of 1501 provided "a specific list of more than forty offices barred to those who could not prove limpieza de sangre," including every civil post in the kingdom.[11] Even the Nobles Doncellas, a school for noble girls founded in Toledo in 1551, required clean blood and legitimacy for admission.[12] Following this trend, the military orders began asking potential candidates about their legitimacy in 1516.[13]

In Europe more broadly, similar transitions are apparent, although without the specific concern over limpieza de sangre that was so characteristic of Castile. Instead, the concern over illegitimacy highlights other social tensions. Judith J. Hurwich argued that the position of noble bastards in

Germany was inferior to that of those in other continental aristocracies, and Heide Wunder noted that some guilds in the Holy Roman Empire rejected apprentices born from concubinage as early as the fourteenth century and that "cathedral chapters increasingly demanded proof of the noble birth of both parents" starting in the fifteenth century. These policies made it difficult for illegitimate sons to take up a trade, become bishops, or obtain high office in the imperial court.[14] Florentine guilds began to exclude bastards in 1414, but the exclusion was inconsistent. The oil merchants' guild included bastards, whereas the notarial guilds excluded them, ranking them with Jews as inherently suspect persons. In the fifteenth century Florence also taxed illegitimates, limited the dowry amounts for illegitimate girls, and tried (somewhat unsuccessfully) to ban illegitimate men from sitting on major executive and legislative councils.[15] In 1569 Venice made an attempt to codify the qualifications for citizenry, passing legislation that required, among other things, legitimate birth, although Jana Byars reported that illegitimate sons of the nobility still succeeded in gaining entrance to the citizen class.[16] According to Matthew Gerber, in France the medieval aristocracy "seemed to mark their strength, courage, and virility through a flagrant transgression of Christian sexual norms, openly acknowledging their extramarital offspring without apparent shame." By the sixteenth century, although illegitimate children were still integral parts of many noble households, the rising importance of the "nobility of the robe" (magistrates who were ennobled through the purchase of a royal office) challenged the more traditional "nobility of the sword," invoking an anxious debate about bastardy and social misalliances that had racial overtones. Gerber commented: "In this context, the customary celebration of an aristocratic bastard's noble blood gave way to growing anxiety over extramarital union."[17] By the seventeenth century the possible consequences of illegitimacy in France included losing noble status and having to pay the *taille*, the principal royal tax, although children born out of wedlock continued to be able to hold public office and were not excluded from the guilds.[18]

In Castile this trend of increasing prejudice continued throughout the sixteenth and seventeenth centuries, leading to serious legal discrimination against conversos and illegitimate children in Spain and its empire by the eighteenth century. But in the fifteenth and sixteenth centuries the rules remained vague, contradictory, and somewhat fluid. By the end of the sixteenth century, San Bartolomé demanded a genealogy from prospective members but did not use the phrase "child of a legitimate marriage" in its entrance requirements. In contrast, the other major colegios gradually annotated their original statutes, adding proof of legitimacy as a way to prove limpieza de sangre.[19] In this ambiguous climate social class became an important factor in overturning concerns about identity, but illegitimate children of the nobility, with tenuous connections to their father's families, could not always claim noble status.[20]

The process of gaining entrance into the prestigious colegios serves as one example of how illegitimacy could impose uncertainty on a man's life and career. Successful entrance into a colegio required economic support, family background, and, increasingly, limpieza de sangre, all of which could be difficult for illegitimate sons to obtain. Juan Sarmiento, illegitimate son of Pedro Sarmiento, the archbishop of Santiago de Compostela, and noblewoman doña María de Guzmán, was taken from his mother at age three-and-a-half and experienced equivocal support from his noble father. The archbishop did not acknowledge Juan publicly but paid meagerly for a series of caretakers for his small son and his education. As soon as Juan had earned the degree of bachiller, the first degree awarded in the Spanish academic system, the archbishop "transferred his obligations to the colegio of San Bartolomé." The witnesses called to verify Juan's identity and upbringing in his application to San Bartolomé did not comment on the fact that the archbishop had fathered a son but were universally critical of the archbishop's stinginess in providing for that son. The powerful archbishop's status and the fact that Juan's mother was known, noble, and of pure blood meant that the archbishop was relieved of further expense for his son. Juan was accepted to San Bartolomé, where he rose to prominence, eventually presiding over the chancery court in Granada as well as the Council of the Indies.[21]

In contrast, Pedro de Portocarrero, the illegitimate grandson of the second Count of Medellín, was not accepted to the colegio mayor of Oviedo at Salamanca. Orphaned at an early age, Pedro was cared for by his grandfather along with his legitimate half-siblings, designated for a church career, and sent to study at Salamanca. By 1549, however, his grandfather had died and his legitimate brother, the third count, was also dying. The responsibility for Pedro's support fell to his widowed sister-in-law, with whom he did not get along, and his economic support became unreliable. Witnesses interviewed for Pedro's application for admission summed up Pedro's problem, stating, "Sometimes she gave it, other times she didn't."[22] Faced with this fiscal uncertainty, Pedro applied for a scholarship from the colegio mayor of Oviedo. The scholarship was not granted because his application revealed that his mother, a lady-in-waiting in the Medellín household, was a conversa.[23] Baltasar Cuart Moner analyzed the ambiguity of Pedro's social class, his illegitimacy, and his lack of limpieza de sangre, stating that Pedro was, in the end, "a victim of a system of social exclusion that, in principle, he should have benefited from." His illegitimacy had not barred him from being considered part of the noble family of Medellín while he was growing up, but as an adult his mother's converso blood eventually barred him from pursuing a career.[24]

These two case studies reveal the potential difficulties that attended illegitimacy. Both boys were children of noblemen, both were designated for a career in the church at an early age, both were educated for that career, and one of them succeeded in it. But both also experienced unstable childhoods and possible stigma. Juan Sarmiento was raised away from his parents, first cared for by "a sister of the archdeacon of Baños," and then educated by "doctor Castillo, a professor at Salamanca," both of whom had to maintain him with help from "small loans from the bishop of Palencia," who was not Juan's father.[25] Pedro was raised and cared for by his father and then his grandfather, but his father failed to provide adequately for him in his will. A series of family deaths deprived him of his brother and protector and made him suddenly dependent on an unwilling sister-in-law.[26] When he fell victim to Spain's rising tide of racial prejudice, Pedro had no economic resources to fall back on. Unlike Juan, who pursued a successful career, he disappeared from the historical records.

The role of blood purity, racism, and illegitimacy in the fifteenth and sixteenth centuries, although important, was also ambiguous, fluid, and inconsistent. As Ann Twinam convincingly demonstrated, by the eighteenth century these prejudices had hardened into widespread discrimination in Spain and its empire against Jews, Muslims, conversos, moriscos, and illegitimate children. Even in the eighteenth-century Hispanic world, however, individuals could pass, overcoming prejudice and discrimination to achieve office, occupations, education, or entrance to the church.[27] This passing was even more ubiquitous in the fifteenth and sixteenth centuries, when policies were still in the process of being codified. Although illegitimate children of the nobility were the most likely to pass, because their social status often overcame their illegitimacy, there were some limits to what could be achieved.[28] Antonio de Montemayor, great-grandson of the second Count of Arcos, failed to gain entrance to San Bartolomé in 1515 not because of his own illegitimacy (his parents were noble and engaged but not married to each other) but because his grandmother was the illegitimate daughter of the second Count of Arcos and his Muslim slave, thus compromising Antonio's purity of blood. On the other hand, the nephew of the powerful secretary Francisco de Eraso was accepted into the college of Oviedo even though his maternal grandmother was the illegitimate daughter of an unnamed hidalgo and an innkeeper.[29] In cases of ambiguity (according to the ideas of the time, the hidalgo and the innkeeper might have had purity of blood whereas an enslaved Muslim woman unequivocally did not), the power of the noble family worked in the candidate's favor. In both these cases, the identities of women became crucially important in determining the lives and career choices of their male descendants.

In addition to a certain amount of legal confusion, social attitudes toward illegitimacy were also ambiguous and often contradictory. Scott Taylor's analysis of the Spanish honor codes found that public insults often included phrases such as *hijo de puta* (son of a whore) and *fue de señora mala* (born of a sinful woman), along with the terms *cabrón* and *cornudo*, "both of which could refer to cuckolds or illegitimacy."[30] These insults were meant more to harass than as a true description of a social situation, but like other insults (calling someone a Jew, a Moor, a *mestizo*, or a thief), they indicated tensions in Spanish society.[31] Again, social class was an important factor in the social perception of illegitimacy. The seventeenth-century commentator Bernabé

Moreno de Vargas distinguished between noble illegitimate children and everyone else, stating, "Children who are bastardos or espúreos inherit the nobility and *hidalguía* that their parents have [because nobility is transmitted] directly, by legitimate or natural male lines . . . if the trunk and branches of the tree are good, the fruit cannot be other than good."[32] Illegitimate children of the nobility had potential access to status and opportunities that even legitimate children of lower social classes would never have, but that potential rested in large part on the willingness of their noble relatives to recognize them as members of the family.

The most straightforward and legally sound establishment of illegitimate children's identity was their father's written recognition of them in a will, usually accompanied by a legacy if a child was male or a dowry if she was female. Occasionally, an illegitimate son was lucky enough to inherit the estate and a title. As noted in chapter 1, many fathers of illegitimate children recognized them and provided for them in their wills, but Alfonso Girón was especially fortunate in this respect. Alfonso's father, Pedro Girón, master of the cavalry for the Order of Calatrava, had no legitimate children. Dying in 1466 on the eve of making a brilliant marriage, Pedro recognized Alfonso and his three illegitimate siblings in his will in a typically gendered fashion. Pedro obtained papal and royal legitimations for Alfonso, his two illegitimate brothers, and his illegitimate sister María. Pedro also created a mayorazgo for Alfonso, appointed his brother, the powerful Marquis de Villena, as the children's guardian, and left Alfonso in charge of the administration of the family funerary chapel.[33] Pedro Girón had taken care to bestow upon Alfonso, his eldest son, an identity as well as a legacy. In addition to the property and money his father left Alfonso, he also legitimated Alfonso, made his connection to the family clear by giving him his uncle as guardian, and made his connection to the lineage clear by making him responsible for the tombs of his ancestors. Alfonso benefited substantially from this, eventually becoming the first Count of Ureña.[34] This type of recognition, in which an illegitimate child became the heir and a titleholder in his own right, was the best-case scenario for illegitimate sons. The three boys were the equal heirs of the estate, with Alfonso inheriting the entail because he was the oldest. In contrast, the boys' illegitimate sister María was acknowledged, legitimated, and received a dowry of 6,000 Aragonese gold florins (618,000 maravedís), but was not named as an heir to the estate. Pedro Girón was able to leave his estate and fortune to his illegitimate sons and dower his illegitimate daughter as though they were legitimate because he had no legitimate children to inherit.[35] Although disrupting the hierarchy imposed by legitimacy, his legacies upheld the hierarchies of birth order and gender and the principles of dynastic succession. Pedro's illegitimate children served as an asset to his lineage, which gained status when his son received the title of Count of Ureña.

In Pedro Girón's case, his illegitimate children took the place of the legitimate children he did not have time to beget because he died unmarried. About a hundred years later, Pedro de Velasco, the third Duke of Frías's surviving illegitimate son, was in a more ambiguous position because he had legitimate half-sisters. Because of the terms of the Frías entail and his sisters' inheritance rights, the bulk of the Frías estate and the title went to Pedro's uncle after his father died. The duke was restricted to providing for his illegitimate son from the remaining fifth of his unentailed goods.[36] To the duke's distress, Pedro could not be the next duke because of his illegitimacy, but his future was nevertheless tied to the Velasco family. In his last will in 1559, the duke left all of his unentailed goods to Pedro on the condition that Pedro marry a woman from the legitimate male line of one of the duke's great-grandfathers.[37] The condition seems to indicate the duke's desire to integrate his illegitimate son and namesake into the legitimate family line. He could not leave Pedro the title, but he could attempt to bind him to the lineage through marriage. A similar move by the Marquises de los Vélez in the early seventeenth century reveals the potential advantages to this type of strategy that kept illegitimate sons connected to their father's family. An illegitimate son of the second Marquis de los Vélez made a good marriage and his legitimate son married a first cousin from the house of Vélez, thus starting a new collateral line with a new title (Marquis de Espinardo). The Marquises de los Vélez thus benefited from this added prestige gained by an illegitimate line.[38]

An interesting aspect of these cases are the royal and papal legitimations that both Pedro Girón and the third Duke of Frías valued and paid for in the hopes of solidifying the status of their illegitimate children. Although Rosa María Montero Tejada stated that "being legitimated was not always a guarantee of having the same rights as other children," it did help demonstrate an individual's identity.[39] The idea of legitimation by rescript dates back to a letter of Pope Innocent II in 1131 and was picked up in the 1160s in Bishop Stephen of Tournai's commentary on Gratian. The practice of legitimation by rescript started with Pope Alexander III in the second half of the twelfth century. According to Sara McDougall, Alexander's text provides "lawyerly discussions of the procedures of legitimation that offered opportunities for parents and children who wished to find ways to correct for illegitimate birth." In an 1156 English case, illegitimacy was used as a weapon against a potential heir, but in general, before the 1170s illegitimacy did not impede inheritance, so it seems that "ecclesiastical authorities began to declare legitimate many of the children of illegal marriages at right around the very moment those born to illegal unions needed designation as legitimate in order to inherit."[40] The result was to maintain an elasticity in the law that allowed both nobles and monarchs to continue to adjust the inheritance rights of their children in ways that benefited their dynasties. An excellent example of this is the first known medieval legitimation by rescript, provided to the French king Philip II by Pope Innocent III in 1201 because of "necessity and utility" and "on the grounds that the kingdom of France needed heirs."[41] In part because of tensions between the crown and the papacy, this power was not widely used after 1201, and the *Siete Partidas* carefully distinguished between papal legitimations, which applied to spiritual matters and allowed illegitimate children to hold sacred office, and royal legitimations, which applied to temporal matters and allowed illegitimate children the right to secular inheritance and titles.[42]

Both kings and popes made only limited use of this power before the fourteenth and fifteenth centuries (and they almost never used it for the purposes of royal succession), but by the fifteenth century in Castile the nobility began to use both papal and royal legitimations more widely, though unevenly. Although, as Montero Tejada noted, legitimations were infrequent in the Manrique family, many other noble fathers across the fifteenth and sixteenth centuries applied for formal legitimations for their sons born out of wedlock.[43] These concerned fathers included the second Count of Niebla (d. 1436), the first Duke of Medina Sidonia (d. 1468), Pedro Girón (d. 1466), the second Count of Arcos (d. 1471), the second Count of Castañeda (d. 1493), Cardinal Mendoza (d. 1495), Pope Alexander VI (d. 1503), and the first and third Dukes of Frías (d. 1512 and 1559, respectively).[44]

Most of these legitimations were purchased for illegitimate sons, not daughters. As adults, illegitimate sons also valued legitimations and applied for them independently of their fathers. In 1460, after the early death of the Lord of Pobo, his son Juan de Molina successfully applied to Enrique IV for a legitimation, and Diego de Rojas Manrique was legitimated by Queen Juana in 1515 after the death of his father in the late 1470s.[45] Like María Girón, Alfonso's sister, some girls and women were legitimated along with their brothers when a father simply purchased legitimations for all of his illegitimate children. The second Count of Arcos, for example, seems to have legitimated most of his illegitimate children, boys and girls alike, and the second Count of Castañeda legitimated his daughters Aldonza and Isabel along with their brothers.[46] The other cases in which a daughter got an official legitimation are directly related to inheritance issues. Doña Catalina Manrique was legitimated by her father, the archdeacon of Valpuesta in Burgos, so that she could be his universal heir.[47] A much more complicated example was that of Francisca Ponce de León, whose father legitimated her and arranged a marriage for her so that her legitimate son could inherit the title of Count of Arcos. In this case, Francisca's legitimation was part of her father's strategy to pass his title on to his grandson even though he had no legitimate children.[48] Evidence suggests that other kinds of papal or royal recognition, such as dispensations, might be enough to establish illegitimate daughters in either a good marriage or a convent without formally legitimating them.[49]

Whereas fathers might find recognition and legitimation important for dynastic purposes, illegitimate children found this kind of recognition to be key to their success in pursuing careers. Like most noble children, illegitimate children's careers were mapped out for them by their parents (most often their fathers) and were restricted by their gender. The vast majority of illegitimate sons joined the army or the church, whereas illegitimate daughters married or joined convents. For the nobility, success in any of these endeavors, regardless of gender, depended heavily on family support and family networks.

MEMBERS OF THE FAMILY: CAREERS FOR BOYS

The nobility still claimed a primarily military role, especially during the civil wars and the end of the Reconquista in the late fifteenth century, bringing their own troops (including their sons and grandsons) to military campaigns in support of their monarch. Because military service was such an integral part of the noble identity, illegitimate sons who became soldiers also became part of revered family traditions.[50] Military service created bonds between male family members as illegitimate sons fought with their fathers and brothers and paid the price for their military endeavors. The second Duke of Medina Sidonia (who was himself illegitimate) fought with his illegitimate brother Alfonso and two illegitimate half-brothers, Juan and Pedro, in the War of the Castilian Succession. Pedro and Alfonso were killed, and Juan was taken prisoner.[51] The Marquis de Cádiz (d. 1492) fought alongside his illegitimate half-brothers Diego, Lope, and Beltrán.[52] The house of Butrón had a long tradition of military service that included generations of illegitimate children. Gomez González Butrón had two illegitimate sons who were killed in battle, and his second legitimate son was killed at the battle of Mondragón in 1448 along with *his* illegitimate son Juan. A century later, Juan Gomez de Butrón, illegitimate son of the third Lord of Butrón, was a captain general in the Armada.[53]

The illegitimate sons who fought alongside their families often enjoyed the support and patronage of their powerful male relatives, and their careers flourished accordingly. Juan Enríquez was the illegitimate son of Alfonso Enríquez y Angulo, the Admiral of Castile (d. 1429). His powerful father helped him gain the post of captain general of the Spanish fleet, and he in turn served with his father during the Reconquista.[54] Juan Benavides (illegitimate son of the Marquis of Javalquinto and a member of the Order of Santiago) fought in the Armada along with his distinguished uncle the first Marquis of Santa Cruz. He survived and went out to the Indies, eventually becoming the captain general of the Fleet of New Spain.[55] In perhaps the most famous example, the third Duke of Alba, "the most famous Spanish soldier of Spain's great epoch of empire" or, alternatively, "the butcher of Flanders," was routinely accompanied by his illegitimate son Hernando de Toledo (b. 1527). Hernando served with his father in Naples and in 1556 became the grand prior of Castile of the Order of St. John of Jerusalem. In 1566 he was sent to relieve the siege of Malta, and from 1567–70 he served as his father's chief cavalry commander in Flanders. Henry Kamen argued that Hernando's presence was a comfort and solace to his father, whose legitimate sons had more troubled careers. García, the eldest legitimate son, died in 1548. When the duke set sail for Flanders in 1567, Fadrique, the second legitimate son, was serving three years forced military service in Oran (North Africa) for seducing a young noblewoman with a promise of marriage that he did not honor.[56]

Another method of earning a living and advancing a military career was by gaining entrance into a military order, which in the fifteenth century required nobility, purity of blood, and legitimacy, and in the sixteenth century slowly began to include the merits of individual candidates.[57] The recognition and support of a noble family made proving all three of the former characteristics easier. Following the pattern we saw earlier in this chapter with entrance into the colegios, in the sixteenth century the military orders were more lenient about legitimacy than about a lack of nobility or purity of blood, but this began to change and by the seventeenth century illegitimacy was more stigmatized.[58] Illegitimate children needed recognition from their noble fathers to demonstrate nobility and purity of blood, and they often needed an expensive papal bull of legitimation to get over the legitimacy requirement. As in all other aspects of early modern Castilian life, family relationships and political patronage were crucial to a candidate's acceptance and to his advancement once he had entered the order.

Across the late fifteenth century and into the sixteenth, the nobility assisted their illegitimate sons to enter the major military orders. Four of the first Duke of Nájera's (d. 1515) illegitimate sons entered the Order of Calatrava, as did an illegitimate son of the third Count of Paredes (d. 1536), Carlos de Bazán, as well as the illegitimate nephew of the first Marquis of

Santa Cruz (d. 1588), and the illegitimate son of the second Marquis de Vélez in the early seventeenth century (who became a military hero).[59] Illegitimate sons of the third and fourth Dukes of Nájera joined the Order of San Juan.[60] In the mid-sixteenth century an illegitimate son of the fourth Count of Valencia de don Juan (d. 1532) entered the Order of Santiago, as did Pablo de Meneses, illegitimate son of Fernan Dalvarez de Menses. Hernan Tello Portocarrero (also illegitimate) was a commander in the order; the illegitimate grandson of the third Count of Paredes joined the order in 1575 with a papal dispensation and the assurance that his mother was an Old Christian; and the illegitimate son of the first Marquis of Auñón became a knight in the order in 1625.[61]

Military orders provided economic support for men who advanced in their ranks through either a salary or a command (*encomienda*) that produced an income.[62] Because the encomiendas were often passed from father to son, family ties were again important to the project of securing a reliable income.[63] Fathers might grant a temporary inheritance that supported and educated a son until he had advanced enough to earn an income from the order. Jorge Manrique, illegitimate son of the first Duke of Nájera, received 50,000 maravedís in annual income from his father until he could be granted an encomienda. The investment that noble families made in getting their illegitimate sons into the military orders often paid off, as illegitimate sons could do well in this environment and reflect prestige back on the larger lineage. Pablo de Meneses became a general in Peru, and Hernan Tello Portocarrero became the governor of Dorlan and the governor and conquistador of Amiens and served with distinction in Flanders under Philip II.[64]

Illegitimate sons also appeared in various governmental capacities, posts that were sometimes the result of military success and often linked to noble background and patronage. Ferdinand and Isabel's Royal Pragmatic of 1501 increased the possibility of discrimination against illegitimate children.[65] In numerous cases, however, nobility seems to have counted more than legitimacy, making the success of illegitimate sons contingent on the recognition of their noble families.[66] For example, Pedro de Castilla, a royally appointed judge (*corregidor*) in Toledo, was simultaneously the illegitimate son of the bishop of Palencia and the great-grandson of Pedro I of Castile.[67] Although his father's commitment to celibacy seems to have been erratic at best (Pedro had at least nine siblings), Pedro's mother was noble, his father recognized him, and he had the blood of kings. Sometimes it was the influence of noble patronage as much as noble blood that helped an illegitimate son rise to an important post. Juan González de Butrón was the illegitimate son of the Lord of Aramayona, and he became the appellate judge (*alcalde mayor*) of the town of Aramayona, a post that his father held the power to fill.[68]

The attitude of church institutions toward the acceptance of illegitimate children was, like the military's, ambiguous, responding as much to the power and influence of the candidate's family as to issues of illegitimacy. Although illegitimacy should have been a barrier to a church career because of concerns over limpieza de sangre, illegitimate sons could be found at all levels of the church hierarchy. From my sample of 245 illegitimate sons recognized by the Castilian nobility in the fifteenth and sixteenth centuries, 52 are recorded as having entered the church.[69] Family support and connections could be crucial to advancing in the church hierarchy. The will of a grumpy father helps reveal some of the behind-the-scenes support that noble fathers provided to advance the church careers of their illegitimate sons. Don Luis Pacheco de Silva, the first Lord of Villarejo de Fuentes and the head of Charles V's household (*maestresala*), had six legitimate children and an illegitimate son, Alonso, who was apparently born before his father married. By 1512 Alonso was a priest with a benefice in Villarejo (which was under his father's control) and by 1530 he had moved up to be the school master and a canon of the cathedral in Cuenca, roughly fifty miles northeast of Villarejo. His father seemed disappointed with this result, remarking, rather acidly, that the costs of obtaining these benefices outweighed the results and requesting that Alonso not ask his legitimate siblings or his father's wife for any more help.[70] This portion of don Luis's will makes it clear that he had supported Alonso's career by paying for Alonso's benefices and presumably by using his influence in Villarejo to help secure the posts. Although the money paid for the benefices is what appeared to bother Luis, the influence that noblemen had over towns and parishes in their jurisdictions was also crucial to the careers of illegitimate children. Bernardino and Alonso de Aguila, the illegitimate sons of a nobleman from Ciudad Rodrigo, became deans of the cathedral of Ciudad Rodrigo, a post previously held by their uncle in a city where their illegitimate first cousin was on the city council.[71]

Although family affection and concern undoubtedly played a role in the financial support that noble families provided for illegitimate sons with church careers, the goal for these aristocratic sons was an influential career that would benefit their father's family. Bishops, archbishops, and cardinals were powerful men with wealth and political influence, some of whom had close relationships with the monarchy. Most of them also identified strongly with their families of origin and worked with the family lineage.[72] In this culture talented men could be a good investment in spite of their illegitimacy, and in the first half of the sixteenth century, the bishops of Zaragoza, Osma, Huesca, Malaga, Sigüenza, and Zamora were illegitimate sons, as were the archbishops of Santiago and Toledo.[73] One individual who demonstrated the success every noble family hoped for in a church career was don Bernardo Manrique, illegitimate son of the third Count of Castañeda, who joined the Dominican Order, became the rector of the college of St. Gregory in Valladolid, and by 1535 was the provincial of Spain, from which post Charles V promoted him to bishop of Malaga.[74]

Noblemen who pursued a religious career took their patriarchal ways of thinking about sexuality, dynasty, and lineage with them into a church that was already indifferent about enforcing celibacy.[75] A twist on the importance of family connections is that powerful prelates in Spain often had illegitimate children of their own, thus serving as noble fathers and exerting their influence and power. When the families involved were powerful enough, the church benefited materially. The cathedral in Zaragoza, "jewel of Spanish gothic architecture in the sixteenth century," thrived under the leadership of "the archbishops of the royal house," Alonso de Aragón, illegitimate son of Ferdinand of Aragón, and his two illegitimate sons, Juan and Hernando. Over seventy years of their combined leadership, they remodeled, rebuilt, and poured their extensive wealth into the cathedral, drawing on all the best artisans that Zaragoza could provide.[76] This was not the only ecclesiastical dynasty. Alfonso de Fonseca was the illegitimate son of the archbishop of Santiago de Compostela and was in his turn the archbishop of Santiago de Compostela (1507–34) and of Toledo (1523–34), with an illegitimate son of his own. Other clerical fathers had sons who advanced into different (but equally prestigious) church positions.[77] Alonso Manrique, bishop of Badajoz y Córdoba, had a son, Geronimo Manrique de Lara, who started a distinguished career as the inquisitor of Murcia, from which position Philip II appointed him as inquisitor and vicar general of the Armada de la Liga Católica that don Juan de Austria (illegitimate son of Charles V) was leading against the Turks. When Geronimo had taken part in the famous battle of Lepanto and celebrated the first thanksgiving mass after the battle, Philip II appointed him as bishop of Cartagena, then later of Ávila, and finally as inquisitor general of Spain. Somewhere in the midst of this illustrious career, Geronimo had an illegitimate daughter of his own, Josepha.[78]

MEMBERS OF THE FAMILY: CAREERS FOR GIRLS

For the Castilian nobility, convents were safe places for daughters, legitimate or not, that also bound them closely to the family lineage and tradition. Noble families patronized local convents and monasteries, declaring their identities visibly both by the entrance of their living children into these institutions and by the establishment of family tombs.[79] In Guadalajara the Mendoza family buried their dead ceremoniously in the monastery of San Francisco and entrusted their daughters to the convent of Santa Clara. When Leonor de Mendoza, illegitimate daughter of the Marquis de Santillana, began her long career in the convent of Santa Clara in Guadalajara some time before 1455, she entered an institution that had been supported by her family for several generations and was presently headed by her aunt, also an illegitimate daughter, who was the abbess. Her father left Leonor 2,000 maravedís for her maintenance in the convent and gave his half-sister the abbess an additional 5,000 maravedís. By 1480 Leonor herself had become the abbess of the convent, where she was still active in 1499 when her legitimate half-sister, Mencía de Mendoza, the Countess of Haro, remembered Leonor in her will.[80] Leonor's successful convent career was undoubtedly partly the result of her own initiative and skill, but it helped to have family connections and ongoing financial support. Leonor and her aunt also both benefited from the strong sibling ties discussed in the previous chapter. The presence of noblewomen in convents reflected the nobility's values of patronage and piety, with noble daughters bringing with them dowries that included rights to lands closely connected to the noble family and the patronage of the powerful noblewomen who were their mothers, aunts, and grandmothers.[81]

The importance of convents to the nobility who patronized them meant that illegitimate daughters did not disappear when they entered convents but remained closely tied to their father's lineage, receiving legacies as Leonor did from her half-sister or experiencing convent life with their female relatives. One of the convents patronized by the Counts of Osorno was Santa Clara de Carrión (see figure 2). Beatriz Manrique, the legitimate daughter of the first count (d. 1482) professed there and was subsequently joined by her legitimate nieces María and Beatriz and by their illegitimate niece Antonia, who rose to the rank of abbess before she died. The illegitimate granddaughter of the third Count of Osorno (d. 1546) also professed in Santa Clara de Carrión along with her legitimate half-sister María, who became the abbess. They were later joined by two illegitimate nieces. By 1559 the position of abbess was held by another, distant relative, Juana de Guevara, the illegitimate daughter of the Lord of Salinillas.[82] In the late sixteenth century, the first Duke of Nájera's daughters created a similar web of female relationships in the convent of Las Huelgas in Burgos (see figure 3). His illegitimate daughter Juana was the prioress of Las Huelgas, by 1570 his legitimate daughter Isabel was the abbess, and two generations later their great-niece Guiomar (descended from their illegitimate sister, another Juana) was the abbess and her sister Francisca was a nun.[83] As Elizabeth Lehfeldt argued, "Convents provided a canvas on which to display a family's good name or social standing." The Castilian nobility regularly included illegitimate daughters within that canvas.[84] Those illegitimate daughters in turn regularly reflected prestige back on their lineage through illustrious convent careers.

For illegitimate daughters, entering the convent meant joining generations of their female family members. Aristocratic women used convents to create what Lehfeldt characterized as "a type of familial home" that could assert their pride in lineage and in family ties, and their success can be seen in the vast and complex networks of relatives that permeated sixteenth-century Castilian convents.[85] Younger daughters, illegitimate daughters, and widows all regularly entered Castilian convents, and other female family members took refuge there when marriages or engagements failed or if they had extreme conflicts with sons and heirs.[86] The convent of Santa María de Consolación de Calabazanos welcomed eleven daughters of the extended Manrique lineage across the sixteenth century (see figure 4). The first Duke of Nájera sent two illegitimate daughters (both named María) there, and their cousins, four legitimate daughters of the fourth Count of Paredes, professed there in the late 1530s and early 1540s. Two illegitimate daughters of the fourth Count of Paredes's son Francisco followed their aunts into the convent, and by 1567 doña Francisca Manrique, legitimate daughter of fourth Lord of Amayuelas (and a distant cousin to both the Dukes of Nájera and the Counts of Paredes) had professed there, quickly followed by her legitimate sister Bernardina and an illegitimate half-sister.[87]

The patterns of daughters joining convents also includes multiple examples of siblings and cousins of the same generation joining the same convent. Ana de Silva, born before her father don Diego López Pacheco de Silva's marriage in 1531, professed in the Dominican convent of Madre de Dios in Toledo along with two of her legitimate half-sisters and her illegitimate first cousin Gerónima.[88] As well as joining convents where their relatives (sisters, aunts, and others) already lived, illegitimate daughters of the nobility joined convents with women in the same situation they were in. For example, in the first half of the sixteenth century, the Dominican convent of Madre de Dios in Toledo had several nuns who were illegitimate daughters of noble families. In addition to Ana and Gerónima de Silva; Guiomar de Silva, the illegitimate daughter of the first Marquis de Montemayor; Margarita de Mendoza, the illegitimate daughter of the second Count of Tendilla; and Giuomar Manrique, the illegitimate daughter of the bishop of Badajoz and Córdoba all joined this particular convent.[89] These women would have had peers with whom they could share, if they

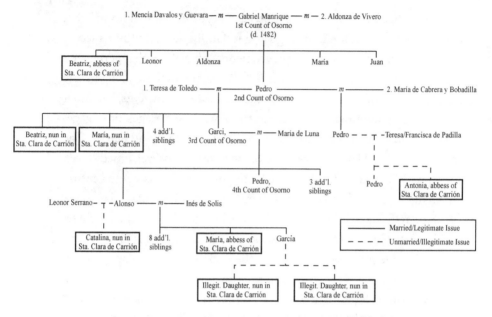

1. Mencía Davalos y Guevara — *m* — Gabriel Manrique — *m* — 2. Aldonza de Vivero
1st Count of Osorno
(d. 1482)

Beatriz, abbess of Sta. Clara de Carrión   Leonor   Aldonza   María   Juan

1. Teresa de Toledo — *m* — Pedro — *m* — 2. María de Cabrera y Bobadilla
2nd Count of Osorno

Beatriz, nun in Sta. Clara de Carrión   María, nun in Sta. Clara de Carrión   4 add'l. siblings   Garci, — *m* — María de Luna   Pedro — — Teresa/Francisca de Padilla
3rd Count of Osorno

Pedro, 4th Count of Osorno   3 add'l. siblings   Pedro   Antonia, abbess of Sta. Clara de Carrión

Leonor Serrano — —Alonso — *m* — Inés de Solis

Catalina, nun in Sta. Clara de Carrión   8 add'l. siblings   María, abbess of Sta. Clara de Carrión   García

——— Married/Legitimate Issue
– – – – Unmarried/Illegitimate Issue

Illegit. Daughter, nun in Sta. Clara de Carrión   Illegit. Daughter, nun in Sta. Clara de Carrión

2. Counts of Osorno family tree. Composed by Grace E. Coolidge from Luis Salazar y Castro, *Historia genealógica de la casa de Lara* (Valladolid: MAXTOR, 2009), 1:611–14, 621, 673–74, 2:85. Drawn by Max Coolidge Crouthamel and Fletcher Coolidge.

wished to, the experience of being illegitimate and what that meant for their identity.

As all these abbesses and prioresses suggest, illegitimacy was not a barrier to succeeding in the convent, and convents could benefit from the presence of the illegitimate daughters of kings and nobles. Isabel Beceiro Pita demonstrated that both legitimate and illegitimate daughters from the noble lineage that patronized the convent often monopolized the role of abbess.[90] An early example of this, the story of Isabel and Inés de Castilla, the "aunt abbesses," is one of successful convent careers bolstered by strong family ties. Illegitimate daughters of Enrique II of Castile, Isabel and Inés joined the convent of Santa Clara in Toledo before 1379, bringing with them substantial dowries granted to them by their father. Their dowries included 100,000 maravedís each along with jewels, objects of art, at least one sacred image, and an annual income of 35 *cahizes de pan*, an allowance of bread. Both women served as abbesses of the convent, and both of them

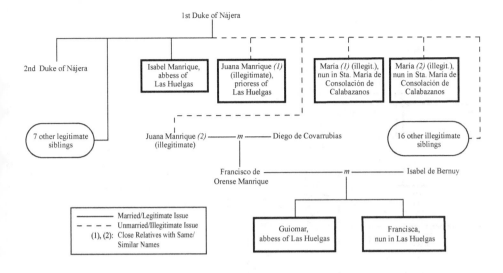

3. Dukes of Nájera family tree. Composed by Grace E. Coolidge from Luis Salazar y Castro, *Historia genealógica de la casa de Lara* (Valladolid: MAXTOR, 2009), 2:149, 152–53. Drawn by Fletcher Coolidge.

maintained strong ties with their royal relations. Their father left them a royal income in 1379 that would revert to the convent after their deaths, their nephew King Enrique III of Castile left them 100,000 maravedís in his will in 1406, and their great-nephew King Juan II of Castile referred to them as the "aunt abbesses" and left them a legacy in his will. In addition to this financial support, Pope Clement VII issued a dispensation that allowed them to hold the office of abbess "in spite of not being legitimate." The aunt abbesses obtained four papal bulls over their tenure, granting them privileges such as the ability to collect parish tithes, and they received the significant honor of keeping the keys of the city of Toledo at night. Long-lived and powerful, they were buried in the convent they had led after Isabel died in 1420 and Inés in 1443.[91] Convent careers served the lineage and coincided with noble values, connecting family members to their heritage through the memory of ancestors of both genders who had donated to and perhaps been buried in the convent as well as sustaining networks of related women who could work toward protecting and promoting the next generation.[92]

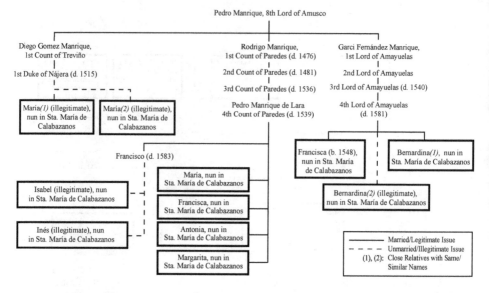

Pedro Manrique, 8th Lord of Amusco

Diego Gomez Manrique,
1st Count of Treviño

1st Duke of Nájera (d. 1515)

María(1) (illegitimate),
nun in Sta. María de
Calabazanos

María(2) (illegitimate),
nun in Sta. María de
Calabazanos

Rodrigo Manrique,
1st Count of Paredes (d. 1476)

2nd Count of Paredes (d. 1481)

3rd Count of Paredes (d. 1536)

Pedro Manrique de Lara
4th Count of Paredes (d. 1539)

Garci Fernández Manrique,
1st Lord of Amayuelas

2nd Lord of Amayuelas

3rd Lord of Amayuelas (d. 1540)

4th Lord of Amayuelas
(d. 1581)

Francisco (d. 1583)

Isabel (illegitimate), nun
in Sta. María de Calabazanos

Inés (illegitimate), nun
in Sta. María de Calabazanos

María, nun in
Sta. María de Calabazanos

Francisca, nun in
Sta. María de Calabazanos

Antonia, nun in
Sta. María de Calabazanos

Margarita, nun in
Sta. María de Calabazanos

Francisca (b. 1548),
nun in Sta. María
de Calabazanos

Bernardina(1), nun in
Sta. María de Calabazanos

Bernardina(2) (illegitimate),
nun in Sta. María de Calabazanos

———— Married/Legitimate Issue
– – – – Unmarried/Illegitimate Issue
(1), (2): Close Relatives with Same/
Similar Names

4. Manrique lineage. Composed by Grace E. Coolidge from Luis Salazar y Castro, *Historia genealógica de la casa de Lara* (Valladolid: MAXTOR, 2009), 2:152, 371–80, 695. Drawn by Fletcher Coolidge.

The other career for girls was marriage. Noble families carefully planned the strategic marriages of their offspring, using them as tools in combination with the use of mayorazgo. If a family had enough economic resources, prestigious marriages of younger siblings and illegitimate children could benefit the entire lineage.[93] My data suggest that illegitimate daughters were slightly less likely to marry than their legitimate half-sisters. In the fifteenth century, studies show, 86 percent of aristocratic women married in Córdoba, while in the Andalucían nobility in general, from 82 to 91 percent of women married.[94] Studying the Manrique family, Rosa María Montero Tejada found a lower rate of 66 percent of women marrying in the fourteenth through sixteenth centuries, but stated that only about 20 percent of illegitimate children (daughters and sons) married.[95] In my study 50 percent of illegitimate daughters are known to have married in the fifteenth century, with the rate dropping to 37 percent in the sixteenth century. Illegitimate daughters also tended to receive smaller dowries than their legitimate sisters.[96]

In spite of this family hierarchy, however, illegitimate daughters often made good marriages to noblemen whose rank was just slightly below that of their fathers and brothers. Juana de la Cerda, the illegitimate daughter of the first Duke of Medinaceli (d. 1501), married the son of the first Count of Monteagudo, while María Pimentel, the illegitimate daughter of the fifth Duke of Benavente (d. 1530) married the Count of Monterrey.[97] Sometimes illegitimate daughters married illegitimate sons from families of equivalent rank. The second Count of Niebla's illegitimate daughter married the illegitimate son of Alfonso Enríquez, the Admiral of Castile, and in 1457 the first Duke of Medina Sidonia arranged a marriage for his illegitimate daughter Leonor with Manuel, the illegitimate son of the Count of Arcos.[98] Among the more minor nobility, for whom the pressure of dowry inflation was less, illegitimate daughters might have an easier time marrying men of their own status. Three generations of the Lords of Butrón married off all of their illegitimate daughters. These alliances culminated with Gomez González (d. 1448), Lord of Butrón and Moxica, who married off his illegitimate daughters María, Mayor, Juana, and two more sisters whose names are not recorded, all to men who were his equivalent in rank.[99]

Like all noble arranged marriages, the marriages of illegitimate daughters were economic transactions, and their families' readiness to accept and support them was part of what made them valuable marriage partners. When María Ponce de León, illegitimate daughter of the third Count of Arcos, married don Rodrigo Messía Carrillo, the Lord of la Guardia, the marriage, according to Ángel Vidma Guzmán, "enormously increased his [the husband's] possessions in Jaén, with houses in the city of Jaén and lands in Fuerte del Rey and Garcíez."[100] Another consideration that could make an accepted and acknowledged illegitimate daughter an attractive marriage partner was social status. If the daughter in question married below the social status of her father's family, her husband could gain prestige and patronship as well as property. Cardinal Mendoza showed his support of Juan Alonso de Moxica, Lord of Butrón and Moxica, by arranging for Juan's eldest son to marry the cardinal's niece, Elvira de Mendoza, an illegitimate daughter of the first Duke of Infantado, in 1468. The Butrón family were noble, but ranked far below the Dukes of Infantado, and the marriage was considered a prestigious alliance for them.[101]

One of the reasons that noblemen and noble families invested in the education and dowry that would enable a daughter to marry a nobleman even if she was illegitimate was because of the nobility's persistent belief in the power of the arranged marriage to convey political advantages and recruit allies.[102] In this strategic game illegitimate daughters were assets. An example of this is Beatriz de Pacheco, the illegitimate daughter of Juan Pacheco, the Marquis of Villena and the first Duke of Escalona. Beatriz was the eldest of Juan Pacheco's seventeen children (twelve legitimate and five illegitimate), and Alfonso Franco Silva analyzed how her father used her marriage to neutralize the power of a potential political rival. In 1448 Juan Pacheco was the influential favorite of the Prince Enrique, heir to the throne of Castile, but Rodrigo de Portocarrero was rapidly rising in the prince's favor. Worried about this rise to power, Pacheco arranged a marriage between his daughter Beatriz and Portocarrero, thus making his potential rival his son-in-law, a member of his immediate family who had obligations and owed deference to him. Pacheco gave Beatriz an extensive dowry consisting of the estate of Villarejo de Fuentes and its land and used his influence with the prince to get Portocarrero the title of Count of Medellín. Rodrigo de Portocarrero was thus converted from rival to client, because he owed all his new wealth and titles to Pacheco's influence.[103] The success of this strategy suggests that although Beatriz was illegitimate, her father, her new husband, and the prince all saw Beatriz as a member of the Pacheco family whose marriage conveyed that status to her husband as well. After Portocarrero's death Beatriz made another prestigious marriage, with the second Count of Cifuentes, and later distinguished herself by fighting alongside her legitimate half-brother Diego against the Catholic Monarchs in the War of the Castilian Succession, thus demonstrating her own loyalty to the Pacheco family.[104]

Beatriz Pacheco's life trajectory resembles that of a legitimate daughter of a noble family and is in fact very similar to those of her legitimate half-sisters, with multiple prestigious marriages and active participation in family politics.[105] Barbara Harris argued that English aristocratic women had careers that "had as much political and economic as domestic importance and were as crucial to the survival and prosperity of their families and class as the careers of their male kin."[106] This concept also applies to noblewomen in Castile, who shared with their royal counterparts what Silvia Mitchell described as a tradition of "legally sanctioned, robust, and effective female leadership."[107] The careers of illegitimate daughters in these examples also had this kind of impact, demonstrating female agency, transmitting wealth and prestige to the families they married into, making strategic alliances that benefited their natal families, and in Beatriz's case even fighting for their families. They eventually became mothers and grandmothers who could convey status and property to their own children and grandchildren. Illegitimate daughters were often valuable assets and consistent allies to their families and, simultaneously, powerful women in their own right.

FAMILIAL HIERARCHIES

The attention and care that the nobility tended to demonstrate toward illegitimate children can in part be understood by the degree to which the nobility valued people as a basis for political power. Thinking in terms of lineage and of patron-client relationships, the nobility valued human resources and saw children as potential assets, pieces of the larger lineage who could benefit the family. According to Rosa Montero Tejada, "One of the sources of the nobility's political power was their capacity to bring together a great number of people who constituted their political clientele." This political clientele included blood relations, servants, vassals, and fictive kin, all of whom made up a noble "house."[108] While illegitimate children were useful in this system because they were part of the family, they had fewer rights of inheritance, making their positions more malleable.

The noble house had a distinct hierarchy, and illegitimate children tended to fill slightly lower positions in the lineage, in part because they were likely to inherit less. The hierarchy in the lives of noble children was both gendered and affected by legitimacy. Heirs to the title (eldest sons) often served as pages in the royal court, while younger legitimate sons who would not inherit the title (*segundones*) and illegitimate sons entered the church or the military.[109] Illegitimate daughters tended to marry men of slightly lower rank than their legitimate sisters or enter convents. An early example of this in the Arcos family is Pedro Ponce de León, the fourth Lord of Marchena, who had a wife, Sancha, and four legitimate children as well as four illegitimate children with a woman named María Sánchez. When he wrote his will in 1374, Pedro had already betrothed his eldest legitimate daughter, Isabel, to a member of the prominent Guzmán family, giving her a dowry of 130,000 maravedís plus the income from the jurisdiction of Mayrena, located on what is today the edge of the Sierra Nevada National Park in Andalusia. He left his other two legitimate daughters dowries of 50,000 maravedís each and his son Pedro as the heir to his entailed estate. Although he recognized, cared for, and provided for his four illegitimate children, their inheritances were only 10,000 maravedís each, much less than those of their legitimate half-siblings, and the will of his adult illegitimate son in 1401 reveals a household with more limited economic resources than that of his father.[110]

Although the occasional illegitimate daughter was given a large dowry and made a brilliant match, this occurred more often when either there were no legitimate daughters or the family was among the very highest nobility and could afford multiple dowries. As we saw in chapter 1, the third Duke of Medina Sidonia (d. 1507) gave his eldest legitimate daughter, Leonor, an extravagant dowry of 26 million maravedís, and her younger legitimate sister Mencía was part of a double-marriage contract that carried a payment from her father of 30 million maravedís.[111] The duke left his still unmarried legitimate daughter Isabel a dowry of 6 million maravedís and his two illegitimate daughters dowries of 2 million maravedís each.[112] The hierarchy in this will was based on birth order and legitimacy, with the eldest legitimate daughters receiving the largest dowries. It was not just the third duke who recognized this family hierarchy. The girls' grandmother Leonor de Mendoza also left them legacies and her will followed a similar pattern, awarding 8 million maravedís to her namesake Leonor, 6 million to Mencía, and 3 million to Isabel. Leonor also left her illegitimate granddaughters 1 million maravedís a piece to augment their dowries.[113] The difference in dowries made a difference in the marriages of this group of sisters and half-sisters. The duke's eldest legitimate daughter, Leonor, married the Duke of Braganza, a nephew of King Manuel I of Portugal, while his second daughter, Mencía, married the Count of Urueña's eldest son and heir. In contrast, the duke's illegitimate daughter Leonor, who had the smallest dowry, married Valencia de Benavides, captain of the royal guard.[114] A hierarchy based in part on age and legitimacy operated within the Duke of Medina Sidonia's family, even though all the daughters (both legitimate and illegitimate) were provided with dowries.

The hierarchy reflected in less prestigious marriages for illegitimate children was a deliberate part of the nobility's strategy of arranging marriages to benefit the larger family lineage.[115] The second Count of Arcos married off almost all of his approximately twenty-eight illegitimate children. The legitimated children of doña Leonor Nuñez (who was noble and eventually became the count's wife) made the most prestigious marriages, forming alliances with the Dukes of Medina Sidonia, the Counts of Cabra, the powerful Pacheco family, and Álvaro de Luna's niece, in addition to a generous selection of the minor noble families from the surrounding area in Andalusia.[116] These alliances were essential pieces of the Arcos family's national and local networks of influence, and they indicate that other noble families accepted the count's marriage and the legitimation of his children. The children of Catalina González (who was a maidservant and not noble) also married, creating another network of influence with the local officials who ranked just below the families that Leonor's children had married into. Their spouses included local castle commanders, councilmen, notaries, judges, a member of Seville's city council, and a member of the military Order of Santiago. The count's other illegitimate children, whose mothers were enslaved or were unknown, married men without titles, local citizens or, in one case, the son of a lawyer.[117] Although all the children were given enough financial support to enable them to make some kind of honorable marriage, there is a hierarchy here based on the status of the children's mothers. These marriages also benefited the Arcos dynasty by creating ties, bonds, and alliances with the Castilian nobility, the local nobility, and many of the local governments and officials for the entire region of Andalusia, including the cities of Seville and Córdoba. This kind of networking demonstrates how a noble dynasty used their illegitimate children to make the family more resilient by giving the Counts of Arcos ties to both local and national elites who could help them when they needed it.[118]

In addition to illegitimacy, birth order had a profound impact on the future prospects of children, so that illegitimate children of younger sons had fewer options than those of the heir simply because their fathers inherited fewer resources. Don Bernardino Manrique de Lara was the tenth son of the third Count of Paredes and was born illegitimate, arriving before his father's controversial second marriage to his mother, a lady-in-waiting in the Paredes household. Bernardino became dean of the cathedral of Granada and the head chaplain of the royal chapel in that cathedral, but when he had an illegitimate daughter of his own (Isabel), she was relegated to marrying the steward of the Paredes's estate (held by her uncle, the fourth count). On one hand, Isabel Manrique's husband was noble enough to carry the honorific title "don," but he did not hold a title of his own. On the other hand, her marriage shows the unmistakable patronage of the house of Paredes, which provided her with a marriage that kept her connected to the family and perhaps rewarded a loyal retainer at the same time.[119]

The noble family's strategic use of their illegitimate children to cement family alliances underscores ways in which those children faced uncertainty, lack of support, and discrimination when embarking on careers. Most illegitimate children were designated to play minor, secondary roles in family strategies, and their opportunities were limited by the strategies of more powerful family members and by the availability of economic resources. For example, marriage dowries began to inflate in the fifteenth century and continued to grow.[120] Studying the Manrique family, Rosa Montero Tejada found that convent entrance rates tended to increase even for legitimate daughters when there were many girls in a family or when the father's title was less prestigious (thus limiting his economic resources) and that this was even more true for illegitimate daughters. She cited the example of the first Duke of Nájera; of his six legitimate daughters, only one entered a convent, while the rest married, whereas of his ten illegitimate daughters, seven entered a convent and only one married.[121] In the mid-sixteenth century the fourth Lord of Javalquinto's family demonstrated a similar hierarchy. He had ten legitimate daughters, eight of whom married, with the ninth becoming a nun, but none of his three illegitimate daughters married. Isabel and Juana became beatas, Brianda professed as a nun, and their illegitimate brother Alonso became a Franciscan friar.[122] In families with fewer resources, the hierarchy was less apparent as all girls, legitimate or not, might have to enter the convent. All three of the second Count of Oñate's legitimate daughters professed as nuns, his illegitimate daughter Isabel was a beata, and the count stated in his will in 1541 that he hoped his youngest illegitimate daughter, Ana, would also become a nun.[123] The number of illegitimate daughters who became beatas, a choice that did not require a convent dowry, also suggests a hierarchy.

Just as joining a convent was generally less expensive and could be a lower-status option for daughters, illegitimate boys did not always advance in their church careers. Rising legal and social concern with racial purity (limpieza de sangre) and the upheavals of the Catholic Reformation in Castile had a more immediate effect on illegitimate men who were eligible for public careers and opportunities that were already denied to women because of their gender. Increased discrimination against illegitimate children could be offset by a supportive and powerful family. Baltasar Cuart Moner asserted that although the ideal candidate for all the major colleges exhibited immaculate purity of blood and descent from a legitimate marriage, "the first was more important than the second." For illegitimate children of the nobility, it all "depended on the family power of the candidate in question," and although noble families routinely saw the church as a career for second-born and illegitimate sons, not all families were willing or could afford to help them advance.[124] Candidates for higher-level church positions had to be educated, a process that required payments for tuition and basic living expenses while they were in school, and it might be some time before young men were able to earn a benefice that provided a living wage. As previously discussed with regard to Pedro de Portocarrero (illegitimate grandson of the Count of Medellín), the period in which young men were training for a church career was one in which illegitimate children were potentially more vulnerable than their legitimate peers because they were not guaranteed an inheritance.[125]

Some noble fathers were generous, hoping for and often getting a good return on their investment in a son's education. Others were less willing or less able to support long-term career goals for sons born out of wedlock, especially if they had legitimate sons to support. Many illegitimate sons are simply listed in the noble genealogies as "cleric," as is the case for Alonso de Guzmán, illegitimate grandson of the second Count of Aguilar.[126] Other illegitimate sons became monks, and in spite of increasing discrimination across the fifteenth and sixteenth centuries and especially after the Council of Trent, all the major religious orders in Castile included illegitimate sons of the nobility into the seventeenth century. Pedro de Velasco, illegitimate grandson of the first Count of Haro, died as a Hieronymite monk in 1502; Domingo, illegitimate son of the third Duke of Medina Sidonia, professed in the Dominican monastery of San Esteban in Salamanca; Alonso de Sandoval, illegitimate son of the third Duke of Nájera, was a Jesuit; Pedro Manrique, illegitimate grandson of the Lord of Butrón, joined the Augustinians; and Francisco de Peralta, illegitimate son of fifth Lord of las Villas de Lixar, was a Franciscan.[127] An illegitimate grandson of the second Count of Osorno joined the new Carthusian monastery in Granada, which was founded in 1506.[128] Even after the Council of Trent stipulated that illegitimate children could not join religious orders, the eighth Count of Castañeda's illegitimate son became a Geronimite monk and the ninth count had two illegitimate sons who were monks, a third illegitimate son who was an abbot, a fourth who was the rector of the University of Salamanca, and an illegitimate daughter who was the abbess of Santa Clara de Aguilar de Campo.[129]

This list of illegitimate monks (and one abbess) tends to support Baltasar Cuart Moner's analysis that support from a noble family overcame any barriers that religious orders might theoretically impose on illegitimate sons, but it also suggests that illegitimate sons might have had trouble moving beyond the rank of monk and advancing to higher positions in the church. Rosa Montero Tejada found that the Manrique family saw the church as a secondary career option, more suitable for illegitimate sons. Legitimate boys in the Manrique family only joined the church if there were more than two of them in a family. If a family had only one legitimate son, illegitimate sons were sent into a church career, and over the course of two centuries Montero Tejada found only four legitimate sons who remained monks and did not advance to higher ranking ecclesiastical posts with political influence.[130]

The expectations that noble boys would make a brilliant career out of the church and the limits that illegitimate boys might face are illustrated by the careers of two illegitimate sons of the second Count of Niebla. Both Fadrique and Enrique de Guzmán went into the church, starting their careers under the patronage of their father as archdeacons of Niebla. Enrique remained an archdeacon, but Fadrique was appointed bishop of Mondoñedo. Fadrique showed little interest in that job. He traveled six hundred miles north to Mondoñedo, where he quickly installed a vicar general to act for him, and then immediately returned to his father and family in Seville. His ambitions lay in Seville, where in 1473 he was nominated to the post of archbishop but did not get the job. Enrique, in his turn, failed to become the bishop of Cádiz.[131] Both boys had received the education and patronage necessary to advance in the church, but neither did. This suggests that they might have suffered some discrimination because of their illegitimate birth, although other factors (including their own abilities) may have influenced whether or not they advanced.

The nobility themselves, with a ruthless focus on their own ascendancy, were ambivalent and inconsistent about the status of illegitimate children. Their attitudes toward these children were affected both by the child's gender and by whether the family had legitimate children. Although their actions toward their own children were often flexible and supportive, noblemen used the formal, legal language of mayorazgos to reinforce the hierarchy for future generations. In 1487 the Lord of Amayuelas created a mayorazgo for his son Bernardino that addressed what would happen if Bernardino had male children with a concubine: "We wish and command that *the legitimate sons and those born from legitimate marriage are preferred* and . . . inherit the said mayorazgo even if they are younger in age than a natural son legitimated by subsequent marriage or by the King or by any other manner, even if the said legitimation took place previously" (emphasis added).[132] What one father could formally create, however, another father could undo. In pursuit of dynastic continuity, a noble father without a legitimate son might turn to his illegitimate son as a substitute heir. As discussed in chapter 1, the second Count of Castañeda, having no legitimate children, legitimated four of his illegitimate children in 1453 and made his eldest son the heir to the title. This action was challenged by his brother the Count of Osorno.[133] Although the Count of Castañeda eventually succeeded and his son inherited the title, the transition was neither smooth nor easy, and it involved a lengthy lawsuit between the brothers. The hierarchy that privileged the eldest legitimate son, although looking clear-cut on paper, was only as effective as the next titleholder's willingness to enforce it. If the next titleholder was more interested in pursuing dynastic succession by having his illegitimate son inherit the title, the situation abruptly became more fluid.

In pursuit of their own advantage, noble fathers rearranged bequests, entails, and inheritances for their illegitimate sons as circumstances evolved. In 1535 the third Duke of Frías donated the valley of Arreba, complete with towns, fortifications, vassals, and civil and criminal jurisdictions, to his illegitimate son Juan. It was a handsome inheritance that would provide economic security for Juan and his heirs. By 1542, however, the duke had changed his mind, revoking his donation to Juan, making the valley of Arreba an entailed estate, and leaving it to Juan's younger illegitimate half-brother Pedro, who had been born sometime after 1535. Adding to the uncertainty of this bequest was the condition that if the duke had legitimate sons, the donation to Pedro would be immediately revoked. Both boys officially agreed to the document, Juan signing it himself while the younger Pedro's guardian ad litem signed for him.[134] It seems probable that Juan was compensated in some way and that there was no ongoing dispute, given that when Juan died before his father did, his father stepped in to raise and provide for Juan's three (legitimate) children.[135] The entire transaction, however, illustrates the tenuous nature of the inheritances of illegitimate sons, as Juan lost his chance to inherit and Pedro's chance to inherit an entailed estate remained entirely dependent on the lack of legitimate male heirs to the larger Frías title.

The legacies to illegitimate sons could be changed, they could be conditional, they favored legitimate sons, and they rested on the whim of noble fathers rather than on the legal rights of the children. Illegitimate children were especially vulnerable to these changes because they had limited rights of inheritance.[136] This lack meant fathers had more control over their children's inheritances, including the right to disinherit them altogether. The first Duke of Nájera disinherited one of his illegitimate sons, revoking a previous legacy of 30,000 maravedís because, he said, his son "had been so disorderly."[137] The tenuous nature of an illegitimate son's right to inheritance (and thus status) helps explain why don Bernardino de Velasco, whose story starts this chapter, felt the need to try to formally preserve legal proof of his identity even as an adult in order, as he put it, that his children "might inherit all and whatever goods remain from the said lord don Bernaldino de Velasco my lord father after his death."[138]

Illegitimate girls were not likely to inherit an entailed estate or title from their noble fathers, but their claims to support and maintenance could also lead to disputes within the noble family.[139] Lady Leonor Manrique had to take legal action to get financial support from her father, don Antonio Manrique de Lara, second Lord of San Leonardo. Because don Antonio was a member of the Order of Calatrava, Leonor's guardian made a formal request to the Council of Military Orders that her father both recognize her and provide financial support. Leonor was fortunate to have a baptismal certificate that not only contained both her parents' names but also named her as an hija natural. This document convinced the council, who decreed in 1605 that her father had to provide for her. Don Antonio duly provided 1,500 ducados for her support in 1605, but in 1609 doña Leonor had to go back to the council, who again took her side, agreeing that she should get an additional 200 ducados.[140] Although doña Leonor succeeded in getting the money she needed, she had to resort to repeated, formal legal procedures to establish her connection to her father and her right to his support. Gender also played a role here for both father and daughter. As an illegitimate daughter, doña Leonor did not provide her father with a potential heir, and her goal was merely a regular living allowance, not an entailed estate. In his turn, her father did not respond willingly to the legal and social pressure to demonstrate his masculinity by caring for his dependents. This might have been because Leonor was a girl, but it could also have reflected a lack of financial resources on don Antonio's part.

Despite the many ways in which noble families benefited from the presence of illegitimate children, illegitimacy always carried risk, both for the lineage and for the illegitimate individual. Miguel Ángel Ladero Quesada's analysis of the first Duke of Medina Sidonia's career holds true for many noblemen. On one hand, don Juan de Guzmán maintained the favor of King Juan II of Castile during the conflict with the Infantes of Aragón from 1443 to 1445, reclaimed the estate of Lepe, developed the estate of Medina Sidonia, and was the first person in Castile who was not the son of a king to obtain the title of Duke of Medina Sidonia. On the other hand, the duke suffered from "risks derived from the failure of his marriage, his lack of legitimate children and the claims that his sister María made on parts of his inheritance [because of his lack of legitimate heirs]." Don Juan negotiated these risks successfully, compensating for his lack of legitimate sons by legitimating one of his illegitimate sons and passing the title on to him. His dispute with his sister was settled with an agreement in 1442, but her descendants, the Counts of Alba de Liste, would revive the claim years later.[141] His situation reveals both the benefits of illegitimate children as substitute heirs and the risks that their presence and their illegitimacy would disrupt the inheritance process.

Illegitimate children who did succeed in inheriting the title inevitably also inherited a disputed status. Although many of them triumphed, almost all of them were sued. The third Count of Castañeda, Garci Fernández Manrique, was illegitimate. Anticipating problems, Garci's father (the second Count of Castañeda, mentioned above) procured three royal legitimations for his son. In spite of this, when Garci's father died, his paternal uncle promptly challenged Garci's right to his father's title, suing him in the chancery court in 1485. Garci won the challenge, but the lawsuit was long and expensive.[142] When Diego de Rivera left his estate to his illegitimate son (and only child), Felipe, in 1520, Diego's brother promptly sued Felipe, and it took the intervention of Charles V to preserve Felipe's inheritance.[143] These lawsuits could be long and were often costly and bitter. Manuel Ponce de León sued his nephew, the first Duke of Arcos, because although the first duke himself was legitimate, his mother had been the illegitimate daughter of the second Count of Arcos. Manuel, as the younger brother of the second count, felt that he had a stronger claim to the title and estates of Arcos, even though both he and his brother (the second count) were illegitimate themselves. The lawsuit lasted from 1494 to 1522, finally culminating in a settlement that granted the estate of Bailén to Manuel along with a settlement of 61,000 ducados and an arranged marriage but left his nephew with the title of duke and the bulk of the Arcos estate.[144] Illegitimate titleholders faced added expenses as they dealt with these issues. To continue the story of the Dukes of Medina Sidonia mentioned above, the second duke, illegitimate son of the first duke, eventually had to pay 90,000 ducados to compensate the other branch of the family (the Counts of Alba de Liste) for dropping their claims to his title. He made the payment in 1510, ending a dispute that had dragged on since at least the 1460s and which had created some substantial bitterness among family members. In the claim filed with the Royal Council in 1487, Alfonso Enríquez, the Count of Alba de Liste, complained that the second duke was nothing more than a bastard, the "son of miller's daughter."[145]

It was not simply the presence of illegitimate children or the lack of legitimate children that was a risk to the noble family. The actions of illegitimate children and the claims they could potentially make on their families were also a risk. Noble culture, with its expectation that noble families would care for their illegitimate members, created a space for illegitimate children to sue for lack of support even when they did not have a strong legal basis for their claims. Thus, despite the best efforts of noble fathers, the relationships between the eldest son who inherited the title and his illegitimate siblings were sometimes disrupted by conflict. In 1518 the second Duke of Nájera was sued by his illegitimate half-brother Luis over Luis's allowance and the estates of Villajimena, Alesanco, and Oruñuela that Luis had inherited from his father. The second Duke of Nájera was in general a conscientious elder brother and patron to his twenty illegitimate half-siblings, but in this case the two brothers apparently disagreed about the terms of their father's will.[146] In this litigious society family lawsuits were common, even unremarkable. Antonio Terrasa-Lozano argued that the nobility (like the monarchy) had two bodies, a natural body that was "obliged to show fraternal and Christian love" and a political body "that was obliged to sue in order to defend the rights of their household."[147] The dichotomy between the two bodies allowed noble families to absorb the tensions that arose between their entangled estates and properties while preserving personal relationships with each other. Analyzing the Dukes of Arcos and Medina Sidonia, Miguel Ladero Quesada noted that they "had frequent lawsuits with other lineages or with other branches of the same lineage."[148] Lawsuits did not necessarily mean a permanent rupture of family relationships, but they were expensive and could produce bitterness.

Illegitimate children could also disrupt noble families when their status was in question. The lack of clarity found in the stages of marriage could create situations in which noble children could claim that they were actually legitimate. As we saw in chapter 2, when the third Duke of Nájera jilted his noble fiancée doña Aldonza de Urrea in 1520, leaving her pregnant and unmarried, doña Aldonza sued him for breach of promise. She lost all three of the lawsuits that she brought against the duke, but this did not deter their son, Manrique de Lara, from continuing the fight. He sued his younger half-brother, the fourth Duke of Nájera, starting in Spain and taking his suit all the way to the Rota, the papal tribunal that heard matrimonial cases that were appealed from the diocesan courts. Claiming that his mother's three failed lawsuits in no way prejudiced his legitimacy, he stated that he should in fact be the duke because he was the third Duke of Nájera's eldest son. In addition, he appealed to the Royal Council to force his half-brother to award him an annual income. Finally, in 1568, Manrique, then forty-eight years old and apparently realizing that this was a lost cause, settled with his half-brother. The settlement reveals what the nobility worried about in relation to illegitimate children. Manrique ceded all the rights he had claimed to the title and promised never to marry, thus effectively shutting down all possibility of future lawsuits from his legitimate descendants. In return, after fifty years of lawsuits, the fourth Duke of Nájera granted Manrique an annual income of 2,000 ducados.[149] The fourth Duke of Nájera was right to be concerned about lawsuits that lasted for generations. Francisco del Aguila, the third Lord of Payo de Valencia y Eliseda, married twice but had only one legitimate child, a daughter named Catalina, who was mentally disabled (*mentecapta*). Although Catalina lived to adulthood and was able to marry, her illegitimate half-brother, Antonio, sued in 1558. Antonio claimed that he should inherit their father's estate and his eldest son carried on the lawsuit in his turn.[150]

Illegitimate litigants were usually at a disadvantage if they wanted to claim the title. One lawsuit over the title of Count of Paredes was dismissed in 1588 because the litigant "was not born in legitimate marriage" and therefore had no legal claim to the title.[151] Don Francisco de Vargas y Silva, illegitimate son of the tenth Lord of Higuera, sued to gain possession of his father's lands and title after the death of his legitimate half-sister but lost his claim because of his illegitimate status.[152] On the other hand, illegitimate children often had some success in claiming that they had a right to an inheritance or an income. In 1510 don Alonso Manrique won a lawsuit against his nephew, the fourth Count of Castañeda, and claimed an inheritance of 600,000 maravedís that don Alonso's brother (the third count) had left him.[153]

Illegitimate adults who had noble fathers and thus connections to titled families occupied an ambiguous space in Castilian society. On one hand, they were intimately connected to the most powerful people in Castilian society and politics. On the other hand, their claim to even the most modest inheritance depended on the goodwill and acknowledgment of those same powerful people. They could be crucial assets or tools to help advance the larger lineage, or their mere existence could be an embarrassment and a burden, and their presence and their claims could complicate family ties and relationships. Gender played a complex role in these uncertainties. Changing ideas about race in the fifteenth and sixteenth centuries created particular vulnerabilities for illegitimate men, but even in the face of this discrimination, men's ability to achieve professions, status, and economic resources outstripped that of their illegitimate sisters. Maternal lineage played an important role in the future of these children, as their mothers might be noble, hidalgo, poor, servants, Native Americans, or enslaved women, and their children's potential status varied accordingly. The diversity of their mothers and the existence of children born outside of the usually endogamous noble marriage alliance introduced a broad range of race and ethnicity into the noble family. This diversity had complex implications for nobility, as noble fathers' status and patronage could overcome discrimination and gain social acceptance, careers, and status for their illegitimate children. At the same time, illegitimate adults were not guaranteed the interest and support of their noble fathers.

The vulnerability of illegitimate adults emphasizes the complex and fluid status of the noble family. Illegitimate adults were a potential source of tension, but they were also sometimes dearly loved as treasured family members who had talents to contribute to the lineage. The nobility valued people as a basis for political power, and illegitimate children had the potential to extend noble family networks and influence. The flexibility of their roles within the family was an immense asset to the lineage but created precarious situations for illegitimate adults themselves. The very nature of that fluidity had an emotional cost. The next chapter attempts to uncover the complex emotions that illegitimacy created within the noble family, exploring a wide of range of potentially contradictory emotions, including affection, love, anxiety, jealousy, rage, grief, and loss.

5

"It Is Such a Burden to Me"

The Emotional Implications of Illegitimacy

As we have seen, illegitimacy was wound into the fabric of the noble families of Castile. Noblemen and, to a lesser extent, noblewomen routinely had extramarital affairs, and illegitimate children were common. But illegitimacy also had emotional consequences. This book has explored the economic consequences and power dynamics of illegitimacy. This chapter aims to analyze the emotional complications produced by the nobility's ruthless adherence to dynastic succession. The use of tactics such as entail and arranged marriages resulted in a system in which many adults had children with multiple sexual partners over long periods of time. In many ways extramarital affairs and illegitimate children are the logical consequences of a system of arranged marriages, so this chapter examines marriages as well as extramarital relationships. The emotional reactions to illegitimacy and extramarital sexuality were not consistent. They ranged from affection and love to anxiety, jealousy, and rage. They sometimes resulted in violence, and they were tempered by grief and loss. It is particularly difficult to determine the degree of coercion, agency, or choice exercised by or upon the women who had sexual relations with the nobility.

This chapter argues that illegitimacy gave the noble family the emotional flexibility needed to make a patrilineal system of arranged marriages function by creating alternate families that provided a space for the emotional attachments and relationships that could not thrive within the arranged marriage. Families that were created informally, for reasons other than dynastic succession, were potential sites for love and affection. Illegitimacy and the alternate families it created could also cushion the grief and loss that accompanied the various stages of evolving noble families. Too often, spouses, partners, and children died young. Surviving family members struggling to rebuild both the patrilineal and the emotional family unit might find themselves relying on their illegitimate members as heirs, guardians, executors, and compassionate family members. At the same time, illegitimacy itself created human complications, conflicting emotions, and disruptions such as failed marriages, jealous spouses, and even violence that led to lawsuits and feuds that threatened the smooth transfer of property within a patrilineal family system.

The presence of illegitimacy and extramarital sexuality in the noble family produced a broad spectrum of emotions that are conflicting, difficult to categorize, and challenging to uncover.[1] Jacqueline Holler approached this problem by using what she called "accidental" documentation of emotional states in Mexican colonial records in which individuals "report, analyze, and speculate upon feeling," in pursuit of other goals. This concept is useful when exploring notarial records for the Spanish nobility.[2] When dictating wills or setting up entails that included illegitimate children, the nobility occasionally revealed motivations and emotions that are not otherwise visible in the records. The range of these emotions was enhanced by the variety of concepts about love and sexuality that were available in early modern culture. Linda A. Curcio-Nagy argued that moral treatises, songs, popular plays, erotic art, and love poetry advanced a wide range of ideas that individuals could draw on as they thought about their own lives and relationships in colonial Mexico, and an equally extensive variety of these sources were available in Castile.[3]

Illegitimacy created enormously complex networks of families and emotions. The late medieval elite nuclear family ate and drank, went fishing, played games, went to the bathhouse, practiced archery, and even went on pilgrimage together.[4] How did one balance this commitment to family life among multiple families? Barbara H. Rosenwein's argument that people occupy multiple "emotional communities" applies particularly well to the complex families that this study examines. Late medieval people recognized the importance of the nuclear family within what Philip Grace termed "concentric circles" of close relatives, members of a larger lineage, and household servants, retainers, and courtiers.[5] Because sexual and romantic partners were often located within those concentric circles (men had sexual relations with their cousins, their wives' ladies-in-waiting, and women who lived on their estates), extramarital relationships created even more complex ties and convoluted emotional communities. Moving between families, each of which was an emotional community, could be complex in multiple ways.

Studying illegitimacy in the noble family over two hundred years also complicates any analysis of the changing patriarchal nature of the Castilian noble family and of Castilian society in general. The late medieval and early modern noble family in Castile was increasingly patrilineal in the sense that men and eldest male children were more likely to benefit economically from the inheritance system at the cost of women and of younger sons. As Castilian nobility moved away from practicing strict partible inheritance, they aimed for success by constructing a patrilineal system of inheritance that depended on arranged marriages and the succession of the eldest son to an entail.[6] This emphasis on patrilineality in turn pushed society in a more patriarchal direction, toward a kind of society that Allan Johnson described as promoting "male privilege by being *male dominated, male identified,* and *male centered.*"[7] But the nobility's increasing emphasis on a patrilineal system of inheritance was risky because of the possibility of the premature death of the male heir or male titleholder. The nobility thus depended heavily on women for practical purposes like the guardianship of younger children left fatherless or the production of illegitimate children who might serve as substitute heirs and useful members of the larger lineage. Patrilineal families, paradoxically, functioned because of the presence and participation of women, younger sons, and illegitimate children, giving these family members added emotional as well as practical importance.

An example of this is that as the use of entail (favoring the eldest son) increased during the fifteenth century, dowries also rose astronomically, to the point where they constituted a substantial part (if not all) of a woman's inheritance from her parents.[8] This might seem to put noblewomen at a disadvantage by cutting them out of an inheritance, but under Castilian law, although the husband administered his wife's dower property during their marriage, it remained legally hers and had to be returned to her when her husband died. Men were accountable for the decisions they made about their wife's property, and women could sue for recovery of their dowry if they felt it was not being well taken care of.[9] As noble dowries grew to the point where the nobility were alienating entailed goods to pay them, the effect on women's economic status was mixed. On one hand, huge noble dowries might take generations to pay (some of them were never completed). But on the other hand, the women who owned these vast dowries, which included movable goods, towns, rents, and slaves, had substantial economic power within their family units and in relation to the children who would inherit from them.[10] Being a mother who controlled property gave women what Susan Broomhall called "an authoritative status," which they often used for the benefit of the lineage, crafting self-presentations that used emotions to accomplish dynastic goals such as filial obedience or advantageous marriages.[11]

This makes it difficult to argue for the solidification of a patriarchal culture in Castile.[12] The noble family did not become a group in which, in the words of Adrienne Rich, "the female was everywhere subsumed by the male," but rather might be more accurately described (to modify the words of Sylvia Walby) as a system in which some men were able to "dominate, oppress and exploit" some women while simultaneously relying heavily on the expertise, resources, emotional support, and agency of other women.[13] Judith Bennett argued that there are many varieties of patriarchy and thus this study presents, in part, a "history of women as survivors, resistors, and agents of patriarchy."[14] It is perhaps problematic to categorize early modern women as "resistors" of the patriarchy, but sources reveal that women in a wide variety of roles (mistresses, wives, mothers, aunts, illegitimate daughters) certainly exerted agency as they negotiated the labyrinth of family and marriage politics and the emotional turmoil surrounding illegitimacy. Allyson Poska's use of the term "domestic power" in relation to peasants in Galicia also applies to noblewomen in Castile, who had "some autonomy in key decisions concerning sexual relations, marriage, residence, divorce, and the lives of children."[15] That authority varied and specific circumstances could at times make it difficult for a woman to claim or exercise it.

ANXIETY, IDENTITY, AND THE ARRANGED MARRIAGE

Castilian nobles defined their identity through a lineage that they constructed by using strategic marriage alliances. Illegitimacy played a surprisingly constant role in developing the identity of a lineage over generations. Several noble houses proudly proclaimed their illegitimate descent from royalty. The first Duke of Medina de Rioseco traced his ancestry back to Alfonso Enríquez, the illegitimate son of an illegitimate son of Alfonso XI (1311–50), King of Castile, and his concubine Leonor de Guzmán. The Dukes of Arcos were descended from Aldonza Alonso, the illegitimate daughter of King Alonso IX (1188–1230) of León.[16] The Dukes of Híjar, who were from Aragón but married into the Castilian nobility, were descended from Pedro Fernández, illegitimate son of Jaime I (1208–76), King of Aragón.[17] Even a level below the great grandee families, nobility such as the Counts of Santisteban del Puerto (who ended up in Andalusia) could trace their ancestry back to an illegitimate son of Alfonso VII of León (1104?–57).[18]

Castilian noble families continued to marry illegitimate royal daughters from across the peninsula, shoring up their prestige, political connections, and finances with these advantageous marriages. In the late fourteenth century, the Admiral of Castile, Diego Hurtado de Mendoza, married María de Castilla, an illegitimate daughter of King Enrique II of Castile (1333–79).[19] The first Count of Niebla married María's half-sister, Beatriz de Castilla, also an illegitimate daughter of King Enrique II, who brought with her a magnificent dowry in 1374. King Enrique stood as godfather to their eldest son, his grandson and namesake, Enrique the second Count of Niebla.[20] The young Enrique grew to adulthood and in about 1420 took as his second wife Violante de Aragón, the illegitimate daughter of the King of Sicily. Violante brought little in the way of dowry except for her royal birth, but Enrique sought the political connection to the Aragonese royal family.[21] Likewise, the first Duke of Medinaceli married Ana de Navarra, an illegitimate daughter of the Infante Carlos, heir to the kingdoms of Navarre and Aragón, and in 1495 the first Duke of Frías married Juana de Aragón, illegitimate daughter of Ferdinand of Aragón (1452–1516), who brought with her a magnificent dowry of 20,000 doblas de oro.[22] In 1507 the third Duke of Gandía married another Juana de Aragón, the illegitimate daughter of the archbishop of Zaragoza, who was, in turn, the illegitimate son of Ferdinand of Aragón.[23]

Many noble families had illegitimacy in their ancestry even when it was not connected to any part of the royal family. Historian Miguel Ladero Quesada argued that noble origin stories, chivalrous biographies, and other late medieval and early modern chronicles "established a model of a knight, poor because of his illegitimate origin, who mounts to the top of the nobility thanks to his bravery, to the wealth obtained in war, to his blood, and, in a later age, to his political capacity."[24] The subjects of Ladero Quesada's research, the Dukes of Medina Sidonia, descended from the legendary "Guzmán el Bueno," an illegitimate son born in 1256 to a royal appellate judge of Castile under Alfonso X (1221–84).[25] The Counts of Oropesa traced their lineage back to an illegitimate son (hijo natural) of García Álvarez de Toledo (d. 1370), master of the Order of Santiago, while the Dukes of Osuna were descended from the illegitimate son of Pedro Girón, master of the Order of Calatrava, who died in 1466.[26] As we have seen throughout this book, after noble titles were established illegitimate children continued to serve as heirs, mending broken links in generations where the eldest son either failed to materialize or died prematurely. The second Duke of Medina Sidonia (d. 1492) was an illegitimate son, as were the third Count of Arcos (d. 1492), the third Count of Castañeda (d. 1506), and the second Duke of Medinaceli (d. 1544).[27]

Illegitimacy was common, a persistent theme in the noble family and an entirely predictable result of a rigid system of arranged marriages, but it was not without consequences for property and for people. The arranged marriage was a key piece of noble family strategy, designed to advance the lineage by extending the property and maintaining the social and political power of the family through its personal connections.[28] In 1696 the genealogist Luis de Salazar y Castro, eulogizing the Lara family, announced proudly, "Nothing is such an explicit sign of the degree of authority of a family as the class of their marriage alliances." He then went on to list two pages of marriage alliances between daughters of the house of Lara and the royal families of Castile, Aragón, Navarre, and Portugal.[29] Precisely because of its importance, marriage was also a focus of anxiety among the nobility, who tended to ignore human emotion when structuring marriages and families.[30] The nobility remained so focused on the well-being and consolidation of their property that they consistently practiced a tightly endogamous system in which they accepted uncle-niece and aunt-nephew marriages as well as marriages between first cousins and also arranged betrothals (and some marriages) for very young children. This practice resulted in marriages that Juan Hernández Franco described as "on the margins of what is permitted by the degrees of consanguinity" and increased the odds that a marriage would fail.[31] Ruy Gómez, Prince of Éboli, worried about the human implications of his own dynastic marriage. Married at age thirty-six to twelve-year-old Ana de Mendoza, with the consummation to be delayed until she was at least fourteen, he accompanied Philip II (1527–98) to England and Flanders while his bride remained in Spain. He wrote to the Duke of Alba, "They write me that my wife has grown up, but I have grown gray and I'm afraid that if we go on like this, I won't even be recognized at home."[32] This kind of anxiety must have attended many of these arranged marriages.

For the noble family, factors that assured dynastic succession such as primogeniture, the nature of the family entail (mayorazgo), and the well-being of the lineage were more important considerations when undertaking the arranging of a noble marriage than mutual attraction or affection between the couple. This was true not just in Castile but across Europe, where noble families fought for the power to arrange their children's marriages even though the Catholic Church did not require parental consent for a marriage to be valid.[33] Gloria Lora Serrano argued that in Castile, a noble marriage needed to "to lift [the couple] to a higher aristocratic circle, increase the political power of the lineage and of course augment the patrimony."[34] As discussed in the introduction, the Castilian nobility reinvented themselves under the Trastámara dynasty, and their systematic use of the arranged marriage and the practice of endogamy aided in their attempts to consolidate power and wealth.[35] Marriage was also an important and increasing financial investment (as previously noted, noble dowries rose dramatically over the fifteenth and sixteenth centuries).[36] Over the course of the fifteenth century the monarchy became progressively more involved in noble marriages by signing on to marriage capitulations and even choosing partners for heirs and heiresses whose marriages had important political implications for the entire realm.[37]

Exploring illegitimacy allows us a glimpse into the human side of the arranged marriage system that was so ruthlessly successful in gaining power for the Castilian nobility. Individual men and women paid an emotional price for their arranged marriages that can be glimpsed in the persistence of extramarital relationships and the nearly constant presence of illegitimate children and alternate families. The dissatisfaction of the people involved could also render an arranged marriage useless for dynastic purposes. All the marriages between noblemen and illegitimate daughters of kings that I cited above were dynastic failures (that is, they did not produce a surviving male heir) except for the fruitful union of the first Count of Niebla and Beatriz de Castilla. The Admiral of Castile and María de Castilla had a son who died in infancy and a daughter. It was not until after María's death that the admiral's second prestigious marriage (also a failure on human terms, as the couple lived mostly apart) produced a son and heir. The second Count of Niebla never lived with Violante de Aragón, his second wife, and tried to leave her in 1428 in favor of his long-term concubine Isabel Mosquera. The count and Violante had no children.[38] Neither did the first Duke of Medinaceli and Ana de Navarra. The estate of Medinaceli was inherited (amid a great deal of conflict) by the duke's illegitimate son with Catalina "of the gate" (del puerto), a nonnoble woman who had been a nurse in his household and who was also his concubine and eventually his third wife.[39] Finally, the first Duke of Frías and Juana de Aragón had a daughter, Juliana, who could not inherit the Frías entail because of her gender, but who was eventually married off to her first cousin, the third Duke of Frías, with whom she had no surviving children. The first Duke of Frías had at least four illegitimate children with two different women, and the third duke (his nephew and son-in-law) had three illegitimate sons.[40] The nobility's progress toward wealth, power, and stability was uneven at best, and creating space for less orthodox family arrangements gave them the flexibility they needed to cope with the tensions between an increasingly rigid system of patrilineal inheritance and incidents of premature death, human frailty, affection, and the potent factor of human sexuality.

Marriage among the nobility was traditionally arranged by parents and other relatives to cement relationships and negotiate the complicated finances of dowries.[41] These arrangements were so critical to the entire lineage and such a focus of noble anxiety that they sometimes took place even before the children who would fulfill them were born. During the Marquis de Villena's rise to power under Juan II of Castile (1405–64) in the late fifteenth century, he formed a marriage alliance with don Beltrán de la Cueva, the master of the Order of Santiago, designed to promote peace and unity between the nobility. In conjunction with the bishop of Calahorra and don Pedro de Velasco, the marquis and don Beltrán agreed that if don Beltrán's unborn child was a girl, she would marry the marquis's son Alonso and that if the child was a boy, he would marry one of the marquis's daughters. The dowry would be determined by the bishop of Calahorra and don Pedro de Velasco. The arrangement was part of the much larger shifting political currents that surrounded the royal court. It reflected parental anxiety about status and political influence and was predicated on the idea that the children involved would, of course, comply with the arrangement.[42] Just over a hundred years later, in 1594, don Enrique de Mendoza's anxiety about the future of his estate influenced his marriage plans for his daughter. Faced with the fact that, in the absence of sons, his daughter was going to inherit his estate, don Enrique's will stipulated that his daughter should marry "the person who appears most convenient for the conservation of my house and estates."[43] This statement makes it evident that noble marriage was designed to serve the lineage, not the particular individuals involved.

Noble culture put a heavy emphasis on children's obligations to obey their parents in all things, including marriage, equating obedience with a harmonious and loving family.[44] In 1560 Catherine de Médicis used emotional language to remind her daughter Elizabeth, the Queen of Spain, that Elizabeth should obey her mother's instructions "if you want me to be content with you and to love you, and to think that you love me as you should."[45] By the seventeenth century the French nobility was equating obedience to the family with obedience to the state and promoting "an ethos of self-sacrifice in service to the collective interest of the house, household, or lineage."[46] In sixteenth-century Castile the degree to which noble parents felt that they had the right to arrange their children's marriages can be seen in their fury when this role was denied them. Don Diego López Pacheco de Silva angered his parents by marrying doña María Dávalos without their permission. Even though María was noble and her status was equivalent to Diego's, his parents were so angry at not being consulted about this marriage that they disinherited Diego, who was the eldest son and the heir.[47] Diego left his parents' house and departed to make his fortune in the Indies, leaving María behind "in the charge of a dependent of his." She died soon after. In the Indies Diego fathered an illegitimate daughter before making a second marriage in 1531 to a Portuguese noblewoman, with whom he had five legitimate children. His parents were not mollified, and they transferred the inheritance of the estate of Villarejo to his younger brother Juan, who made a suitably arranged marriage with doña Gerónima de Mendoza. Juan and Gerónima had no legitimate children, although Juan did have an illegitimate daughter.[48]

The marriages in this family had been a catastrophic failure leading to disappointing results from a dynastic perspective. The second marriage of the disinherited eldest son produced a legitimate son, but the approved marriage of the second son produced no legitimate children and thus no heir for the estate. What to do? The second son, Juan, turned back to the arranged marriage, attempting to marry his illegitimate daughter to his brother's eldest son and thus pass the estate down through the bloodline. When his nephew refused to cooperate, Juan's daughter joined the Dominican convent of Madre de Dios in Toledo and became a nun, and Juan left the estate of Villarejo to his sister's eldest son.[49] Behind this story of disrupted inheritance, there is also a story of human passions and emotions. Diego was so passionate about marrying María that he rushed into the marriage without his parents' permission. Diego's parents were so angry about his first marriage, arranged without their consent, that they disinherited him (an unusual move in regard to an eldest son). In turn, Diego was so furious about being disinherited that he threatened his widowed mother, sued his younger brother who had inherited in his stead, and encouraged his eldest son to continue the lawsuit even after Diego had accepted a settlement of five thousand ducados de oro. Juan's peace offering of a marriage between his illegitimate daughter and his brother's legitimate son (which would have put the estate under Diego's son's control) was rejected in favor of continuing the quarrel. The legal dispute in this family dragged on for sixty years, involving two generations and finally ending in 1591.[50]

Marriage was a locus of anxiety for the Castilian nobility. They relied on it as a mechanism with which to advance their dynasties, but its failure or disruption could shatter their long-term plans, often leading to more violent emotions than anxiety.[51] In addition, they shared formal control over what marriage should look like and how it should be structured with the Catholic Church. The nobility and the church did not agree on either the purpose or the structure of marriage. In theory, the church privileged individual consent and saw marriage as a sacrament, thus making it indissoluble and permanent.[52] The nobility in Spain and across Europe saw it as more flexible, with an emphasis on parental consent.[53] This disagreement divided the two institutions, creating a situation in which, according to Rafael Sánchez Saus, "the moral standard emanating from the ecclesiastical authorities" existed in tandem with "the moral standard of the lineage, whose only apparent end [was] the obsession to ensure the endurance of that lineage and the preservation of the integrity of the goods received from the previous generation."[54]

Historian Miguel Ángel Ladero Quesada made a similar distinction between the moral logic and the socioeconomic logic of noble thinking. Morally, the nobility saw adultery as a sin, though one that could be compensated for through military service; as a matter of honor; and as an action that could damage a marriage. Socioeconomically, they saw adultery as problematic behavior that could impede good financial management, alienate wives whose skills and talents were needed to run the estate, and produce illegitimate children who might have claims on noble property and who needed to be raised and cared for at the expense of the noble estate.[55] The hardheaded way in which the nobility assessed the problems caused by adultery was focused, again, on the importance of dynastic succession in the context of the lineage as a whole. Another layer that complicated how early modern Castilians viewed adultery was the "language of desire" that was articulated both by the church and by writers of popular entertainments, which Linda A. Curcio-Nagy argued allowed individuals to "articulate their own ideas about their romantic and sexual feelings." In addition to the paradox between moral logic and socioeconomic logic, Curcio-Nagy highlighted a personal paradox: "A person could feel desire, engage in sexual relations, and view such emotions and actions as positive; yet, he or she could also worry about salvation and turn to the Church to repair any spiritual damage."[56]

The failure of an arranged marriage was thus an emotional event that could generate anxiety, fear, disappointment, and tension on multiple levels (spiritual, familial, personal), both for the family and for the couple involved. When reports reached Pope Alexander VI that his young son, Juan de Borja, had failed to consummate his marriage with María Enríquez, an Aragonese noblewoman, he expressed to his son that he was "discontented and indignant." Juan's older brother Cesar wrote that both he and his father were "consumed by melancholy" because of Juan's bad behavior. Alex Mizumoto-Gitter analyzed Juan's marriage troubles as threatening to disrupt a family networking strategy in which "power flowed multidirectionally through interpersonal connections" and the ultimate goal was "the creation of a familial dynasty, one that was very capable of spanning other territories."[57] Juan's failure to consummate his marriage threatened the dynastic succession that his father and older brother were counting on him to perpetuate and, by their own account, generated the negative emotions of discontent, indignation, and even melancholy.[58]

In another example of the difficulties of dynastic marriage, the emotional burden fell on the wife who was credited with spiritual distress because of the failure of her marriage. Doña Mencía de Guevara, Lady of Osorno, became engaged to the second Count of Castañeda in 1422, but the couple was unable to consummate their marriage and were obliged to separate. In 1432 Mencía contracted a second marriage with the Count of Castañeda's younger brother. Her mother objected because of the earlier engagement, but the second marriage was celebrated and consummated anyway for dynastic reasons. Marriage to Mencía (who brought with her the estate of Osorno) enabled her husband, a younger son, to eventually become the first Count of Osorno. By 1451, however, Mencía had given birth to and lost two sons. In her grief she decided that God was punishing her for the irregularities of her second marriage. According to Salazar y Castro, the seventeenth-century genealogist, Mencía was "frightened of the danger to her conscience and persuaded that her offspring would not live in punishment for the sin she had committed."[59] She persuaded her husband to apply for an annulment, which was granted on the grounds that the first engagement rendered the second marriage invalid (and thus Mencía's children illegitimate). Mencía's first marriage had remained in that socially liminal state of an engagement (palabras de futuro) that the nobility could conveniently ignore when it suited them, and it was not allowed to stop her second marriage. But when the second marriage did not produce a living heir, it was judged a failure, and for the sake of the lineage needed to end. Mencía's previously ignored first marriage was now conveniently remembered, and her second marriage was annulled. Mencía ceded her rights to the town of Osorno (part of the basis of her husband's title) to her ex-husband and took vows in the monastery of Amusco, which subsequently became El Real Monasterio de Nuestra Señora de la Consolación in Calabazanos, a convent of the Franciscan Poor Clares. The Count of Osorno remarried and fathered two sons and four daughters, all of whom lived to adulthood, and the line of the Counts of Osorno continued.[60]

This story illustrates how convenient it was for the noble lineage, which needed a live son and heir, to treat marriage more flexibly than the church would have liked. It also presents a series of events with potential emotional connotations that are very hard to trace. After twenty years of marriage and probably more failed pregnancies than are recounted in the genealogy's record of two sons who "died at a tender age," Mencía was reported to be frightened of the sin on her conscience.[61] We can deduce grief, pain, and moral uncertainty or fear in this situation. But it was also extremely convenient for her husband's ambitions that Mencía should have a crisis of conscience, designate her husband as her universal heir, legally dissolve their marriage, and retire unobtrusively to a monastery. This allowed him to skip the complications of illegitimacy, marry again, and produce a legitimate heir. Was Mencía truly frightened of the sin on her conscience? Was she tired of being married? Was she weary of the continuous pregnancies and saddened by the deaths of her two little boys? Did she consider them illegitimate and blame herself for the irregularities of her marriage? How did she feel about her spouse? Was the monastery a refuge or a prison for her in these circumstances?

There are complex emotions in this story of three different marriages, but they are hard to uncover or to understand accurately. Women's anxieties about their moral choices could be acute. An unusually poignant lament of a woman who was anxious about her own moral standing and the future of her children is captured in 1513 in the will of Inés de Mendoza y Delgadillo, an excellent example of the "accidental" documentation of an emotional state.[62] Inés de Mendoza y Delgadillo had four illegitimate children with the first Duke of Nájera. In her will she expressed her anxiety about the morally ambiguous position she found herself in as she lay dying. She reminded the duke that he had an obligation to her ("since I was a virgin in word, fact, and thought") and to their children ("because it is God's will that he [the duke] look after and provide for his children and mine as is just"). She went on to add, "The way I am faring, it is such a burden to me, as if I were in a room in chains."[63] The phrasing evokes the mental burden and the anxiety that were tormenting Inés as she composed her will and tried to protect her illegitimate children. The emotion in these phrases elucidates the burden that Mencía de Guevara might also have been carrying if she was genuinely tormented about the legal and moral status of her marriage and of her dead sons. Her crisis of conscience might have been both convenient and real.

Another side of the story of illegitimacy and adultery concerns unexpected families, some of them loving and affectionate, that sprang up in the shadows of the noble system of arranged marriages and absorbed some of the nobility's emotional energy. The duality of these families is an interesting illustration of Rosenwein's concept of emotional communities. Rosenwein argued that people move between multiple emotional communities and systems of feeling, adjusting their emotional displays and judgments as they go.[64] Noblemen with both marriages and extramarital relationships had multiple emotional communities (families) that they and sometimes their children traveled between. The dynamics of the different families could encompass a wide range of emotions and modes of behavior. The first Duke of Medina Sidonia had multiple contrasting emotional communities in his multiple families. All the duke's children were illegitimate, so his paternity was enacted entirely outside the bonds of marriage. The duke's official family life was undoubtedly difficult. He stated, "Against my will, I am and will remain apart from my wife and my married life." And thus, he admitted, because of "the weakness of the human flesh," he had "engendered" no fewer than eight illegitimate children with at least six different women. In words that connect back to the early modern ideas of paternity explored in chapter 1, the duke testified to the family that he had formed outside his marriage. He eloquently expressed the affection and love that could form in these complex families in the mayorazgo that he formed for his illegitimate son Enrique, stating, "To love and cherish intensely one's descendants is the most natural inclination, innate to all reasonable creatures, because wise men say that paternal love descends through our species and conquers all other love." The duke had cared for all his children in his home since their births and had been involved in their daily lives, and he attributed some of his intense paternal love to this fact: "It is because I have been near them that I love and cherish them."[65]

The duke's ideas about paternal love had a larger cultural resonance, echoing the *Siete Partidas*, which spoke of the "natural affection" that parents have for their children. The *Partidas* added that a father's natural affection for his child "increases much more by reason of the nurture which he affords it."[66] Silvia Nora Arroñada's study of noblemen and their children found, "The relationship between fathers and children was warm and close: this can be seen most clearly in the expressions of affection with which children are mentioned in the chronicles, in the demonstrations of joy when children are born, and in the manifestations of sorrow in the face of their illness or death."[67] In the case of the first duke, his illegitimate children provided this emotional satisfaction.

Women could also find fulfillment in parenting children whom they bore outside of a legal marriage. In January of 1592 doña Juana Manrique de Lara left her post as lady-in-waiting to Princess Isabel Clara Eugenia, daughter of Philip II, to marry don Manrique de Lara, the Count of Valencia. It was an advantageous marriage from a practical point of view. Don Manrique was the eldest son of Juana's first cousin (and guardian) the fourth Duke of Nájera, and Juana was destined to be an heiress, although that may not have been obvious in 1592 when her only brother was still alive. By 1593 Juana was a widow, don Manrique having died of his various illnesses without being able to consummate their marriage. The young widow went back to the palace and her post until the princess left for Flanders, at which time Juana retired to her own estate. Juana never remarried, but she gradually developed a close relationship with don Francisco de Rojas, the married Marquis de Poza, with whom she had a daughter, María, in 1600.[68]

The affair, and the subsequent child, were kept as secret as possible. The drama was minimized. When María was old enough to leave her wet nurse, Juana, claiming her as a niece, brought the child into her home where she raised and cared for her. Juana arranged a prestigious marriage for María, who became the Countess of Monclova. Upon her father's death in 1605, young María was publicly recognized as his illegitimate daughter, but she was apparently unaware of her mother's identity until March of 1629, when Juana became gravely ill. Juana called María, María's legitimate half-sister Mariana, her confessor, Father Juan de la Puente, and a notary to her bedside. She formally recognized María as her daughter and that of the Marquis de Poza, asking all the witnesses not to reveal the secret publicly.[69]

An illegitimate child, María was nevertheless raised by her own mother in comfort and luxury and given a secure future with a prestigious marriage. After the discovery of her identity, she maintained close ties with the mother who had raised her. Juana appears in this story as a widow with a carefully managed private pregnancy who was able to be a mother and then a grandmother in spite of having only a brief, unconsummated marriage.[70] Her will, written in 1630, left her daughter as an executor and as her universal heir while still claiming her as a niece. On a more personal note, Juana left María a silver flask and a walnut prayer desk, and she stated that María's children, Luis, Francisca, and Juana, should each receive a desk or a chest from among her possessions. Finally, she left her granddaughter Catalina (a lady-in-waiting to Queen Isabel) a farm.[71] Her bequests were substantial yet also personal markers of the affectionate relationships that were an important part of her family.

María's illegitimacy caused her some legal problems. Her mother had to secretly procure two dispensations from the pope to enable María's marriage to take place legally because of consanguinity issues, and María's claim to her mother's goods was promptly challenged in a series of lawsuits with the extended Manrique family. Apart from these difficulties, however, this story is one of an apparently loving family with close ties in spite of the lack of legitimacy. María knew and was recognized by her half-sister Mariana, who inherited their father's title, and she and her children had a strong relationship with her mother, who remembered them lovingly in her will. The family formed by Juana, the Marquis de Poza, and their illegitimate daughter María was never an official family, but it did have bonds of love and affection as well as the shared property interests that marked most noble families. Like official families, this unconventional family unit gradually evolved so that it eventually included the Marquis de Poza's older, legitimate daughter Mariana as well as María's husband and nine children.[72]

Although many noblemen simply indulged in casual liaisons, others developed stable family units which, although irregular, fulfilled the human need for continuity and affection that was so often unfulfilled in the arranged marriage. Enrique de Guzmán, the second Count of Niebla, married Teresa de Orozco, the daughter of the master of Santiago. The match "was the fruit of the political alliances that the Count Juan Alfonso [his father] had been arranging for some years," although the family chronicler went to some pains to describe it as a love match in which Enrique entertained the royal court by his pursuit of Teresa.[73] The couple had two children, and after Teresa's death (in about 1420), Queen María of Aragón (1403–45) stepped in to arrange a second marriage for Enrique, with Violante de Aragón, the illegitimate daughter of the King of Sicily. This second marriage seems to have been an abject failure, with Enrique neither treating his wife as she deserved because of her royal lineage nor living with her. The failure of Enrique's second arranged marriage occurred in part because Enrique (who had four illegitimate children) had already formed a stable liaison with Isabel Mosquera, mother to two of those children. In 1418 he made a public declaration of his concubinage with Isabel and recognized their two sons, Fadrique and Alonso.[74] By 1428 he went so far as to attempt to annul his marriage to Violante in order to marry Isabel.[75]

According to Miguel Ladero Quesada, the reason Enrique married Violante de Aragón was "to connect the count to the former royal family of Aragón." This political expediency did not translate into a meaningful personal relationship.[76] Unfortunately for the nobility's assumptions about the dynastic effectiveness of arranged marriages, the two individuals involved had to get along well enough to produce a child (preferably a son) or the marriage failed in its ultimate purpose. In this case Enrique had built a stable family, but it was with the wrong woman. His relationship with Isabel Mosquera lasted at least ten years (from the public declaration of their concubinage in 1418 to his attempt to marry her in 1428) and produced two male children. Enrique's attempt to regularize that relationship and recognize that family in 1428 indicates his value for his partner and children. He had a legitimate son from his first marriage who inherited his title and extended the lineage into the future, so his value for Isabel and their illegitimate sons seems to have been an affective one. Enrique's most meaningful relationship later in his life was with his concubine and their illegitimate sons, the stable family whom he apparently loved.

Although Enrique seems to have valued and loved his concubine Isabel Mosquera and their two children, it is almost impossible to discover Isabel's side of the story. This is an example of the difficulty of uncovering the degree of coercion, agency, or choice exercised by or upon women involved in extramarital relationships. There are factors that suggest a potential for stable affection, including the length of the relationship and the status of the woman involved. As we saw with doña Juana Manrique de Lara above, wealthy noble widows had more freedom than married women, although they also might incur the wrath of their noble relatives when they made choices that interfered with inheritance and succession. Widows with limited economic resources had fewer choices. For example, Vincenza Spinello was a widow when she began a relationship with Pedro Álvarez de Toledo, Marquis de Villafranca. The couple lived together for about a decade and were married shortly before Pedro's death in 1553.[77] The length of the relationship and the fact that it ended in marriage suggest affection and stability, as it seems likely that Vincenza and Pedro's relationship began in Naples (where Pedro was the viceroy) after the death of Pedro's wife in 1539. The affair might have provided both the widow and the widower with companionship and support, but it is impossible to know the emotional dynamics or what role economic necessity played in Vincenza's choices.

On the other hand, doña Margarita Manuel was the daughter of the Count of Montealegre, the widow of the fifth Lord of Mejorada, and the guardian of her two sons from her first marriage when she had sexual relations and two children with don Álvaro de Luna. Álvaro de Luna provided for both their illegitimate children, founding mayorazgos for them in 1440.[78] It seems probable that as a noblewoman in her own right, the widow of a nobleman, and a guardian, Margarita had sufficient economic resources and might thus have had the luxury of entering into a long-term sexual relationship to find love or companionship, but again we cannot really know. The ambiguity facing historians trying to understand women's choices and the limits on them is highlighted by María Pilar Manero Sorolla's analysis of the sexual relations between Luisa de la

Cerda (d. 1596) and the Prince of Mélito. Their liaison produced an illegitimate daughter but did not prevent Luisa from making a good marriage to someone else several years later. Manero Sorolla wrote, "This liaison could be interpreted as a sign of the power and freedom of a highborn lady such as Luisa. Closer examination of the stage of life in which the event occurred, however, reveals a disparity between the powerful position of her lover and her own youth and status as an orphan."[79] The degree of choice exercised by women was affected by their age, marital status, and command of economic resources, and must have had an important (although difficult to trace) impact on their feelings and the emotional repercussions of the extramarital relationship.

The issue of women's agency is an important reason for approaching the analysis of relatively stable concubinous families with caution. As discussed in chapters 1 and 2, Catalina de Ribera was the long-term concubine and then the second wife of the second Count of Castañeda, with whom she had four children. The couple were together for at least thirty years. Catalina's liaison with the count began, however, when he kidnapped her in the town of Tordehumos to prevent her marrying someone else and sequestered her in his fortress of Villalumbroso, where their four children were born.[80] Catalina might have been passionately in love with the second Count of Castañeda and happy to be rescued from an unwanted arranged marriage, or she might have made the best of the circumstances she found herself in and created a new life with the count because she had to. Whether or not she wanted to be kidnapped must have made an emotional difference to the life of this family, which was certainly durable and might have been loving.

Noblemen's power is perhaps most obvious in situations like Catalina's, where the count could not only kidnap her but also had a fortress handy to keep her in. In an example that more clearly illustrates the difficult choices women might have faced, doña Mencía de Lemos, the widow of a Portuguese nobleman and a lady-in-waiting to Queen Juana of Castile (wife of Enrique IV) was also stowed away in a castle. When the nobility rebelled against Enrique IV in favor of his half-brother Alfonso in 1465 and Queen Juana was given as a hostage to the nobility, her ladies-in-waiting found themselves in an awkward situation.[81] In the flirtatious atmosphere of Juana's court, Mencía had been the object of the amorous bishop of Calahorra's admiration, but she had apparently not rewarded him in spite of costly gifts and anguished poetry. The bishop wailed:

Where service [of love] suffers hardship,
and disservice love,
the greatest who fails to serve,
enjoys the best life.

But it was not until the court dissolved and he found Mencía alone and defenseless that he was able to carry her off to his brother's castle in Manzanares, where the couple subsequently had two children.[82] Although Mencía and the bishop were together for almost a decade, the story implies that Mencía might have made other choices if the bishop had not come upon her at a vulnerable moment, and the relationship did not last. The bishop (now Cardinal Mendoza of Spain) provided generously for Mencía and their sons, but by 1476 he was involved with a different young woman, Inés de Tovar, with whom he had a third son. Mencía lived until 1536, remarried, and is buried in Toledo, suggesting that she might have lived in that city after her sojourn in Manzanares.[83]

Although men's emotional attachments to their concubines are also elusive, they at least exercised more clearly discernible choices. It was not uncommon for noblemen to have multiple families rather than (or sometimes in addition to) short-term sexual relationships. Fernán Dalvarez de Meneses married Catalina de Herrera sometime after the death of his first wife in 1497. The couple already had four children at the time of their marriage, suggesting a long-term, stable family.[84] Likewise, don Pedro Manuel appears to have sought female companionship after the death of his wife in 1458, the evidence being the existence of four illegitimate children who appeared in his will in 1469 in addition to his three legitimate daughters. In this case no information at all is available about the children's mother.[85] The sheer length of some of these relationships is telling. The Count of Castañeda had a fifty-year marriage to Mencía Enríquez as well as a thirty-year concubinage with Catalina after he kidnapped her.[86] His marriage was sterile but his relationship to Catalina ensured his succession by producing four children. He also married Catalina as soon as Mencía died, obtaining three separate legitimations for their children, the eldest of whom inherited his title.[87]

In spite of Mencía's vigorous efforts to prevent the count's relationship with Catalina, the count's two families coexisted over many years and intertwined at least once in a moment of crisis. The count and Mencía were married in 1430, and by 1453 the count was applying to King Juan II of Castile to legitimize his children with Catalina. In 1456 the count was taken prisoner by the Muslims of Granada and held for ransom. His wife, Mencía, raised the money to free him by selling her own jewelry and mortgaging several properties. After seventeen months in captivity the count was able to return to Castile by paying about half of the demanded ransom and leaving his eldest son with his concubine Catalina hostage in his place.[88] Isabel Beceiro Pita and Ricardo Córdoba de la Llave argued that the stable families that existed "on the margin of marriage, although they could include physical pleasure, sexual attraction, and love, were also influenced by the social and mental habits of the Castilian aristocracy for whom the maintaining of lovers was as usual and normal as having a legitimate spouse."[89] The Count of Castañeda's two families illustrate this point of view, as he drew on resources from both families (his wife's money and his concubine's son) when he needed rescuing. This story also suggests the complex array of emotions that these noble families could include, encompassing the stability and probable affection of his long-term relationship with Catalina and their children, the active jealousy of his wife Mencía when she tried to end that relationship, and the later loyalty and cooperation of that same wife when he needed ransoming.

LUST, ADULTERY, JEALOUSY, AND RAGE

As convenient as illegitimate children may have been as means of extending the power and influence of the noble family, and as important, valued, and stable as some of these extramarital families were, adultery and illegitimacy caused endless emotional, moral, and economic complications in the noble family. Chapter 4 explored some of the economic complications caused by illegitimate children's claims on inheritance and the long, drawn-out lawsuits that were typical of the early modern period. Adultery and illegitimacy also had emotional implications for the people involved. A persistent double standard meant that noblemen did not often feel bound by their marriage vows to fidelity to their wives. Neither were they restricted by Catholic ideas of morality or even religious vows from claiming a right to sexual access to other women, especially those below them in rank, and there was no social stigma attached to male extramarital liaisons. The term "adultery" (*adulterio*) was solely used to describe the extramarital relationships of married women. The affairs of married men were described as concubinage (*amancebado*) and added to their masculinity by demonstrating virility and sexual prowess.[90] Salazar y Castro, the seventeenth-century genealogist, said admiringly of the first Duke of Nájera (d. 1515): "He loved women very much, and was so fortunate in his offspring, that he arrived at the hour of his death with twenty-seven children of both sexes."[91]

The same author also commented on the virility of Cardinal Alonso Manrique (d. 1538), who flagrantly disregarded his vows of celibacy, stating, "In the greenness of his young and most robust age, the Cardinal was not so careful of his purity that he could free his spirit of a passionate liaison that produced three children."[92] This kind of lifestyle on the part of leading churchmen complicated the message that the church was trying to send to laypeople. Although ecclesiastical writers equated feelings of lust and sexual desire with spiritual danger,[93] church leaders (who were usually also noblemen) displayed a mindset closer to that of the nobility themselves. A common response was that of the bishop of Mondoñedo, who in 1527 wrote a letter to don Francisco Manrique (who was married to the bishop's niece), calling him to order. The letter, which began, "very magnificent knight and very naughty boy," scolded don Francisco for forcing his wife, doña Teresa de Bazan, to endure "the irritations that don Francisco caused with his amorous diversions."[94] In spite of his active intervention, the bishop's tone was light and there is no further indication of punishment of don Francisco.

At the same time, the nobility's concern for the welfare of the lineage meant that they expected men to conduct their extramarital relationships in such a way as to inflict minimal damage on their marriages (and thus the lineage), and they had an unwritten expectation that men would support and provide for their illegitimate children. When adultery and the ensuing illegitimacy caused severe problems in noble marriages, the monarchy or other males in the family might intervene. In truly egregious cases, noblemen could be imprisoned for adultery or bad management, two problems that were often conflated by the nobility and the monarchy. In 1491 don Diego Gómez de Sandoval, son of the Count of Denia, was imprisoned by Ferdinand and Isabel "because of his excesses and bad government." Diego's will, written just before he died of an illness while incarcerated in the fortress of the Pardo, recognized five illegitimate children, all of whom were classified as hijos bastardos, meaning that they had been born during his marriage.[95]

Diego would not have been imprisoned simply for having five children out of wedlock. It took excesses and bad government in addition to marital infidelity to create a situation severe enough for the monarchs to intervene. In 1531 don Pedro de Luna, the third of Lord of Fuentidueña, was disciplined in the royal court by his peers, his brother (captain of the royal guard), and the Count of Miranda. At issue was both don Pedro de Luna's behavior toward his wife, doña Aldonza, and his management of a lawsuit that he was conducting with the Count of Santisteban. Don Pedro de Luna's sentence tells a story of illegitimacy but also of spousal abuse and neglect. He was told to treat doña Aldonza as her rank deserved, giving her liberty to come and go as her health demanded, and to provide her with the economic support she was entitled to. Furthermore, he was to give up concubines and "women who damaged his conscience." Any future maids hired in his house had to be preapproved by doña Aldonza. His two illegitimate sons were clearly the least of his offenses. The penalties threatened if he did not reform were severe, including serving a year in Oran, Algeria (with the Spanish army fighting against the Turks), for the first offense with two years of additional service possible for a second offense.[96]

Don Pedro de Luna's affairs might have passed unnoticed except for his abuse of his wife, which led to the perception that his house was not in order.[97] In spite of the potential severity of his sentence, don Pedro de Luna does not seem to have served any time in Oran. In the later sixteenth century, however, don Pedro Girón, the third Duke of Osuna, was exiled and imprisoned by the Council of Castile for his excessive affairs with women. By 1620 his career as viceroy of Naples ended abruptly and he was sent home in disgrace because of his "intense erotic activity."[98] Scandalous and highly public sexual relationships with at least eight different women, some of whom were actresses and at least one of whom was married, pushed the tolerance of the Spanish monarchy to the limit.[99] Unhappy marriages had emotional implications, and the concept of the *mala vida* was used in colonial Mexico to "refer to a persistent and miserable state of marital discord," something that Jacqueline Holler analyzed as "honor[ing] the notion of happiness in the breach."[100]

Cases in which noblemen were formally punished for adultery were rare, but they leave evidence of the damage that noble affairs could do to family relationships and the variety of ways in which noblewomen reacted to male adultery. The accusations against don Pedro de Luna in 1531 shed some light on the nature of his long marriage. Doña Aldonza's life as a wife was a difficult one. She endured thirty-six years of marriage and had five children with a man who restricted her liberties, conducted multiple public extramarital liaisons, had two children with another woman during their marriage, did not provide her with adequate economic support or access to health care, and refused to pay their daughters' convent dowries. Even the intervention of her brother-in-law and the Count of Miranda, which was meant to help her gain her rights, must have been humiliatingly public, making her and her marriage the subject of gossip throughout the court and the nobility. Yet, in testimony to the awkward economic bonds that often connected feuding noble spouses, don Pedro de Luna seems to have trusted Aldonza to look after his interests, as he left her as one of the executors of his will in 1542.[101] It was technically possible to get a divorce in Castile when a marriage was abusive, but it rarely happened.[102] Rosa María Montero Tejada found no divorces in her study of the extensive Manrique family (which included the titles of Duke of Nájera and Counts of Osorno, Castañeda, and Paredes, among many others).[103] In this case Aldonza was the daughter of the second Count of Osorno, and she had two illegitimate half-brothers as well as two illegitimate nephews. Although none of them were the products of adultery, illegitimacy was common in these noble families.[104] Don Pedro was exposed to the censure of his peers when the presence of his illegitimate children was combined with the neglect of his legitimate family, his flagrant adultery, and his abuse of his wife. The breakdown of this family allows us a glimpse into the emotional complications that adultery and illegitimacy sometimes created within noble marriages.

Doña Aldonza's difficulties were not unique. The third Duke of Osuna's wife, doña Catalina Enríquez de Ribera, daughter of the second Duke of Alcalá and granddaughter of Hernán Cortés, also dealt with a difficult marriage and her husband's public adultery. Doña Catalina was able to assert her own position and authority when dealing with her erring husband, defending him publicly and taking a high hand with the exasperated king, Philip IV. In 1596 during the early years of their marriage Catalina instituted a judicial process against the duke's current concubine, accusing Jerónima de Salcedo (in addition to Jerónima's husband and father) of concubinage, procurement, and complaisance.[105] After that intervention, however, she seems to have stepped back from direct confrontation, responding to the duke's repeated and flagrant infidelities by developing her own role as the manager of the Osuna estates during his absence in Flanders and as a patroness of the arts. In 1600 Cristóbal González de Perales dedicated his study of the life of St. Bernard of Clairvaux to Catalina. When the duke was appointed as viceroy to Sicily, Catalina, as his duchess, accompanied him to Italy and, continuing her interest in the arts, served as a highly effective vicereine. Her loyalty to the Osuna interests kept her in Italy when the duke was recalled in disgrace, thus impeding the new viceroy's access to the viceregal seat. When recalled by the king herself in 1621, she ensured that the couple's rich acquisitions during their years in Italy were preserved and transported, and she haughtily informed the king, "It is not possible that the duke could alone be guilty of these [numerous extramarital relationships he was accused of], since I am also and without doubt committed in them, as the one who has been living with him the whole time."[106] By 1623 Catalina was living in Madrid with "all of her children," a household that included her two legitimate children and the duke's four illegitimate children, a deliberate public stance that once again supported her husband, in whose defense she sent a *Memorial* (a public written statement) to King Philip IV.[107]

Catalina's strategy highlighted her own identity and power as the daughter of a duke, the wife of a duke (however badly behaved), and the manager of a rich and powerful estate. She appears to have taken the high road emotionally, asserting herself as an individual and, in the words of the scholar Encarnación Sánchez García, reconstructing the role of tolerant wife "by the personality and elegance with which she defined her space as a vicereine and her official representation of that post."[108] Catalina and Aldonza's different responses to their husband's public infidelity reflect some of the variety of circumstances that could define women's power. Caught in a situation where she suffered from bad health and apparently did not have access to sufficient economic resources of her own, Aldonza had fewer options than Catalina when it came to dealing with the practical consequences of her husband's actions.

Male adultery was not the only way that noble marriages could be disrupted. In spite of higher social penalties for female adultery, noblewomen were not always faithful to their marriage vows nor were they always chaste as widows. According to historian Miguel Ángel Ladero Quesada, the high nobility could tolerate only one kind of female adultery or concubinage and that was with royalty. Even a liaison with a royal, however, had a cost, because it "augmented the quality of the lineage at the cost of the moral and personal discredit of the corresponding husband."[109] That basic principle (adultery that enhanced the lineage, though at a price) can also be seen when the lesser nobility tolerated female adultery with the grandees on whose patronage they depended. An example of this is María de Sandoval, who, while married to Ramiro Guzmán, had sexual relations with the Duke of Nájera. The duke, in turn, granted Ramiro rights to the estate and houses of Villajimena.[110] Outside of this formula, however, and even without the unrealistic drama of the wife-murder plays, women often paid a higher price for extramarital sexuality than men did, and noblemen were especially incensed when they perceived the sexual behavior of their female relatives as threatening their own reputation, property rights, or lineage. The fear of this reaction created difficult choices for adulterous women. Doña María de Ribera, for instance, surrendered custody of her illegitimate baby daughter Magdalena, conceived and born in 1504 while her husband was out of town, first to her sister and then to the convent of Santo Domingo el Real in Toledo, where Magdalena spent the rest of her life.[111]

It was difficult, however, to completely ostracize powerful noblewomen who had property rights of their own (especially if they were widows) when their behavior did not meet the approval of their male relatives. A particularly dramatic example is that of María de Sandoval, the thirty-eight-year-old widowed Countess of Treviño, who was left as guardian of her five children after her husband's death in 1458.[112] Her husband's powerful brothers contested the guardianship and tried to take their nephew's considerable property into their own hands. Afraid that she would lose the guardianship and control of her children's estate, María called in her two brothers to help defend the town of Amusco, where she and her children were besieged.[113] One of the noblemen who came to help in the defense was Diego López de Stúñiga, the Count of Miranda, who, in the process of rescuing María, also became her lover. When María's teenage son, the new Count of Treviño, discovered that his widowed mother was living in sin with the Count of Miranda, he was angry. Anger, one of the seven deadly sins, was considered a "spiritual" problem connected to the soul, a "poison of the heart." By the fifteenth century, however, Renaissance scholars in Castile and across Europe were recognizing factors that could lessen the vice of anger, including the difficulty in controlling one's impulses. Fray Luis de Granada argued that displays of anger might be necessary to maintain public order and that social superiors might be justified in using anger to punish the words and deeds of those below them.[114]

In accordance with this interpretation of anger, the Count of Treviño applied for the king's permission and then stormed the castle where the couple was living to remove his mother by force.[115] After that attempt failed he began to systematically try to deprive her of some of her lands. His actions could be interpreted as efforts to restore order in his family and assert his control over his female relatives (both appropriately masculine goals and acceptable outcomes of male anger), but they did not meet with complete success. The Count of Miranda left his wife (with whom he had several adult children) and applied to have their marriage annulled on the grounds of consanguinity.[116] He apparently succeeded, because on

September 5, 1470, María and the Count of Miranda were married. She was fifty years old and he was close to seventy, and their relationship was of long standing by that time. Her son did not attend her wedding personally but did send his *alcalde mayor*, and the Count of Miranda's eldest son was present at the veiling, which took place the next day.[117]

How do we understand the emotions involved in this story? To apply a modern term, the marriage between María and the count rendered both their former families dysfunctional. There was no possibility of blending these two families in any conventional way. María and her son had a notoriously difficult relationship. "There still has not been in Castile a guardianship more disputed or vexatious," announced the genealogist Luis de Salazar y Castro.[118] Only three days after her wedding, María's son forced her to renounce a long list of her estates, and by August of 1479 María had ceded additional properties to her son.[119] María's love affair threatened her son's masculinity just at the moment when he was attempting to assert control over the house and lineage of Nájera. Her guardianship of the heir gave María much of the power and responsibility that the adolescent duke needed to claim in order to become an adult male.

The Count of Miranda's children were also incensed, angered by the insult to their mother and worried that their new stepmother would disrupt their inheritance because the annulment of their parents' marriage made them technically illegitimate.[120] The count's ex-wife lived until 1476, a lasting reminder of his former life. The count's eldest son (whose legitimacy was now in doubt) took his father, María, and María's daughters captive, killing the mayor of Aza in the scuffle and forcing them to renounce the estate of Miranda to him. At this point it seems that the nobility felt that anger had been allowed to go too far, for other nobles intervened and rescued the pair. The Count of Miranda indignantly revoked the renunciation and, in turn, waged war upon his son. Salazar y Castro concluded that long years of violent, armed dispute meant that "neither the count or the countess had thereafter one hour of peace."[121] Neither, it would seem, did any other member of their immediate families, all of whose lives had been upended by this liaison and the subsequent marriage. By 1479 María was widowed for a second time, signing herself "the *most* sad countess," on the documents that ceded her property to her son.[122] Her emphasis on her sorrow might also have carried a political connotation, signaling that she felt she was being badly treated.[123] By this time she was losing the battle with her eldest son, now the first Duke of Nájera. He took away her jewelry and imprisoned her first in the convent of Santa Ana de Amusco and then in his own house, until in 1491 she took vows in the convent of Santa María de Consolación de Calabazanos, where she remained until her death.[124] In his turn, the first Duke of Nájera created a family of byzantine complexity, fathering twenty-nine children (nine legitimate and twenty illegitimate).

The preserved documents mostly record the nobility's concern with assuring the smooth transmission of property, but the appetite of lust, the emotions of anger, jealousy, and fear, and the insult of wounded honor also swirl through this story.[125] Under all of that is the question of the nature of María's relationship with her second husband, the Count of Miranda. Was this couple's willingness to unleash chaos and break all acceptable social bonds an indication of love? Of lust? Of an abiding trust and affection? It is impossible to know exactly what their relationship was, but they took dramatic risks to achieve and maintain it. In spite of her troubles, María lived a long life, outliving both her husbands and joining a convent at age seventy-one. Another interesting question is how this emotional upheaval affected her son, who seems to have been as passionate and headstrong as she was herself. His own family structure was as unconventional but more peaceful than her own, in part because, though it was possible for women to break society's rules (as María demonstrated), it was simply easier for men to exploit the double standard.

Although this book has downplayed the importance of the famous Castilian honor codes in favor of a more nuanced examination of how men and women experienced ideas of honor and good reputation in their daily lives, honor was occasionally a direct factor in how noblemen viewed themselves, their wives, and their jurisdiction over their families. Perceived injuries to honor could escalate emotions like rage. The 1505 *Leyes de Toro* allowed for a man to kill his wife and her lover if he caught them in the act, and the 1567 *Nueva recopilación* law code stated that a man could kill both (but not just one of them) if he caught them in the act.[126] I found a handful of examples of men who murdered their wives because of suspected adultery, but rather than their peers justifying their actions, all of them faced severe legal consequences. This supports Sonya Lipsett-Rivera's claim that in the early modern world jealousy was "not a socially acceptable emotion" and needed to be controlled.[127] In 1436 don Diego Suárez Gómez de Sandoval reportedly carried out the murder of his wife on suspicion of adultery even though he was exiled in Aragón at the time. Don Diego sent his nephew and a group of retainers to the convent where his wife was staying to suffocate her in her bed.[128] Another such violent incident occurred in the late fifteenth century, when Gonçalo Muñoz de Castañeda caught the aptly named don Juan Manrique with Gonçalo's wife, Isabel de Silva. Gonçalo reportedly killed both of them on the spot, an action that exactly mirrored the plot lines of the wife-murder plays. Although this murder adhered to the literary version of the honor codes that demanded murderous revenge as the only solution to damaged honor, it was not well received by Gonçalo's peers, and Gonçalo was exiled to Portugal as a result of his actions. By 1696, when the incident was recorded by Luis de Salazar y Castro, the genealogist remarked rather dubiously that the story "strain[ed] . . . credulity."[129]

In a similar case study, the eighteenth-century genealogist Diego Gutiérrez Coronel reported that don Francisco de Silva killed his wife, doña Catalina Dávila y Mendoza, on "imprudent and vain suspicions about her conjugal purity."[130] Condemned to death, don Francisco fled to Valencia, and the courts decided that his estate was to be put in trust for his daughter. He died in exile without regaining his property. Ironically, his actions to defend his honor later caused inheritance problems for his son from a second marriage that he contracted while in exile. After his father's death, his son returned to Castile, where he had to sue his half-sister in order to inherit his father's Castilian estate. He won the lawsuit but later had to flee back to Valencia after he murdered a vassal on the estate. The violent actions of this father and son meant that they lost their Castilian lands permanently.[131] This brings the total number of men who murdered their wives on suspicion of adultery during the entire two hundred years covered by this study to four, and all of them faced consequences.

Moreover, although several of the women in this study who had children out of wedlock with noblemen had actually committed adultery, it is not clear that any of the four women who were killed had done so. Rather than endorsing the more violent parts of the honor code, fellow nobles (often the family of the murdered woman) objected to this method of redressing male honor, and the monarchy simply could not afford to allow the nobility to routinely take the law into their own hands, especially when murder was involved.[132]

Another reason that noblemen might not have opted for murder when noblewomen committed adultery was that they had other choices. The first Duke of Medina Sidonia, Juan de Guzmán, sued his wife, María, daughter of the Count of Medinaceli, for adultery. Married in 1434, the pair lived together "a little and badly" until their final separation 1448. In September 1448 the duke appeared before the municipal judge in the town of Huelva and accused María of having repeated affairs with many different men. He submitted documentation with witnesses who detailed the occasions of María's adultery, adding, "[She] always was and is a very dissolute and amorous woman."[133] María fled Huelva, passing through lands owned by the military order of Alcántara. She was further accused of having sex with the master of Alcántara, don Gutierre de Sotomayor, whom she had known since childhood. María's complete absence from the court proceedings led to her being declared rebellious, and by the end of May 1449 she was also declared guilty of adultery and condemned to the loss of all her goods, both those contained in her dowry and any others she owned. María was forced to take refuge in her brother's house and then, after his death, in her nephew's house, and her estranged husband retained all her property (which included her dowry of 30,000 florines de oro and the town and jurisdiction of Huelva) with the ability to pass it on to his heirs.[134]

From an emotional standpoint it seems clear that María and the duke disliked and maybe even hated each other. The sixteenth-century commentator Barrantes Maldonado recorded that the duke was intensely jealous of his wife.[135] It seems unlikely that María could possibly have received a fair trial when she was absent from the proceedings and had no chance to present her side of the story in a court and with a municipal judge who was subject to her angry husband's authority. As Ladero Quesada points out, however, the charge of adultery was a very serious one for a woman and the sentence was never appealed.[136] Instead of contesting the charge of adultery, María's nephew claimed that under her dowry contract, the estate of Huelva should return to the Medinaceli family if María and the duke had no legitimate heirs. María lived another twenty years under the protection of her own family, dying in 1468. After her death her dower property of Huelva became the subject of an intense dispute between her nephew and her estranged husband that encompassed a lawsuit, an armed standoff, and the intervention of King Enrique IV, which finally resulted in compensation for María's nephew and the incorporation of the town of Huelva into the entail of Medina Sidonia.[137]

The Duke of Medina Sidonia did not need to murder his wife (thus risking the wrath of the monarch and potential exile) to end his marriage and conduct his personal life to suit himself. He had a court system at his disposal. Whether he was jealous of María, simply disliked her from the start, or was badly treated by her, he could banish her from his home, accuse her of adultery, and confiscate her property. In the end, whatever may have happened to his honor, he gained a rich addition to his own estate, was able to have eleven children with at least six different women, and could leave one of his illegitimate sons as his heir.[138] The duke was, from all accounts, a violent man, perhaps in modern eyes even a sexual predator. As discussed in chapter 2, he destroyed his uncle's family, kidnapping his illegitimate first cousin and having two sons with her before she died at a young age.[139] He seems to have been more invested in having his own way than in any abstract idea of honor, and the court system that was under his jurisdiction could deliver a more certain victory than personal violence. María thus spent the next twenty years in exile and lost all her property, but she was not killed either by her husband or by her own male relatives, who took her in and provided for her.

Noblemen also used the language of honor to justify sexual violence. The few examples I have found where an idea of honor was cited by the nobility include aberrant sexual behavior by noblemen such as incest or predatory violence. Even in a society that granted noblemen almost unlimited sexual access to women, there were boundaries to what was considered accept-able sexual behavior. For example, don Fadrique de Castro, the Duke of Arjona, married Aldonza de Mendoza, eldest daughter of the Admiral of Castile, Diego Hurtado de Mendoza, in 1405. The marriage was a troubled one. The couple had no children and Fadrique was both abusive toward Aldonza and a notorious womanizer, in part, at least, because he ardently desired a male heir.[140] Contemporary sources report that Fadrique was also in love with his illegitimate half-sister Constanza, reportedly killing a bear in order to impress her. When Constanza married Diego Dávalos in 1423, a spiral of violence erupted. On her wedding night, rather than consummating her marriage with her husband, Constanza reported, "the duke, her brother, had had her instead."[141] Diego was so incensed by this flagrant violation of his honor that he broke off all communication with his wife, and waiting until Fadrique's wife Aldonza was traveling in León, waylaid and raped her as a revenge. According to the sixteenth-century text that reported the incident, Diego stated that because Fadrique had given him grave affront by raping his wife, he (Diego) had no other option than to rape Fadrique's wife.[142] The language of honor employed in the text makes no mention of the incest committed when Fadrique raped his half-sister.

Here is the honor code employed with a vengeance, playing out in a scenario where women are perceived as passive objects, the carriers of their husband's honor, doomed to suffer for any violation of that honor even if they are vulnerable and innocent. In spite of the horrific sexual violence in this story, however, neither Aldonza nor Constanza died and the men involved faced severe legal consequences. By 1429 Fadrique's numerous offenses and repeated violence had caught up with him, and Juan II ordered him imprisoned and his belongings confiscated.[143] Diego died soon after raping Aldonza, but his actions played a role in the subsequent exile of his father, the Constable Ruy López Dávalos because, in the words of Fernán Pérez de Guzmán, writing in 1517, "the countess was the wife of a great lord and related by marriage to the monarchs."[144] These words emphasize the importance of social status in determining the punishments for sexual violence. Noblemen's sexual access to women of lower social status was not considered rape by their contemporaries and did not merit exile as a punishment, in part because lower-status families were not powerful enough to pursue legal or political vengeance against these men.

The story of the women involved encompasses pain, abuse, frustration, and sorrow, but is ultimately one of determined survival rather than passivity. Constanza retreated to the monastery of San Domingo Real in Toledo, where she stayed until Fadrique's death in prison in 1430.[145] At this point she emerged and married Pedro Álvaro Osorio, Lord of Cabrera y Rivera, who, ironically, had been Fadrique's *mayordomo*.[146] Before Fadrique's death, Aldonza continued to suffer physical abuse at his hands. He forced her to travel to Galicia, where he imprisoned her in the fortress of Ponferrada, and took control of her property. Of all her numerous, high-ranking family, only her aunt, Juana de Mendoza, and her aunt's second husband tried (unsuccessfully) to intervene to protect her. After Fadrique's death in 1430, however, the widowed Aldonza sued for possession of Ponferrada, the fortress where Fadrique had imprisoned her.[147] Not content to leave the lawsuit to the lawyers, Aldonza mounted a loud and vigorous public campaign that reminded the court and her peers of her status as the granddaughter of a king, claimed her rights to her dowry and *arras* (the bride's portion paid by the groom at the time of marriage), and detailed the abuses she had endured at Fadrique's hands. She won her lawsuit and lived until 1435. Aldonza's life encompassed abuse, sexual violence, and neglect, but she was also a proud, quarrelsome, brave woman who was a noted patron of the Hieronymites and a thorn in the side of her stepmother and half-siblings after the death of her father.[148]

GRIEF AND MOURNING

The story of the double rape of Constanza and Aldonza, compounded as it was by incest and the long history of Aldonza's troubled and abusive marriage, shows the darkest side of the noble family and uncovers some of the violence, disruption, and dramatic emotional consequences of adultery and illegitimacy. Another more subtle emotion that can be found in the background of many of these family dramas is grief. The stories of illegitimate children are not just about an anxious preoccupation with lineage, succession, property, and honor. They also reveal how the late medieval and early modern family was torn apart by death and rebuilt in ways that created complex family structures. From 17 to 20 percent of Castilian households in the sixteenth century had children from at least one previous marriage that had ended in the death of one spouse, in addition to illegitimate children from extramarital relationships.[149] This was complicated by the reality that the extramarital relationships could be ongoing or have ended in separation of the partners or the death of one parent. Death, remarriage, and extramarital relationships made for complex households, as covered in chapter 3, but it also meant that children and parents alike often experienced grief and loss as their families evolved.

To return to the Pacheco family, whose eldest son, as mentioned above, married without permission, a closer look at Diego Pacheco's tumultuous marital career reveals another side of the passionate, angry, disinherited eldest son. Before Diego's first marriage, which had been so unwelcome to his parents, he had considered himself engaged to Inés de la Parra, an honorable woman from the city of Toledo, with whom he had a daughter. It is not clear what happened to Inés, but it seems likely that she died in childbirth before the couple could finalize their marriage, as Diego treated this daughter, Ana de Silva, "as though she was legitimate," a phrase that suggests both affection and respect.[150] This couple adhered to the social understanding of marriage that accepted it as a multistage institution, but Inés's untimely death interrupted their plans. Although it cannot be documented, it is possible that Diego experienced grief after Inés's death, and the life course of his family encompassed much human loss. Diego was estranged from his parents and brother and he had survived the loss of his fiancée and his first wife, leaving him to care for his motherless illegitimate daughter, Ana. He and his second wife, Felipa, lost two sons of their own at an early age. Their family life seems to have been disrupted, as their eldest son was born in Mexico but raised by his cousin the Duchess of Medinaceli back in Spain, and they surrendered another daughter to the monastery of Madre de Dios in Toledo at the young age of two.[151] The grief that early modern parents felt over the deaths of children is well documented in both their own letters and chronicles and in a wealth of advice literature at the time designed to comfort grieving parents. In 1422 the writer Juan Fernández de Valera wrote to Enrique de Villena to console him over the deaths of family members from the plague, advising him not to grieve too passionately because his young daughter had been spared the pains and troubles of a long life in this world. Attempts to support grieving parents suggest that the relationship between many parents and children was both warm and close, and their grief subsequently heartfelt.[152]

Behind the façade of the entail, the hope for an orderly succession, and the dynastic concerns of the arranged marriage lay the tumult of human lives and emotions, disrupted by death and feuds. What is remarkable, perhaps, about this whole scenario is the nobility's reliance on the lineage as the symbol of their larger identity, something that (even more perhaps than their religion) would outlast the confusion of the moment. This vision can be seen most clearly when comparing the world constructed by the noble will with the reality of family life. Historian Juan Luis Carriazo Rubio described the noble will as an exercise in creating memory and lineage, "inscribing the testator in the collective memory of their heirs and beneficiaries,"[153] and it extended the lineage forward by creating and sustaining the mayorazgo or entail, which dictated future generations of inheritance. The first Duke of Arcos, facing death in the spring of 1530, included the formulaic language of the mayorazgo that was so common in noble wills. After his death his entailed property was to go to his eldest son, Luis Cristóbal, and after Luis Cristóbal the will stated: "*His* eldest son will have and inherit the goods of the entail, and in defect of a son, his eldest daughter." The entail would thus continue down the generations of heirs who were "legitimate and born of legitimate marriage, always preferring the male over the female." If, God forbid, his son died without heirs, the entail would go to his daughter and then to her descendants who were "legitimate and born of legitimate marriage, always preferring the male over the female."[154]

In the will, the sense of order is palpable and the succession straightforward. But of course, it did not really work that way. The first Duke of Arcos had used (as had all his ancestors and would all his successors) the notarial formula for the straightforward, male-dominated succession born of legitimate marriage that they wished were true. In reality the first Duke of Arcos was descended from an illegitimate daughter of the Marquis of Cádiz, who was himself an illegitimate son of the second Count of Arcos.

Moreover, the first Duke of Arcos had been married four times, had already lost a daughter, had an illegitimate son of his own, and was leaving his title and extensive estates to a boy not yet two years old whose mother had died giving birth to him. Set in that context, the first duke's will reads less like a confirmation of an orderly patriarchy and more like a desperate attempt to finally get on with the business of establishing a secure lineage.

The first Duke of Arcos, did, after all, succeed. His four marriages over the course of ten years produced one male heir. Luis Cristóbal, the second Duke of Arcos, was orphaned before he was two, raised by his maternal grandparents, and lived to become the second Duke of Arcos and father three legitimate and three illegitimate children of his own, continuing the family tradition of complex households. A clause in the first duke's will, however, gives a glimpse of the human cost of that success. The duke's first wife died childless in 1521, his second wife died after giving birth to a daughter who also died young, and his third wife, María Girón, died in 1528 right after she gave birth to Luis Cristóbal, the long-awaited son and heir. María died without signing a final copy of her will, although she had prepared a simple copy of it before giving birth.[155] Coping with the problems that her unsigned will created, the duke's will states that everyone had assumed she had signed her will and that she was doing so well after the baby was born that "nobody thought about the necessity of signing."[156] But María quickly became ill and in the confusion and distress that engulfed the household, nobody remembered to have her sign her will before she died. The phrasing shows the chaos that quickly overwhelmed a household facing death just after rejoicing over the long-awaited birth of an heir. Within two years of María's death, her husband had remarried and then quickly died, leaving their children orphaned.[157] The lineage survived, but the immediate family proved remarkably transient. The first Duke of Arcos lost three wives and a daughter within a decade and then died himself. His entire adult life must have been dominated by grief and loss.

Illegitimacy and illegitimate children were an ordinary and consistent part of the noble lineage in fifteenth- and sixteenth-century Castile, part of the "social and mental habits of the Castilian aristocracy for whom the maintaining of lovers was as usual and normal as having a legitimate spouse."[158] Unpacking the emotional implications of illegitimacy, however, opens a window into the messy individual lives that lie behind the genealogical records. Pedro de Luján, the popular sixteenth-century moralist, maintained that a loving marriage was a good antidote to lust.[159] This advice effectively undercut the moral foundation of the arranged marriage, with its focus on families rather than individuals. The structure of the arranged marriage imposed order on the lineage, but it could also create affective chaos for individual couples, making marriage a focus of intense anxiety on the part of the noble family. The failure of marriages and the existence of alternate families could simultaneously create chaos and discord and provide emotional stability, love, and affection for the adults and children who were part of them. The strength of the feelings involved in these relationships that lay beyond the bonds of marriage can also be seen in the violence, rage, and jealousy that could erupt in reaction to them. The emotional impact of illegitimacy could sometimes get caught up in the infamous Castilian honor code, leading to rape, murder, and revenge. Underlying all this turbulence were grief and loss, as changing family structures and the high mortality rates of these centuries took their inevitable toll on individual people and families. The flexibility that illegitimacy gave the noble lineage simultaneously provided unexpected emotional benefits and extracted a high emotional price.

Conclusion

Noble families were complex, fluid, and emotionally challenging. Molded by the arranged marriage, broken by death, infidelity, and incompatibility, reshaped by remarriage, specific noble family units within the larger lineage evolved and changed. Nevertheless, in spite of the chaos, the early modern Castilian nobility functioned largely within the context of family and lineage. Generations of individual family units worked together to promote the lineage as a whole by providing service to the crown, making strategic alliances with other powerful members of the Castilian nobility, and consolidating land and other economic assets into powerful entails that could be passed down through the generations. Within the noble family itself a gendered hierarchy stretched from the firstborn male titleholder down to the lowliest female cousin, younger daughter of a younger son. There was no attempt at equality, but family members of various ranks and stations could be valued for their contributions to the corporate whole.

One persistent and potentially destabilizing characteristic of the noble family was sexual promiscuity. Most noblemen and some noblewomen had premarital sex, extramarital affairs, and liaisons during widowhood. This power-hungry social class made up of complex families with only a loose adherence to Catholic sexual mores created a space and a role for illegitimate children. Noble families used the illegitimate children they produced as tools to protect the lineage and consolidate family power. They loved these children and resented them, provided for them and struggled to incorporate them into the immediate family. Because illegitimate children did not fit into the prescribed structure of a family based on the sacrament of Christian marriage, their presence and their fates give a window into the economic and emotional inner workings of the noble family as it negotiated power and status. The nobility's intense focus on the importance of dynastic succession caused them to modify prescriptive gender roles, the honor code, the civil law codes, and Catholic morality in order to promote the lineage. The nobility used, even depended on, the agency of women, extramarital sexuality, and illegitimate children to preserve their power and extend their family into the future.

One of my goals in this book has been to study not just individual illegitimate children but illegitimacy itself. Because illegitimate children of the nobility were so numerous and such a constant presence across the fifteenth and sixteenth centuries, the phenomenon of illegitimacy was an integral part of the noble family. Illegitimacy affected all family members, from the titleholder who had illegitimate children to his mother who might remember an illegitimate grandchild in her will to his heir who might be left responsible for raising and educating an illegitimate half-sibling. The presence of illegitimate children also highlights the ways in which the nobility was not, in fact, a class apart at the top of the social hierarchy. In spite of their wealth, power, and status, some of the nobility's most intimate relationships were with women far below them in the social hierarchy. Some noblemen had affairs with noblewomen, but others had sexual relations with or raped maids, enslaved women, townswomen, or the workers on their vast estates. Because noble fathers often assumed responsibility for their illegitimate children, both out of affection and as a way to demonstrate successful masculinity, they also maintained relationships with women of disparate social status. These relationships varied from minimal economic support to marriage. The ability to be fathers and to support women and children was an important part of demonstrating noble masculinity that depended heavily on the ability to produce more men who could continue the lineage.

Examining how noblemen treated their illegitimate children reveals contradictory aspects of noble manhood. Noblemen raped, assaulted, and sexually coerced women of all ranks with very little in the way of repercussions, but they were also often affectionate, caring fathers who demonstrated attachment to their sexual partners and enjoyed sustained family relationships outside of their marriages. This was perhaps in part because illegitimate children served a variety of functions for the male titleholder, including demonstrating his virility, expanding the family connections through advantageous marriages, and providing the lineage with substitute heirs.

Illegitimacy also has immense implications for women. The presence of illegitimate children sheds some light on rape, sexual coercion, and the vast power differentials between noblemen and women across the social spectrum. Paradoxically, if we look beyond the infamous Castilian honor code, illegitimate children could be assets for their mothers. Questioning the honor code compels us to come to grips with the complex reality of women's lives across the social spectrum as they faced issues such as unplanned parenthood, complex extended families, strained relationships with their partners, difficult economic situations, legal challenges, marriage, widowhood, convent careers, and relationships with their grown children.

Studying illegitimacy makes the women who had illegitimate children visible within the family structure, because it shows their lives as they actually were rather than as honor codes, Catholic doctrine, or Castilian literature suggested they should be. Studying illegitimacy in fact makes a multitude of women visible. Although it reveals much about the lives of women who had illegitimate children, it also shows the grandmothers, aunts, sisters, and stepmothers who coped with the presence and needs of illegitimate children. Illegitimacy illuminates unexpected partnerships between women, who often worked together, contributing both economic resources and labor to the expensive and time-consuming task of raising and educating illegitimate children. The importance of women's labor makes the nonnoble women in the noble household visible as both mothers and caregivers of illegitimate children.

The issue of women's visibility connects to the challenges and opportunities provided by the sources. Although archives are traditionally organized around a male structure (grouped by noble title, for example) and documents are filed in relation to the patriarchal family, archival documents such as wills, legitimations, dowry agreements, guardianships, and property transactions are rich sources for the lives and, especially, economic activities of women. Because Castilian women had the legal power and religious obligation to write wills, their wills are in the archives, documenting their economic resources, their religious preoccupations, their marital alliances, and their children.[1] In addition, early modern genealogists such as Luis de Salazar y Castro documented women's lives because of the importance of strategic marriage alliances between noble families. These sources record illegitimate children (also for dynastic reasons), thus adding the mothers of illegitimate children to the list of women whose lives can be partially uncovered.

There are limitations to these sources, the most obvious being that, though they obsessively document the transfer and transmission of property between people and generations, they rarely discuss how anybody felt about anything. Very occasionally a noblewoman broke the formula and recorded emotions, as Inés de Mendoza y Delgadillo did in her will when pleading with her partner, the Duke of Nájera, to take care of their illegitimate children, telling him that her uncertainty was "such a burden."[2] Otherwise, one is left wondering how many widows were actually sad ("la triste doña Ana"), how many spouses were really beloved ("mi muy cara y amada muger"), how many women were forced into sexual relationships they did not want, and how many illegitimate children fell victim to infanticide.[3] But using archival documents and genealogies to study the lives of people who are not noblemen is possible and it is important. The more historians uncover about the wide variety of people who populated the noble household and noble family, the more accurately we will understand the history of the family itself. Studying illegitimacy, extramarital sexuality, remarriage, stepfamilies, and the lives of women adds an important depth to our understanding of families and of the ways in which patriarchy functioned. More research needs to be done in the archives on people who are harder to find such as wives, unmarried women, maids, servants, enslaved women, younger siblings, and illegitimate children. Families in the past, even among the nobility, were as fragmented and diverse as our own.

When turning the focus to the lives of illegitimate children themselves, we encounter a less optimistic, more troubled picture of illegitimacy. Being born out of wedlock created a group of adults with complex social, racial, and gender identities, a subset of the nobility who sometimes achieved power but had no guaranteed rights to either power or economic resources. The changing standards of fifteenth- and sixteenth-century Castilian society, which slowly came to privilege supposed purity of blood, made the status of illegitimate children even more precarious. Over the early modern period, illegitimate adults had increasing trouble gaining entrance to institutions of higher education, becoming priests or advancing in the service of the church, getting access to civil posts, or entering military orders. Although this discrimination would become codified, legal, and increasingly formal by the eighteenth century, the rules and social strictures of the fifteenth and sixteenth centuries remained fluid, ambiguous, and contradictory. Social status often overcame other issues of identity, but illegitimate children could not always claim the noble status of their fathers. Studying the lives and careers of illegitimate children thus gives a glimpse into the ways that markers of identity changed and developed in the fifteenth and sixteenth centuries as well as the growing presence of systemic, institutionalized racism in Castile and early modern Europe in general.

This complex process again highlights the identity and agency of women. For children of noble fathers, the mother's identity might affect her child's class status and religious and ethnic identity. Many illegitimate children thrived within the context of the large, often loving noble family, but their liminal position offered no guarantee of success and their mother's identity might affect their place in the hierarchy. Sibling relationships could also reflect this ambiguity. Siblings alternately reached across generations to support and care for illegitimate children or competed with half-siblings whose presence made their own claims to status and resources more precarious. Even when recognized and supported by their noble families, illegitimate children usually occupied lower rungs on the family hierarchy.

This competition for power and emphasis on the larger corporate identity of the lineage produced endless emotional complications for members of noble families. Contradictory, inconsistent, and difficult to uncover, the emotional implications of illegitimacy are nevertheless as important as the economic structures it affected. The creation of alternate families outside the bonds of marriage gave the noble family the emotional flexibility needed to make a system of arranged marriages work. Alternate families provided love, warmth, affection, and useful children who could make good marriage alliances, succeed in prestigious church careers, or even inherit the title in times of crisis. Alternate families also caused social disorder, stirring up jealousy, straining economic resources, and, occasionally, leading to the violence predicted by the Castilian honor codes. Studying these families can bring to light some of the emotional aspects of the noble family that are often hidden behind dowry arrangements and property transactions. Uncovering more of the hidden history of families is one of the most exciting challenges facing historians.

NOTES

INTRODUCTION

1. Carriazo Rubio, *Los testamentos,* 42–45.

2. Archivo Histórico de la Nobleza (hereafter AHNOB), fondo Osuna, C. 118, D. 9d.

3. See, for example, the Marquises de Vélez, who skillfully used the power of the entail, strategic marriages, membership in military orders, military service, and recognition and promotion of illegitimate sons to turn their land and seigneurial power into social and political advancement. Hernández Franco and Rodríguez Pérez, "Bastardía," 331–62.

4. As Barbara Harris found for the late fifteenth- and early sixteenth-century aristocracy in England, the Castilian patriarchy "consisted of a series of social structures and practices that converged to produce and sustain male dominance rather than an integrated, unified system." Harris, *English Aristocratic Women,* 10–11. For the resilience of the nobility, see Helen Nader's analysis of the Marquises of Mondéjar, which found that their real income did not decline during the sixteenth century, making them "typical: the income of the Castilian nobility kept up with prices during the sixteenth century." Nader, "Noble Income," 412. More recently, Hamish Scott argued that the historiography of the nobility has moved away from the metaphor of "crisis" to one of "consolidation." Scott, "The Early Modern European Nobility," 34.

5. Crawford, *The Fight for Status and Privilege,* 2. Jonathan Dewald used the term "nobles" to refer to the class of people who have preeminence over others and

"aristocracy" to refer to the most powerful members of that group who have a governing role, but he acknowledged that the terms "cover overlapping realities," which is true for this study also. Dewald, *The European Nobility*, xiii.

6. McDougall, *Royal Bastards*, 191. Barbara Harris noted that in England one "of the primary functions of aristocratic families was, of course, to reproduce the next generation." Harris, *English Aristocratic Women*, 7.

7. Romaniello and Lipp, "The Spaces of Nobility," 2.

8. Nader, *Mendoza Family*, 36.

9. Nader, *Mendoza Family*, 38–41; Dewald, *The European Nobility*, 19.

10. The list of their offices highlights both their power and the importance of their marriage alliances. Pedro González de Mendoza was *mayordomo mayor* (high steward) to Juan I of Castile (1405–54), his brother-in-law Pedro López de Ayala was the *canciller mayor* (high chancellor) of Castile, and both of them were members of the king's council. Pedro's son-in-law Diego Gómez de Manrique served as *adelantado mayor* (royal appellate judge) of Castile, and his other son-in-law, Díaz Sánchez de Benavides, was *caudillo mayor* (military governor) of Jaén. Nader, *Mendoza Family*, 41–42; Dewald, *The European Nobility*, 19.

11. Nader, *Mendoza Family*, 15–16.

12. Phillips, *Ciudad Real*, 106; McKendrick, "Honour/Vengeance," 325.

13. Dewald, *The European Nobility*, xvii; Romaniello and Lipp, "The Spaces of Nobility," 6, 10.

14. Nader, *Mendoza Family*, 46–47, 49, 53, 120–21. Similar examples of shifting noble allegiances exist in France. Chronicler Jean Froissart related how Godfrey of Harcourt was banished from France, was welcomed in England where he fought against France, and then later returned to France and was restored to his estates. Dewald, *The European Nobility*, 135.

15. The number remained about the same from 1541 to 1600, while the proportion for Spain as a whole was about 3.8 percent of the population by 1797. In comparison, about 1 percent of France's and Bohemia's populations were noble. Dewald, *The European Nobility*, 23.

16. Elliott, *Imperial Spain*, 112–13. By comparison, the aristocracy had less control of land in England, although it still a substantial amount; 1 percent of the population controlled 15 to 20 percent of the cultivated land. Harris, *English Aristocratic Women*, 7.

17. Lynch, *Spain*, 6–7; Elliott, *Imperial Spain*, 88–89.

18. Elliott, *Imperial Spain*, 113; Lynch, *Spain*, 144–45; Liang, *Family and Empire*, 21–22; Casey, *Early Modern Spain*, 145.

19. Dewald, *The European Nobility*, xiv–xv; Nader, "Noble Income," 411–12; Scott, "The Early Modern European Nobility," 34.

20. Dewald, *The European Nobility*, 36–40. Raimundo A. Rodríguez Pérez identified this shift as a crucial focus for future studies of the Spanish nobility. Rodríguez Pérez, "La historia social," 132. For a parallel shift among the Portuguese nobility, see Humble Ferreira, "Inventing the Courtier in Early Sixteenth-Century Portugal," 100.

21. Dewald, *The European Nobility*, 108, 124–26. Military service remained an important part of noble success. See Hernández Franco and Rodríguez Pérez, "El linaje," 399. The change in the image of the noble paralleled changes in the ideals of masculinity that are discussed in chapter 1.

22. Crawford, *The Fight for Status and Privilege*, 29–30; Nader, *Mendoza Family*, 49.

23. Rickman, *Love, Lust, and License*, 44.

24. Lynch, *Spain*, 18–19.

25. Elliott, *Imperial Spain*, 114. Although second sons did not inherit the main title, family strategies sometimes created new titles and entails for them, starting collateral branches of major families. Rodríguez Pérez, "La historia social," 129.

26. For Habsburg family strategies and how they often paralleled those of the elite across Europe, see Cruz and Galli Stampino, *Early Modern Habsburg Women*; and Palos and Sánchez, *Early Modern Dynastic Marriages*.

27. Burns, *Las Siete Partidas*, vol. 4, partida 2, title 9, law 6, 314. See Barton, *Conquerors, Brides, and Concubines*, 8–12, for the ideologically charged nature of the term Reconquista. Because of its political overtones, I have tried to avoid using it.

28. Precioso Izquierdo and Gutiérrez de Armas, "De padres nobles," 378; Nader, *Liberty in Absolutist Spain*, 30; Rodríguez Pérez, "La historia social," 137.

29. Dewald, *The European Nobility*, 28–29; Nader, *Mendoza Family*, 37.

30. Dewald, *The European Nobility*, 60; García Hernán, *La nobleza en la España moderna*, 29; Rodríguez Pérez, "La historia social," 134.

31. Dewald, *The European Nobility*, 33–36.

32. Crawford, *The Fight for Status and Privilege*, 147–48. James Casey noted the "sheer impreciseness and confusion of status," in Castile. Casey, *Early Modern Spain*, 142.

33. Dewald, *The European Nobility*, 168; Precioso Izquierdo and Gutiérrez de Armas, "De padres nobles," 378; Gaston, "All the King's Men," 168. This emphasis on lineage was a common trait of the European nobility. See, for example, Soldat, "Sepulchral Monuments"; Haddad, "The Question of the Imprescriptibility of Nobility," 150.

34. McDougall, *Royal Bastards*, 273.

35. Precioso Izquierdo and Gutiérrez de Armas, "De padres nobles," 365.

36. Nader, *Mendoza Family*, 3; Dewald, *The European Nobility*, 160; Casey, *Family and Community in Early Modern Spain*, 168–69; Precioso Izquierdo and Gutiérrez de

Armas, "De padres nobles," 375. Pablo Ortego Rico noted how the Mendoza used their funerary chapels to cement the image of their lineage, its hierarchy, and the bonds between the family and its clients: "El linaje mendocino principal en la capilla mayor, y los clientes y familiares nobles en capillas circundantes—se convertían en expresión *post mortem* de los lazos políticos habidos en vida de estos nobles." Ortego Rico, "El patrocinio religioso de los Mendoza," 283. See also Soldat, "Sepulchral Monuments," 111–12.

37. Sabean and Teuscher, "Kinship in Europe," 2–3, 14. An important difference here is that Sabean and Teuscher argued that during the early modern period marriage alliances were sought with "strangers," whereas the Castilian nobility remained heavily endogamous throughout the late medieval and early modern period. Sabean and Teuscher, "Kinship in Europe," 3.

38. Bastress-Dukehart, "Negotiating for Agnes' Womb," 42.

39. Sabean and Teuscher, "Kinship in Europe," 15.

40. Shiba, "Rasgos de la familia," 70; and Rodríguez Pérez, "La historia social," 136. The Castilian nobility also systematically married into the nobilities of the other Spanish kingdoms. Although other Iberian regional nobilities had distinct economic and political powers and marriage and inheritance patterns, my evidence suggests that illegitimacy rates were also high for these other groups. For more context on the nobilities of the other Spanish kingdoms, see Lynch, *Spain*, 62–63, 296. For the practice of arranging marriages among the English aristocracy, see Harris, *English Aristocratic Women*, 43–59.

41. Davidoff, *Thicker Than Water*, 5.

42. Davidoff, *Thicker Than Water*, 5.

43. Erler and Kowaleski, "Introduction," 2.

44. Kuehn, *Illegitimacy*, 35; Twinam, "The Negotiation of Honor," 74–76, 77–79; Archivo Histórico Nacional, Consejos, legajo 4480, no. 57; Burns, *Las Siete Partidas*, vol. 4, partida 4, title 15, law 3, 953.

45. Kuehn, *Illegitimacy*, viii.

46. Kuehn, *Illegitimacy*, ix.

47. Kuehn, *Illegitimacy*, 33; Lewin, *Surprise Heirs I*, xiii–xiv; Gerber, "Bastardy, Race, and Law," 581; Korpiola, "Marriage in Sweden," 235; Hurwich, *Noble Strategies*, 178. English law does seem to have made a basic distinction between "general bastardy," where parents did not marry, and "special bastardy," where parents later married, but that second category was only recognized by the common law courts, not the church, making most "special bastards" legally legitimate. Macfarlane, "Illegitimacy and Illegitimates in English History," 73. This ranking by degree of sin is also found in canon law. Kuehn, *Illegitimacy*, 35–36.

48. Twinam, *Public Lives*, 128; Bacó, *Suma de los preceptos*, 74. In Sweden children born after a betrothal or a trothplight were legitimate even if their parents were not subsequently able to complete the marriage. Korpiola, "Marriage in Sweden," 235.

49. Burns, *Las Siete Partidas*, vol. 4, partida 4, title 15, law 1, 952; Bacó, *Suma de los preceptos*, 74–75. "Llamanse naturales, porque los engendró solo la naturaléza y no la honestidad del matrimonio."

50. Espinosa, *Leyes de Toro*, law 9, 11; Bacó, *Suma de los preceptos*, 75; Twinam, *Public Lives*, 128. Twinam noted, "[I have] avoided the use of the term *espúreo*, because the meaning varied. Some colonists used it to refer to both *adulterinos* and *sacrílegos*, while others used it exclusively in reference to the offspring of clerics." I have encountered the same confusion in my documents, especially in lawsuits where the status of an illegitimate child is under question. Twinam, *Public Lives*, 128n5. Roisin Cossar found that in Venice, *spuria*, or children of clerics, had no legal inheritance rights at all. Cossar, *Clerical Households*, 78.

51. Nader, introduction to *Power and Gender*, 3–4. For more on women's roles as guardians, see Coolidge, *Guardianship*. A similar pattern of relying on wives existed in the English aristocracy. Harris, *English Aristocratic Women*, 8, 64–70.

52. Poska, "Upending Patriarchy," 195.

53. See, for example, Matthew Gerber's excellent book on bastards in France: Gerber, *Bastards*.

54. Mangan, *Transatlantic Obligations*, 4.

55. For sixteenth-century Peru see Mangan, *Transatlantic Obligations*; for seventeenth-century Peru see Mannarelli, *Private Passions and Public Sins*; for the eighteenth century, see Twinam, *Public Lives*; for late colonial Brazil, see Nazzari, "An Urgent Need to Conceal," 103–26.

56. Exceptions to this are article-length studies by Ricardo Córdoba de la Llave and Frederico R. Aznar Gil, along with the interesting articles written by Juan Hernández Franco and Raimundo A. Rodríguez Pérez on the Fajardo lineage and the ways in which they used illegitimate children as part of their family strategy. Aznar Gil, "Los ilegitimos," 9–48; Córdoba de la Llave, "Las relaciones," 571–619; Hernández Franco and Rodríguez Pérez, "El linaje"; Hernández Franco and Rodríguez Pérez, "Bastardía." The classic study on illegitimacy in Europe does not include Spain. See Laslett, Oosterveen, and Smith, *Bastardy and Its Comparative History*.

57. Maltby, *Alba*, 14–15; Kamen, *The Duke of Alba*, 3, 76–77, 83; Elliott, *The Count-Duke of Olivares*, 618–19, 630–32, 638, 669; Vaquero Serrano, "Garcilaso traicionado," 57–68.

58. Maltby, *The Reign of Charles V*, 26, 59.

59. See, for example, the illegitimate children of Cardinal Pedro González de Mendoza in Nader, *Mendoza Family*, 124–25; or the illegitimate children of the first Duke of Medina Sidonia in Ladero Quesada, *Guzmán*, 158–63; or the illegitimate children of the first Count of Alcaudete and his sons in Liang, *Family and Empire*, 77n13. For noblewomen who were mothers of illegitimate children, see Manero Sorolla, "On the Margins of the Mendozas," 114; and Bilinkoff, *The Avila of Saint Teresa*, 41–42. For an overview of European women's sexuality outside of marriage, see Mazo Karras, "Sex and the Singlewoman," 127–42.

60. For the legal aspects of illegitimacy in Spain, see Aznar Gil, "La califación de 'hijos naturales,'" 623–38. For illegitimacy in European canon law, see Mayali, "Note on the Legitimation," 55–75. For illegitimacy and its implications for *conversos*, see Cuart Moner, "El bastardo de Medellín," 29–61; and Cuart Moner, "Bastardos en el estudio," 307–14.

61. Twinam, "The Negotiation of Honor," 74–75.

62. Armstrong-Partida, *Defiant Priests*. For illegitimacy among the clergy, see also Aznar Gil, "Pensas y sanciones," 501–20; Kelleher, "'Like Man and Wife,'" 349–60; Jimeno Aranguern, "Concubinato, matrimonio y adulterio de los clérigos," 543–74; Haboucha, "Clerics, Their Wives, and Their Concubines." For similar situations in medieval Italy, see Cossar, *Clerical Households*.

63. Poska, *Women and Authority*, 76.

64. Dyer, "Seduction by Promise of Marriage," 439, 441.

65. Taylor, *Honor and Violence*, 165.

66. Barahona, *Sex Crimes*, 121–22.

67. Poska, *Women and Authority*, 8.

68. Although many women were publicly known to have illegitimate children, with their names appearing most often in the wills of their noble partners but also frequently in the early modern genealogies, 123 of the 258 women in this study remain anonymous, making it difficult to define their social status. Of the 135 women whose names appear in the sources, 67 of them are identified as carrying the honorific title "doña" (loosely translated as "lady") which indicates that they had at least enough status to be defined as *hidalgas*.

69. Poska, *Women and Authority*, 76–77.

70. The number of illegitimate children is somewhat distorted by the exceptional numbers provided by a couple of noblemen in the fifteenth century. Álvaro de Bracamonte, the second Lord of Peñaranda y Fuente el Sol, had twenty illegitimate children, while the second Count of Arcos had about twenty-eight, and the first Duke of Nájera also had twenty. Most noblemen in the fifteenth and sixteenth centuries had from one to four illegitimate children. The number of women in the

study is undoubtedly lower than the actual number of women who were sexually involved with the nobility, because often it is impossible to tell how many sexual partners a nobleman had outside of marriage. For example, a nobleman with four acknowledged illegitimate children may have had any number of sexual partners.

1. COMPLEX MASCULINITY

1. Nader, *Mendoza Family*, 172.
2. Rodríguez Posilio, "La casa del Infantado," 183.
3. Quoted in and translated by Nader, *Mendoza Family*, 184.
4. Rodríguez Posilio, "La casa del Infantado," 168–69, 183.
5. Layna Serrano, *Historia de Guadalajara*, 3:131.
6. Gutiérrez Coronel, *Historia genealógica*, 2:236. For the legitimate children, see the third duke's will, AHNOB, fondo Osuna, C. 1763, D. 1–2; an emancipation of his eldest son, AHNOB, fondo Osuna, C. 1769, D. 9; and the marriage of his second son, AHNOB, fondo Osuna, C. 1776, D. 19. For the illegitimate children see the duke's will, AHNOB, fondo Osuna, C. 1763, D. 1–2; for María's marriage, AHNOB, fondo Osuna, C. 1776, D. 23; and for Martín, the best documented of the illegitimate children, AHNOB, fondo Osuna, C. 1976, C. 1761, D. 5, C. 1969, D. 2, D. 13, C. 1966, D. 25, D. 30, C. 1967, D. 7–8, C. 1968, D. 1.
7. Layna Serrano, *Historia de Guadalajara*, 3:142. Another example of this predicament for historians is Pedro Enríquez, Conde de Lemos (d. 1400), who had four legitimate children, seven illegitimate children, and two children whose legitimacy is in doubt. Pardo de Guevara y Valdés, *Los señores de Galicia*, 1:246–50.
8. This analysis is based on R. W. Connell's theory that hegemonic masculinity can be complicated, disrupted, and contested, which draws on social psychologist Erich Fromm's identification of different categories of masculinity (authoritarian and democratic). Connell, *Masculinities*, 18, 37. Hendrix and Karant-Nunn, "Introduction," provides a good overview of how these ideas have recently been applied to early modern masculinity. Jane Mangan found similar contradictions in the behaviors of Spanish fathers of illegitimate children in colonial Peru. Mangan, *Transatlantic Obligations*, 174.
9. Tosh, "The History of Masculinity," 29.
10. Poska, "'A Married Man Is a Woman,'" 4–5.
11. For gender as a performance in sixteenth-century Castile, see Barlow, "Love and War," 384–85.
12. Mirrer, "Representing 'Other' Men," 171; Lehfeldt, "Ideal Men," 464–65.
13. Lehfeldt found that the seventeenth-century discourse about masculinity in Spain also provided different models separated by social class, and Poska argued that noble birth made a man more manly. Lehfeldt, "Ideal Men," 467; Poska, "'A

Married Man Is a Woman,'" 9. For more on the existence of multiple masculinities, see Lees, "Introduction," xx–xxi.

14. Villaseñor Black, *Creating the Cult of St. Joseph*, 87.
15. Mirrer, "Representing 'Other' Men," 172–79; Bullough, "On Being a Male," 31–32, 37.
16. Bullough, "On Being a Male," 41.
17. Armstrong-Partida, *Defiant Priests*, 105–6, 123; Bullough, "On Being a Male," 43. Medical treatises on various topics were widely available in Castile. Solomon, *Fictions of Well-Being*.
18. Villaseñor Black, *Creating the Cult of St. Joseph*, 43–47.
19. Armstrong-Partida, *Defiant Priests*, 123.
20. Mirrer, "Representing 'Other' Men," 169; Barton, *Conquerors, Brides, and Concubines*, 147.
21. Mirrer, "Representing 'Other' Men," 171–72. Poska argues that Spanish masculinity was "essentially antifeminine." Poska, "'A Married Man Is a Woman,'" 4.
22. Villaseñor Black, *Creating the Cult of St. Joseph*, 112; Mirrer, "Representing 'Other' Men," 181.
23. Fox, *Hercules and the King of Portugal*, 2.
24. Salazar y Castro, *Casa de Silva*, 1:381. "Siempre con mi persona, vassallos, criados, y amigos he servido, e seguido á la Corona Real destos Reynos." AHNOB, fondo Osuna, C. 125, D. 99–104, http://pares.culturaydeporte.gob.es/inicio.html. "Y al dicho mi successor y a los que despues de el lo fueren en la dicha mi Casa y Mayorazgo Ruego y Encargo y debajo de mi Maldizión y la de Dios les mando sean siempre obedientes a la Santa Fe de Apostolica y sirvan a sus Reyes con toda lealtad y fidelidad poniendo su Sangre y Vidas a todo el Riesgo que Conbenga por la defensa de la dicha Santa Fe de Apostolica y de la fee Cathólica y Servicio de sus Reyes y de la Corona de Castilla como Siempre lo an hecho nuestros Antecesores dejandonos en esto la mayor hazienda que nos pudieran dejar."
25. Barlow, "Love and War," 385, 391.
26. Lehfeldt, "Ideal Men," 470–71; Donahue, "Good Boys," 209–10.
27. Nader, *Mendoza Family*, 3.
28. Lehfeldt, "Ideal Men," 470–71, 477–79. Matthew Gerber found a similar transformation in France, where medieval aristocrats openly acknowledged illegitimate children as marks of their fathers' "strength, courage, and virility," but after the Treaty of Cateau-Cambrésis (1559) ended decades of war in France, the role of the nobility changed and a rhetoric of heredity and racial purity gradually made illegitimate children more of a threat. Gerber, *Bastards*, 51–53.
29. Strasser, "'The First Form and Grace,'" 51, 55; Dewald, *The European Nobility*, 12. In the early seventeenth century, the Spanish crown invited the Jesuit order

to start a school designed to reform the education of noblemen with a view to making them more useful to the crown. The nobility remained unconvinced and the school soon failed. Gaston, "All the King's Men," 171, 178.

30. Villaseñor Black, *Creating the Cult of St. Joseph*, 17.

31. Lehfeldt argued that the seventeenth-century discourse of masculinity "failed due to nostalgia and lack of creativity." Lehfeldt, "Ideal Men," 466, 486. See also Dewald, *The European Nobility*, 126; Gaston, "All the King's Men," 170, 182–83.

32. McKendrick, "Honour/Vengeance," 316. Vives provided multiple examples from antiquity and from the sixteenth century of fathers, brothers, and husbands killing sexually deviant female relations. Vives, *The Education of a Christian Woman*, 84. Other examples of the honor code in literature appear in the early seventeenth century in Alonso Gerónimo de Salas Barbadillo's *El caballero perfecto (1620)* and in Pedro Calderón de la Barca's *El medico de su honra* (1620). See Poska, "'A Married Man Is a Woman,'" 6. This was also an issue in Italy, where in 1425 the Duke of Este had his son and his young wife (his son's stepmother) executed for forming a romantic attachment. Fifteenth-century humanists were critical of his decision. Vitullo, *Negotiating the Art of Fatherhood*, 102.

33. McKendrick, "Honour/Vengeance," 316; Taylor, *Honor and Violence*; Poska, "'A Married Man Is a Woman'"; Villaseñor Black, *Creating the Cult of St. Joseph*, 122.

34. Taylor, *Honor and Violence*, 7–8.

35. Quoted in Arnold and Brady, "Introduction," 1.

36. Armstrong-Partida, *Defiant Priests*, 82; Mosher Stuard, "Burdens of Matrimony," 63. This was true across Europe (e.g., in Geneva, Germany, and France), where marriage and heading a household were remarkably consistent markers of masculinity in Catholic and Protestant countries alike. Puff, "The Reform of Masculinities," 22; and Mentzer, "Masculinity and the Reformed Tradition in France."

37. Armstrong-Partida, *Defiant Priests*, 83; Rickman, *Love, Lust, and License*, 73; Cossar, *Clerical Households*, 77.

38. Armstrong-Partida, *Defiant Priests*, 91; Taylor, *Honor and Violence*, 111. Alexandra Shephard affirmed the importance of this aspect of masculinity in early modern England and provided a provocative analysis of how difficult it could be for men to achieve it. Shephard, "Manhood, Credit and Patriarchy," 75–106.

39. AHNOB, fondo Osuna, C. 1763, D. 15.2. "Bienes recebidos de dios"; "hacer testamento donde dellos disponga a suya y provecho propio y de sus proximos y descargue la propia consciencia y dexo orden y claridad en sus cosas." His will is dated 1559.

40. Armstrong-Partida, *Defiant Priests*, 110, 122; Cossar, *Clerical Households*, 79. A similar definition appears in the writing of the German pastor Justus Menius in 1528. Hendrix, "Masculinity and Patriarchy," 71.

41. Bullough, "On Being a Male," 40.

42. "Assi descenda de grado en grado por los varones majores que descendieren por la linia derecha," entail founded by Pedro González de Mendoza in favor of his son Diego, quoted in Layna Serrano, *Historia de Guadalajara*, 1:282. These documents are very formulaic, following a basic notarial protocol that did not vary much across the entire early modern period or the entire Spanish empire. Burns, *Into the Archives*, 37–39.

43. AHNOB, fondo Osuna, C. 1872, D. 2.1–3, quoted in Beceiro Pita and Córdoba de la Llave, *Parentesco, poder y mentalidad*, 111. See also Franco Silva, *Entre los reinados*, 185.

44. Salazar y Castro, *Casa de Lara*, 1:278. The humanist Francesco Barbaro articulated a similar view for the Venetian nobility in his treatise *De re uxoria* (1415–16), arguing that the goal of noble marriage was "the continuance and prosperity" of the noble regime. Chojnacki, *Women and Men in Renaissance Venice*, 247–48.

45. Dewald, *The European Nobility*, 173.

46. Morant Deusa and Bolufer Peruga, *Amor, matrimonio y familia*, 28–29, 73; Poska, "'A Married Man Is a Woman,'" 13. For more on this topic, see Barahona, *Sex Crimes*; and Dyer, "Seduction by Promise of Marriage," 439–55. Historian Johanna Rickman found that sixteenth-century English noblemen did not consider their extramarital sexuality as a serious sin and that the political consequences they might suffer from it were usually reversable. Rickman, *Love, Lust, and License*, 34, 162, 60. Reformation Geneva also struggled with the conflict over the nature of masculinity demonstrated by the existence of illegitimate children in a godly society. Spierling, "Father, Son, and Pious Christian," 104.

47. Barton, *Conquerors, Brides, and Concubines*, 61–62.

48. Armstrong-Partida, *Defiant Priests*, 104–5.

49. Vitullo, *Negotiating the Art of Fatherhood*, 82; Bullough, "On Being a Male," 34, 41; Armstrong-Partida, *Defiant Priests*, 104.

50. Precioso Izquierdo and Gutiérrez de Armas, "De padres nobles," 368–69; Villaseñor Black, *Creating the Cult of St. Joseph*, 114; Rodríguez Pérez, "La historia social," 134. This analogy also appears in France, where John Calvin eventually put a reformed twist on it by comparing "the household to a small individual church," with the father as the head. Gerber, *Bastards*, 15. See also Mentzer, "Masculinity and the Reformed Tradition in France," 125.

51. Burns, *Las Siete Partidas*, vol. 4, partida 4, title 12, 960; Usunáriz, "Asistir la madre," 117. Fathers reclaiming their children from Indigenous mothers in the Americas also exercised this power. Mangan, *Transatlantic Obligations*, 51, 54.

52. Usunáriz, "Asistir la madre," 109. This kind of recognition could also be seen in Italy. Vitullo, *Negotiating the Art of Fatherhood*, 187–88.

53. Mothers supported children until three years of age (while they were still nursing) and fathers assumed the responsibility for supporting the child after age three. See chapter 2 for more on maternal responsibilities. Burns, *Las Siete Partidas*, vol. 4, partida 4, title 19, laws 2–3, 972–73; Espinosa, *Leyes de Toro*, law 10, 11; Usunáriz, "Asistir la madre," 114–15; Mangan, *Transatlantic Obligations*, 5. Similar expectations existed in other parts of Europe. Spierling, "Father, Son, and Pious Christian," 99.

54. Usunáriz, "Asistir la madre," 110–11; Mangan, *Transatlantic Obligations*, 148. Armstrong-Partida argued that a Catalan priest who provided for a concubine "as if she were his wife" was considered by his parishioners to be publicly committed to the concubinage. Armstrong-Partida, *Defiant Priests*, 89, 100, 115.

55. Blumenthal, *Enemies and Familiars*, 188–89.

56. Quoted in and translated by Donahue, "Good Boys," 218.

57. Precioso Izquierdo and Gutiérrez de Armas, "De padres nobles," 369; Byars, "From Illegitimate Son," 660–61. For the role of fathers in the education of daughters see Donahue, "Good Boys," 212, where she cites Luján's *Coloquios matrimoniales* for a father who was so exemplary that his daughter could articulate the paternal ideal. Sir Thomas More's daughters in England and Luisa Sigea (1522–60) in exile in Portugal received robust humanist educations from their respective fathers, and Mencía de Mendoza (1508–54), Marquise of Cenete, inherited a substantial library from her father, who was the illegitimate son of Cardinal Pedro González de Mendoza. Cruz, "Introduction," 3–4; and Cruz, "Reading over Men's Shoulders."

58. Precioso Izquierdo and Gutiérrez de Armas, "De padres nobles," 369; These ideas led to a rising level of education in the Portuguese court at about the same time. Humble Ferreira, "Inventing the Courtier in Early Sixteenth-Century Portugal," 96.

59. Donahue, "Good Boys," 209–11; Vives, *The Education of a Christian Woman*; Álvarez Cora, "Compañía matrimonial y prejuicio del sexo," 161.

60. Vitullo, *Negotiating the Art of Fatherhood*, 58–59, 71, 75. Protestant countries interpreted this paternal responsibility in light of a child's religious education. Spierling, "Father, Son, and Pious Christian," 107.

61. Coolidge, "Investing in the Lineage," 234–36.

62. Armstrong-Partida, *Defiant Priests*, 113; Mangan, *Transatlantic Obligations*, 149.

63. See the conflicts over the Council of Trent's refusal to invalidate marriages made without parental consent in chapter 2. Noble fathers often controlled the marriage choices of both their sons and their daughters, while marriages further down the social scale were more likely to reflect the choice of the bride and groom. Gerber, *Bastards*, 92; Morant Deusa and Bolufer Peruga, *Amor, matrimonio y familia*, 28.

64. Vives, *The Education of a Christian Woman*, 155–56; Vitullo, *Negotiating the Art of Fatherhood*, 118–20.

65. Rickman, *Love, Lust, and License*, 194.

66. Byars noted a similar self-interest among the Venetian nobility who used their illegitimate sons to gain entrance to the citizen class in an effort to expand the family's influence. "The Venetian nobility did not opt to provide for their sons solely because they felt it was the right thing to do. In addition, there must have been some benefit for the greater kin group." Byars, "From Illegitimate Son," 661.

67. Korth and Flusche, "Dowry and Inheritance," 398.

68. Clavero, *Mayorazgo*, 21–22. The *Siete Partidas*, issued by Alfonso X (1221–84), was popular with the nobility because the concept of the "universal heir" made it easier to establish primogeniture and to set up an entail. Entail had obvious advantages for noble families trying to build power and wealth over the generations, because it prevented large estates from being broken up every time the titleholder died. Castilian entail was regulated by royal license until the *Leyes de Toro* was issued in 1505, and even then the *Leyes de Toro* drew on the *Siete Partidas* and authorized the continued use of entail. In addition, the nobility retained the right to access the royal appellate courts, called the *chancillerías*, which fell under the jurisdiction of the *Siete Partidas*. O'Callaghan, "Alfonso X and the *Partidas*," xxxix; Burns, "Introduction," xii–xiv; Burns, *Las Siete Partidas*, vol. 5, partida 6, titles 3–4, 1193–216; Villalon, "The Law's Delay," 526, 530; Korth and Flusche, "Dowry and Inheritance," 396.

69. Lynch, *Spain*, 17–18. For the issue of entail and the *Leyes de Toro*, see Bermejo Castrillo, *Entre ordenamientos y códigos*, 549–603.

70. Korth and Flusche, "Dowry and Inheritance," 398; Montero Tejada, *Nobleza y sociedad*, 98.

71. Burns, *Las Siete Partidas*, vol. 5, partida 6, title 13, laws 8–10, 1272–73. Illegitimate children were also entitled to inherit from their mothers. Burns, *Las Siete Partidas*, vol. 5, partida 6, title 13, law 11, 1273–74.

72. Burns, *Las Siete Partidas*, vol. 5, partida 6, title 13, law 10, 1273.

73. Aznar Gil, "Los ilegítimos," 12.

74. Burns, *Las Siete Partidas*, vol. 4, partida 4, title 14, 950.

75. Burns, *Las Siete Partidas*, vol. 4, partida 4, title 15, law 3, 953; Raúl Estrella, "En los márgenes del matrimonio," 184.

76. Armstrong-Partida, "Priestly Marriage," 235.

77. Armstrong-Partida, "Priestly Marriage," 232, 245.

78. Aznar Gil, "Penas y sanciones," 502; Aznar Gil, "Los ilegítimos," 34.

79. Mangan, *Transatlantic Obligations*, 49.

80. Mangan, *Transatlantic Obligations*, 47. For an example of how the social hierarchy might affect these decisions, Julian Vitullo found that 60 percent of children left at

the foundling hospital in Florence were children of wealthy fathers and enslaved mothers. Vitullo, *Negotiation the Art of Fatherhood*, 170.

81. Casey, *Early Modern Spain*, 146.

82. Maltby, *The Reign of Charles V*, 26. Although I have not made an extensive study of Castilian royalty and their attitudes toward illegitimacy, there are parallels between their family strategies and those of the nobility, and they have in common the intense focus on dynastic succession. For ways in which noble and royal family strategies overlapped, see Palos, "Bargaining Chips," 1–18.

83. Usunáriz, "Asistir la madre," 109, 111. See also chapter 3 for ways in which fathers acknowledged paternity through actions.

84. Cuart Moner, "El bastardo de Medellín," 42–43; Hernández Franco and Rodríguez Pérez, "Bastardía," 357–58.

85. Burns, *Las Siete Partidas*, vol. 4, partida 4, title 19, law 2, 972; Espinosa, *Leyes de Toro*, law 10, 11; Usunáriz, "Asistir la madre," 114–15; Bacó, *Suma de los preceptos*, 80–81.

86. AHNOB, fondo Frías, C. l663, D. 19.

87. AHNOB, fondo Osuna, C. 1765, D. 1.4. "E Ynstituio e establesco por mi hija legitima universal heredera en todos mis bienes A la dicha mi hija Dona Leonor de Mendoza e hija de la dicha mi muger Da. Mencia de toledo."

88. García Oro, *Testamento*, 7.

89. In Venice, Jana Byars found some illegitimate children living with their fathers in the family palazzo but others residing with their mothers in a separate apartment paid for by the father. Her records indicate some degree of instability as fathers went back and forth between residences. Byars, "From Illegitimate Son," 656.

90. AHNOB, fondo Osuna, C. 123, D. 2.

91. AHNOB, fondo Osuna, C. 1765, D. 1.4.

92. Beceiro Pita and Córdoba de la Llave, *Parentesco, poder y mentalidad*, 111.

93. AHNOB, fondo Osuna, C. 423, D. 12.

94. AHNOB, fondo Osuna, C. 538, D. 3, fol. 23.

95. Montero Tejada, *Nobleza y sociedad*, 98. For papal and royal dispensations in medieval Spain, see Aznar Gil, "Los ilegítimos," 19–22, 27–28.

96. Ann Twinam found 2,300 legitimation petitions in the Archivo General de Simancas from 1475 to 1543 (in addition to an unknown number from the seventeenth century) and 244 from the Archivo General de Indias in Seville. There are 300 more from the eighteenth century in the Archivo Histórico Nacional in Madrid. Twinam, *Private Lives*, 6, 50–51. I occasionally found copies of the petitions in the noble archives, but this study does not draw on the petitions in Simancas.

97. AHNOB, fondo Frías, C. 394, D. 11; Franco Silva, *Entre los reinados*, 202–3.

98. Salazar y Castro, *Casa de Lara*, 1:390. He was the eldest son of the Lord of Villar de Torre, which is located in what is today La Rioja in northern Spain. A censo was "an annual percentage payment for a larger sum," which by the sixteenth century had become a secured mortgage loan, redeemable at a fixed term. The nobility used them to arrange extended payments over time, and they often appear as bequests because they provided an income. Phillips, *Ciudad Real*, 61.

99. Matilla Tascon, *Testamentos de 43 personajes*, 78.

100. AHNOB, fondo Frías, C. 600, D. 16, D. 19.

101. Salazar y Castro, *Casa de Silva*, 1:412.

102. AHNOB, fondo Frías, C. 663, D. 19.

103. Berco, "Juana Pimentel, the Mendoza Family, and the Crown," 30, 34; Gutiérrez Coronel, *Historia genealógica*, 1:65.

104. Pedro's descendants became the Counts of Feuntidueña in the early seventeenth century. It was unusual, but not unheard of, for a woman to inherit a formal entail, but Álvaro founded one for his illegitimate daughter in 1440. Gutiérrez Coronel, *Historia genealógica*, 1:62, 65.

105. Liang, *Family and Empire*, 3, 43.

106. Ladero Quesada, *Guzmán*, 291, 295.

107. Galán Parra, "El linaje," 63.

108. Salazar y Castro, *Casa de Lara*, 1:460.

109. AHNOB, fondo Osuna, C. 423, D. 12, fol. 1.

110. Steen, *Margaret of Parma*, 8–9.

111. Alessandro may have been the illegitimate son of Pope Clement VII. Steen, *Margaret of Parma*, 12.

112. Steen, *Margaret of Parma*, 25–28, 28n61, 34.

113. Steen, *Margaret of Parma*, 9.

114. AHNOB, fondo Osuna, C. 121, D. 13ñ.

115. AHNOB, fondo Osuna, C. 117, D. 6–54, http://pares.culturaydeporte.gob.es/inicio .html. It is possible that this was a family strategy agreed upon by Rodrigo and his father to get Rodrigo out of a marriage that they no longer wanted to go through with.

116. García Hernán, "Los grandes de España," 336.

117. Naya Franco, "El ajuar funerario del arzobispo de Zaragoza y Valencia," 336.

118. AHNOB, fondo Osuna, C. 932, D. 3. Ana first married the fifth Duke of Medina Sidonia, but after he was declared mentally incompetent the marriage was annulled and Ana married his brother, the sixth duke. Galán Parra, "El linaje," 65.

119. Aznar Gil, "Los ilegítimos," 9; Gutiérrez Coronel, *Historia genealógica*, 1:134. Sherrin Marshall recorded similar examples in the Netherlands, where the sixteenth-century dean of the Dom cathedral of Utrecht, Adriaen van Renesses, had a

mistress and several children, one of whom joined the church in his turn. Marshall, *The Dutch Gentry*, 83.

120. For illegitimate daughters in Toledo entering at a younger age, see Martz, *A Network of Converso Families*, 226.

121. Salazar y Castro, *Casa de Silva*, 1:392, 409–10.

122. Salazar y Castro, *Casa de Silva*, 1:392, 409–10. For the strong connections between convents and noble families, see Atienza López, "Nobleza, poder señorial y conventos," 235–69.

123. Claire Walker discussed this mix of motivations, noting that though families used convents for social and financial reasons, nuns themselves often expressed vocations. Walker, *Gender and Politics in Early Modern Europe*, 30–37.

124. There is an ongoing historiographical debate about the nature of forced monarchization for all early modern nuns, whether legitimate or illegitimate, which is concisely summarized in Lehfeldt, "The Permeable Cloister," 34–35. For the benefits of having relatives in the convent, see Lehfeldt, "The Permeable Cloister," 30–31.

125. De Cruz Medina, "An Illegitimate Habsburg," 113.

126. Ortego Rico, "El patrocinio religioso de los Mendoza," 285.

127. Salazar y Castro, *Casa de Lara*, 2:150.

128. Kamen, *The Duke of Alba*, 77. See also Maltby, *Alba*. Another example of this is Juan Enríquez, captain general of the sea and illegitimate son of Alonso Enríquez, Admiral of Castile, who served with his father in the war against Granada. Salazar y Castro, *Casa de Lara*, 2:463; Ortega Gato, "Los Enríquez," 27.

129. The Affair of the Princes convulsed eighteenth-century France after the death of Louis XIV but did not result in the king's illegitimate children inheriting the throne. Gerber, *Bastards*, 72–73, 82–88.

130. Salazar y Castro, *Casa de Lara*, 1:385–86.

131. Galán Parra, "El linaje," 49; Ladero Quesada, *Guzmán*, 158–63.

132. Barrantes Maldonado, "Ilustraciones de la casa de Niebla," 216.

133. Layna Serrano, *Historia de Guadalajara*, 3:134. The title of Count of Medinaceli was first given to an illegitimate son in 1368 by King Enrique II. Romero Medina, "Leonor de la Vega y Mendoza," 138.

134. Montero Tejada, *Nobleza y sociedad*, 99–100.

135. AHNOB, fondo Frías, C. 606, D. 26. "Un hidalgo mui honrrado."

136. Lehfeldt, "Ideal Men," 471.

137. AHNOB, fondo Frías, C. 606, D. 26.

138. AHNOB, fondo Frías, C. 606, D. 26. "Yo ponia duda en ello porque el Señor Don Juan le tenian en la Corte en reputacion de Capon."

139. AHNOB, fondo Frías, C. 606, D. 26. "Me dijo mira el capon que decia, que dejó preñada la hija del Huesped."

140. AHNOB, fondo Frías, C. 606, D. 26.

141. Jonathan Dewald argued that there was a dark side to European court life that required nobles to exercise self-control and conceal their inner thoughts for fear of misrepresentation. Dewald, *The European Nobility*, 127–28. See also Starkey, "The Court," 232–39.

142. Gutiérrez Coronel, *Historia genealógica*, 2:373.

143. Liss, *Isabel the Queen*, 89, 203; Nader, *Mendoza Family*, 119–23.

144. Nader, *Mendoza Family*, 120.

145. Gutiérrez Coronel, *Historia genealógica*, 2:195, 251, 379; AHNOB, fondo Osuna, C. 1858, D. 7.

146. AHNOB, fondo Osuna, C. 1762, D. 15, and C. 1858, D. 7; Gutiérrez Coronel, *Historia genealógica*, 2:379; Nader, *Mendoza Family*, 120.

147. AHNOB, fondo Frías, C. 606, D. 37.

148. Burns, *Las Siete Partidas*, vol. 4, partida 4, title 19, laws 2–3, 972–73; Espinosa, *Leyes de Toro*, law 10, 11; Usunáriz, "Asistir la madre," 114–15.

149. In her study of transatlantic families, Jane Mangan pointed out that "enacting the responsibilities of fatherhood" does not necessarily imply physical proximity. Mangan, *Transatlantic Obligations*, 47.

150. AHNOB, fondo Osuna, C. 423, D. 12, fol. 1.

151. García Oro, *Testamento*, 8. "Y tenga e administer su persona e vienes asta que sea de hedad, y tenga cargo de la hazer estudiar y aprender y ordenar a clerigo."

152. A beata or beguine was a woman who lived in a community of pious women who observed "such religious ideals as poverty and chastity, but without taking formal religious vows or living under a monastic rule." Lehfeldt, *Religious Women*, 111.

153. Belén Rubio Ávila, "María de Mendoza," 437–38.

154. Salazar y Castro, *Casa de Lara*, 2:143–53.

155. Quoted in Spivakovsky, *Son of the Alhambra*, 354.

156. García Oro, *Testamento*, 8; AHNOB, fondo Osuna, C. 538, D. 3, fol. 23.

157. AHNOB, fondo Frías, C. 606, D. 37.

158. Barrantes Maldonado, "Ilustraciones de la casa de Niebla," 199. "É á los hijos que él mas quiso fueron tres"; "porque no tuvo otra hija."

159. Barrantes Maldonado, "Ilustraciones de la casa de Niebla," 199. "É los hijos no tuvieron aquellas maneras para contentar al padre."

160. Barrantes Maldonado, "Ilustraciones de la casa de Niebla," 219.

161. Salazar y Castro, *Casa de Silva*, 2:199.

162. Salazar y Castro, *Casa de Lara*, 1:390.

163. Quoted in Layna Serrano, *Historia de Guadalajara*, 3:119. "Ni consume el matrimonio por sus muchas enfermedades, flaqueza y vejez."

164. Layna Serrano, *Historia de Guadalajara*, 3:119–24.

1. Under Castilian law, four-fifths of a parent's estate had to go to the direct descendants (legitimate children). The mother or father could allocate the remaining one-fifth (called the quinto) for funeral expenses, pious works, and free bequests to any person, thus enabling many men to provide for their illegitimate children and any partners they were not married to. In this case, Juan de Mendoza (who was a younger son with a smaller portion) seems to have felt that the quinto was not sufficient to provide for Ana and their children. Korth and Flusche, "Dowry and Inheritance," 398.

2. "La triste doña Ana," Layna Serrano, *Historia de Guadalajara*, 2:229–30, 229n2.

3. Layna Serrano, *Historia de Guadalajara*, 2:230. This was a very gendered charge that was often leveled at women who were perceived as having too much influence over men. For another example, see Silleras-Fernández, "Money Isn't Everything," 81.

4. Layna Serrano, *Historia de Guadalajara*, 2:229.

5. Layna Serrano, *Historia de Guadalajara*, 2:231.

6. Layna Serrano, *Historia de Guadalajara*, 2: 235–36.

7. For expectations of women's behavior throughout the lifecycle, see contemporary manuals such as Vives, *The Education of a Christian Woman*; or León, *A Bilingual Edition*. See also Taylor, *Honor and Violence*, 2.

8. Poska, *Women and Authority*; Taylor, *Honor and Violence*; Dyer, "Seduction by Promise of Marriage"; Nader, *Power and Gender*; Fink De Backer, *Widowhood*; Mitchell, *Queen, Mother, and Stateswoman*; Lehfeldt, *Religious Women*.

9. Poska, "The Case for Agentic Gender Norms," 354.

10. Poska, "The Case for Agentic Gender Norms," 355.

11. McDougall, *Royal Bastards*, 6, 49.

12. Of these seventy-four women who are identified as noble, either I have concrete information on their parents and families of origin or their contemporaries gave them the honorific title doña or referred to them specifically as noble. Some of them, of course, may have been passing as noble. See Twinam, *Public Lives*, 29 (for a discussion of the phenomenon of passing), 253 (for a discussion of the importance of the honorific doña).

13. Their status varied widely and includes maids in noble households, daughters of laborers or townspeople, and enslaved women.

14. Many of those whose status is unclear are never mentioned in the documents. I know they exist because an illegitimate child exists, but I can find no records of them. Sometimes their names are mentioned with no explanation or clarification of social status, and sometimes they are simply referred to as a "doncella" or a "mujer." If they are identified as coming from a specific town ("vecina de") I have

counted them as nonnoble because the implication is that they don't carry a title. For issues of women's archival obscurity, see Cossar, *Clerical Households*, 95.

15. Helen Ettlinger's study of mistresses in Italian Renaissance courts confirms this for Italy. Ettlinger, "Visibilis et Invisibilis," 781. Out of a total of 258 women in my database, 8 had no recorded children with their noble partners. The third Count of Osuna, who had sexual relations with multiple actresses, accounts for 3 of those 8. Sánchez García, "La marquesa de Campolattaro," 109–30. Most of the women in my study did not leave lawsuits against their seducers, perhaps because there was a disparity of rank and status and little or no expectation of marriage in most of these relationships. In contrast, other Spanish women aggressively took their seducers to court. See Dyer, "Seduction by Promise of Marriage"; Barahona, *Sex Crimes*; Poska, *Women and Authority*, 88–89.

16. Fantazzi, "Introduction," 1–2.

17. Vives, *The Education of a Christian Woman*, 47, 85.

18. León, *A Bilingual Edition*, 31, 33, quoted in Poska, *Women and Authority*, 3.

19. Quoted in Dyer, "Seduction by Promise of Marriage," 440.

20. Espinosa, *Reglas de bien vivir*, 2.

21. Dyer, "Seduction by Promise of Marriage," 440.

22. Perry, *Gender and Disorder in Early Modern Seville*, 39–41; Villaseñor Black, *Creating the Cult of St. Joseph*, 110.

23. Morant Deusa and Bolufer Peruga, *Amor, matrimonio y familia*, 49–50.

24. Taylor, *Honor and Violence*, 6; McKendrick, "Honor/Vengeance," 313–35.

25. Poska, *Women and Authority*, 7. Abigail Dyer found one case of "what may have been an honor-based filicide" in the court records in Navarre, in contrast to 1,804 women and their families who sued for seduction. Dyer, "Seduction by Promise of Marriage," 441. McKendrick found eight cases of wife-murder in Valencia from 1598 to 1638, none of which appear to be honor-based killings, and all of which were punished. McKendrick, "Honor/Vengeance," 315. The research for this study found four men who killed their wives on suspicion of adultery, all of whom faced severe legal and social consequences, which are discussed in more detail in chapter 5.

26. Morant Deusa and Bolufer Peruga, *Amor, matrimonio y familia*, 51; Vives, *The Education of a Christian Woman*, 270–71, 275–76.

27. Vives, *The Education of a Christian Woman*, 54, 275.

28. Quoted in Morant Deusa and Bolufer Pergua, *Amor, matrimonio y familia*, 52. "Bárbaras mujeres que, por no tener un poco de paciencia y reprimir su amor de fieras, quieren que sus hijos se críen para necios, embarazando que el padre los corrijas, que el maestro los castigue como merecen sus travesuras."

29. Morant Deusa and Bolufer Peruga, *Amor, matrimonio y familia*, 50–52; Pérez-Toribio, "From Mother to Daughter," 59. "El amor maternal se consideraba un sentimiento natural, sobre el que poco había que decir."

30. Vives, *The Education of a Christian Woman*, 279.

31. Casey, *The History of the Family*, 113.

32. Poska, "The Case for Agentic Gender Norms," 356. In Iberia the rates of women who were permanently single varied widely by region. Bennett and Froide, *Singlewomen in the European Past*, 54.

33. The importance of lineage to kings and nobility persisted throughout the medieval and early modern periods and led to numerous compromises, such as the extraordinary story of Ramiro, the monk-king of Aragón, who temporarily left his monastery, married, and sired a daughter to perpetuate the lineage. McDougall, *Royal Bastards*, 199.

34. Although St. Anne's cult was suppressed by the church after the Council of Trent, it remained at its height from 1450 to 1550. Villaseñor Black, "St. Anne Imagery," 4–6, 19.

35. Usunáriz, "Asister la madre," 111–14.

36. Broomhall, "'The King and I,'" 339; Pérez-Toribio, "From Mother to Daughter," 60.

37. Once again, the Council of Trent put an end to this depiction of Mary in Spain, labeling it "indecorous and disrespectful to the mother of God." Villaseñor Black, *Creating the Cult of St. Joseph*, 107–8; Burns, *Las Siete Partidas*, vol. 4, partida 4, title 19, law 3, 973; Bacó, *Suma de los preceptos*, 80–81; Usunáriz, "Asistir la madre," 115.

38. Vives, *The Education of a Christian Woman*, 269–70. By the eighteenth century, doctors were telling women that breastfeeding was the best thing they could do for their infants as well as the best way to prevent postpartum illness for themselves. Sherwood, "The Ideology of Breast-Feeding," 98–103.

39. For elite wet-nursing practices, see Harris, *English Aristocratic Women*, 104; Klapisch-Zuber, *Women, Family, and Ritual in Renaissance Italy*, 132–35; Beam, "Turning a Blind Eye," 269; Winer, "The Enslaved Wet Nurse as Nanny," 303–19; Dewald, *The European Nobility*, 173. The Duchess of Medina de Rioseco, writing her will in 1565, left a legacy to her daughter's wet nurse, who had been a part of the ducal household for fifteen years. AHNOB, fondo Osuna, C. 1763, D. 16, fol. 2.

40. Howe, *Education and Women*, 94.

41. Villaseñor Black, "St. Anne Imagery," 6, 12.

42. Pérez-Toribio, "From Mother to Daughter," 62, 69. This role for noble mothers can also be seen in England, where noblewomen "supervised their children's educations and care and cooperated with their husbands to settle them in appropriate careers and marriages." Harris, *English Aristocratic Women*, 99.

43. The Countess of Palamós (1479–1546), for example, wrote to her daughter Estefania (1504–49), who had married into the Castilian nobility, advising her on domestic tasks as well as on how to run a profitable business in silk manufacturing. Pérez-Toribio, "From Mother to Daughter," 68.

44. Howe, *Education and Women*, 99, 102–3; Cruz, "Introduction," 4–5.

45. Pérez-Toribio, "From Mother to Daughter," 66; Broomhall, "'My Daughter, My Dear,'" 557–60.

46. Coolidge, *Guardianship*; Fink De Backer, *Widowhood*; Harris, *English Aristocratic Women*, 111–17.

47. Twinam, *Public Lives*, 65.

48. Dyer, "Seduction by Promise of Marriage," 441. Just the fact that they could sue on these grounds suggests some flexibility in legal and social approaches to chastity. For similar lawsuits in eighteenth-century France, see Lefebvre-Teillard, "Marriage in France," 271.

49. Poska, "Elusive Virtue," 136; Poska, *Women and Authority*, 75–111.

50. Taylor, *Honor and Violence*, 165.

51. Taylor, *Honor and Violence*, 166–67.

52. Poska, *Women and Authority*, 6–8; Taylor, *Honor and Violence*, 165.

53. Twinam, *Public Lives*, 63. A similar dynamic existed in early modern England. Barbara Harris found that though adulterous aristocratic wives probably suffered more than their cheating husbands did, the penalties against them focused on loss of property and did not include "complete ruin of their character, abandonment by their lovers, or permanent banishment from aristocratic society." Harris, *English Aristocratic Women*, 85. Johanna Rickman argued that chastity was not the only, or even the most important, ingredient in female honor, and that in fact noblewomen's high status "carried with it an inherent notion of honor" that could lessen the impact of immoral behavior. Rickman, *Love, Lust, and License*, 175–76.

54. Ladero Quesada, *Guzmán*, 29, 31.

55. Dyer, "Seduction by Promise of Marriage," 447.

56. Lombardi, "Marriage in Italy," 94; Morant Deusa and Bolufer Pergua, *Amor, matrimonio y familia*, 35; McDougall, *Royal Bastards*, 55, 191. Even the two people involved might have trouble knowing at what point their marriage became legal and indissoluble. See Wunder, "Marriage in the Holy Roman Empire," 66.

57. Donahue, "The Legal Background," 34.

58. Heath Dillard noted that in medieval Castile, "Formal betrothal with endowment remained . . . the irreversible step in the secular marriage process, and sexual relations were not unusual or even reprehensible before the wedding." In 1215 the Fourth Lateran Council moved toward the need for a church wedding

with bans, witnesses, and a public ceremony, but even then it did not invalidate clandestine marriages but merely penalized the participants. Dillard, *Daughters of the Reconquest*, 143; Brundage, *Law, Sex, and Christian Society*, 499.

59. Burns, *Las Siete Partidas*, vol. 4, partida 4, title 1, law 4, 880. The *Leyes de Toro* (1505) and the *Nueva Recopilación* (1563) retained a slightly modified version of the *Siete Partidas*'s language on marriage, so those laws along with the decrees of the Council of Trent were the legal requirements in Spain until 1776. Usunáriz, "Marriage and Love," 203.

60. Montero Tejada, *Nobleza y sociedad*, 80. Even as late as 1564, Jutta Sperling found that 20 percent of engaged couples and 72 percent of clandestinely married couples who applied to the papal office of the Penitentiary for a dispensation to legalize their marriage had already consummated their relationships. Sperling, "Marriage at the Time of the Council of Trent," 86, 88.

61. Dillard, *Daughters of the Reconquest*, 57; Brundage, *Law, Sex, and Christian Society*, 502. In early modern Castile, Renato Barahona noted, promises of marriage or betrothal "dramatically changed the nature of the couples' relationships . . . sexual intercourse and loss of virginity occurred only *after* receiving pledges of marriage." Barahona, *Sex Crimes*, 17. Jesús M. Usunáriz found this to be true into the seventeenth century. Usunáriz, "Marriage and Love," 216. See also Lacarra Lanz, "Changing Boundaries," 162.

62. Seidel Menchi, *Marriage in Europe*, provides a sense of how persistent this opinion was. The German writer Joachim von Beust (1522–97), who studied in Bologna, concluded that betrothal (future tense) followed by sexual intercourse made a marriage even in post-Reformation Saxony (the same was true in Lutheran Sweden until the seventeenth century), and Samuel Stryk was still making this argument as late as 1690 in Frankfurt. Donahue, "The Legal Background," 44–45, 52–53; Korpiola, "Marriage in Sweden," 226, 237. The concept remained a subject of controversy, with the Holy Roman Empire legally abolishing the practice during the Reformation but still struggling with it in rural areas in the late sixteenth century; in Switzerland banning the practice in rural areas "had no visible effect on sexual behavior." Wunder, "Marriage in the Holy Roman Empire," 72, 78; Burghartz, "Competing Logics," 189. In Italy, Daniela Lombardi argued, "this conception of the promise explains why premarital sexuality was so well tolerated," and did not necessarily damage a woman's honor. By the late sixteenth century, sexual activity before marriage was being attacked from the confessional in Italy, but lay people continued to believe that sexual intercourse after an engagement was acceptable into the eighteenth century. Lombardi, "Marriage in Italy," 99, 109, 117. The idea persisted in England into the sixteenth century, and though the Political Act of 1580 made all sexual intercourse outside of marriage punishable by law in

the Netherlands, Manon van der Heijden noted that "long-standing traditions hindered the effective implementation of such rules for decades." Helmholz, "The Legal Regulation of Marriage," 134; Van der Heijden, "Marriage Formation," 163.

63. The difference between a wife and a concubine, though never completely clear, evolved over the Middle Ages. McDougall, *Royal Bastards*, 55–56.

64. Salazar y Castro, *Casa de Silva*, 1:179. Pope Innocent III set the rules for marriages of close relatives at the Fourth Lateran Council in 1215, prohibiting marriages between kin related in the fourth degree. This meant that the perpetually endogamous Castilian nobility increasingly needed a dispensation (both a papal bull and a license from a local bishop or ecclesiastical judge) in order to consummate their marriages legally under canon law. Montero Tejada, *Nobleza y sociedad*, 68.

65. The Fifth Lateran Council finally declared it illegal in 1514. Brundage, *Law, Sex, and Christian Society*, 514. Italy also had a long-standing tradition of concubinage that was affected by this. Seidel Menchi, "Conclusion," 337.

66. Lacarra Lanz, "Changing Boundaries," 163, 163n9. In theory, these relationships were formalized with a legal contract signed by both parties, but the contracts themselves have not been found in the archives. Córdoba de la Llave, "Las relaciones," 579. For an interesting reevaluation of these contracts, see Shadis, "'Received as a Woman,'" 38–54.

67. McDougall, *Royal Bastards*, 262; Córdoba de la Llave, "Las relaciones," 577–78. For the prevalence of medieval concubinage in Iberia, see Shadis, "'Received as a Woman,'" 2; Kelleher, "'Like Man and Wife,'" 356–57; Dillard, *Daughters of the Reconquest*, 127–32; Silleras-Fernández, "Money Isn't Everything," 70–71; Calderón Medina, "Las otras mujeres del rey," 4, 6. Discussions of concubines and the status of their children are found in medieval canon law. See McDougall, *Royal Bastards*, 39. Brundage noted that concubinage remained a common practice across Europe "long after systematic measures were taken to repress it." Brundage, *Law, Sex, and Christian Society*, 516. For the range of terms used to describe the concubines of Catalan priests and their implications, see Armstrong-Partida, *Defiant Priests*, 46–47.

68. Only Portugal had a higher rate, with 88 percent of petitioners reporting they had married clandestinely. Sperling, "Marriage at the Time of the Council of Trent," 69–70, 93. German law allowed polygamy by recognizing secondary but still legal marriages. In the medieval period, these were marriages by mutual consent (*Friedelehe*) which translated to morganatic marriage after the Reformation. Sperling, "Marriage at the Time of the Council of Trent," 82; Seidel Menchi, "Conjugal Experiments in Europe," 326–27.

69. Poska, *Women and Authority*, 86–88; Sperling, "Marriage at the Time of the Council of Trent," 70; Lacarra Lanz, "Changing Boundaries," 163, 163n9. Concubinage

could also be unstable and women and children could suffer if a man abandoned them. Michelle Armstrong-Partida found records of deadbeat fathers in medieval Catalunya and Jane Mangan acknowledged the same issue in transatlantic relationships, but both studies also found a substantial number of men who remained committed to their partners and/or children. Armstrong-Partida, *Defiant Priests*, 120; Mangan, *Transatlantic Obligations*, 47.

70. Shadis, "'Received as a Woman,'" 10–11. For studies on the lives of some of these women, see Calderón Medina, "Las otras mujeres del rey"; Rodríguez González, "Concubina o esposa," 143–68.

71. To further complicate this story, Enrique II of Castile was the illegitimate son of Alfonso XI of Castile. The second Lord of Marchena was an ancestor of the Dukes of Arcos. Ladero Quesada, *Guzmán*, 62–63, 62n16. It was not only medieval kings who could have concubines or lovers. Queen Urraca of Castile-León had a lover and two illegitimate children in the twelfth century. McDougall, *Royal Bastards*, 195–96; Martin, *Queen as King*, 18.

72. For an example of the benefits, Alfonso XI ceded the estate of Huelva to Alfonso Méndez de Guzmán, Leonor's brother. Ladero Quesada, *Los señores de Andalucía*, 102; Silleras-Fernández, "Money Isn't Everything," 71; Salazar y Castro, *Casa de Silva*, 1:476.

73. Silleras-Fernández, "Money Isn't Everything," 71.

74. Montero Tejada, *Nobleza y sociedad*, 87. María's illegitimate daughter entered the church, and the estate of Villajimena eventually came to her illegitimate son. Salazar y Castro, *Casa de Lara*, 2:149, 152.

75. Poska, *Women and Authority*, 88.

76. Waterworth, *The Canons and Decrees*, 196–97; Donahue, "The Legal Background," 36.

77. Trent also condemned marriages of minors without parental consent, but expressly declared that these marriages remained valid. Lacarra Lanz, "Changing Boundaries," 185; Brundage, *Law, Sex, and Christian Society*, 521; Donahue, "The Legal Background," 36; Morant Deusa and Bolufer Pergua, *Amor, matrimonio y familia*, 47.

78. Burghartz, "Competing Logics," 178.

79. Sperling, "Marriage at the Time of the Council of Trent," 78. Other European countries also struggled with the decrees of Trent, especially *Tametsi*, the decree on marriage. The French monarchy wanted Trent to declare that both marriages without parental consent and marriages not publicly celebrated in a church with posting of banns were invalid. When *Tametsi* did not require banns or invalidate marriages made without parental consent, the French refused to promulgate it. Donahue, "The Legal Background," 36–37. Protestant countries did not promulgate the Tridentine rules either, but changes to marriage law and the creation of

new Protestant marriage courts led to similar bans on prostitution, concubinage, and all premarital and extramarital sexual relations. See Wunder, "Marriage in the Holy Roman Empire," 72. Italy saw a slow change in attitudes similar to that which can be traced in Spain. Lombardi, "Marriage in Italy," 104.

80. Schoenrich, *The Legacy*, 1:293–94. Bigamy was considered a particularly serious crime and fell under the jurisdiction of the Inquisition because it violated the doctrine of the marriage sacrament. Usunáriz, "Marriage and Love," 217.

81. AHNOB, fondo Osuna, C. 4, D. 2; Schoenrich, *The Legacy*, 1:297.

82. Twinam, *Public Lives*, 37. The Council of Trent stated specifically: "Furthermore, the same holy synod exhorts the bridegroom and bride not to live together in the same house until they have received the sacerdotal benediction, which is to be given in a church." Waterworth, *The Canons and Decrees*, 198. See also Donahue, "The Legal Background," 38.

83. AHNOB, fondo Osuna, C. 4, D. 2. "El concilio se avia publicado en estos Reynos en Abril o Mayo del mismo ano de 64."

84. AHNOB, fondo Osuna, C. 4, D. 2. "Y para ser legitima no hasta que la madre tuviesse buena fee, al tiempo que se caso, sino que esta le avia de durar al tiempo de la concepcion porque si le concibo en mala fee no sera legitimo; pues digo que al tiempo de la concepción es ymposible que Da. Luisa tuviesse buena fee."

85. The decrees of the Council of Trent are quite specific about the problem with clandestine marriages: "The grievous sins which arise from the said clandestine marriages, and especially the sins of those parties who live on in a state of damnation, when, having left their former wife, with whom they had contracted marriage secretly, they publicly marry another, and with her live in perpetual adultery." Waterworth, *The Canons and Decrees*, 196–97. These issues created opposition to clandestine marriages across Europe. Donahue, "The Legal Background," 36. Luis Colón had, in fact, been married three times simultaneously and seems to have spent most of his life dealing with the results of his bigamy. He also had two illegitimate daughters. See Schoenrich, *The Legacy*, 1:253–303, for the complete history of Luis's marital adventures.

86. AHNOB, fondo Osuna, C. 2418, D. 13. "Por ser (como es) espurio y adulterino; y como tal incapaz de la dicha sucesión." It isn't immediately obvious that he was espurio, which was a pejorative term often used more loosely than adulterino and which implied that one parent had been bound by religious vows. Twinam, *Public Lives*, 128n5.

87. Dyer, "Seduction by Promise of Marriage," 444–45. The Spanish scholar Tomás Sánchez devoted an entire volume of his massive work on marriage, *Disputationum de sancto matrimonii sacramento tomi tres* (1626), to the issue of clandestine

consent. Donahue, "The Legal Background," 46. The *Siete Partidas* also admitted the possibility of clandestine marriages. Usunáriz, "Marriage and Love," 202.

88. AHNOB, fondo Osuna, C. 4, D. 2.

89. Shoenrich quotes the lawsuit here. Shoenrich, *The Legacy*, 1:300–303.

90. For the dowry, see Schoenrich, *The Legacy*, 1:299.

91. Women's fertility was especially important to the European nobility as a way to ensure dynastic continuity. Ladero Quesada, *Guzmán*, 29, 31; Harris, *English Aristocratic Women*, 99; Broomhall, "'My Daughter, My Dear,'" 560.

92. A good example of this is the marriage capitulations that the Duke of Medinaceli signed when his daughter married Rodrigo de Mendoza, Marquis de Cenete, in 1492. The duke stated that he would finish paying his daughter's dowry when, and only when, the young couple had produced a male child who lived more than sixty days. Beceiro Pita and Córdoba de la Llave, *Parentesco, poder y mentalidad*, 111n4. The Count of Niebla and the master of Santiago made a similar agreement in 1396. In the marriage arrangements for their children, the dowry of the count's daughter was to be restored to the master of Santiago if her marriage with his son produced no children. Casey, *The History of the Family*, 88.

93. Cuart Moner, "El bastardo de Medellín," 49–53.

94. Harris, *English Aristocratic Women*, 5.

95. Salazar y Castro, *Casa de Lara*, 1:522–23, 4:96, 133. "Con sus rentas, é pechos, y derechos." The count obtained another royal legitimation in 1484 after Mencía's death, but his eldest son still faced considerable legal difficulty about his inheritance. Catalina's official husband must have died sometime before 1480 to make her second marriage possible. Another example of this kind of situation is doña Leonor Nuñez, who had nine illegitimate children with the second Count of Arcos and married him after the death of his first (childless) wife, to whom she had been a lady-in-waiting. Carriazo Rubio, *Los testamentos*, 42; AHNOB, fondo Osuna, C. 4165; C. 3476, D. 16; C. 121, D. 13ñ.

96. Ladero Quesada, *Guzmán*, 158, 168, 168n151; Galán Parra, "El linaje," 49; Barrantes Maldonado, "Ilustraciones de la casa de Niebla," 216.

97. Cuart Moner, "Bastardos en el estudio," 310.

98. Owning slaves was common among the Castilian nobility. In the medieval period, the Iberian Peninsula was a crossroad where, as the balance of power shifted during the Reconquista, "Spanish Muslims were enslaved in Christian Spain and sold throughout the northwestern Mediterranean." Constable, "Muslim Spain and Mediterranean Slavery," 264. By 1550 the slave population in Spain may have been as high as 100,000, and it was concentrated in southern Spain, where the Dukes of Arcos had their seat. Black slaves were often used as "exotica" to denote

status and confer prestige in both Aragón and Castile. Silleras-Fernández, "*Nigra sum sed formosa,*" 553, 555. The Dukes of Medina Sidonia had more than 200 slaves in 1507, the Counts of Arcos had at least 52, and a little further down the social scale Martín Dávila (in Jerez) had 15 slaves in 1502. Ladero Quesada, *Los señores de Andalucia*, 245; Sánchez Saus, "De los patrimonios nobiliarios," 480–81.

99. Carriazo Rubio, *Los testamentos*, 226. "Se han criado conmigo de mui luengo tienpo, e con mis fijos e fijas, e saben mucho el estilo e costunbre de mi casa e entiended e saben mucho en la gouernación de la salud de los ninnos mis fijos e fijas, por tanto yo les ruego e mando que commo quiera que ellas sean forras estén con los dichos mis fijos e fijas e de la dicha Catalina González en tanto que se crían, e más sy más quisyeren, ayudándolos a criar e curando de su salud dellos." For information on the enslaved persons (including women) in the household of the Dukes of Medina Sidonia, see Ladero Quesada, *Los señores de Andalucía*, 81. According to François Soyer, the stipulation that slaves "continued to serve surviving family members for a determined period of time" was a fairly common testamentary condition of freedom through the twelfth century in Castile, and Ruth Pike found examples of this in sixteenth-century Seville. Soyer, "Muslim Freedmen," 139; Pike, "Sevillian Society," 352.

100. The laws of Soria and the *Fuero Real* (1256) are both concerned that children from these liaisons be brought up as Christians, which was clearly the case in the Arcos household. Barton, *Conquerors, Brides, and Concubines*, 59–60. See also Pike, "Sevillian Society," 357. This practice was not unique to Spain, as elite men in Renaissance Italy also raped their female slaves or took them as concubines. Vitullo, *Negotiating the Art of Fatherhood*, 170. Iberian slaves came from a wide variety of backgrounds, and it isn't always easy to tell from the documents what their actual identity was. They could be Muslim or Christian and included "Tartar, Circassian, Russian and Greek Orthodox Christian women and children, as well as black Africans and Canary Islanders," as well as Moriscos. Blumenthal, *Enemies and Familiars*, 1; Pike, "Sevillian Society," 344.

101. Pike, "Sevillian Society," 349; Silleras-Fernández, "*Nigra sum sed formosa,*" 563. Enslaved women provided similar kinds of labor in Italy. Vitullo, *Negotiating the Art of Fatherhood*, 152.

102. Vaquero Serrano, "Doña María de Ribera," 76, 80, 83–84.

103. Fernando stated (somewhat cryptically), "Por buen debdo que con ella he, dos mill marauedís." Carriazo Rubio, *Los testamentos*, 126; Franco Silva, *Entre los reinados*, 113.

104. AHNOB, fondo Frías, C. 606, D. 37.

105. The term *amiga conoscida* was historically used in Castile to indicate the concubine of a married man. Dillard, *Daughters of the Reconquest*, 132; AHNOB, fondo Frías, C. 600, D. 16, C. 606, D. 37.

106. For the legal powers that noblewomen had, see Nader, *Power and Gender*; Coolidge, *Guardianship*. Fink de Backer and Poska also discuss the legal power and responsibilities of nonelite widows. Fink de Backer, *Widowhood*, 158–68, 176–84; Poska, *Women and Authority*, 163–92.

107. All Spaniards, both men and women, were theoretically required to make a will because dying intestate could cause spiritual and legal problems. Eire, *From Madrid to Purgatory*, 20. For an analysis of women's will-making strategies in late sixteenth-century Toledo, see Coolidge, "Death and Gender," 59–79.

108. Montero Tejada, *Nobleza y sociedad*, 87–88; Salazar y Castro, *Casa de Lara*, 2:363–65.

109. Salazar y Castro, *Casa de Lara*, 4:438. "Mis hijos legitimos, que al presente tengo, é de dicho Conde Don Rodrigo Manrique, mi Señor, é marido, que yo ove, durante el matrimonio, y tiempo que yo fuy casada con el dicho Conde Don Rodrigo Manrique, mi Señor." Rosa Montero Tejada states that all six children were illegitimate. Montero Tejada, *Nobleza y sociedad*, 87–88.

110. Spanish women made extensive use of the courts to address what was called "seduction by promise of marriage." See Dyer, "Seduction by Promise of Marriage"; Barahona, *Sex Crimes*; Usunáriz, "Asistir la madre."

111. The duke announced in October of 1501 that Pedro, the couple's third son, "was born and conceived after the said dispensation was brought and [that they were] married and veiled according to the order of the Sainted Mother Church of Rome," so Leonor must have either been pregnant or have already given birth to their second son in April of 1500. Quoted in Ladero Quesada, *Guzmán*, 293. "Fue habido y engendrado después de ser traida la dicha dispensación y ser casados y velados segund order de la Santa Madre Iglesia de Roma."

112. Ladero Quesada, *Guzmán*, 292–93, 293n23. For details of the papal dispensation issued by Pope Alexander VI on April 13, 1500, see 307n74. For more on the rules of consanguinity, see Donahue, "The Legal Background," 35. The issue of incest was a recurrent one for the Castilian high nobility, a small group who practiced endogamous marriage. Both church and civil law prohibited marriage between people who were related in the fourth degree (*cuarto grado de parentesco*). A legal marriage to close kin needed a papal bull and a license from the bishop or a judge in a church court, a process that could take from six months to a year and cost 35,000–40,000 maravedís in the fifteenth century. Montero Tejada, *Nobleza y sociedad*, 67–69. Another example of the importance of the dispensation was the marriage of doña Beatriz Castro to her nephew Pedro Álvarez Osorio in 1433. The marriage was celebrated before the dispensation arrived, so the couple was ordered to separate and "abstain from the conjugal act" until August of 1434, when Pope Eugenio IV granted the dispensation "with attention to the honor of this high-ranking lady and the scandal which will result among the family."

Pardo de Guevara y Valdés, *Los señores de Galicia*, 1:303n756. This type of retroactive dispensation was declared illegal by the Council of Trent when it abolished clandestine marriages. Sperling, "Marriage at the Time of the Council of Trent," 70–71.

113. Galán Parra, "El linaje," 59–60.

114. Ladero Quesada, *Guzmán*, 318n108.

115. In spite of Leonor's success, this story has a tragic coda because her son Alonso, the fifth duke, was mentally incapacitated (*mentecapto*) and could not govern his estates or consummate his marriage. Eventually the marriage had to be annulled and control of the estates passed to Alonso's younger brother Juan Alonso. Ana de Aragón made a second marriage to Juan Alonso, who became the sixth duke, governing the estates successfully until his death in 1558. Galán Parra, "El linaje," 60, 64–65.

116. Salazar y Castro, *Casa de Lara*, 2:184. Jesús M. Usunáriz found multiple examples of these written promises to marry in the Spanish archives for the sixteenth and seventeenth centuries, and he found that they were important to formalize the relationship in the eyes of the community and to serve as legal proof in court. Usunáriz, "Marriage and Love," 212.

117. In Italy this rule had been in force since the fifteenth century. Lombardi, "Marriage in Italy," 104.

118. There appears to be some slight confusion over the dates and order of events here. Salazar y Castro, *Casa de Lara*, 2:185.

119. "Vows worded in the future tense (*de futuro*) became binding upon consummation. Until 1563, promises alone, without church services, banns, clergy, or witnesses, constituted valid, if legally problematic, 'clandestine marriages.'" Dyer, "Seduction by Promise of Marriage," 444. Aldonza's case seems to have fallen under the "legally problematic" category and was undoubtedly influenced by the social status of the parties involved.

120. Salazar y Castro, *Casa de Lara*, 2:186–87; 192.

121. Salazar y Castro, *Casa de Lara*, 2:185, 192. The Spanish monarchy (like the French monarchy) strongly objected to children marrying without parental and royal approval and exerted considerable pressure on the high nobility to avoid clandestine marriages. Philip II, Charles V's son, punished the Duke of Feria (1577) and the Duke of Alba and his son (1578) with house arrest and exile for contracting marriages against his wishes. Morant Deusa and Bolufer Peruga, *Amor, matrimonio y familia*, 34; Sperling, "Marriage at the Time of the Council of Trent," 73–74.

122. Salazar y Castro, *Casa de Lara*, 2:185. Doña Luisa's disinheritance for marrying without consent was legal under the *Leyes de Toro*, but the same law stated that illegitimate children could not legally inherit the estate in Castile if they had

legitimate siblings, so her father's effort to leave the estate to her illegitimate half-brother did not succeed. Usunáriz, "Marriage and Love," 203; Espinosa, *Leyes de Toro*, law 9, 10–11.

123. Fink De Backer, *Widowhood*, 125–32, 155; Coolidge, *Guardianship*, 119–39.

124. Ettlinger, "Visibilis et Invisibilis," 771; Calderón Medina, "Las otras mujeres del rey," 5. This route to power was rarely as straightforward as the nobility wanted it to be. Silleras-Fernández, "Money Isn't Everything," 67, 71, 76.

125. Ettlinger, "Visibilis et Invisibilis," 770–71.

126. See Broomhall, "'The King and I,'" 339; and Potter, "The Life and After-Life of a Royal Mistress," 323–24.

127. Usunáriz, "Asistir la madre," 114. "Cuando la madre es pobre el padre es obligado de alimentar al hijo y a la madre."

128. Cuart Moner, "El bastardo de Medellín," 52–53.

129. Salazar y Castro, *Casa de Lara*, 4:314. Salazar y Castro, *Casa de Lara*, 2:162. "Aver tenido comunicación con." The word *comunicación* had clear sexual connotations. Barahona, *Sex Crimes*, 51.

130. AHNOB, fondo Osuna, C. 1765, D. 4.3. Another example of this is a woman named Ana who inherited "a certain estate" from her partner, Sancho de Rojas, the Lord of Monçón, when he died in 1500. Salazar y Castro, *Casa de Lara*, 1:481.

131. The clause continues with the details of the inheritance and its derivation. Carriazo Rubio also interpreted this as a sexual relationship. Carriazo Rubio, *Los testamentos*, 43, 221. "Porque yo ove moça donzella a Mençía de Fojeda, fija del jurado [Garci] González de Fojeda e de Marina Sánchez, su muger, con voluntad de su padre e madre e della, a la qual yo he dad en la mi villa de Marchena un heredamiento." A *jurado* was a representative from a parish to the municipal council, so Mencía's father had standing in the local community but was not on a social or economic level with the Count of Arcos. Nader, *Liberty in Absolutist Spain*, 229.

132. Bilinkoff, *The Avila of Saint Teresa*, 41–42.

133. Blumenthal, *Enemies and Familiars*, 174; Catlos, *Muslims of Medieval Latin Christendom*, 266–67.

134. Carriazo Rubio, *Los testamentos*, 225–26; Catlos, *Muslims of Medieval Latin Christendom*, 267.

135. Catlos, *Muslims of Medieval Latin Christendom*, 266; Soyer, "Muslim Freedmen," 139; Pike, "Sevillian Society," 356–57.

136. Usunáriz, "Asistir la madre," 103. Rewarding a woman with a dowry as compensation for her loss of virginity happened in other European countries also. See Korpiola, "Marriage in Sweden," 247; Lefebvre-Teillard, "Marriage in France," 274.

137. AHNOB, fondo Frías, C. 606, D. 26. "Un hidalgo mui honrrado." In practice, hidalgos could range from poor but noble individuals to men and women of substantial property and importance. Renato Barahona recorded that in 1628 Marina Léniz was awarded a dowry of 200 ducados by a Bilbao justice of the peace in her lawsuit against a man that she claimed had seduced her with promises of marriage and then abandoned her with damaged honor, which suggests that the amount of Anna's dowry might have been fairly standard for her social status. Barahona, *Sex Crimes*, 5–6.

138. AHNOB, fondo Frías, C. 606, D. 26.

139. Viña Brito, "El testamento de don Pedro Girón," 494, 504. "E que si la dicha doña Isabel su madre se casará e quisiere vivir honestamente, quel dicho don Alfonso mi fijo la aya de sostener en su vida en manera que ella viva honrada-mente." Examples of women who went on to marry after public affairs include doña Mencía de Ayala, who lived with the Admiral of Castile and subsequently married Ruy Sánchez Zapata, "copero mayor de Enrique III y Juan II." She left part of her legacy from the admiral (the town of Barajas) to her husband. Layna Serrano, *Historia de Guadalajara* 1:144n16. Luisa de la Cerda, daughter of the second Duke of Medinaceli, had an illegitimate daughter with the prince of Mélito and subsequently married Anontio Arias Pardo, one of the richest men in Castile. Manero Sorolla, "On the Margins of the Mendozas," 114. In the late sixteenth century, doña Victoria de Mendoza had two illegitimate children with the brother of the first Marquis of Santa Cruz and went on to marry a minor nobleman, the Lord of los Señores de Prejamo. Salazar y Castro, *Casa de Lara*, 1:596. Doña Mencía de Lemos married a Portuguese noble after her relationship with Cardinal Mendoza. Salazar y Castro, *Casa de Silva*, 2:227.

140. León, *A Bilingual Edition*, 41.

141. Salazar y Castro, *Casa de Lara*, 4:379. Salazar y Castro, *Casa de Lara*, 2:152. Marina did marry. Montero Tejada, *Nobleza y Sociedad*, 421.

142. Salazar y Castro, *Casa de Lara*, 2:744.

143. Lorenzo seems to have gotten into extensive trouble with the law, culminating in his murder of a hunting guard (*guarda de caza*) in 1546 after his mother's death. Vaquero Serrano, "'El desdichado [poeta] don Lorenzo Laso,'" 61, 63, 69; López de la Fuente and Vaquero Serrano, "¿Garcilaso traicionado?," 64.

144. Lehfeldt, *Religious Women*, 2–3.

145. Lehfeldt, *Religious Women*, 23, 32. For more on the connections between elite families and convents, see Atienza López, "Nobleza, poder señorial y conventos," 235–69; Beceiro Pita, "Los conventos de clarisas," 319–41.

146. A *beaterio* was a place for a group of women who had dedicated their lives to religion but had not taken formal vows with the church.

147. Bilinkoff, *The Avila of Saint Teresa*, 42.

148. Salazar y Castro, *Casa de Silva*, 2:154.

149. Salazar y Castro, *Casa de Lara*, 2:187.

150. Lehfeldt, *Religious Women*, 5.

151. Lehfeldt, *Religious Women*, 5. Not all of these women became abbesses. Ana de Bustamante had an illegitimate son with the third Count of Castañeda and later became a nun, although where is not recorded. Salazar y Castro, *Casa de Lara*, 1:533. María Sánchez had at least one illegitimate child with the second Lord of Marchena and later became a nun in the convent of Santa María de las Dueñas. Carriazo Rubio, *Los testamentos*, 32, 126. For a medieval precedent, see Silleras-Fernández, "Money Isn't Everything," 81.

152. Montero Tejada, *Nobleza y sociedad*, 87–88; Salazar y Castro, *Casa de Lara*, 2:363–65.

3. "SEND THE BABY TO ME"

1. Belén Rubio Ávila, "María de Mendoza," 433–37.

2. A *beata* or *beguine* was a woman who "lived a religiously inspired ascetic or philanthropic life outside of" a convent. They developed in the twelfth and thirteenth centuries across Europe, often took simple vows of chastity and poverty, and were not enclosed. They could be found in Germany, France, and Italy as well as Spain. Wickersham, "Beguines," 45; Belén Rubio Ávila, "María de Mendoza," 428, 434–35.

3. Belén Rubio Ávila, "María de Mendoza," 437, 441–42.

4. Belén Rubio Ávila, "María de Mendoza," 438.

5. Belén Rubio Ávila, "María de Mendoza," 445–46.

6. Ladero Quesada, *Guzmán*, 437; García Hernán, "Los grandes de España."

7. De la Pena Marazuela and León Tello, *Archivo de los duques de Frías*; Franco Silva, *Entre los reinados*; Gutiérrez Coronel, *Historia genealógica*.

8. Rosa Montero Tejada found that more minor branches of the Manrique family (younger sons and brothers) were less fertile in general, producing 3.8 legitimate children per marriage compared to 4.7 for the higher-ranking nobles and fewer illegitimate children in general (she did not give a number). Montero Tejada, *Nobleza y sociedad*, 96–97; Gerbert, *La nobleza en la corona de Castilla*, 94, quoted in Montero Tejada, *Nobleza y sociedad*, 97n222.

9. Twinam, *Public Lives*, 128. For a more specific breakdown of the complex categories of illegitimacy, see the introduction.

10. Ladero Quesada, *Guzmán*, 95, 95n22. See Sánchez Saus, *La nobleza andaluza*, 358–60, 359n6, for the debate about the legality of Alfonso's marriage to Leonor. Although his relationship with Mencía seems to have functioned as a marriage for the family, it was probably not technically legal.

11. Ladero Quesada, *Guzmán*, 96. For more on the political chaos in Castile, see Ruiz, *Spain's Centuries of Crisis*, 87–94.

12. Ladero Quesada, *Guzmán*, 165.

13. Ladero Quesada, *Guzmán*, 292–93.

14. Salazar y Castro, *Casa de Lara*, 2:744.

15. Garcia was the third Lord of las Torres de Alozayna. Salazar y Castro, *Casa de Lara*, 2:737.

16. Salazar y Castro, *Casa de Lara*, 2:419. For stepfamily puzzles, see Warner, "Seeing Stepfamilies in European Visual Culture," 205–25, 227.

17. The Mendoza family cared for the girls (María married and Antonia entered a local convent), but there is little evidence about where they spent their childhood. Baños Gil, "Ana de Mendoza de Luna y de la Vega," 291–92, 295–97; Layna Serrano, *Historia de Guadalajara*, 3:260, 294.

18. The fate of many illegitimate children is captured in the genealogist Salazar y Castro's description of the illegitimate son of Pedro Gomez de Silva: "Little is known of him and he died young" ("Que supo poco, y murió moço"). Salazar y Castro, *Casa de Silva*, 2:18. The concept of a "subset" is from Mangan, *Transatlantic Obligations*, 47. Mangan used it in relation to the fathers who cared for their illegitimate children, but it can also be applied to the children themselves.

19. Casey, *Family and Community in Early Modern Spain*, 156. Casey's work centers on the seventeenth century, but earlier noble households were at least as complex as the later ones. See, for example, Miguel Ángel Ladero Quesada's enumeration of the personnel of the Dukes of Medina Sidonia's vast households. Ladero Quesada, *Los señores de Andalucía*, 80–81. Leonore Davidoff pointed out the "hitherto undervalued vast amounts of labor—physical, mental, and emotional—financial responsibility, caring, and support provided by siblings and extended kin," in her study of nineteenth-century English families, and a similar pattern is visible in this earlier time period in Castile. Davidoff, *Thicker Than Water*, 9. See also Beceiro Pita and Córdoba de la Llave, *Parentesco, poder y mentalidad*, 224.

20. Harris, *English Aristocratic Women*, 61.

21. Salazar y Castro, *Casa de Lara*, 1:373. "Reparamos ya en el Capitulo VI del Libro I. la felicidad que consiguió la Casa de Lara en la produccion de muchas, y muy excelentes hijas, que contribuyeron altamente à mantener con sus alianças, y con su grande posteridad el anciano splendor de tan heroyca familia."

22. Quoted in Ladero Quesada, *Guzmán*, 28. "Caer en algunos pecados de la carne"; "Por aver hijos de bendiçión en quien suçediese su hazienda y su memoria."

23. Salazar y Castro, *Casa de Silva*, 2:580. "Governó, con acierto notable, los Estados de su marido, en las jornadas de Francia, Portugal, y Roma. Administró igualmente la tutorial de sus hijos. Cuydó mucho de la major direccion de sus

costumbres, y finalmente puso à todos en estado correspondiente à la grandeza de su nacimiento."

24. Matilla Tascon, *Testamentos de 43 personajes*, 19. "Y mando a mi hijo Don Juan y a mi hija Da. Mencia, y a calquier otros mis hijos que Dios me diere, que reverencien, sirvan y acaten a la dicha señora, mi amada mujer, a quien yo he querido y amado entrañablemente, como lo debia a la calidad de su persona, y al mucho amor con que hemos vivido, y asi mando, y ruego a los dichos mis hijos que la sirvan y obedezcan."

25. Ladero Quesada, *Guzmán*, 33–34.

26. Terence, *The Mother-in-Law*, quoted in Vives, *The Education of a Christian Woman*, 233–35.

27. Vives, *The Education of a Christian Woman*, 232.

28. García-Fernández, "Mujeres luchando," 55n84. English aristocratic men made similar requests. Harris, *English Aristocratic Women*, 84.

29. Kamen, *The Duke of Alba*, 9. For María Enríquez's acceptance of Hernando, see Maltby, *Alba*, 18.

30. Fitz James Stewart y Falco, "Biografía de doña María Enríquez," 9; Vives, *The Education of a Christian Woman*, 234.

31. AHNOB, fondo Osuna, C. 1762, D. 8, fol. 1. "Haba en su casa y compañía a las dichas mys fijas doña elvyra y doña maryna fasta en tanto que casen por que yo confio de su amor y bondad que las ella guardará y castigará y honrrará como conviene." Layna Serrano, *Historia de Guadalajara*, 2:233.

32. Layna Serrano, *Historia de Guadalajara*, 2:20–23.

33. For the guardianship, see AHNOB, fondo Frías, C. 97, D. 7, http://pares .culturaydeporte.gob.es/inicio.html.

34. Layna Serrano, *Historia de Guadalajara*, 2:21; AHNOB, fondo Osuna, C. 1840, D. 10 and fondo Frías, C. 97, D. 9, http://pares.culturaydeporte.gob.es/inicio.html.

35. Ladero Quesada, *Guzmán*, 39, 50–51.

36. Salazar y Castro, *Casa de Lara*, 2:206, 4:346. Barabara Harris found examples of women remembering their husband's illegitimate children in their wills in Tudor England. Harris, *English Aristocratic Women*, 84.

37. Quoted in Franco Silva, *Entre los reinados*, 113. "Su hacienda es poca y al dicho don Pedro le será buena." In the end, Pedro did not inherit Juana's goods, which went instead to her legitimate daughter Juliana.

38. Quoted in Ladero Quesada, *Guzmán*, 160, 168. "Desde que nacieron." See also Arroñada, "Algunas notas," 24.

39. Carriazo Rubio, *Los testamentos*, 42–43. For more on the roles of enslaved women in noble households, see Pike, "Sevillan Society," 348–49; Winer, "The Enslaved Wet Nurse as Nanny," 303–19.

40. Carriazo Rubio, *Los testamentos*, 221; AHNOB, fondo Osuna, C. 118, D. 9d.

41. Lehfeldt, "Ideal Men," 478.

42. Salazar y Castro, *Casa de Lara*, 1:521–23.

43. Salazar y Castro, *Casa de Lara*, 2:162.

44. Salazar y Castro, *Casa de Lara*, 2:162. His eldest daughter, Isobel, was already a beata and he left provisions for Ana to become a nun in the convent of Santa Clara in Burgos.

45. She married don Gómez Butrón y Mogica. Layna Serrano, *Historia de Guadalajara*, 2:233.

46. AHNOB, fondo Osuna, C. 1762, D. 8, fol. 1. "Como ser legitimo."

47. AHNOB, fondo Osuna, C. 1762, D. 8, fol. 1. "Una hija mia . . . se llama Leonor y disponga della agora de matrimonio o de religión aquello que a ellos major visto sera."

48. Salazar y Castro, *Casa de Lara*, 2:525; Gutiérrez Coronel, *Historia genealógica*, 2:421. Ana de Mendoza was the widowed Marquise de Cogolludo, born in 1505, the legitimate daughter of the third Duke of Infantado, and thus sister to Mariana's grandfather, the first Marquis de Montesclaros. Layna Serrano, *Historia de Guadalajara*, 3:138.

49. Salazar y Castro, *Casa de Lara*, 2:525.

50. For more on the rights and powers of female guardians in Castile, see Coolidge, *Guardianship*. Elite widows across Europe exercised similar responsibilities. See Harris, *English Aristocratic Women*, 127–74; Calvi, "Reconstructing the Family," 275–96; Van Aert, "The Legal Possibilities of Antwerp Widows," 282–95; Cavallo and Warner, *Widowhood*.

51. Fink De Backer, *Widowhood*, 150–52, 151n225.

52. Reed, "Mother Love in the Renaissance," 164.

53. The Venetian nobility also felt an obligation towards illegitimate children. In 1591 Franceschina Corner left her illegitimate grandson a legacy designed to pay for his education and upkeep. Byars, "From Illegitimate," 657.

54. Usunáriz, "Asistir la madre," 116–17.

55. Vaquero Serrano, "'El desdichado [poeta] don Lorenzo Laso,'" 63; Goodwin, *Spain*, 22; Vaquero Serrano, *Garcilaso*, 19–22.

56. Ladero Quesada, *Guzmán*, 291–92.

57. Fink De Backer, *Widowhood*, 150n225; Belén Rubio Ávila, "María de Mendoza," 433–35.

58. Salazar y Castro, *Casa de Lara*, 1:524.

59. Korth and Flusche, "Dowry and Inheritance," 398.

60. In book 3, title 2 discusses unlawful marriages, title 3, rape, and title 4, adultery; in book 4, title 2 discusses the laws of inheritance but does not distinguish between legitimate and illegitimate children. Scott, *The Visigothic Code*.

61. Pérez Martín, *Fuero Real*, book 3, title 6, law 1, 78.

62. Burns, *Las Siete Partidas*, vol. 4, partida 4, title 15, law 3, 953.

63. Burns, *Las Siete Partidas*, vol. 5, partida 6, title 13, laws 8–9, 1272–74. The *Fuero Real* also states that natural children whose parents are free to marry can inherit after their parents do in fact marry each other. Pérez Martín, *Fuero Real*, book 3, title 6, law 2, 79.

64. The *Leyes de Toro* also kept the hierarchy that ranked hijos naturales above children of incest or adultery. Espinosa, *Leyes de Toro*, law 9, 10–11. Jane Mangan provided a helpful summary of how these distinctions played out when Spanish men had children in colonial Spanish America. Mangan, *Transatlantic Obligations*, 149.

65. For the role of customary law, see Mangan, *Transatlantic Obligations*, 5; as well as Dillard, *Daughters of the Reconquest*. An example of a father manipulating both law and status can be found in the case of the Count of Castañeda in chapter 1 of this volume. Montero Tejada, *Nobleza y sociedad*, 99–100.

66. Carriazo Rubio, *Los testamentos*, 200.

67. Precioso Izquierdo and Gutiérrez de Armas, "De padres nobles," 378.

68. AHNOB, fondo Osuna, C. 538, D. 3, fol. 23.

69. Matilla Tascon, *Testamentos de 43 personajes*, 78.

70. The importance of siblings in the noble family existed across Europe. Bastress-Dukehart, "Sibling Conflict," 61–80; Broomhall, "Letters Make the Family," 25–44; Ruppel, "Subordinates, Patrons, and Most Beloved," 85–110; Tillyard, *A Royal Affair*; Chojnacka, "Women, Men, and Residential Patterns," 9–12.

71. Quoted in Casey, *Early Modern Spain*, 145. This emphasis on the responsibilities that the heir to an entailed estate had toward his younger siblings helped compensate for the pressure that the increased reliance on entail placed on family structures. Sabean and Teuscher, "Kinship in Europe," 2–3.

72. Salazar y Castro, *Casa de Lara*, 4:433.

73. Montero Tejada, *Nobleza y sociedad*, 189, 246. "Que en las bacantes que de aquí adelante hubiere se acuerde que el duque mi padre dexó muchos hijos y parientes muy gastados por serbir a su alteza y que yo asy mesmo tengo hijos."

74. Ladero Quesada, *Guzmán*, 174–75, 440.

75. Salazar y Castro, *Casa de Lara*, 4:346.

76. Isabel seems to have died before 1616. Salazar y Castro, *Casa de Lara*, 2:198, 200, 206.

77. Salazar y Castro, *Casa de Lara*, 4:341, 2:186, 239.

78. Salazar y Castro, *Casa de Lara*, 2:378–80. The convent of Nuestra Señora de Consolación in Calabazanos was closely connected to this branch of the Manrique family. Beceiro Pita, "Los conventos de clarisas," 329.

79. Carriazo Rubio, *Los testamentos*, 243, 259–60.

80. Salazar y Castro, *Casa de Lara*, 4:445, 2:366.

81. Salazar y Castro, *Casa de Lara*, 2:368.

82. Ladero Quesada, *Guzmán*, 294n29.

83. The specific crisis, in this case, was the transfer of power between Ferdinand of Aragón and his daughter Juana and her husband Philip of Burgundy. Elliott, *Imperial Spain*, 130; Phillips and Rahn Phillips, *A Concise History of Spain*, 126–27.

84. Ladero Quesada, *Guzmán*, 342.

85. See chapter 2 of this volume.

86. Salazar y Castro, *Casa de Lara*, 4:429.

87. Salazar y Castro, *Casa de Lara*, 2:362, 365. "D. Geronimo debió de lograr la gracia de sus hermanos."

88. Salazar y Castro, *Casa de Lara*, 2:366, 4:440.

89. Salazar y Castro, *Casa de Lara*, 2:262.

90. Ladero Quesada, *Guzmán*, 342.

91. Juan Rodríguez de Rojas was the Lord of Requena. Don Iñigo was the bishop of Oviedo, Coria, and Jaén, and later archbishop of Seville. Salazar y Castro, *Casa de Lara*, 2:46, 563–64.

92. Isabel was the illegitimate daughter of the Prince of Mélito. Vaquero Serrano, "Books in the Sewing Basket," 103.

93. Belén Rubio Ávila, "María de Mendoza," 574.

94. Carvajal, "Ana de Mendoza y de la Cerda," 583.

95. Cruz Gil, "María de Mendoza," 407, 409, 415–16.

96. María's father was don Agustin Mejia, "Comendador de Alhange, y Trece de Santiago, Maestro de Campo general de España, de los Consejos de Estado, y Guerra de Felipe IV." Her mother was doña Juana Vallejo. Salazar y Castro, *Casa de Lara*, 2:370, 842.

97. Salazar y Castro, *Casa de Silva*, 2:200.

98. Salazar y Castro, *Casa de Lara*, 2:640.

99. There was a similar trend in the early modern Venetian nobility. Byars, "From Illegitimate Son," 660.

100. Ladero Quesada, *Guzmán*, 142.

101. Ladero Quesada, *Guzmán*, 142.

102. Ladero Quesada, *Guzmán*, 438.

103. Salazar y Castro, *Casa de Lara*, 2:187. "Justicia ordinaria."

104. Hernández Franco and Rodríguez Pérez, "Bastardía," 348–49.

105. Vives Torija and Ayuso Blas, "Guiomar de Mendoza y Borbón," 680.

106. García Oro, *Testamento*, vii, 8.

107. Her grandfather was the fourth Count of Castañeda and she was married to the fifth Count of Paredes. Salazar y Castro, *Casa de Lara*, 1:531–33. See also Montero Tejada, *Nobleza y sociedad*, 100.

108. Salazar y Castro, *Casa de Lara*, 2:365, 374.

109. Salazar y Castro, *Casa de Lara*, 1:678–80.

110. Möller Recondo and Carabias Torres, *Historia de Peñaranda de Bracamonte*, 69–70; Gutiérrez Coronel, *Historia genealógica*, 1:140.

111. Ladero Quesada, *Guzmán*, 94, 170–71. "Cargado de simbolismo sobre el origen y la jerarquía de los poderes y el fundamentos de su ejercicio, donde queda clara la preeminencia del oficio y justicia del señor sobe todos los demás, que dependen de él."

112. Ladero Quesada, *Guzmán*, 171.

113. Salazar y Castro, *Casa de Lara*, 2:626–27.

114. Hernández Franco and Rodríguez Pérez, "El linaje," 398n59.

115. Fernan Yañez's grandmother was the illegitimate daughter and the heiress of don Gomez Manrique, archbishop of Toledo. Salazar y Castro, *Casa de Lara*, 1:331.

4. NOT BORN OF LAWFUL MARRIAGE

1. AHNOB, fondo Frías, C. 606, D. 37. "Terciópelo carmesí, y otras veces de otras sedas, y le críaban como a hijo del dicho Señor Condestable." In a parallel case from about one hundred years later, when Francisco Fajardo Melgarejo, illegitimate son of the fourth Marquis de Vélez, applied for membership in the Order of Santiago, the witnesses attesting to his paternity stated that they knew he was his father's son because his father had cared for him in his own house, he sat at his father's table, and his father had verbally claimed that Francisco was his son. Hernández Franco and Rodríguez Pérez, "Bastardía," 357–58. Further discussion on the ways in which fathers acknowledged paternity is in chapter 1.

2. AHNOB, fondo Frías, C. 606, D. 37. This story appears from the point of view of Bernaldino's father in chapter 1.

3. Recent historiography has emphasized the importance of familial networks, especially among the elite. For networks among Spanish royalty, see Sánchez, *The Empress, the Queen, and the Nun*; and for royalty across Europe, see Cruz and Galli Stampino, *Early Modern Habsburg Women*. These royal networks and noble family networks regularly included illegitimate children. See, for example, Mangan, *Transatlantic Obligations*; Mizumoto-Gitter, "From Rome to Gandía," 57–76; Beceiro Pita, "Los conventos de clarisas," 319–41.

4. Twinam, *Public Lives*, 41–42.

5. McDougall, *Royal Bastards*, 6, 19, 128.

6. This was true in other places across Europe as well. For example, the Holy Roman Empire required "noble descent on both the paternal and maternal sides" to achieve noble status, thus excluding legitimate and illegitimate children of non-noble mothers from both tournaments and cathedral chapters. Hurwich, *Noble Strategies*, 229–30.

7. Burns, *Las Siete Partidas*, vol. 5, partida 7, title 6, laws 2 and 7, 1333, 1335–36; Twinam, *Public Lives*, 44.

8. Dewald, *The European Nobility*, 36–38, 144.

9. Twinam, *Public Lives*, 45. *Colegios* were small, semiautonomous institutions that existed within Spanish universities and were originally designed to provide poor students with the chance to attend university, although the income restrictions were relaxed in the early sixteenth century. San Bartolomé was the oldest of the *colegios mayores*. Kagan, *Students and Society*, 65–67, 129, 131, 135.

10. Twinam, *Public Lives*, 42, 44.

11. Twinam, *Public Lives*, 46.

12. Howe, *Education and Women*, 107.

13. Hernández Franco and Rodríguez Pérez, "Bastardía," 355.

14. Wunder, "Marriage in the Holy Roman Empire," 67; Hurwich, *Noble Strategies*, 228–29, 240–41, 244. Thomas Kuehn also singles out Germany as "taking a decidedly tough moral stand on illegitimacy." Kuehn, *Illegitimacy*, 81.

15. Kuehn, *Illegitimacy*, 79–84.

16. Byars, "From Illegitimate," 645.

17. Gerber, *Bastards*, 15, 51, 53.

18. Louis XIV created a tax on bastards in 1697 that, if paid, technically made them legitimate but without the right to inherit. Gerber, *Bastards*, 50, 98, 102–3.

19. The colegios of Cuenca, Oviedo, and Arzobispo all added legitimacy requirements to their original statutes. Cuart Moner, "Bastardos en el estudio," 309.

20. We see a similar focus on social class in France, where Avocat-Général Cardin Le Bret wrote in 1632 that though the bastards of gentleman were commoners and had to pay the *taille*, he "would not extend this rule to include the bastards of great and illustrious houses whose nobility [was] known to everyone." Gerber, *Bastards*, 54.

21. Cuart Moner, "Bastardos en el estudio," 310–11, 313; Kagan, *Students and Society*, 91. The *bachiller* would be roughly equivalent to a modern bachelor's degree or BA.

22. Cuart Moner, "Bastardos en el estudio," 310; Cuart Moner, "El bastardo de Medellín," 50.

23. Cuart Moner, "Bastardos en el estudio," 310.

24. Cuart Moner, "El bastardo de Medellín," 40. "Fue víctima de un sistema de exclusion social que, en principio, le debería haber beneficiado."

25. Cuart Moner, "Bastardos en el estudio," 310.

26. Cuart Moner, "El bastardo de Medellín," 42–43.

27. Twinam, *Public Lives*, 48–49.

28. Twinam attributes this to the fact that "early modern Spaniards practiced both negative and also positive forms of discrimination in order to establish a hierarchy of status," so that *hijosdalgo* and the nobility were more likely to be "positively recognized because of their lineage." Twinam, *Public Lives*, 41.

29. Cuart Moner, "Bastardos en el estudio," 311–12.

30. Taylor, *Honor and Violence*, 118–19. In Venice, illegitimate children were referred to as *muli*, which translates to the uncomplimentary term mule, "the sterile offspring produced by the mismatched congress of a horse and a donkey." Byars, "From Illegitimate Son," 643.

31. For more analysis of insults and how they relate to gender and racial tensions, see Villa-Flores, *Dangerous Speech*.

32. Quoted in Cuart Moner, "Bastardos en el estudio," 308. "Que los hijos bastardos y espúreos sucedan a sus padres en la nobleza e hidalguía que tuvieron"; "por líneas rectas y legítimas o naturales de varón . . . y siendo las raíces y el tronco del árbol Bueno no pueden dexar de ser Buenos los frutos." *Hidalguía* designates the social status of a tax-exempt elite who did not carry a title. Crawford, *The Fight for Status and Privilege*, 2.

33. Viña Brito, "El testamento de don Pedro Girón," 498–505.

34. Clavero, *Mayorazgo*, 44.

35. Legitimate children figured as "necessary" or "forced" heirs who could not be disinherited. Korth and Flusche, "Dowry and Inheritance," 398. Illegitimate children born from an unmarried man who died intestate and had an established, monogamous relationship with the children's mother could inherit one-sixth of their father's property, or could inherit all, but only in the absence of legitimate children. Burns, *Las Siete Partidas*, vol. 5, partida 6, title 13, law 8, 1272–73.

36. Korth and Flusche, "Dowry and Inheritance," 398; Montero Tejada, *Nobleza y sociedad*, 98.

37. Failing this, Pedro had to marry a woman of good, clean lineage who was a hidalgo. Franco Silva, *Entre los reinados*, 217–18.

38. Hernández Franco and Rodríguez Pérez, "Bastardía," 349–50.

39. Montero Tejada, *Nobleza y sociedad*, 99. "El ser legitimado no siempre era garantía de tener los mismos derechos que los otros hijos."

40. McDougall, *Royal Bastards*, 43, 140, 169–70, 174.

41. McDougall, *Royal Bastards*, 224.

42. McDougall, *Royal Bastards*, 232; Burns, *Las Siete Partidas*, vol. 4, partida 4, title 15, law 4, 953.

43. Montero Tejada, *Nobleza y sociedad*, 98; McDougall, *Royal Bastards*, 232–33. There is an excellent analysis of what a formal legitimation could mean for the eighteenth-century Colombian elite at the beginning of Ann Twinam's book on illegitimacy in Spanish America. Twinam, *Public Lives*, 3–5.

44. For the legitimation of Pope Alexander VI's son (born before his father was pope), see Mizumoto-Gitter, "From Rome to Gandía," 60 and 60n14.

45. Salazar y Castro, *Casa de Lara*, 1:274. His father, Gómez de Rojas, was Lord of Villa de Requena and a member of the royal council of Castile under Henry IV and again under Ferdinand and Isabel. Salazar y Castro, *Casa de Lara*, 1:470–71.

46. Carriazo Rubio, *Los testamentos*, 42; AHNOB, fondo Osuna, C. 118, D. 9; Montero Tejada, *Nobleza y sociedad*, 98.

47. This meant that she could inherit all his goods. Salazar y Castro, *Casa de Lara*, 2:563.

48. García Hernán, "Los grandes de España," 336.

49. See, for example, the case of Enrique II's illegitimate daughters, the "aunt abbesses" who got a papal dispensation to hold their office. Pérez de Tudela y Bueso, "El Monasterio," 301–2.

50. Montero Tejada, *Nobleza y sociedad*, 241. The nobility's value for their military role lasted into the eighteenth century. Precioso Izquierdo and Gutiérrez de Armas, "De padres nobles," 376–77; Coolidge, "Investing in the Lineage," 241–42.

51. Ladero Quesada, *Guzmán*, 186.

52. Salazar y Castro, *Casa de Lara*, 2:670.

53. Salazar y Castro, *Casa de Lara*, 2:350, 355.

54. Ortega Gato, "Los Enríquez," 27.

55. Salazar y Castro, *Casa de Lara*, 2:420.

56. In 1568 Fadrique was allowed to complete the rest of his punishment by serving with his father in Flanders. Kamen, *The Duke of Alba*, vii, 76–77.

57. Montero Tejada, *Nobleza y sociedad*, 259, 267; Hernández Franco and Rodríguez Pérez, "Bastardía," 341–42. The three military-religious orders were the Orders of Santiago, Calatrava, and Alcántara, which had been founded in the twelfth century. They controlled huge estates and vast revenues and exercised jurisdiction over a million vassals. By the late fifteenth century, Ferdinand and Isabel had incorporated all three orders into the crown, a process that was finalized by a papal bull in 1523. Elliott, *Imperial Spain*, 88–89.

58. Hernández Franco and Rodríguez Pérez, "Bastardía," 348, 355.

59. Montero Tejada, *Nobleza y sociedad*, 262; Salazar y Castro, *Casa de Lara*, 2:149–52, 365, 383–84, 443; Hernández Franco and Rodríguez Pérez, "Bastardía," 348.

60. Salazar y Castro, *Casa de Lara*, 2:187, 198.

61. Salazar y Castro, *Casa de Silva*, 2:155; Salazar y Castro, *Casa de Lara*, 2:189; Salazar y Castro, *Casa de Silva*, 1:421; Salazar y Castro, *Casa de Lara*, 2:383; Burke and Cherry, *Collections of Paintings in Madrid*, 361.

62. Elliott, *Imperial Spain*, 89.

63. Montero Tejada, *Nobleza y sociedad*, 245–46, 254, 261.

64. Salazar y Castro, *Casa de Silva*, 1:421; Salazar y Castro, *Casa de Silva*, 2:155.

65. Twinam, *Public Lives*, 46.

66. For an interesting analysis of the complicated relationship between nobility, illegitimacy, and limpieza de sangre, see Hernández Franco and Rodríguez Pérez, "Bastardía," 361–62.

67. Gutiérrez Coronel, *Historia genealógica*, 2:360; Salazar y Castro, *Casa de Lara*, 2:438.

68. Salazar y Castro, *Casa de Lara*, 2:353; Nader, *Liberty in Absolutist Spain*, 228.

69. One hundred and eleven illegitimate sons' careers are unknown, forty-nine entered the military and/or royal service, and twenty-eight inherited the title.

70. He made the comment in his second will. Salazar y Castro, *Casa de Silva*, 1:387. "Y dize su padre, que avia gastado por él en los pleytos de estos Beneficios, mas de lo que avia percibido de sus frutos."

71. Their illegitimate cousin was a *regidor* (councilman). Salazar y Castro, *Casa de Silva*, 2:198–200; Ladero Quesada, *Guzmán*, 94.

72. Montero Tejada, *Nobleza y sociedad*, 298–302; Elliott, *Imperial Spain*, 99–100.

73. Aznar Gil, "Los ilegítimos," 9; Salazar y Castro, *Casa de Lara*, 1:532; Montero Tejada, *Nobleza y sociedad*, 289.

74. Salazar y Castro, *Casa de Lara*, 1:532–33. Another good example of this is Juan de Rivera, illegitimate son of the first Duke of Alcalá, who became bishop of Badajoz, then patriarch of Alexandria, and eventually archbishop of Valencia. In the late eighteenth century he was beatified, and he was then canonized by Pope John XXII in 1959. Gutiérrez Coronel, *Historia genealógica*, 1:134; Benedictine Monks of St. Augustine's Abbey, Ramsgate, *The Book of Saints*, 379.

75. Frederico Aznar Gil made this case for the Iberian clergy in general. Aznar Gil, "Los ilegítimos," 9. Michelle Armstrong-Partida demonstrated that priests in fourteenth-century Catalunya were sexually active in a variety of ways that ranged from casual sexual relationships to long-term, marriage-like concubinage. Episcopal officials in Catalunya "were lenient in their policies of tolerating and punishing concubinage, and repeat offenders were not removed from their benefice or deprived of their clerical status." Armstrong-Partida, *Defiant Priests*, 25, 32.

76. Morte García, "Los arzobispos de la Casa Real," 177.

77. Luis de Acuña, the bishop of Burgos, had a son, Antonio, who became the bishop of Zamora. Aznar Gil, "Los ilegítimos," 9.

78. Salazar y Castro, *Casa de Lara*, 2:455–56.

79. Lehfeldt, *Religious Women*, 32; Rodríguez Pérez, "La historia social," 135; Liang, *Family and Empire*, 178–79.

80. Beceiro Pita, "Los conventos de clarisas," 325; Ortego Rico, "El patrocinio religioso de los Mendoza," 281–85; Perea Rodríguez, "Mencía de Mendoza," 128. Perea Rodríguez named her as abbess of Las Huelgas in Burgos, but her father's will states that she entered the convent of Santa Clara in Guadalajara. Layna Serrano, *Historia de Guadalajara*, 1:330–31.

81. Beceiro Pita, "Los conventos de clarisas," 320, 329–30.

82. Montero Tejada, *Nobleza y sociedad*, 319, 414–15; Salazar y Castro, *Casa de Lara*, 1:621, 673–74, 2:85.

83. Salazar y Castro, *Casa de Lara*, 2:149, 152–53.

84. Lehfeldt, *Religious Women*, 32.

85. Lehfeldt, *Religious Women*, 32.

86. Beceiro Pita, "Los conventos de clarisas," 334–35. For a dramatic example of this kind of conflict, see the story of María de Sandoval and her fight with her son, the Count of Treviño and later the first Duke of Nájera, in chapter 5. María ended up taking vows in the convent of Santa María de Consolación de Calabazanos.

87. Amayuelas was also a title held by the Manrique family. Salazar y Castro, *Casa de Lara*, 2:371–73, 380, 695.

88. Salazar y Castro, *Casa de Silva*, 1:390, 410. Other examples include the first Duke of Nájera's other two illegitimate daughters, who were both nuns in Santa Clara de Burgos (Salazar y Castro, *Casa de Lara*, 2:152); Francisca and Inés Manrique, illegitimate daughters of the third Count of Paredes who both joined the Monastery of the Magdalene in Alcaráz (Salazar y Castro, *Casa de Lara*, 2:366); Ana de Arellano, illegitimate daughter of the fifth Count of Aguilar (d. 1590) who joined the Cistercian convent of Santa María de Erce along with two of her legitimate half-sisters (Salazar y Castro, *Casa de Lara*, 1:398); and Isabel de Cardenas, illegitimate daughter of the fifth Duke of Nájera (by marriage) who professed in the convent of the Concepción in Torrijos at the same time as her first cousin Mariana Manrique, the illegitimate daughter of the son of the fourth Duke of Nájera (Salazar y Castro, *Casa de Lara*, 2:200, 206). For more examples of multiple women from the same lineage (including the Manrique) in convents, see Beceiro Pita, "Los conventos de clarisas," 338–40.

89. I cannot prove that all these women were in the convent at the same time. The only dates I have for them are their fathers' death dates, which range from 1515–85, making it probable that their convent careers overlapped to some degree. Salazar y Castro, *Casa de Silva*, 1:390–92, 409–10, 475; Layna Serrano, *Historia de Guadalajara*, 2:236; Salazar y Castro, *Casa de Lara*, 2:455–56.

90. Beceiro Pita, "Los conventos de clarisas," 337.

91. A *cahiz* is about twelve bushels. The Spanish reads, "No obstante no ser legítima." Pérez de Tudela y Bueso, "El Monasterio," 184, 188, 301–4.

92. Beceiro Pita, "Los conventos de clarisas," 340.

93. Hernández Franco and Rodríguez Pérez, "El linaje," 392.

94. Quintanilla Raso, "Estructuras sociales y familiares y papel político," 342; Ladero Quesada, *Los señores de Andalucía*, 29.

95. Her sample size was very small, including only seven illegitimate males and eleven illegitimate females. Montero Tejada, *Nobleza y sociedad*, 57–58. Beceiro Pita also found that illegitimate daughters were more likely to enter the convent. Beceiro Pita, "Los conventos de clarisas," 335.

96. An important caveat here is the number of illegitimate daughters whose status I do not know. Out of ninety-seven illegitimate daughters in the fifteenth century, forty-nine married and the marital status of thirty-five is unknown; out of ninety-four illegitimate daughters in the sixteenth century, thirty-five married and the marital status of twenty-one is unknown. The rest joined convents or died young. A good example of smaller dowries for illegitimate daughters is the family of the third Duke of Medina Sidonia, referenced in chapter 1 and below.

97. AHNOB, fondo Osuna, C. 423, D. 12; Gutiérrez Coronel, *Historia genealógica*, 2:438.

98. Ladero Quesada, *Guzmán*, 94, 143. The marriage between Leonor and Manuel did not take place because Leonor died in childhood. Ladero Quesada, *Guzmán*, 143n58. Matthew Gerber found a similar trend for a slightly later period (1697) in France, where one out of twenty of the illegitimate daughters identified by Louis XIV's tax on bastards had married another illegitimate child. Gerber, *Bastards*, 104. Jana Byars cited a seventeenth-century example in Venice. Byars, "From Illegitimate Son," 659.

99. Salazar y Castro, *Casa de Lara*, 2:350.

100. Vidma Guzmán, "El señorío y el marquesado de la guardia (Jaén)," 116.

101. Salazar y Castro, *Casa de Lara*, 2:350. This is possibly another example of two illegitimate noble children marrying each other, as I cannot find a record that Juan Alonso was married.

102. Palos, "Bargaining Chips," 1.

103. Franco Silva, "Las mujeres," 177–78; Cuart Moner, "El bastardo de Medellín," 44.

104. Franco Silva, "Las mujeres," 178.

105. Franco Silva, "Las mujeres," 179–80.

106. Harris, *English Aristocratic Women*, 5.

107. Mitchell, *Queen, Mother, and Stateswoman*, 8.

108. Montero Tejada, *Nobleza y sociedad*, 152.

109. The Manrique family, for example, followed this pattern, and before his premature death Prince don Juan, the heir to the Catholic Monarchs, included among his court the firstborn sons of the Duke of Nájera, the Duke of Alba, the Marquis of Priego, and the Count of Ureña. Montero Tejada, *Nobleza y sociedad*, 189.

110. Carriazo Rubio, *Los testamentos*, 32, 114–15.

111. Ladero Quesada, *Guzmán*, 291, 295.

112. Galán Parra, "El linaje," 63.

113. Ladero Quesada, *Guzmán*, 292.

114. Of the legitimate daughters with 6-million-maravedís dowries, one became a nun and the other died young. One of the illegitimate daughters also died young. Ladero Quesada, *Guzmán*, 291–92, 295.

115. Ladero Quesada, *Los señores de Andalucia*, 30; Hernández Franco and Rodríguez Pérez, "El linaje," 396.

116. Carriazo Rubio, *Los testamentos*, 44.

117. Carriazo Rubio, *Los testamentos*, 44.

118. Ladero Quesada, *Los señores de Andalucía*, 79; Hernández Franco and Rodríguez Pérez, "El linaje," 393.

119. Salazar y Castro, *Casa de Lara*, 2:364.

120. Casey, *Early Modern Spain*, 147. Dowry inflation was a problem across Europe. See Chojnacki, *Women and Men in Renaissance Venice*, 125–27.

121. The fates of the other two illegitimate daughters are unknown. Montero Tejada, *Nobleza y sociedad*, 317.

122. Salazar y Castro, *Casa de Lara*, 2:419. A *beata* or *beguine* was a woman who lived in a community of pious women who observed "such religious ideals as poverty and chastity, but without taking formal religious vows or living under a monastic rule." Lehfeldt, *Religious Women*, 111. Less formally organized than nuns in convents, they required less in the way of dowry and were open to women from middle or lower ranks of society. Wickersham, "Beguines," 45.

123. Salazar y Castro, *Casa de Lara*, 2:162.

124. The colegios of Cuenca, Oviedo, and Arzobispo all added legitimacy requirements to their original statutes. Cuart Moner, "Bastardos en el estudio," 309. "Pero lo primero era más importante que lo segundo." "Todo iba a depender del poder familiar del candidato en cuestión." Montero Tejada, *Nobleza y sociedad*, 289.

125. Cuart Moner, "Bastardos en el estudio," 310.

126. Salazar y Castro, *Casa de Lara*, 1:392. Other examples of this vague designation of *clerigo* include Lorenzo de Guzmán, illegitimate son of the first Duke of Medina Sidonia (d. 1468), Juan de Vargas, illegitimate son of the ninth Lord of Higuera, and Antonio Manrique, illegitimate son of the third Duke of Nájera. Barrantes Maldonado, "Ilustraciones de la casa de Niebla," 219; Salazar y Castro, *Casa de*

Silva, 1:604; Salazar y Castro, *Casa de Lara*, 2:187. Rodrigo de Borja, illegitimate son of the sixth Duke of Gandía, is listed simply as "religioso en Valencia," and Alonso, son of the fourth Lord of Javalquinto and brother to Isabel, Juana, and Beatriz discussed above is described only as "Frayle Francisco." AHNOB, fondo Osuna, C. 538, D. 3, fol. 8b; C. 539, D. 2, fol. 25; Salazar y Castro, *Casa de Lara*, 2:419.

127. AHNOB, fondo Frías, C. 274, D. 6; Barrantes Maldonado, "Ilustraciones de la casa de Niebla," 376; Salazar y Castro, *Casa de Silva*, 1:397; Salazar y Castro, *Casa de Lara*, 2:187, 353. Other monks include Enrique, illegitimate son of the fifth Count of Coruña, who also joined the Augustinians. Gutiérrez Coronel, *Historia genealógica*, 2:353.

128. His illegitimate sister was Antonia Manrique, who became abbess of St. Clara de Carrión. Salazar y Castro, *Casa de Lara*, 1:621.

129. Salazar y Castro, *Casa de Lara*, 1:565, 568.

130. Montero Tejada, *Nobleza y sociedad*, 291, 316.

131. Neither Ladero Quesada nor I can find him in the list of bishops of Cádiz. Ladero Quesada, *Guzmán*, 94.

132. Quoted in Montero Tejada, *Nobleza y sociedad*, 99. Emphasis added. "Queremos e mandamos que los tales fijos legítimos e naturales e nacidos de legítimo matrimonio varones sean preferidos e ayan y hereden el dicho maiorazgo aunque sean menores en edad al tal hijo natural legitimado por el matrimonio subsequente o por el Rey o por otra manera qualesquier, aunque la tal legitimación sea fecha antes."

133. The brother was already the Count of Osorno in his own right. Montero Tejada, *Nobleza y sociedad*, 99–100.

134. AHNOB, fondo Frías, C. 394, D. 11, D. 12; Franco Silva, *Entre los reinados*, 203. A guardian ad litem was temporarily appointed to manage the property of a minor. Coolidge, *Guardianship*, 23–25.

135. Franco Silva, *Entre los reinados*, 217.

136. Montero Tejada, *Nobleza y sociedad*, 98. Illegitimate children could be provided for from the quinto of the parental estate that remained after the legitimate children had inherited the other four-fifths of the estate, but could only inherit the entire estate if they had no legitimate siblings and were hijos naturales. For a more specific discussion of the legal aspects of this, see chapter 3. Burns, *Las Siete Partidas*, vol. 5, partida 6, title 13, laws 8 and 10, 1272–73; Korth and Flusche, "Dowry and Inheritance," 398.

137. Quoted in Montero Tejada, *Nobleza y sociedad*, 98.

138. AHNOB, fondo Frías, C. 606, D. 37.

139. Fathers were legally required to provide basic maintenance for illegitimate children. Espinosa, *Leyes de Toro*, law 10, 11.

140. Salazar y Castro, *Casa de Lara*, 2:262.

141. Ladero Quesada, *Guzmán*, 490. "A los riesgos derivados de la ruptura de su matrimonio, la falta de hijos legítimos y las reclamaciones de su hermana María a partes de la herencia."

142. Montero Tejada, *Nobleza y sociedad*, 98; Salazar y Castro, *Casa de Lara*, 1:607, 616.

143. Allende-Salazar, "Don Felipe de Guevara," 189.

144. Ladero Quesada, *Los señores de Andalucía*, 79.

145. Ladero Quesada, *Los señores de Andalucía*, 77; Ladero Quesada, *Guzmán*, 165.

146. It is not altogether clear what the disagreement was. The duke did leave these properties to Luis in his will. Salazar y Castro, *Casa de Lara*, 2:171, 4:300.

147. Terrasa-Lozano, "Legal Enemies, Beloved Brothers," 729.

148. Ladero Quesada, *Los señores de Andalucía*, 83.

149. Salazar y Castro, *Casa de Lara*, 2:184, 186–87, 192.

150. Salazar y Castro, *Casa de Silva*, 2:198–99.

151. Salazar y Castro, *Casa de Lara*, 2:231.

152. Salazar y Castro, *Casa de Silva*, 1:507.

153. Salazar y Castro, *Casa de Lara*, 1:524.

5. "IT IS SUCH A BURDEN TO ME"

1. For some of the challenging aspects of writing the history of emotions, see Plamper, *The History of Emotions*, 33–39. For an excellent overview of the historiography of emotions starting with Lucien Febvre in the 1930s, see Villa-Flores and Lipsett-Rivera, "Introduction," 4–5. For a critique of this historiography, see Rosenwein, "Worrying about Emotions," 821–28.

2. Holler, "Of Sadness and Joy," 18–19.

3. Curcio-Nagy, "The Language of Desire," 55–56. For the immense popularity of commercial theater in early modern Spain, see Ball, *Treating the Public*.

4. Grace, "Family and Familiars," 201.

5. Rosenwein, "Worrying about Emotions," 842; Grace, "Family and Familiars," 196.

6. Casey, *Early Modern Spain*, 145. Analysis of this trend for the European-wide nobility can be found in Sabean and Teuscher, "Kinship in Europe," 14.

7. Johnson, *The Gender Knot*, 5, quoted in Bennett, *History Matters*, 55. Emphasis is in the original.

8. Korth and Flusche, "Dowry and Inheritance," 399; Casey, *Early Modern Spain*, 147. Dowry inflation was also a concern in Venice, Florence, and Rome. Chojnacki, "Nobility, Women and the State," 141; Cohn, "Marriage in the Mountains," 188; Fosi and Visceglia, "Marriage and Politics at the Papal Court," 199.

9. Korth and Flusche, "Dowry and Inheritance," 399–401. For women's control over and access to their dowries, see also Wessell-Lightfoot, *Women, Dowries, and Agency*.

10. Montero Tejada, *Nobleza y sociedad*, 70–77. I define women's power as the "ability to act effectively, to influence people or decisions, and to achieve goals" in their families and communities. Erler and Kowaleski, "Introduction," 2.

11. Broomhall, "'My Daughter, My Dear,'" 558.

12. In both Spain and Portugal, women had more access to family property than in England or Italy because of the traditions of partible inheritance (even when those were modified by the use of entail). For the difference that dowry regimes make in women's freedom and ability to control their own lives, see Sperling, "The Economics and Politics of Marriage," 221.

13. Rich, *Of Woman Born*, 57, quoted in Bennett, *History Matters*, 55. Walby's original quote defines patriarchy as "a system of social structures and practices in which men dominate, oppress and exploit women." Walby, *Theorizing Patriarchy*, 20, quoted in Bennett, *History Matters*, 56. Early modern Iberia continued to rely heavily on the contributions and expertise of women of all social classes. See, for example, Poska, *Women and Authority*; Coolidge, *Guardianship*; Fink De Backer, *Widowhood*; Sánchez, *The Empress, the Queen, and the Nun*; Mitchell, *Queen, Mother, and Stateswoman*.

14. Bennett, *History Matters*, 59.

15. Poska, *Women and Authority*, 10.

16. Gutiérrez Coronel, *Historia genealógica*, 1:125; Salazar y Castro, *Casa de Silva*, 1:143; Ladero Quesada, *Los señores de Andalucía*, 88.

17. Their marriage alliances included a daughter of the Counts of Alba de Liste and the sister of the second Duke of Infantado. Casaus Ballester, "La casa ducal de Híjar," 102–4.

18. Quintanilla Raso, "Aportación al studio de la nobleza en la Edad Media," 168; Quintanilla Raso, "La casa señorial de Benavides en Andalucía," 476.

19. Layna Serrano, *Historia de Guadalajara*, 1:140.

20. Ladero Quesada, *Guzmán*, 49, 63, 71.

21. Ladero Quesada, *Guzmán*, 93.

22. Gutiérrez Coronel, *Historia genealógica*, 2:185, 383; Nuñez Bespalova, "Origen del linaje," 11; Franco Silva, *Entre los reinados*, 111.

23. Real Academia de la Historia, "Juan de Borja Enríquez."

24. Ladero Quesada, *Guzmán*, 17. "Establece un modelo de caballero, pobre por su origen bastardo, que alcanza la cima de la nobleza gracias a su valor, a las riquezas que obtiene en la guerra, a su sangre y, en un etapa de madurez, también a su capacidad política." Sara McDougall noted that by the twelfth and thirteenth

centuries, literary works took an interest in bastard kings, thus linking them to older traditions of hero stories that credited the hero with irregular birth or abandonment. McDougall, *Royal Bastards*, 187.

25. Ladero Quesada, *Guzmán*, 14. Taking the family origins even further back, the Guzmán also claimed descent from (among others) an illegitimate daughter of the Infante Ordoño. Ladero Quesada, *Los señores de Andalucía*, 88.

26. Hernández Franco, "Matrimonio," 48; Clavero, *Mayorazgo*, 44; Viña Brito, "El testamento de don Pedro Girón," 493; AHNOB, fondo Osuna, C. 2, D. 10.

27. Ladero Quesada, *Guzmán*, 168–69, 172; Carriazo Rubio, *Los testamentos*, 42; Salazar y Castro, *Casa de Lara*, 1:526, 530; Layna Serrano, *Historia de Guadalajara*, 3:138.

28. Precioso Izquierdo and Gutiérrez de Armas, "De padres nobles," 364. For an excellent example of how royalty expected dynastic marriages to function to their advantage, see Broomhall, "'My Daughter, My Dear,'" 552–53.

29. Salazar y Castro, *Casa de Lara*, 1:8.

30. The nobility's focus was on the good of the group (the lineage) rather than the wishes of the individual. Precioso Izquierdo and Gutiérrez de Armas, "De padres nobles," 364.

31. Hernández Franco, "Matrimonio," 44. "En los márgenes que permiten los grados de consanguinidad."

32. Reed, "Mother Love in the Renaissance," 155.

33. Brundage, *Law, Sex, and Christian Society*, 498–99. The king of France was so indignant that the Council of Trent did not require parental consent that he pulled his bishops out of the council, refused to promulgate the decrees of the council in France, and instigated severe punishments for children who married without parental permission (although he could not invalidate those marriages). Morant Deusa and Bolufer Peruga, *Amor, matrimonio y familia*, 33; Lefebvre-Teillard, "Marriage in France," 263–64.

34. Lora Serrano, "Estrategia matrimonial y fiscalidad señorial," 187. "Y debía servir para ascender a un círculo aristocrático superior, para incrementar el poder político del linaje y por supuesto para aumentar el patrimonio." See also Ladero Quesada, *Los señores de Andalucía*, 306; Montero Tejada, *Nobleza y sociedad*, 56. In addition to social advancement, much of Christian Europe believed that "the purpose of Christian marriage was to establish a new alliance between two families, to reconcile battling factions, to bring peace wherever there was war." Lombardi, "Marriage in Italy," 100. Wedding festivities, as well as the choice of partner, were important markers of social advancement. Burghartz, "Competing Logics," 185.

35. Hernández Franco, "Matrimonio," 44.

36. Sánchez Saus, *La nobleza andaluza*, 336–37; Casey, *Early Modern Spain*, 146–47; Montero Tejada, *Nobleza y sociedad*, 71–72.

37. Montero Tejada, *Nobleza y sociedad*, 59, 66; Morant Deusa and Bolufer Peruga, *Amor, matrimonio y familia*, 33. A good example of royal involvement in a noble marriage is the marriage of Eleanora de Toledo to Cosimo I de'Medici, Duke of Florence, in 1539. Palos, "A Spanish Barbarian and an Enemy of Her Husband's Homeland," 165–87.

38. Layna Serrano, *Historia de Guadalajara*, 1:66; Beceiro Pita and Corodoba de la Llave, *Parentesco, poder y mentalidad*, 216–17; Ladero Quesada, *Guzmán*, 93–94.

39. Núñez Bespalova, "Origen del linaje," 12.

40. AHNOB, fondo Frías, C. 600, D. 16, D. 19, C. 606, D. 1, D. 49, C. 609, D. 2.

41. Morant Deusa and Bolufer Peruga, *Amor, matrimonio y familia*, 34; García-Fernández, "Mujeres luchando," 51.

42. Salazar y Castro, *Casa de Lara*, 2:300.

43. AHNOB, fondo Osuna, C. 1765, D. 14, fol. 1. Enrique de Mendoza was the younger brother of the Duke of Infantado.

44. Early seventeenth-century commentators like Luisa de Padilla (Countess of Aranda) and Juan de Soto (Augustinian) emphasized the importance of filial obedience. Precioso Izquierdo and Gutiérrez de Armas, "De padres nobles," 369–70.

45. Broomhall, "'My Daughter, My Dear,'" 551.

46. Gerber, *Bastards*, 42.

47. Clandestine marriages (which Trent punished but declared valid) were a source of tension between noble families and the church across Europe, while most Protestant churches (England was an exception) required parental consent. Donahue, "The Legal Background," 36–37; Lefebvre-Teillard, "Marriage in France," 264–66; Lombardi, "Marriage in Italy," 99–100; Van der Heijden, "Marriage Formation," 156; Korpiola, "Marriage in Sweden," 246; Wunder, "Marriage in the Holy Roman Empire," 72–75; Helmholz, "The Legal Regulation of Marriage," 134. In Spain the *Leyes de Toro* prescribed confiscation of goods and exile for everyone who participated in a clandestine marriage, as well as giving fathers permission to disinherit daughters who contracted marriage without their permission. However, the law did not state that fathers could disinherit their sons. Usunáriz, "Marriage and Love," 203; Espinosa, *Leyes de Toro*, law 49, 23–24.

48. Salazar y Castro, *Casa de Silva*, 1:388–90, 408–10.

49. Salazar y Castro, *Casa de Silva*, 1:388–90, 408–10.

50. Salazar y Castro, *Casa de Silva*, 1:392.

51. Ladero Quesada, *Los señores de Andalucía*, 76.

52. Even in the context of the church, however, there was an extensive debate about the nature of consent and the role of consummation. Brundage, *Law, Sex, and Christian Society*, 236–38.

53. Gerber, *Bastards*, 7.

54. Sánchez Saus, *La nobleza andaluza*, 378. "En convivencia con la norma moral emanada de authoridad eclesiástica existe otra, obsesión por asegurar la perduración del mismo y la preservación de la integridad de los bienes recibidos de la generación anterior."

55. Ladero Quesada analyzes the story of how María Coronel handled the discovery of her husband Guzmán el Bueno's adultery which was recounted by the sixteenth-century commentator Barrantes Maldonado. Ladero Quesada, *Guzmán*, 34. The nobility's practical and legalistic mindset was in some ways not that far of from that of the church, which had a very complicated and detailed definition of which activities (and with whom and when) constituted the sin of lust. Curcio-Nagy, "The Language of Desire," 46–47.

56. Sixteenth-century Castilian preachers such as fray Luis de Granada preached about lust as one of the seven deadly sins. Curcio-Nagy, "The Language of Desire," 46.

57. Mizumoto-Gitter, "From Rome to Gandía," 68–69, 59. Juan did eventually do his duty and father a son, and the Dukes of Gandía became a powerful noble family in early modern Castile.

58. Melancholy was understood to be an emotional condition of sadness that carried spiritual, ethical, and medical significance. It was diagnosed by medical practitioners and was more serious and complex than simply being sad. See Gowland, "The Problem of Early Modern Melancholy," 77–120.

59. Salazar y Castro, *Casa de Lara*, 1:608–9.

60. Salazar y Castro, *Casa de Lara*, 1:612.

61. Salazar y Castro, *Casa de Lara*, 1:608–9.

62. Holler, "Of Sadness and Joy," 18.

63. Salazar y Castro, *Casa de Lara*, 4:379. "Suplico al Duque, que el cargo que de mi tiene, que por el passo que voy, que me es tanto cargo, como si estuviera en una cámara con cadenas; y mas, que estaba virgen en dicho, hecho e pensamiento; pues me es tanto cargo, que muero, porque es la voluntad de Dios, que mire, e procure por sus hijos, e mios, como es razon."

64. Rosenwein, "Worrying about Emotions," 842.

65. Quoted in Arroñada, "Algunas notas," 23–24. "Que sin mi voluntad ha estado y está apartada de mi consorcio e vida maridable, por lo qual ynclinado e atraido por la flaqueza de la carne humana, ove de engendrar"; "Para querer e ama yntensamente a sus descendientes, quanto mas esta natural ynclinacion es ynata a las criaturas razonables, porque dizen los sabios quel amor paternal desciende en

sus especies y vence a todo otro amor"; "Ha sido y es causa muy propinqua para que yo ame e quiera a vos."

66. Burns, *Las Siete Partidas*, vol. 4, partida 4, title 19, law 1, 972.

67. Arroñada, "Algunas notas," 23. "La relación entre padres e hijos era bastante cercana y cálida: lo vemos claramente en las expresiones de afecto con las que se mencionan a los niños en las crónicas, en las demostraciones de alegría por su llegada y en las manifestaciones de dolor ante su enfermedad o muerte." The history of daily life has been a valuable tool for uncovering and studying premodern emotions. See Villa-Flores and Lipsett-Rivera, "Introduction," 10.

68. Salazar y Castro, *Casa de Lara*, 2:263–64.

69. Salazar y Castro, *Casa de Lara*, 2:264. They were so successful at keeping this secret that the Real Academia de la Historia lists María as the legitimate daughter of the Marquis de Poza. Real Academia de la Historia, "Francisco de Rojas y Enríquez."

70. For an analysis of the phenomenon of private pregnancies among elite women in eighteenth-century colonial Spanish America, see Twinam, *Public Lives*, 60–82.

71. Salazar y Castro, *Casa de Lara*, 4:377–78.

72. Salazar y Castro, *Casa de Lara*, 2:264–65.

73. Ladero Quesada, *Guzmán*, 91–92. "Fueron fruto de las alianzas políticas que el conde Juan Alfonso anudaba por aquellos años."

74. AHNOB fondo Osuna, C. 214, D. 97, http://pares.culturaydeporte.gob.es/inicio .html. Ladero Quesada claimed that the document is dated 1428, but the online image that I consulted is clearly dated 1418. Ladero Quesada, *Guzmán*, 93–94.

75. Ladero Quesada, *Guzmán*, 94.

76. Ladero Quesada, *Guzmán*, 93. "Enlazaba al conde con la anterior familia real aragonesa."

77. Kamen, *The Duke of Alba*, 173.

78. Salazar y Castro, *Casa de Lara*, 2:544; Gutiérrez Coronel, *Historia genealógica*, 1:62, 2:448.

79. Manero Sorolla, "On the Margins of the Mendozas," 114.

80. The seventeenth-century text spells it "Tor de Humos and Villa-Lumbroso." Salazar y Castro, *Casa de Lara*, 1:523.

81. Ruiz, *Spain's Centuries of Crisis*, 98–99.

82. Layna Serrano, *Historia de Guadalajara*, 2:63–65. "Do sufren serviçios pena/ y desserviçios amor, / el mayor desservidor/ tiene la vida mas buena." Translated by Dr. Diane Wright. The castle belonged to the bishop's brother, the Duke of Infantado.

83. Layna Serrano, *Historia de Guadalajara*, 2:65, 82n25; Salazar y Castro, *Casa de Silva*, 2:227.

84. Salazar y Castro, *Casa de Silva*, 1:421.

85. Salazar y Castro, *Casa de Lara*, 1:453.

86. Salazar y Castro, *Casa de Lara*, 1:522.

87. Montero Tejada, *Nobleza y sociedad*, 98.

88. Salazar y Castro, *Casa de Lara*, 1:518.

89. Beceiro Pita and Córdoba de la Llave, *Parentesco, poder y mentalidad*, 220.

90. Beceiro Pita and Córdoba de la Llave, *Parentesco, poder y mentalidad*, 220; Barahona, *Sex Crimes*, 97. There is also evidence that sexual activity was believed to "cure" sadness or melancholy. Holler, "Of Sadness and Joy," 26.

91. Salazar y Castro, *Casa de Lara*, 2:139. "Amó mucho las mugeres, y fue tan dichoso en la sucesion, que se hallava al tiempo de su muerte con 27 hijos de ambos sexos."

92. Salazar y Castro, *Casa de Lara*, 2:455. "En los verdores de la primera, y mas robusta edad no fue el Cardenal tan cuidadoso de su pureza, que pudiesse librar el animo de una apasionada correspondencia, que le produjo tres hijos."

93. Curcio-Nagy, "The Language of Desire," 45.

94. Salazar y Castro, *Casa de Lara*, 2:688.

95. Gutiérrez Coronel, *Historia genealógica*, 2:329.

96. Don Pedro's brother was Álvaro de Luna, Capitán de los Continos. Salazar y Castro, *Casa de Lara*, 1:620. Other nobles who faced exile to Oran as a result of sexual and marital misconduct include the Duke of Veragua (see chapter 2), and the Duke of Braganza (nephew of the king of Portugal), who murdered his wife. Ladero Quesada, *Guzmán*, 291n17.

97. Edward Behrend-Martínez argued that child abuse in early modern Spain was defined, in part, as "the material neglect of a child (food and clothing)," and don Pedro was accused of (among other things) refusing to pay his daughters' convent dowries and not providing his wife with sufficient economic support. Behrend-Martínez, "The Castigation and Abuse," 252.

98. Sánchez García, "La marquesa de Campolattaro," 112. "Intensa actividad erótica."

99. The limits on noble behavior had much to do with politics, social status, and privilege. In England, Johanna Rickman found that the nobility were morally privileged and not subject to either the same punishments or the same sermons about sexual sins that people further down the social scale had to endure. On the other hand, Elizabeth I faced more pressure than her successors did to contain the sexual behavior of her courtiers because of her status as a single woman. Rickman, *Love, Lust, and License*, 4, 14–15.

100. Holler, "Of Sadness and Joy," 37. The problem of unhappy marriages (and thus the power of the concubinous family) can be found across Europe. The case of Andrea Mora, who married Caterina di Gratiani in 1577 in Veneto but returned to his concubine within a month, is just one example. Byars, "The Long and Varied Relationship," 671.

101. Salazar y Castro, *Casa de Lara*, 1:620.

102. Beceiro Pita and Córdoba de la Llave, *Parentesco, poder y mentalidad*, 217. Wives could also sue husbands for battery in ecclesiastical and secular courts to secure a separation. Behrend-Martínez, "The Castigation and Abuse," 253. For an example of an abused wife who took her case to the crown, see García-Fernández, "Mujeres luchando," 58–63.

103. Montero Tejada did say that divorce and separation for physical violence were common among the nobility (although she didn't find them in the Manrique family), but she did not give any examples, and I have found very few cases of divorce. Montero Tejada, *Nobleza y sociedad*, 85. See also Beceiro Pita and Córdoba de la Llave, *Parentesco, poder y mentalidad*, 216–17.

104. All four of these children are identified as hijos naturales. Salazar y Castro, *Casa de Lara*, 1:621.

105. Sánchez García, "La marquesa de Campolattora," 113, 113n12.

106. Sánchez García, "La marquesa de Campolattora," 116. "Si han sido tan grandes los excesos . . . no puede ser el Duque solo culpado de ellos, sino que yo también y sin duda debo haver incurrido también en ellos, como quien ha vivido con él tanto tiempo."

107. Sánchez García, "La marquesa de Campolattora," 116.

108. Sánchez García, "La marquesa de Campolattora," 116. "Por la personalidad y la elegancia con que ella define su espacio de virreina y su representación oficial del cargo."

109. Ladero Quesada, *Guzmán*, 33. "Pues aumentaban la calidad del linaje aun a costa del descrédito personal y moral del marido correspondiente."

110. Montero Tejada, *Nobleza y sociedad*, 87; Salazar y Castro, *Casa de Lara*, 2:149. See chapter 2 for more on María.

111. Vaquero Serrano, "Doña María de Ribera," 76.

112. This is not the same María de Sandoval who had sexual relations with the Duke of Nájera in the previous paragraph.

113. Salazar y Castro, *Casa de Lara*, 2:67–68.

114. Flynn, "Taming Anger's Daughters," 865, 871.

115. Montero Tejada, *Nobleza y sociedad*, 93. The Count of Treviño was fourteen when his father died in 1458. Salazar y Castro, *Casa de Lara*, 2:99.

116. Salazar y Castro, *Casa de Lara*, 2:68–69.

117. Salazar y Castro, *Casa de Lara*, 4:278.

118. Salazar y Castro, *Casa de Lara*, 2:69.

119. Salazar y Castro, *Casa de Lara*, 2:69, 4:282.

120. It is not entirely clear, however, that this threatened their inheritance rights (and, in fact, the count's son did inherit). Sara McDougall noted that in the medieval

period, annulment of a marriage on grounds of consanguinity did not necessarily render the children illegitimate, although the issue remained confusing, giving the count's son grounds for concern. McDougall, *Royal Bastards*, 132.

121. Salazar y Castro, *Casa de Lara*, 2:69.

122. The phrase is formulaic, but not all women added the "most." The emphasis is mine. Salazar y Castro, *Casa de Lara*, 4:282.

123. Rosenwein, "Worrying about Emotions," 841.

124. Montero Tejada, *Nobleza y sociedad*, 94–95; Salazar y Castro, *Casa de Lara*, 2:71.

125. Whether lust is an emotion or an appetite is subject to some debate. See Herzberg, "Sexual Lust as an Emotion," 271–302.

126. Espinosa, *Leyes de Toro*, laws 81–82, 30; Taylor, *Honor and Violence*, 197. The local *fueros* had a wider variety of opinions on the legality of killing one or the other of the adulterous couple. Bermejo Castrillo, *Entre ordenamientos y códigos*, 160–61.

127. Lipsett-Rivera, "'If I Can't Have Her, No One Else Can,'" 70–71.

128. Beceiro Pita and Córdoba de la Llave, *Parentesco, poder y mentalidad*, 219–20.

129. Taylor, *Honor and Violence*, 3; Salazar y Castro, *Casa de Lara*, 1:578–79.

130. Gutiérrez Coronel, *Historia genealógica*, 2:514. Salazar y Castro used almost the same language: "Por vanas, y imprudentes sospechas, de aver faltado á la pureza conjugal." Salazar y Castro, *Casa de Silva*, 1:550.

131. Gutiérrez Coronel, *Historia genealógica*, 2:545; Salazar y Castro, *Casa de Silva*, 1:550–52. The only other example I have found of a murdered wife is the case of Leonor Guzmán, daughter of the third Duke of Medina Sidonia, who was murdered by her husband, the Duke of Braganza and the nephew of the King of Portugal, "without reason" (*sin razón*). He was punished by being sent to do military service in North Africa in 1515. Ladero Quesada, *Guzmán*, 291n17.

132. Ferdinand and Isabel, in particular, made concerted and coordinated efforts to limit the power of the nobility by making alliances with the municipalities, reorganizing the *hermandades* under direct royal control, incorporating the masterships of the military orders into the crown, reorganizing the royal council, and passing a new law code, the *Leyes de Toro*. Elliott, *Imperial Spain*, 86–90; Phillips and Rahn Phillips, *A Concise History of Spain*, 116–17.

133. Ladero Quesada, *Guzmán*, 166.

134. Ladero Quesada, *Guzmán*, 166.

135. Barrantes Maldonado, "Ilustraciones de la casa de Niebla," part seven, chapter 6, quoted in Ladero Quesada, *Guzmán*, 166n145.

136. Ladero Quesada, *Guzmán*, 166.

137. Ladero Quesada, *Guzmán*, 167.

138. Ladero Quesada, *Guzmán*, 160–64, 168–69, 174, 186.

139. Ladero Quesada, *Guzmán*, 96.

140. Beceiro Pita, "Aldonza de Mendoza," 80, 83–85.

141. Beceiro Pita, "Aldonza de Mendoza," 83. Miguel García-Fernández suggested that these accusations might be more malevolent than they were true but accepted that Fadrique was an abusive husband. García-Fernández, "Mujeres luchando," 49.

142. Galíndez de Carvajal, "Adiciones genealógicas," 448–49. Galíndez de Carvajal's account gives the woman involved as Beatriz, Fadrique's legitimate sister, but Beceiro Pita said this was an error. Beceiro Pita, "Aldonza de Mendoza," 83.

143. Beceiro Pita, "Aldonza de Mendoza," 85.

144. Galíndez de Carvajal, "Adiciones genealógicas," 448–49.

145. Beceiro Pita, "Aldonza de Mendoza," 85.

146. Galíndez de Carvajal, "Adiciones genealógicas," 448–49.

147. García-Fernández, "Mujeres luchando," 48.

148. Beceiro Pita, "Aldonza de Mendoza," 85–88; Coolidge, *Guardianship*, 87–88; Nader, *Liberty in Absolutist Spain*, 228.

149. Vassberg, "Widows in Sixteenth-Century Castile," 184, cited in Warner, "Introduction," 4.

150. Salazar y Castro, *Casa de Silva*, 1:390.

151. Salazar y Castro, *Casa de Silva*, 1:391.

152. Arroñada, "Algunas notas," 20–23. For a compelling example in which a mother's grief pushed her close to committing blasphemy, see Holler, "Of Sadness and Joy," 17.

153. Carriazo Rubio, *Los testamentos*, 21. "Rubricaba la inclusión del testador en la memoria colectiva de sus herederos y beneficiados."

154. Carriazo Rubio, *Los testamentos*, 310.

155. For other examples of women writing wills in anticipation of childbirth, see Coolidge, "Death and Gender," 65; Eire, *From Madrid to Purgatory*, 64.

156. Carriazo Rubio, *Los testamentos*, 311–12. "Que nadie pensó que avia nesçesydad de otorgallo."

157. Carriazo Rubio, *Los testamentos*, 54–55. María, in addition to being a wife and a mother, was a daughter, potentially adding another layer of grief to her death. For Catherine de Médici's intense grief when her daughter, Elizabeth of Valois (Queen of Spain), died in childbirth, see Broomhall, "'My Daughter, My Dear,'" 562.

158. Beceiro Pita and Córdoba de la Llave, *Parentesco, poder y mentalidad*, 220.

159. Curcio-Nagy, "The Language of Desire," 51.

CONCLUSION

1. Eire, *From Madrid to Purgatory*, 20. For a brief study on some Castilian wills, see Coolidge, "Death and Gender," 59–79.
2. Salazar y Castro, *Casa de Lara*, 4:379.
3. Layna Serrano, *Historia de Guadalajara*, 2:229–30 and 229n2; AHNOB, fondo Osuna, C. 1764, no. 1.

BIBLIOGRAPHY

MANUSCRIPTS AND ARCHIVES

Archivo Histórico de la Nobleza, Toledo, Spain (AHNOB)
    Fondo Frías
    Fondo Osuna
Archivo Histórico Nacional, Sección Consejos, Madrid, Spain

PUBLISHED WORKS

Allende-Salazar, J. "Don Felipe de Guevara: Coleccionista y escritor de arte del siglo XVI." *Archivo español de arte y arquelogia*, 1925, 189–92.

Álvarez Cora, Enrique. "Compañía matrimonial y prejuicio del sexo (siglos XVI–XIX)." In *Organización social y familias*, edited by Franciso Chacón Jiménez and Juan Hernández Franco, 153–72. Murcia, Spain: Universidad de Murcia, 2019.

Armstrong-Partida, Michelle. *Defiant Priests: Domestic Unions, Violence, and Clerical Masculinity in Fourteenth-Century Catalunya*. Ithaca NY: Cornell University Press, 2017.

———. "Priestly Marriage: The Tradition of Clerical Concubinage in the Spanish Church." *Viator* 40, no. 2 (2009): 221–53.

Arnold, John H., and Sean Brady. "Introduction." In *What Is Masculinity? Historical Dynamics from Antiquity to the Contemporary World*, edited by John. H. Arnold and Sean Brady, 1–14. New York: Palgrave Macmillan, 2011.

Arroñada, Silvia Nora. "Algunas notas sobre la infancia noble en la baja edad media castellana." *HID* 34 (2007): 9–27.

Atienza López, Ángela. "Nobleza, poder señorial y conventos en la España moderna. La dimension política de las fundaciones nobiliarias." In *Estudios sobre señorío y feudalismo: Homenaje a Julio Valdeón*, edited by Esteban Sarasa Sánchez and Eliseo Serrano Martín, 235–69. Zaragoza, Spain: Institución Fernando el Católico, 2010.

Aznar Gil, Frederico R. "La califación de 'hijos naturales' en el derecho histórico español a los habidos de sólo matrimonio canónico (1872)." *Revista española de derecho canónico* 51, no. 137 (1994): 623–38.

———. "Los ilegítimos en la Península Ibérica durante la Baja Edad Media." *Revista española de derecho canónico* 50, no. 134 (1993): 9–48.

———. "Pensas y sanciones contra los clérigos concubinarios en la Península Ibérica (ss. XIII–XVI)." In *Studia Gratiana XXIX Life, Law and Letters: Historical Studies in Honour of Antonio García y García*, edited by Peter Linehan, 501–20. Rome: Libreria Ateneo Salesiano, 1998.

Bacó, Juan Antonio. *Suma de los preceptos del decalogo y de la Iglesia*. Madrid: Bernardo de Villa-Diego, 1667. Google Books.

Ball, Rachael. *Treating the Public: Charitable Theater and Civic Health in the Early Modern Atlantic World*. Baton Rouge: Louisiana State University Press, 2016.

Baños Gil, María Ángeles. "Ana de Mendoza de Luna y de la Vega, VI duquesa del Infantado." In *Damas de la casa de Mendoza: Historias, leyendas y olvidos*, edited by Esther Alegre Carvajal, 287–317. Madrid: Ediciones Polifemo, 2014.

Barahona, Renato. *Sex Crimes, Honour, and the Law in Early Modern Spain, Vizcaya, 1528–1735*. Toronto: University of Toronto Press, 2003.

Barlow, Jennifer E. "Love and War: Male Friendship and the Performance of Masculinity in the Poetry of Garcilaso de la Vega (1501–1536)." *Bulletin of Hispanic Studies* 95, no. 4 (2018): 383–98.

Barrantes Maldonado, Pedro. "Ilustraciones de la casa de Niebla." In *Memorial histórica español: Coleccion de documentos, opúsculos y antigüedades*, vol. 10. Madrid: Imprenta Nacional, 1857.

Barton, Simon. *Conquerors, Brides, and Concubines: Interfaith Relations and Social Power in Medieval Iberia*. Philadelphia: University of Pennsylvania Press, 2015.

Bastress-Dukehart, Erika. "Negotiating for Agnes' Womb." In *Contested Spaces of Nobility in Early Modern Europe*, edited by Matthew P. Romaniello and Charles Lipp, 41–60. Farnham, UK: Ashgate, 2011.

———. "Sibling Conflict within Early Modern German Noble Families." *Journal of Family History* 33, no. 1 (2008): 61–80.

Beam, Sara. "Turning a Blind Eye: Infanticide and Missing Babies in Seventeenth-Century Geneva." *Law and History Review* 39, no. 2 (2021): 255–76.

Beceiro Pita, Isabel. "Aldonza de Mendoza, duquesa de Arjona." In *Damas de la casa de Mendoza: Historias, leyendas y olvidos*, edited by Esther Alegre Carvajal, 71–95. Madrid: Ediciones Polifemo, 2014.

———. "Los conventos de clarisas y sus patronas. Medina de Pomar, Palencia y Calabazanos." *Sémata* 26 (2014): 319–41.

Beceiro Pita, Isabel, and Ricardo Córdoba de la Llave. *Parentesco, poder y mentalidad: La nobleza castellana, siglos XII–XV*. Madrid: Consejo Superior de Investigaciones Científicas, 1990.

Behrend-Martínez, Edward. "The Castigation and Abuse of Children in Early Modern Spain." In *The Formation of the Child in Early Modern Spain*, edited by Grace E. Coolidge, 249–72. Farnham, UK: Ashgate, 2014.

Belén Rubio Ávila, María. "María de Mendoza, 'La Blanca,' Catalina de Mendoza." In *Damas de la casa de Mendoza: Historias, leyendas y olvidos*, edited by Esther Alegre Carvajal, 427–47. Madrid: Ediciones Polifemo, 2014.

Benedictine Monks of St. Augustine's Abbey, Ramsgate. *The Book of Saints: A Dictionary of Persons Canonized or Beatified by the Catholic Church*. New York: Thomas Y. Crowell, 1966.

Bennett, Judith. *History Matters: Patriarchy and the Challenge of Feminism*. Philadelphia: University of Pennsylvania Press, 2006.

Bennett, Judith M., and Amy M. Froide, eds. *Singlewomen in the European Past, 1250–1800*. Philadelphia: University of Pennsylvania Press, 1999.

Berco, Christian. "Juana Pimentel, the Mendoza Family, and the Crown." In *Power and Gender in Renaissance Spain: Eight Women of the Mendoza Family, 1450–1650*, edited by Helen Nader, 27–47. Urbana: University of Illinois Press, 2004.

Bermejo Castrillo, Manuel Ángel. *Entre ordenamientos y códigos: Legislación y doctrina sobre familia a partir de las leyes de Toro de 1505*. Madrid: Editorial Dykinson, 2009.

Bilinkoff, Jodi. *The Avila of Saint Teresa: Religious Reform in a Sixteenth-Century City*. Ithaca NY: Cornell University Press, 2015.

Blumenthal, Debra. *Enemies and Familiars: Slavery and Mastery in Fifteenth-Century Valencia*. Ithaca NY: Cornell University Press, 2009.

Borrero Fernández, Mercedes. "Peasant and Aristocratic Women: Their Role in the Rural Economy of Seville at the End of the Middle Ages." In *Women at Work in Spain: From the Middle Ages to Early Modern Times*, edited by Marilyn Stone and Carmen Benito-Vessels, 11–31. New York: Peter Lang, 1998.

Broomhall, Susan. "'The King and I': Rhetorics of Power in the Letters of Diane de Poitiers." In *Women and Power at the French Court, 1483–1563*, edited by Susan Broomhall, 335–55. Amsterdam: Amsterdam University Press, 2018.

———. "Letters Make the Family: Nassau Family Correspondence at the Turn of the Seventeenth Century." In *Early Modern Women and Transnational Communities of Letters*, edited by Julie Campbell and Anne Larsen, 25–44. Aldershot, UK: Ashgate, 2009.

———. "'My Daughter, My Dear': The Correspondence of Catherine de Médicis and Elisabeth de Valois." *Women's History Review* 24, no. 4 (2015): 548–69.

———, ed. *Women and Power at the French Court, 1483–1563*. Amsterdam: Amsterdam University Press, 2018.

Brundage, James A. *Law, Sex, and Christian Society in Medieval Europe*. Chicago: University of Chicago Press, 1987.

Bullough, Vern L. "On Being a Male in the Middle Ages." In *Medieval Masculinities: Regarding Men in the Middle Ages*, edited by Clare A. Lees, 31–45. Minneapolis: University of Minnesota Press, 1994.

Burghartz, Susanna. "Competing Logics of Public Order: Matrimony and the Fight against Illicit Sexuality in Germany and Switzerland from the Sixteenth to the Eighteenth Century." In *Marriage in Europe, 1400–1800*, edited by Silvana Seidel Menchi, 176–200. Toronto: University of Toronto Press, 2016.

Burke, Marcus B., and Peter Cherry. *Collections of Paintings in Madrid, 1601–1755, Spanish Inventories Part 1*. Los Angeles: J. Paul Getty Museum, 1997.

Burns, Kathryn. *Into the Archives: Writing and Power in Colonial Peru*. Durham NC: Duke University Press, 2010.

Burns, Robert I. "Introduction." In *Las Siete Partidas*, vol. 5: *Underworlds: The Dead, the Criminal, and the Marginalized*, edited by Robert I. Burns, translated by Samuel Parsons Scott, ix–xlvi. Philadelphia: University of Pennsylvania Press, 2001.

———, ed. *Las Siete Partidas*. 5 vols. Translated by Samuel Parsons Scott. Philadelphia: University of Pennsylvania Press, 2001.

Byars, Jana. "From Illegitimate Son to Legal Citizen: Noble Bastards in Early Modern Venice." *Sixteenth Century Journal* 43, no. 3 (2011): 643–63.

———. "The Long and Varied Relationship of Andrea Mora and Anzola Davide: Concubinage, Marriage and the Authorities in the Early Modern Veneto." *Journal of Social History* 41, no. 3 (2008): 667–90.

Calderón Medina, Inés. "Las otras mujeres del rey: El concubinato regio en el reino de León (1157–1230)." Published as proceedings of Seminário Medieval 2009–2011, CEPESE–Universidade do Porto. http://ifilosofia.up.pt/gfm/seminar/docs/CALDERN%20Las%20otras%20mujeres.pdf.

Calvi, Giulia. "Reconstructing the Family: Widowhood and Remarriage in Tuscany in the Early Modern Period." In *Marriage in Italy, 1300–1650*, edited by Trevor Dean and K. J. P. Lowe, 275–96. Cambridge: Cambridge University Press, 1998.

Carriazo Rubio, Juan Luis. *Los testamentos de la casa de Arcos (1374–1530)*. Seville: Diputación Provincial de Sevilla, 2003.

Carvajal, Esther Alegre. "Ana de Mendoza y de la Cerda, princesa de Éboli y duquesa de Pastrana." In *Damas de la casa de Mendoza: Historias, leyendas y olvidos*, edited by Esther Alegre Carvajal, 578–617. Madrid: Ediciones Polifemo, 2014.

———, ed. *Damas de la casa de Mendoza: Historias, leyendas y olvidos*, Madrid: Ediciones Polifemo, 2014.

Casaus Ballester, María José. "La casa ducal de Híjar y sus enlaces con linajes castellanos." *Boletín Millares Carlo* 27 (2008): 101–27.

Casey, James. *Early Modern Spain: A Social History*. New York: Routledge, 1999.

———. *Family and Community in Early Modern Spain: The Citizens of Granada, 1570–1739*. Cambridge: Cambridge University Press, 2007.

———. *The History of the Family*. New York: Basil Blackwell, 1989.

Catlos, Brian. *Muslims of Medieval Latin Christendom, c. 1050–1614*. Cambridge: Cambridge University Press, 2014.

Cavallo, Sandra, and Lyndan Warner, eds. *Widowhood in Medieval and Early Modern Europe*. Harlow, UK: Longman, 1999.

Chojnacka, Monica. "Women, Men, and Residential Patterns in Early Modern Venice." *Journal of Family History* 25, no. 1 (2000): 6–25.

Chojnacki, Stanley. "Nobility, Women and the State: Marriage Regulation in Venice, 1420–1553." In *Marriage in Italy, 1300–1650*, edited by Trevor Dean and K. J. P. Lowe, 128–54. Cambridge: Cambridge University Press, 1998.

———. *Women and Men in Renaissance Venice: Twelve Essays on Patrician Society*. Baltimore: Johns Hopkins University Press, 2000.

Clavero, Bartolomé. *Mayorazgo: Propiedad feudal en Castilla (1369–1836)*. Madrid: Siglo Veintiuno de España, 1974.

Cohn, Samuel Kline, Jr. "Marriage in the Mountains: The Florentine Territorial State, 1348–1500." In *Marriage in Italy, 1300–1650*, edited by Trevor Dean and K. J. P. Lowe, 174–96. Cambridge: Cambridge University Press, 1998.

Connell, R. W. *Masculinities*. Berkeley: University of California Press, 1995.

Constable, Olivia Remie. "Muslim Spain and Mediterranean Slavery: The Medieval Slave Trade as an Aspect of Christian-Muslim Relations." In *Christendom and Its Discontents: Exclusion, Persecution, and Rebellion, 1000–1500*, edited by Scott L. Waugh and Peter D. Diehl, 264–84. Cambridge: Cambridge University Press, 1996.

Coolidge, Grace E. "Death and Gender in Late Sixteenth-Century Toledo." In *Women and Community in Medieval and Early Modern Iberia*, edited by Michelle Armstrong-Partida, Alexandra Guerson, and Dana Wessell Lightfoot, 59–79. Lincoln: University of Nebraska Press, 2020.

———. *Guardianship, Gender, and the Nobility in Early Modern Spain*. Farnham, UK: Ashgate, 2011.

———. "Investing in the Lineage: Children in the Early Modern Spanish Nobility, 1350–1750." In *The Formation of the Child in Early Modern Spain*, edited by Grace E. Coolidge, 223–47. Farnham, UK: Ashgate, 2014.

———. "'Neither Dumb, Deaf, nor Destitute of Understanding': Women as Guardians in Early Modern Spain." *Sixteenth Century Journal* 36, no. 3 (2005): 673–93.

Coontz, Stephanie. *Marriage, a History: How Love Conquered Marriage*. New York: Penguin, 2006.

Córdoba de la Llave, Ricardo. "Las relaciones extraconyugales en la sociedad castellana bajomedieval." *Anuarios de estudios medievales* 16 (1986): 571–619.

Cossar, Roisin. *Clerical Households in Late Medieval Italy*. Cambridge MA: Harvard University Press, 2017.

Crawford, Michael. *The Fight for Status and Privilege in Late Medieval and Early Modern Castile, 1465–1598*. University Park: Pennsylvania State University Press, 2014.

Cruz, Anne J. "Introduction." In *Women's Literacy in Early Modern Spain and the New World*, edited by Anne J. Cruz and Rosilie Hernández, 1–16. Farnham, UK: Ashgate, 2011.

———. "Reading over Men's Shoulders: Noblewomen's Libraries and Reading Practices." In *Women's Literacy in Early Modern Spain and the New World*, edited by Anne J. Cruz and Rosilie Hernández, 41–77. Farnham, UK: Ashgate, 2011.

Cruz, Anne J., and Maria Galli Stampino, eds. *Early Modern Habsburg Women: Transnational Contexts, Cultural Conflicts, Dynastic Continuities*. Farnham, UK: Ashgate, 2013.

Cruz Gil, Ángeles. "María de Mendoza." In *Damas de la casa de Mendoza: Historias, leyendas y olvidos*, edited by Esther Alegre Carvajal, 403–26. Madrid: Ediciones Polifemo, 2014.

Cuart Moner, Baltasar. "Bastardos en el estudio: Algunas consideraciones sobre la bastardía en expedientes de colegiales mayores salmantinos durante el s. XVI." In *Historia y perspectivas de investigación: Estudios en memoria del profesor Angel Rodríguez Sánchez*, edited by Junta de Extremadura, 307–14. Mérida, Badajoz, Spain: Editora Regional de Extremadura, 2002.

———. "El bastardo de Medellín: Las vicisitudes de un noble, bastardo y converso en la Castilla del s. XVI." *Salamanca: Revista de estudios* 31–32 (1993): 29–61.

Curcio-Nagy, Linda A. "The Language of Desire in Colonial Mexico." In *Emotions and Daily Life in Colonial Mexico*, edited by Javier Villa-Flores and Sonya Lipsett-Rivera, 44–65. Albuquerque: University of New Mexico Press, 2014.

Davidoff, Leonor. *Thicker Than Water: Siblings and Their Relations 1780–1920*. Oxford: Oxford University Press, 2012.

de Cruz Medina, Vanessa. "An Illegitimate Habsburg: Sor Ana Dorotea de la Concepción, Marquise of Austria." In *Early Modern Habsburg Women: Transnational*

Contexts, Cultural Conflicts, Dynastic Continuities, edited by Anne J. Cruz and María Galli Stampino, 96–117. Farnham, UK: Ashgate, 2013.

de la Pena Marazuela, María Teresa, and Pilar León Tello. *Archivo de los duques de Frías*. Madrid: Blass, S.A. Tip, 1955.

Dewald, Jonathan. *The European Nobility, 1400–1800*. Cambridge: Cambridge University Press, 1996.

Dillard, Heath. *Daughters of the Reconquest: Women in Castilian Town Society, 1000–1300*. Cambridge: Cambridge University Press, 1984.

Donahue, Charles, Jr. "The Legal Background: European Marriage Law from the Sixteenth to the Nineteenth Century." In *Marriage in Europe, 1400–1800*, edited by Silvana Seidel Menchi, 33–60. Toronto: University of Toronto Press, 2016.

Donahue, Darcy. "Good Boys: The Fifth Dialogue in Pedro Luján's *Coloquios matrimoniales.*" In *The Formation of the Child in Early Modern Spain*, edited by Grace E. Coolidge, 209–21. Farnham, UK: Ashgate, 2014.

Dyer, Abigail. "Seduction by Promise of Marriage: Law, Sex, and Culture in Seventeenth-Century Spain." *Sixteenth Century Journal* 34, no. 2 (2003): 439–55.

Eire, Carlos. *From Madrid to Purgatory: The Art and Craft of Dying in Sixteenth-Century Spain*. Cambridge: Cambridge University Press, 2002.

Elliott, J. H. *The Count-Duke of Olivares: The Statesman in an Age of Decline*. New Haven CT: Yale University Press, 1986.

———. *Imperial Spain*. Reprint. London: Penguin, [1963] 2002.

Erler, Mary, and Maryanne Kowaleski. "Introduction." In *Women and Power in the Middle Ages*, edited by Mary Erler and Maryanne Kowaleski, 1–17. Athens: University of Georgia Press, 2004.

Espinosa, Diego de, ed. *Leyes de Toro*. Salamanca, Spain: Casa de Diego de Cussio, 1605. https://babel.hathitrust.org/cgi/pt?id=ucm.5319100409&view=1up&seq=4.

Estrella, Jorge Raúl. "En los márgenes del matrimonio: Los hijos bastardos." *Fundación para la Historia de España* 4, no. 4 (2001): 173–202.

Ettlinger, Helen S. "Visibilis et Invisibilis: The Mistress in Italian Renaissance Court Society." *Renaissance Quarterly* 47, no. 4 (1994): 770–92.

Fantazzi, Charles. "Introduction: Prelude to the Other Voice in Vives." In Juan Luis Vives, *The Education of a Christian Woman: A Sixteenth-Century Manual*, edited and translated by Charles Fantazzi, 1–42. Chicago: University of Chicago Press, 2000.

Fink De Backer, Stephanie. *Widowhood in Early Modern Spain: Protectors, Proprietors, and Patrons*. Leiden, Netherlands: Brill, 2010.

Fitz James Stewart y Falco, Jacobo. "Biografía de doña María Enríquez, mujer del Gran Duque del Alba." *Boletín de la Real Academia de Historia* 121 (1947): 7–39.

Flynn, Maureen. "Taming Anger's Daughters: New Treatment for Emotional Problems in Renaissance Spain." *Renaissance Quarterly* 51, no. 3 (1998): 864–86.

Fosi, Irene, and Maria Antonietta Visceglia. "Marriage and Politics at the Papal Court in the Sixteenth and Seventeenth Centuries." In *Marriage in Italy, 1300–1650*, edited by Trevor Dean and K. J. P. Lowe, 197–226. Cambridge: Cambridge University Press, 1998.

Fox, Dian. *Hercules and the King of Portugal: Icons of Masculinity and Nation in Calderón's Spain*. Lincoln: University of Nebraska Press, 2019.

Franco Silva, Alfonso. *Entre los reinados de Enrique IV y Carlos V: Los condestables del linaje Velasco (1461–1559)*. Jaén, Spain: Universidad de Jaén, 2006.

———. "Las mujeres de Juan Pacheco y su parentela." *HID* 36 (2009): 161–82.

Galán Parra, Isabel. "El linaje y los estados señoriales de los duques de Medina Sidonia a comienzos del siglo XVI." *En la España medieval* 11 (1988): 45–78.

Galíndez de Carvajal, L. "Adiciones genealógicas a los Claros Varones de Fernán Pérez de Guzmán, escritas hacia 1517." In *Colección de documentos inéditos para la historia de España (CODOIN)*, vol. 18, 423–536. Madrid: Academia de la Historia, 1851. https://babel.hathitrust.org/cgi/pt?id=uva.x030531345&view=1up&seq=477.

García-Fernández, Miguel. "Mujeres luchando por sí mismas. Tres ejemplos para el estudio de la toma de conciencia feminina en la Galicia bajomedieval." *Revista de estudios históricos*, 2012, 33–70.

García Hernán, David. *La nobleza en la España moderna*. Madrid: Istmos, 1992.

———. "Los grandes de España en la época de Felipe II: Los duques de Arcos." PhD diss., Universidad Complutense de Madrid, 1992.

García Oro, José. *Testamento y codicilos de don Fernando de Andrade*. Galicia, Spain: Xunta de Galicia, 1995.

Gaston, Ryan. "All the King's Men: Education Reform and Nobility in Early Seventeenth-Century Spain." In *Contested Spaces of Nobility in Early Modern Europe*, edited by Matthew P. Romaniello and Charles Lipp, 167–88. Farnham, UK: Ashgate, 2011.

Gerber, Matthew. *Bastards: Politics, Family, and Law in Early Modern France*. Oxford: Oxford University Press, 2012.

———. "Bastardy, Race, and Law in the Eighteenth-Century French Atlantic: The Evidence of Litigation." *French Historical Studies* 36, no. 4 (2013): 571–600.

Gerbert, Marie-Claude. *La nobleza en la corona de Castilla: Sus estructuras sociales en Extremadura (1454–1516)*. Cáceres, Spain: Institución Cultural "El Brocense," 1989.

Goodwin, Robert. *Spain: The Centre of the World, 1519–1682*. London: Bloomsbury, 2015.

Gowland, Angus. "The Problem of Early Modern Melancholy." *Past and Present* 191 (2006): 77–120.

Grace, Philip. "Family and Familiars. The Concentric Household in Late Medieval Penitentiary Petitions." *Journal of Medieval History* 35 (2009): 189–203.

Gutiérrez Coronel, Diego. *Historia genealógica de la casa de Mendoza.* Edited by Ángel González Palencia. 2 vols. Madrid: CSIC and Ayuntamiento de Cuenca, 1946.

Haboucha, Reginetta. "Clerics, Their Wives, and Their Concubines in the 'Partidas' of Alfonso el Sabio." In *Acta, Homo Carnalis: The Carnal Aspect of Medieval Human Life* vol. 14, edited by Helen Rodite Lemay, 85–104. Binghamton: SUNY Binghamton, Center for Medieval and Early Renaissance Studies, 1990.

Haddad, Elie. "The Question of the Imprescriptibility of Nobility in Early Modern France." In *Contested Spaces of Nobility in Early Modern Europe,* edited by Matthew P. Romaniello and Charles Lipp, 147–66. Farnham, UK: Ashgate, 2011.

Harris, Barbara. *English Aristocratic Women, 1450–1550.* Oxford: Oxford University Press, 2002.

Helmholz, Richard H. "The Legal Regulation of Marriage in England from the Fifteenth Century to the 1640s." In *Marriage in Europe, 1400–1800,* edited by Silvana Seidel Menchi, 122–52. Toronto: University of Toronto Press, 2016.

Hendrix, Scott H. "Masculinity and Patriarchy in Reformation Germany." In *Masculinity in the Reformation Era,* edited by Scott H. Hendrix and Susan C. Karant-Nunn, 71–91. Kirksville MO: Truman State University Press, 2008.

Hendrix, Scott H., and Susan C. Karant-Nunn. "Introduction." In *Masculinity in the Reformation Era,* edited by Susan C. Karant-Nunn and Scott H. Hendrix, ix–xix. Kirksville MO: Truman State University Press, 2008.

Hernández Franco, Juan. "Matrimonio, consanguinidad y la aristocracia nueva castellana: Consolidación de la casa de Alba (1440–1531)." *Medievalismo* 28 (2018): 43–74.

Hernández Franco, Juan, and Raimundo A. Rodríguez Pérez. "Bastardía, aristocracia y órdenes militares en la Castilla moderna: El linaje Fajardo." *Hispania: Revista española de historia* 69, no. 232 (2008): 331–62.

———. "El linaje se transforma en casas: De los Fajardo a los marqueses de los Vélez y de Espinardo." *Hispania: Revista Española de historia* 74, no. 247 (2004): 385–410.

Herzberg, Larry A. "Sexual Lust as an Emotion." *Humana.Mente Journal of Philosophical Studies* 35 (2019): 271–302.

Hodes, Martha. *White Women, Black Men: Illicit Sex in the 19th Century South.* New Haven CT: Yale University Press, 1997.

Holler, Jacqueline. "Of Sadness and Joy in Colonial Mexico." In *Emotions and Daily Life in Colonial Mexico,* edited by Javier Villa-Flores and Sonya Lipsett-Rivera, 17–43. Albuquerque: University of New Mexico Press, 2014.

Howe, Elizabeth Teresa. *Education and Women in the Early Modern Hispanic World.* Aldershot, UK: Ashgate, 2008.

Howell, Martha C. *The Marriage Exchange: Property, Social Place, and Gender in Cities of the Low Countries, 1300–1550.* Chicago: University of Chicago Press, 1998.

Humble Ferreira, Susannah. "Inventing the Courtier in Early Sixteenth-Century Portugal." In *Contested Spaces of the Nobility in Early Modern Europe*, edited by Matthew P. Romaniello and Charles Lipp, 85–102. Farnham, UK: Ashgate, 2011.

Hurwich, Judith. *Noble Strategies: Marriage and Sexuality in the Zimmern Chronicle.* Kirksville MO: Truman State University Press, 2006.

Jago, Charles. "The Influence of Debt between Crown and Aristocracy in Seventeenth-Century Castile." *Economic History Review* 26, no. 2 (1973): 218–36.

Jimeno Aranguern, Roldan. "Concubinato, matrimonio y adulterio de los clérigos: Notas sobre la regulación jurídica y praxas en la Navarra medieval." *Anuario de historia del derecho español* 71 (2011): 543–74.

Johnson, Allan. *The Gender Knot: Unraveling Our Patriarchal Legacy.* Rev. ed. Philadelphia: Temple University Press, 2005.

Kagan, Richard. *Students and Society in Early Modern Spain.* Baltimore: Johns Hopkins University Press, 1974.

Kamen, Henry. *The Duke of Alba.* New Haven CT: Yale University Press, 2004.

Kelleher, Marie A. "'Like Man and Wife': Clerics' Concubines in the Diocese of Barcelona." *Journal of Medieval History* 28 (2002): 349–60.

Klapisch-Zuber, Christiane. *Women, Family, and Ritual in Renaissance Italy.* Translated by Lydia G. Cochrane. Chicago: University of Chicago Press, 1985.

Korpiola, Mia. "Marriage in Sweden 1400–1700: Formalism, Collectivism, and Control." In *Marriage in Europe 1400–1800*, edited by Silvana Seidel Menchi, 225–57. Toronto: University of Toronto Press, 2016.

Korth, Eugene H., and Della M. Flusche. "Dowry and Inheritance in Colonial Spanish America: Peninsular Law and Chilean Practice." *Americas* 43, no. 4 (1987): 395–410.

Kuehn, Thomas. *Illegitimacy in Renaissance Florence.* Ann Arbor: University of Michigan Press, 2002.

Lacarra Lanz, Eukene. "Changing Boundaries of Licit and Illicit Unions: Concubinage and Prostitution." In *Marriage and Sexuality in Medieval and Early Modern Iberia*, edited by Eukene Lacarra Lanz, 158–94. New York: Routledge, 2002.

Ladero Quesada, Miguel Ángel. *Guzmán: La casa ducal de Medina Sidonia en Sevilla y su reino. 1282–1521.* Madrid: Dykinson, 2015.

———. *Los señores de Andalucía: Investigaciones sobre nobles y señoríos en los siglos XIII a XV.* Cádiz, Spain: Universidad de Cádiz, 1998.

Laslett, Peter, Karla Oosterveen, and Richard M. Smith, eds. *Bastardy and Its Comparative History.* Cambridge MA: Harvard University Press, 1980.

Layna Serrano, Francisco. *Historia de Guadalajara y sus Mendozas en los siglos XV y XVI.* 2nd ed. 4 vols. Guadalajara, Spain: Aache Ediciones, 1993.

Lees, Clare A. "Introduction." In *Medieval Masculinities: Regarding Men in the Middle Ages*, edited by Clare A. Lees, xv–xxv. Minneapolis: University of Minnesota Press, 1994.

Lefebvre-Teillard, Anne. "Marriage in France from the Sixteenth to the Eighteenth Century: Political and Juridical Aspects." In *Marriage in Europe, 1400–1800*, edited by Silvana Seidel Menchi, 261–93. Toronto: University of Toronto Press, 2016.

Lehfeldt, Elizabth A. "Ideal Men: Masculinity and Decline in Seventeenth-Century Spain." *Renaissance Quarterly* 61, no. 2 (2008): 463–94.

———. "The Permeable Cloister." In *The Ashgate Companion to Women and Gender in Early Modern Europe*, edited by Jane Couchman, Allyson M. Poska, and Katherine A. McIver, 28–45. New York: Routledge, 2016.

———. *Religious Women in Golden Age Spain: The Permeable Cloister*. Aldershot, UK: Ashgate, 2005.

León, Luis de. *A Bilingual Edition of Fray Luis de León's "La Perfecta Casada": The Role of Married Women in Sixteenth-Century Spain*. Edited and translated John A. Jones and Javier San José Lera. Lewiston NY: Edwin Mellen, 1999.

Lewin, Linda. *Surprise Heirs I: Illegitimacy, Patrimonial Rights, and Legal Nationalism in Luso-Brazilian Inheritance, 1750–1821*. Stanford CA: Stanford University Press, 2003.

Liang, Yuen-Gen. *Family and Empire: The Fernández de Cordoba and the Spanish Realm*. Philadelphia: University of Pennsylvania Press, 2011.

Lipsett-Rivera, Sonya. "'If I Can't Have Her, No One Else Can': Jealousy and Violence in Mexico." In *Emotions and Daily Life in Colonial Mexico*, edited by Javier Villa-Flores and Sonya Lipsett-Rivera, 66–88. Albuquerque: University of New Mexico Press, 2014.

———. "A Slap in the Face of Honor: Social Transgression and Women in Late-Colonial Mexico." In *The Faces of Honor: Sex, Shame and Violence in Colonial Latin America*, edited by Lyman L. Johnson and Sonya Lipsett-Rivera, 179–200. Albuquerque: University of New Mexico Press, 1998.

Liss, Peggy. *Isabel the Queen: Life and Times*. Philadelphia: University of Pennsylvania Press, 2004.

Lombardi, Daniela. "Marriage in Italy." In *Marriage in Europe, 1400–1800*, edited by Silvana Seidel Menchi, 94–121. Toronto: University of Toronto Press, 2016.

López de la Fuente, Juan, and María Carmen Vaquero Serrano. "¿Garcilaso traicionado? María de Jesús, hija de Guiomar Carrillo." *Lemir* 14 (2010): 57–68.

Lora Serrano, Gloria. "Estrategia matrimonial y fiscalidad señorial: Las bodas de Isabel de Estúñiga y Fadrique Álvarez de Toledo." HID 29 (2002): 187–215.

Lynch, John. *Spain 1516–1598: From Nation State to World Empire*. Oxford: Blackwell, 1991.

Macfarlane, Alan. "Illegitimacy and Illegitimates in English History." In *Bastardy and Its Comparative History*, edited by Peter Laslett, Karla Oosterveen and Richard M. Smith, 71–85. Cambridge MA: Harvard University Press, 1980.

Maltby, William S. *Alba: A Biography of Fernando Alvarez de Toledo, Third Duke of Alba, 1507–1582*. Berkeley: University of California Press, 1983.

————. *The Reign of Charles V*. New York: Palgrave, 2002.

Manero Sorolla, María Pilar. "On the Margins of the Mendozas: Luisa de la Cerda and María de San José (Salazar)." In *Power and Gender in Renaissance Spain: Eight Women of the Mendoza Family, 1450–1650*, edited by Helen Nader, 113–31. Urbana: University of Illinois Press, 2004.

Mangan, Jane. *Transatlantic Obligations: Creating the Bonds of Family in Conquest-Era Peru and Spain*. Oxford: Oxford University Press, 2016.

Mannarelli, María Emma. *Private Passions and Public Sins: Men and Women in Seventeenth-Century Lima*. Translated by Sidney Evans and Meredith D. Dodge. Albuquerque: University of New Mexico Press, 2007.

Marshall, Sherrin. *The Dutch Gentry, 1500–1650: Family, Faith, and Fortune*. New York: Greenwood, 1987.

Martin, Therese. *Queen as King: Politics and Architectural Propaganda in Twelfth-Century Spain*. Leiden, Netherlands: Brill, 2006.

Martz, Linda. *A Network of Converso Families in Early Modern Toledo: Assimilating a Minority*. Ann Arbor: University of Michigan Press, 2003.

Matilla Tascon, Antonio. *Testamentos de 43 personajes del Madrid de los Austrias*. Madrid: Instituto de Estudios Madrileños, 1983.

Mayali, Laurent. "Note on the Legitimation by Subsequent Marriage from Alexander III to Innocent III." In *The Two Laws: Studies in Medieval Legal History Dedicated to Stephan Kuttner*, edited by Laurent Mayali and Stephanie A. J. Tibbetts, 55–75. Washington DC: Catholic University of America Press, 1990.

Mazo Karras, Ruth. "Sex and the Singlewoman." In *Singlewomen in the European Past, 1250–1800*, edited by Judith M. Bennett and Amy M. Froide, 127–45. Philadelphia: University of Pennsylvania Press, 1999.

McDougall, Sara. *Royal Bastards: The Birth of Illegitimacy, 800–1230*. Oxford: Oxford University Press, 2012.

McKendrick, Melveena. "Honour/Vengeance in the Spanish 'Comedia': A Case of Mimetic Transference?" *Modern Language Review* 79, no. 2 (1984): 313–35.

Mentzer, Raymond A. "Masculinity and the Reformed Tradition in France." In *Masculinity in the Reformation Era*, edited by Susan C. Karant-Nunn and Scott H. Hendrix, 120–39. Kirksville MO: Truman State University Press, 2008.

Mirrer, Louise. "Representing 'Other' Men: Muslims, Jews, and Masculine Ideals in Medieval Castilian Epic and Ballad." In *Medieval Masculinities: Regarding Men in the Middle Ages*, edited by Clare A. Lees, 169–86. Minneapolis: University of Minnesota Press, 1994.

Mitchell, Silvia Z. *Queen, Mother, and Stateswoman: Mariana of Austria and the Government of Spain*. Philadelphia: Penn State University Press, 2019.

Mizumoto-Gitter, Alex. "From Rome to Gandía: Family Networks in the Early Modern Mediterranean World." *Royal Studies Journal* 7, no. 1 (2020): 57–76.

Möller Recondo, Claudia, and Ana María Carabias Torres. *Historia de Peñaranda de Bracamonte (1250–1836)*. Salamanca, Spain: Ediciones de la Diputación de Salamanca y Ediciones Bracamonte, n.d.

Montero Tejada, Rosa. *Nobleza y sociedad en Castilla: El linaje Manrique (siglos XIV–XVI)*. Madrid: Caja de Madrid, 1996.

Morant Deusa, Isabel, and Mónica Bolufer Peruga. *Amor, matrimonio y familia: La construcción histórica de la familia moderno*. Madrid: Editorial Síntesis, 2009.

Morte Garcia, Carmen. "Los arzobispos de la Casa Real: Don Alonso, don Juan y don Hernando de Aragón, 1478–1575." *La Seo de Zaragoza*, 1998, 175–247.

Mosher Stuard, Susan. "Burdens of Matrimony: Husbanding and Gender in Medieval Italy." In *Medieval Masculinities: Regarding Men in the Middle Ages*, edited by Clare A. Lees, 61–71. Minneapolis: University of Minnesota Press, 1994.

Nader, Helen. *Liberty in Absolutist Spain: The Habsburg Sale of Towns, 1516–1700*. Baltimore: Johns Hopkins University Press, 1990.

———. *The Mendoza Family in the Spanish Renaissance, 1350 to 1550*. New Brunswick NJ: Rutgers University Press, 1979.

———. "Noble Income in Sixteenth-Century Castile: The Case of the Marquises of Mondéjar, 1480–1580." *Economic History Review* 30, no. 3 (1977): 411–28.

———, ed. *Power and Gender in Renaissance Spain: Eight Women of the Mendoza Family, 1450–1650*. Urbana: University of Illinois Press, 2004.

Naya Franco, Carolina. "El ajuar funerario del arzobispo de Zaragoza y Valencia, don Alonso de Aragón (1470–1520)." *Archivo español del arte* 90, no. 360 (2017): 335–46.

Nazzari, Muriel. "An Urgent Need to Conceal: The System of Honor and Shame in Colonial Brazil." In *Sex, Shame, and Violence: The Faces of Honor in Colonial Latin America*, edited by Lyman L. Johnson and Sonya Lipsett-Rivera, 103–26. Albuquerque: University of New Mexico Press, 1998.

Nuñez Bespalova, María. "Origen del linaje de la Cerda y de las casas y mayorazgos que de ella proceden: BNE; MS 3454." *Revista de literatura medieval* 20 (2008): 7–27.

O'Callaghan, Joseph F. "Alfonso X and the *Partidas*." In *Las Siete Partidas*, vol. 1: *The Medieval Church: The World of Clerics and Laymen*, edited by Robert I. Burns, translated by Samuel Parsons Scott, xxx–xl. Philadelphia: University of Pennsylvania Press, 2001.

Ortega Gato, Esteban. "Los Enríquez, Almirantes de Castilla." *Publicaciones de la Institución Tello Téllez de Meneses*, no. 70 (1999): 23–65.

Ortego Rico, Pablo. "El patrocinio religioso de los Mendoza: Siglos XIV y XV." *En la España medieval* 31 (2008): 275–307.

Palos, Joan-Lluís. "Bargaining Chips: Strategic Marriages and Cultural Circulation in Early Modern Europe." In *Early Modern Dynastic Marriages and Cultural Transfer*, edited by Joan-Lluís Palos and Magdalena S. Sánchez, 1–18. Farnham, UK: Ashgate, 2016.

———. "'A Spanish Barbarian and an Enemy of Her Husband's Homeland': The Duchess of Florence and Her Spanish Entourage." In *Early Modern Dynastic Marriages and Cultural Transfer*, edited by Joan-Lluís Palos and Magdalena S. Sánchez, 165–88. Farnham, UK: Ashgate, 2016.

Palos, Joan-Lluís, and Magdalena S. Sánchez, eds. *Early Modern Dynastic Marriages and Cultural Transfer*. Farnham, UK: Ashgate, 2016.

Pardo de Guevara y Valdés, Eduardo. *Los señores de Galicia: Tenentes y condes de Lemos en la Edad Media*. 2 vols. A Coruña, Spain: Fundación Pedro Barrié de la Maza, 2000.

Perea Rodríguez, Óscar. "Mencía de Mendoza, condesa de Haro." In *Damas de la casa de Mendoza: Historias, leyendas y olvidos*, edited by Esther Alegre Carvajal, 97–132. Madrid: Ediciones Polifemo, 2014.

Pérez de Tudela y Bueso, María Luisa. "El Monasterio de Santa Clara la Real de Toledo: Estudio sobre un encomienda regia monástica, 1376–1779." PhD diss., Universidad Complutense de Madrid, 2002.

Pérez Martín, Antonio, ed. *Fuero Real de Alfonso X el Sabio*. Madrid: Agencia Estatal Boletín Oficial del Estado, 2015.

Pérez-Toribio, Montserrat. "From Mother to Daughter: Educational Lineage in the Correspondence between the Countess of Palamós and Estefania de Requesens." In *Women's Literacy in Early Modern Spain and the New World*, edited by Anne J. Cruz and Rosilie Hernández, 59–77. Farnham, UK: Ashgate, 2011.

Perry, Mary Elizabeth. "Finding Fatima: A Slave Woman of Early Modern Spain." *Journal of Women's History* 20, no. 1 (2008): 151–67.

———. *Gender and Disorder in Early Modern Seville*. Princeton NJ: Princeton University Press, 1990.

Phillips, Carla Rahn. *Ciudad Real 1500–1750: Growth, Crisis, and Readjustment in the Spanish Economy*. Cambridge MA: Harvard University Press, 1979.

Phillips, William D., Jr., and Carla Rahn Phillips. *A Concise History of Spain*. Cambridge: Cambridge University Press, 2010.

Pike, Ruth. "Sevillian Society in the Sixteenth Century: Slaves and Freedmen." *Hispanic American Historical Review* 47, no. 3 (1967): 129–43.

Plamper, Jan. *The History of Emotions: An Introduction*. Oxford: Oxford University Press, 2012.

Poska, Allyson. "The Case for Agentic Gender Norms for Women in Early Modern Europe." *Gender & History* 30, no. 2 (2018): 354.

———. "Elusive Virtue: Rethinking the Role of Female Chastity in Early Modern Spain." *Journal of Early Modern History* 8, nos. 1–2 (2004): 135–46.

———. "'A Married Man Is a Woman': Negotiating Masculinity in Early Modern Northwestern Spain." In *Masculinity in the Reformation Era*, edited by Scott Hendrix and Susan Karant-Nunn, 3–20. Kirksville MO: Truman State University Press, 2008.

———. "Upending Patriarchy: Rethinking Marriage and Family in Early Modern Europe." In *The Ashgate Research Companion to Women and Gender in Early Modern Europe*, edited by Allyson Poska, Jane Couchman, and Katherine A. McIver, 198–214. Farnham, UK: Ashgate, 2013.

———. *Women and Authority in Early Modern Spain: The Peasants of Galicia.* Oxford: Oxford University Press, 2005.

Poska, Allyson, Jane Couchman, and Katherine A. McIver, eds. *The Ashgate Research Companion to Women and Gender in Early Modern Europe.* Farnham, UK: Ashgate, 2013.

Potter, David. "The Life and After-Life of a Royal Mistress: Anne de Pisseleu, Duchess of Etampes." In *Women and Power at the French Court, 1483–1563*, edited by Susan Broomhall, 309–34. Amsterdam: Amsterdam University Press, 2018.

Precioso Izquierdo, Francisco, and Judit Gutiérrez de Armas. "De padres nobles a hijos nobles. Apuntes sobre las obligaciones filialies a través de las previsiones testamentarias de la aristocracia hispánica (1580–1718)." *Tiempos modernos* 38, no. 1 (2019): 362–79.

Puff, Helmet. "The Reform of Masculinities in Sixteenth-Century Switzerland: A Case Study." In *Masculinity and the Reformation Era*, edited by Scott H. Hendrix and Susan C. Karant-Nunn, 21–44. Kirksville MO: Truman State University Press, 2008.

Quintanilla Raso, María Concepción. "Aportación al studio de la nobleza en la Edad Media: La casa señorial de Benavides." *Historia. Instituciones. Documentos* 1 (1974): 165–220.

———. "Estructuras sociales y familiares y papel político de la nobleza cordobesa (siglos XIV y XV)." *En la España medieval* 3 (1982): 331–52.

———. "La casa señorial de Benavides en Andalucia." *Historia. Instituciones. Documentos* 3 (1976): 443–84.

Raúl Estrella, Jorge. "En los márgenes del matrimonio: Los hijos bastardos." *Fundación para la Historia de España* 4, no. 4 (2001–2): 173–202.

Real Academia de la Historia. "Álvaro de Bracamonte." http://dbe.rah.es/biografias/59802/alvaro-de-bracamonte. Accessed November 1, 2020.

———. "Francisco de Rojas y Enríquez." http://dbe.rah.es/biografias/20811/francisco-de-rojas-y-enriquez. Accessed November 10, 2020.

———. "Juan de Borja Enríquez." http://dbe.rah.es/biografias/28025/juan-de-borja-enriquez. Accessed November 1, 2020.

Reed, Helen. "Mother Love in the Renaissance: The Princess of Éboli's Letters to Her Favorite Son." In *Power and Gender in Renaissance Spain: Eight Women of the Mendoza Family, 1450–1650*, edited by Helen Nader, 152–76. Urbana: University of Illinois Press, 2004.

Rich, Adrienne. *Of Woman Born*. New York: W. W. Norton, 1976.

Rickman, Johanna. *Love, Lust, and License in Early Modern England: Illicit Sex and the Nobility*. Aldershot, UK: Ashgate, 2008.

Rodríguez González, María Carmen. "Concubina o esposa: Reflexiones sobre la unión de Jimena Muñiz con Alfonso VI." *Studia historica. Historia medieval* 25 (2007): 143–68.

Rodríguez Pérez, Raimundo A. "La historia social de la aristocracia hispánica durante la Edad Moderna: Un análisis historiográfico." In *Organización social y familias*, edited by Francisco Chacón Jiménez and Juan Hernández Franco, 121–38. Murcia, Spain: Universidad de Murcia, 2019.

Rodríguez Posilio, Montserrat. "La casa del Infantado." In *Damas de la casa de Mendoza: Historias, leyendas y olvidos*, edited by Esther Alegre Carvajal, 170–86. Madrid: Ediciones Polifemo, 2014.

Romaniello, Matthew P., and Charles Lipp. "The Spaces of Nobility." In *Contested Spaces of Nobility in Early Modern Europe*, edited by Matthew P. Romaniello and Charles Lipp, 1–10. Farnham, UK: Ashgate, 2011.

Romero Medina, Raúl. "Leonor de la Vega y Mendoza, condesa de Medinaceli." In *Damas de la casa de Mendoza: Historias, leyendas y olvidos*, edited by Esther Alegre Carvajal, 133–49. Madrid: Ediciones Polifemo, 2014.

Rosenwein, Barbara. "Worrying about Emotions in History." *American Historical Review* 107, no. 3 (2002): 821–45.

Ruiz, Teofilo F. *Spain's Centuries of Crisis: 1300–1474*. Oxford: Wiley-Blackwell, 2011.

Ruppel, Sophie. "Subordinates, Patrons, and Most Beloved: Sibling Relationships in Seventeenth-Century German Court Society." In *Sibling Relations and the Transformations of European Kinship, 1300–1900*, edited by Christopher Johnson and David Sabean, 85–110. New York: Berghahn, 2011.

Sabean, David Warren, and Simon Teuscher. "Kinship in Europe: A New Approach to Long-Term Development." In *Kinship in Europe: Approaches to Long-Term Development (1300–1900)*, edited by David Warren Sabean, Simon Teuscher, and Jon Mathieu, 1–32. New York: Berghahn, 2007.

Salazar y Castro, Luis. *Historia genealógica de la casa de Lara*. 4 vols. Reprint, Valladolid, Spain: MAXTOR, [1696] 2009.

———. *Historia genealógica de la casa de Silva*. 2 vols. Reprint, Valladolid, Spain: MAXTOR, [1685] 2012.

Sánchez, Magdalena. *The Empress, the Queen, and the Nun: Women and Power at the Court of Philip III of Spain*. Baltimore: Johns Hopkins University Press, 1998.

Sánchez García, Encarnación. "La marquesa de Campolattaro y el virrey Osuna: Los diarios de Zazzera y otros rastros sobre su escandalosa relación." In *Perspectives on Early Modern Women in Iberia and the New World: Studies in Law, Society, Art and Literature in Honor of Anne J. Cruz*, edited by Adrienne L. Martín and María Cristina Quintero, 109–30. New York: Escribana, 2015.

Sánchez Saus, Rafael. "De los patrimonios nobiliarios en la Andalucía del siglo XV: Los bienes del caballero jerezano Martín Dávila." *Anuario de estudios medievales* 18 (1988): 469–85.

———. *La nobleza andaluza en la Edad Media*. Granada, Spain: Editorial Universidad de Granada, 2005.

Schoenrich, Otto. *The Legacy of Christopher Columbus*. 2 vols. Glendale CA: Arthur H. Clark, 1949.

Scott, Hamish. "The Early Modern European Nobility and Its Contested Historiographies, c. 1950–1980." In *Contested Spaces of Nobility in Early Modern Europe*, edited by Matthew P. Romaniello and Charles Lipp, 11–39. Farnham, UK: Ashgate, 2011.

Scott, S. P., ed. and trans. *The Visigothic Code (Forum judicum)*. Boston: Boston Book Company, 1910. https://libro.uca.edu/vcode/visigoths.htm.

Seidel Menchi, Silvana. "Conclusion." In *Marriage in Europe, 1400–1800*, edited by Silvana Seidel Menchi, 333–45. Toronto: University of Toronto Press, 2016.

———. "Conjugal Experiments 1400–1800." In *Marriage in Europe, 1400–1800*, edited by Silvana Seidel Menchi, 333–45. Toronto: University of Toronto Press, 2016.

———, ed. *Marriage in Europe, 1400–1800*. Toronto: University of Toronto Press, 2016.

Shadis, Miriam. "'Received as a Woman': Rethinking the Concubinage of Aurembiaix of Urgell." *Journal of Medieval Iberian Studies* 8 (2016): 38–54.

Shephard, Alexandra. "Manhood, Credit and Patriarchy in Early Modern England c. 1580–1640." *Past and Present* 167 (2000): 75–106.

Sherwood, Joan. "The Ideology of Breast-Feeding: Deconstructing Spanish Medical Texts Concerning Nursing Women at the End of the Eighteenth Century." In *Religion, Body and Gender in Early Modern Spain*, edited by Alain Saint-Saëns, 94–107. San Francisco: Mellen Research University Press, 1991.

Shiba, Hiroko. "Rasgos de la familia y sociedad española vistos desde la onomástsica." In *Organización social y familias*, edited by Francisco Chacón Jiménez and Juan Hernández Franco, 61–96. Murcia, Spain: Universidad de Murcia, 2019.

Silleras-Fernández, Núria. "Money Isn't Everything: Concubinage, Class, and the Rise and Fall of Sibil·la de Fortiá, Queen of Aragon (1377–87)." In *Women and Wealth in Late Medieval Europe*, edited by Teresa Earenfight, 67–88. New York: Palgrave Macmillan, 2010.

———. "*Nigra sum sed formosa*: Black Slaves and Exotica in the Court of a Fourteenth-Century Aragonese Queen." *Medieval Encounters* 13 (2007): 546–65.

Soldat, Cornelia. "Sepulchral Monuments as a Means of Communicating Social and Political Power of Nobles in Early Modern Russia." In *Contested Spaces of Nobility in Early Modern Europe*, edited by Matthew P. Romaniello and Charles Lipp, 103–26. Farnham, UK: Ashgate, 2011.

Solomon, Michael. *Fictions of Well-Being: Sickly Readers and Vernacular Medical Writing in Late Medieval and Early Modern Spain*. Philadelphia: University of Pennsylvania Press, 2010.

Soyer, François. "Muslim Freedmen in León, Castile and Portugal (1100–1300)." *Al-Masâq* 18, no. 2 (2006): 129–43.

Sperling, Jutta. "The Economics and Politics of Marriage." In *The Ashgate Research Companion to Women and Gender in Early Modern Europe*, edited by Allyson Poska, Jane Couchman, and Katherine McIver, 213–32. New York: Routledge, 2016.

———. "Marriage at the Time of the Council of Trent (1560–70): Clandestine Marriages, Kinship Prohibitions, and Dowry Exchange in European Comparison." *Journal of Early Modern History* 8, nos. 1–2 (2004): 67–108.

Spierling, Karen A. "Father, Son, and Pious Christian: Concepts of Masculinity in Reformation Geneva." In *Masculinity and the Reformation Era*, edited by Scott H. Hendrix and Susan C. Karant-Nunn, 95–119. Kirksville MO: Truman State University Press, 2008.

Spivakovsky, Erika. *Son of the Alhambra: Don Diego Hurtado de Mendoza, 1504–1575*. Austin: University of Texas Press, 1970.

Starkey, David. "The Court: Castiglione's Ideal and Tudor Reality." *Journal of the Warburg and Courtauld Institutes* 45 (1982): 232–39.

Steen, Charlie R. *Margaret of Parma: A Life*. Leiden, Netherlands: Brill, 2013.

Strasser, Ulrike. "'The First Form and Grace': Ignatius of Loyola and the Reformation of Masculinity." In *Masculinity in the Reformation Era*, edited by Scott Hendrix and Susan Karant-Nunn, 45–70. Kirksville MO: Truman State University Press, 2008.

Taylor, Scott K. *Honor and Violence in Golden Age Spain*. New Haven CT: Yale University Press, 2008.

Terrasa-Lozano, Antonio. "Legal Enemies, Beloved Brothers: High Nobility, Family Conflict, and the Aristocrats' Two Bodies in Early-Modern Castile." *European Review of History* 17, no. 5 (2010): 719–34.

Tillyard, Stella. *A Royal Affair: George III and His Troublesome Siblings*. London: Chatto and Windus, 2006.

Tosh, John. "The History of Masculinity: An Outdated Concept?" In *What Is Masculinity? Historical Dynamics from Antiquity to the Contemporary World*, edited by John. H. Arnold and Sean Brady, 17–34. New York: Palgrave Macmillan, 2011.

Twinam, Ann. "The Negotiation of Honor." In *Sex, Shame, and Violence: The Faces of Honor in Colonial Latin America*, edited by Lyman L. Johnson and Sonya Lipsett-Rivera, 68–102. Albuquerque: University of New Mexico Press, 1998.

———. *Public Lives, Private Secrets: Gender, Honor, Sexuality, and Illegitimacy in Colonial Spanish America*. Stanford CA: Stanford University Press, 1999.

Usunáriz, Jesús M. "Asistir la madre y cuidar de la criatura: El reconocimiento de paternidad en los siglos XVI y XVIII." *Revista historia autónoma* 16 (2020): 101–19.

———. "Marriage and Love in Sixteenth- and Seventeenth-Century Spain." In *Marriage in Europe, 1400–1800*, edited by Silvana Seidel Menchi, 201–24. Toronto: University of Toronto Press, 2016.

Van Aert, Laura. "The Legal Possibilities of Antwerp Widows in the Late Sixteenth Century." *History of the Family* 12, no. 4 (2007): 282–95.

Van der Heijden, Manon. "Marriage Formation: Law and Custom in the Low Countries 1500–1700." In *Marriage in Europe, 1400–1800*, edited by Silvana Seidel Menchi, 155–75. Toronto: University of Toronto Press, 2016.

Vaquero Serrano, María del Carmen. "Books in the Sewing Basket: María de Mendoza y de la Cerda." In *Power and Gender in Renaissance Spain: Eight Women of the Mendoza Family, 1450–1650*, edited by Helen Nader, 93–112. Urbana: University of Illinois Press, 2004.

———. "Doña María de Ribera, esposa de Hernando Dávalos: Otra dama en el entorno de Garcilaso." In *Perspectives on Early Modern Women in Iberia and the Americas: Studies in Law, Society, Art and Literature in Honor of Anne J. Cruz*, edited by Adrienne L. Martín and María Cristina Quintero, 72–89. New York: Escribana, 2015.

———. "'El desdichado [poeta] don Lorenzo Laso': Vida del primogénito de Garcilaso de la Vega." *Lemir* 15 (2011): 59–134.

———. *Garcilaso: Poeta del amor, caballero de la guerra*. Madrid: Espasa-Calpe, 2002.

———. "Garcilaso traicionado. Vida de Guiomar Carrillo: Sus hijos Lorenzo Laso, María de Jesús y de Guzmán y María de Ponce de León." *Lemir* 14 (2010): 121–203.

Vassberg, David. "Widows in Sixteenth-Century Castile." In *Poor Women and Children in the European Past*, edited by John Henderson and Richard Wall, 180–95. London: Routledge, 1994.

Vidma Guzmán, Ángel. "El señorío y el marquesado de la guardia (Jaén), a través de su documentos: Relación de los señores y marqueses de la villa." *Boletín: Instituto de Estudios Giennenses* 215 (2017): 99–148.

Villa-Flores, Javier. *Dangerous Speech: A Social History of Blasphemy in Colonial Mexico*. Tucson: University of Arizona Press, 2006.

Villa-Flores, Javier, and Sonya Lipsett-Rivera, "Introduction." In *Emotions and Daily Life in Colonial New Mexico*, edited by Javier Villa-Flores and Sonya Lipsett-Rivera, 1–14. Albuquerque: University of New Mexico Press, 2014.

Villalon, A. J. "The Law's Delay: The Anatomy of an Aristocratic Property Dispute (1350–1577)." PhD diss., Yale University, 1984.

Villaseñor Black, Charlene. *Creating the Cult of St. Joseph: Art and Gender in the Spanish Empire*. Princeton NJ: Princeton University Press, 2006.

———. "St. Anne Imagery and Maternal Archetypes in Spain and Mexico." In *Colonial Saints: Discovering the Holy in the Americas, 1500–1800*, edited by Allan Greer and Jodi Bilinkoff, 3–29. New York: Routledge, 2003.

Viña Brito, Ana. "El testamento de don Pedro Girón." *Anuario de estudios medievales* 19 (1989): 493–505.

Vitullo, Juliann. *Negotiating the Art of Fatherhood in Late Medieval and Early Modern Italy*. New York: Palgrave Macmillan, 2019.

Vives, Juan Luis. *The Education of a Christian Woman: A Sixteenth-Century Manual*. Edited and translated by Charles Fantazzi. Chicago: University of Chicago Press, 2000.

Vives Torija, Ana, and Amparo Ayuso Blas. "Guiomar de Mendoza y Borbón, I condesa de Oropesa; Isabel de Mendoza y Borbón, señora de Orgaz." In *Damas de la casa de Mendoza: Historias, leyendas y olvidos*, edited by Esther Alegre Carvajal, 673–86. Madrid: Ediciones Polifemo, 2014.

Walby, Sylvia. *Theorizing Patriarchy*. Oxford: Blackwell, 1990.

Walker, Claire. *Gender and Politics in Early Modern Europe: English Convents in France and the Low Countries*. New York: Palgrave Macmillan, 2003.

Warner, Lyndan. "Introduction." In *Stepfamilies in Europe, 1400–1800*, edited by Lyndan Warner, 1–19. London: Routledge, 2018.

———. "Seeing Stepfamilies in European Visual Culture." In *Stepfamilies in Europe, 1400–1800*, edited by Lyndan Warner, 204–25. London: Routledge, 2018.

Waterworth, J., ed. and trans. *The Canons and Decrees of the Sacred and Oecumenical Council of Trent*. London: Dolman, 1848.

Wessell-Lightfoot, Dana. *Women, Dowries, and Agency: Marriage in Fifteenth-Century Valencia*. Manchester, UK: Manchester University Press, 2016.

Wickersham, Jane. "Beguines." In *Encyclopedia of Women in the Renaissance: Italy, France, and England*, edited by Diana Robin, Anne R. Larsen, and Carole Levin, 45–47. Santa Barbara CA: ABC CLIO, 2007.

Winer, Rebecca Lynn. "The Enslaved Wet Nurse as Nanny: The Transition from Free to Slave Labor in Childcare in Barcelona after the Black Death (1348)." *Slavery and Abolition* 38, no. 2 (2017): 303–19.

Wunder, Heidi. "Marriage in the Holy Roman Empire of the German Nation from the Fifteenth to the Eighteenth Century: Moral, Legal, and Political Order." In *Marriage in Europe, 1400–1800*, edited by Silvana Seidel Menchi, 61–93. Toronto: University of Toronto Press, 2016.

INDEX

Page numbers in italics indicate figures.

González de Medina, Elvira, 95, 100
Granada, conquest of, 8, 198
Granada, Fray Luis de, 204, 272n56
grandees, 25, 69, 181, 203
guardians, 141, 192; illegitimate children
    as, 4, 56–57, 131–32, 178–79; women as,
    3, 5, 16, 88, 110–12, 118, 195, 204–5
guardianship, 19, 220; failed, 90, 126, 204–
    5; of illegitimate children, 40, 41, 130,
    146, 170, 171
Guzmán, Leonor de, 79, 181
Guzmán, María de, 86, 143
Guzmán "el Bueno," 106, 110–11, 182

Habsburg dynasty, 10, 49
happiness, 110, 201; and women's agency,
    82
Haro, Countess of (Mencía de Mendoza),
    156
Híjar, Dukes of, 181
hijos bastardos. See bastard
Holy Roman Empire: and discrimination
    against illegitimates, 142, 260n6; and
    marriage, 243n62
honor, 10, 13, 17, 53, 56, 97, 108, 112, 187–88,
    206–11; code, 3, 29–30, 145, 206, 215,
    218–19, 222; and illegitimacy, 141, 145;
    plays, 71, 74; women's, 18–19, 66, 68,
    69, 74–76, 88, 94, 98
household, 88, 144, 164, 166; in France,
    186; and grief, 212, 214; headed by
    women, 72; and illegitimate children,
    21, 40, 55–59, 84, 104–5, 126, 128, 138;
    linens, 98; and masculinity, 20, 30–31,
    125; and maternity, 102; noble, 1–2, 11,
    73, 84, 142, 173–74, 179, 202, 220; and
    paternity, 39, 62; royal, 153; and sexual
    assault, 84, 101–2; and slavery, 86–87,
    121; and women's labor, 105–20, 184,
    219

illness, 61, 133, 200; of children, 192; and
    maternity, 73, 214n38
Infantado, Dukes of, 8, 10; and illegiti-
    macy, 106
Infantado, first Duchess of (Isabel
    Enríquez), 112, 116–17
Infantado, first Duke of, 54; as father, 112,
    116–17, 161
Infantado, second Duchess of (María de
    Luna), 65, 117
Infantado, second Duke of (Iñigo López
    de Mendoza), 117
Infantado, sixth Duchess of (Ana de
    Mendoza), 109
Infantado, sixth Duke of (Juan Hurtado
    de Mendoza), 104
Infantado, third Duchess of (María Mal-
    donado), 23, 61
Infantado, third Duke of (Diego Hurtado
    de Mendoza), 23–25, 52, 61
inheritance: and entail, 53, 122, 179–80,
    213; and illegitimate children, 13, 15–18,
    40, 42–44, 52, 56, 88, 113, 126, 131, 138,
    149, 164, 167; law, 35–37, 78, 120–21,
    148; and masculinity, 31; and maternal
    lineage, 69; and military orders, 152;
    and mothers of illegitimate children,
    84, 95, 101, 117; as noble strategy, 3, 5, 9,
    12, 14, 163, 170–71, 185; partible, 12–13,
    179–80; problems, 77, 91, 93, 106, 139–
    40, 147, 172, 175, 186–87, 199, 205–7. *See
    also* disinheritance
Isabel I (Queen of Castile), 8, 23, 35, 52,
    54, 100, 126, 129, 132, 152; and mater-
    nity, 74
Isabel Clara Eugenia (daughter of Philip
    II), 192
Isabel of Bourbon (Queen of Castile), 193
Isabel of Valois (Queen of Castile), 129,
    277n157

Pedro I (King of Castile), 6–7, 153; illegitimate great-grandson of, 153

Peñaranda y Fuente del Sol, second Lord of (Álvaro de Bracamonte), 132, 228n70

The Perfect Wife (León), 70. *See also* León, Luis de

Philip II (King of France), 148

Philip II (King of Spain), 38, 93, 111, 152, 155, 183; and the Council of Trent, 80

piety, 99, 156

Ponce de León, Manuel, 172–73

Ponce de León family. *See* Arcos, Dukes of

Portugal, 90, 110–11, 183, 207; and concubinage, 78, 244n68

pregnancy, 53, 73, 84, 193

primogeniture, 12, 183; and the law, 35

Ramírez, Isabel, 95

rape, 2, 46, 94, 96–97, 215, 218–19; and masculinity, 25, 210–11; and women's agency, 80, 83–85

Reconquista, 10, 17, 26–27, 150, 247n98

Reformation, 77, 232n46, 243n62. *See also* Catholic Reformation

remarriage, 2, 108–9, 212, 217, 220

Renaissance, 28–29; and emotion, 204; and fatherhood, 33–34; and illegitimacy, 14–15; and women, 94

Ribera, María de, 87–88, 203–4

Roman law, 35

royal court, 54, 185, 194, 200; as career, 41, 126, 142, 163; and concubinage, 78

Ruiz de la Vega, Gonzalo, 95; as father, 40

Sandoval, María de, 79

Santa Cruz, first Marquis de (Álvaro de Guzmán), 150, 152; as father, 42, 122

Santiago, Order of, 59, 89, 123, 129, 150, 152, 165, 182, 185, 194. *See also* military orders

sewing, 74

sexual assault. *See* sexual violence

sexuality: and Christian norms, 142, 154, 199, 218; and convents, 99; and emotion, 188, 198; female, 29–30, 36, 68–71, 75–85, 101–2, 114, 181; and the law, 36–37; and masculinity, 53–54, 60–62, 199; premarital, 18, 75, 80, 91, 217, 243n62; and sexual satisfaction, 5

sexual violence, 9, 19, 71, 96, 209–11, 219–20; and masculinity, 20, 27, 29, 32, 203. *See also* abuse; rape; sexuality

Siete Partidas: and adultery, 70; and concubinage, 36–37, 86, 120–21; and entail, 35; and illegitimacy, 15, 36–37, 120–21, 141, 148; and marriage, 76–77, 132; and maternity, 73; and nobility, 10; and paternity, 33, 39, 191–92. *See also* law

Silva, Ana de, 157, 212. *See also* Villarejo de Fuentes, third Lord of

Silva, Ana de (daughter of Count of Cifuentes), 118–19

slaves, 2, 11, 19, 30, 33, 68, 96, 113, 121, 180, 221; children of, 21, 139–40, 145, 165, 175; and maternity, 86–87, 105, 110, 114–15, 134; and sexual violence, 96, 101, 218

Soma, second Duke of, 133

Spanish Empire, 17, 38, 151; and discrimination, 145; and patriarchy, 32

Sweden, 15; and marriage, 227n48, 243n62

taxation, noble exemption from, 11, 35, 142

taxes, 118, 142

Tendilla, Counts of, 10

Tendilla, fourth Count of (Iñigo López de Mendoza), 119–20; as father, 57, 103–4

Tendilla, second Count of (Iñigo López de Mendoza), 23, 66, 128, 157; as father, 59

Tendilla, third Countess of (Catalina de Mendoza y Zúñiga), 103, 120

In the Women and Gender in the Early Modern World series:

To order or obtain more information on these or other University
of Nebraska Press titles, visit nebraskapress.unl.edu.